Boys' Love, Cosplay, and Androgynous Idols

Queer Asia

The Queer Asia series opens a space for monographs and anthologies in all disciplines focusing on non-normative sexuality and gender cultures, identities and practices across all regions of Asia. Queer Studies, Queer Theory, and Transgender Studies originated in, and remain dominated by, North American and European academic circles. Yet, the separation between sexual orientation and gender identity, while relevant in the West, does not neatly apply to all Asian contexts, which are themselves complex and diverse. Growing numbers of scholars inside and beyond Asia are producing exciting and challenging work that studies Asian histories and cultures of trans and queer phenomena. The Queer Asia series—first of its kind in publishing—provides a valuable opportunity for developing and sustaining these initiatives.

Editorial Collective

Chris Berry (King's College London), John Nguyet Erni (Hong Kong Baptist University), Peter Jackson (Australian National University), and Helen Hok-Sze Leung (Simon Fraser University)

International Editorial Board

Dennis Altman (La Trobe University, Australia), Evelyn Blackwood (Purdue University), Tom Boellstorff (University of California, Irvine), Pimpawan Boonmongkon (Mahidol University), Judith Butler (University of California, Berkeley), Ding Naifei (National Central University, Taiwan), David Eng (University of Pennsylvania), Neil Garcia (University of the Philippines, Diliman), David Halperin (University of Michigan, Ann Arbor), Josephine Chuen-juei Ho (National Central University, Taiwan), Annamarie Jagose (University of Auckland, New Zealand), Yinhe Li (Chinese Academy of Social Sciences), Song Hwee Lim (University of Exeter), Kam Louie (UNSW, Australia), Lenore Manderson (Monash University, Australia), Fran Martin (University of Melbourne), Mark McLelland (University of Wollongong), Meaghan Morris (Lingnan University, Hong Kong), Dede Oetomo (University of Surabaya, Indonesia), Cindy Patton (Simon Fraser University), Ken Plummer (University of Essex), Elspeth Probyn (University of Sydney), Lisa Rofel (University of California, Santa Cruz), Megan Sinnott (Georgia State University), John Treat (Yale University, USA), Carol Vance (Columbia University, USA), and Audrey Yue (University of Melbourne)

Selected titles from the series

As Normal as Possible: Negotiating Sexuality and Gender in Mainland China and Hong Kong
Edited by Yau Ching

Conditional Spaces: Hong Kong Lesbian Desires and Everyday Life
Denise Tse-Shang Tang

Contact Moments: The Politics of Intercultural Desire in Japanese Male-Queer Cultures
Katsuhiko Suganuma

Falling into the Lesbi World: Desire and Difference in Indonesia
Evelyn Blackwood

First Queer Voices from Thailand: Uncle Go's Advice Columns for Gays, Lesbians and Kathoeys
Peter A. Jackson

Gender on the Edge: Transgender, Gay, and Other Pacific Islanders
Edited by Niko Besnier and Kalissa Alexeyeff

Obsession: Male Same-Sex Relations in China, 1900–1950
Wenqing Kang

Philippine Gay Culture: Binabae to Bakla, Silahis to MSM
J. Neil C. Garcia

Queer Bangkok: 21st Century Markets, Media, and Rights
Edited by Peter A. Jackson

Queer Politics and Sexual Modernity in Taiwan
Hans Tao-Ming Huang

Queer Singapore: Illiberal Citizenship and Mediated Cultures
Edited by Audrey Yue and Jun Zubillaga-Pow

Shanghai Lalas: *Female* Tongzhi *Communities and Politics in Urban China*
Lucetta Yip Lo Kam

Undercurrents: Queer Culture and Postcolonial Hong Kong
Helen Hok-Sze Leung

Boys' Love, Cosplay, and Androgynous Idols

Queer Fan Cultures in Mainland China, Hong Kong, and Taiwan

Edited by Maud Lavin, Ling Yang, and Jing Jamie Zhao

Hong Kong University Press
The University of Hong Kong
Pokfulam Road
Hong Kong
www.hkupress.org

© 2017 Hong Kong University Press

ISBN 978-988-8390-80-9 (*Hardback*)

All rights reserved. No portion of this publication may be reproduced or transmitted in any form or by any means, electronic or mechanical, including photocopy, recording, or any information storage or retrieval system, without prior permission in writing from the publisher.

An earlier version of Chapter 10 was published under the title "Girls Who Love Boys' Love: Japanese Homoerotic Manga as Transnational Taiwan Culture" in *Inter-Asia Cultural Studies* 13, no. 3 (2012): 365–83. Reprinted by permission of Taylor & Francis Ltd, http://www.tandfonline.com/.

British Library Cataloguing-in-Publication Data
A catalogue record for this book is available from the British Library.

10 9 8 7 6 5 4 3 2 1

Printed and bound by Paramount Printing Co., Ltd. in Hong Kong, China

Contents

Acknowledgments vii
Note on Romanization and Chinese and Japanese Names x
Introduction xi
    Jing Jamie Zhao, Ling Yang, and Maud Lavin

I. Mainland China

1. Chinese *Danmei* Fandom and Cultural Globalization from Below 3
    Ling Yang and Yanrui Xu

2. Cosplay, Cuteness, and *Weiniang*: The Queered *Ke'ai* of Male Cosplayers as "Fake Girls" 20
    Shih-chen Chao

3. "The World of Grand Union": Engendering Trans/nationalism via Boys' Love in Online Chinese *Hetalia* Fandom 45
    Ling Yang

4. Queering the Post-*L Word* Shane in the "Garden of Eden": Chinese Fans' Gossip about Katherine Moennig 63
    Jing Jamie Zhao

5. From Online BL Fandom to the CCTV *Spring Festival Gala*: The Transforming Power of Online Carnival 91
    Shuyan Zhou

6. Dongfang Bubai, Online Fandom, and the Gender Politics of a Legendary Queer Icon in Post-Mao China 111
    Egret Lulu Zhou

II. Hong Kong

7. Desiring Queer, Negotiating Normal: Denise Ho (HOCC) Fandom before and after the Coming-Out 131
    Eva Cheuk Yin Li

8. Hong Kong–Based Fans of Mainland Idol Li Yuchun: Elective Belonging, Gender Ambiguity, and Rooted Cosmopolitanism 157
   Maud Lavin

III. Taiwan

9. Exploring the Significance of "Japaneseness": A Case Study of *Fujoshi*'s BL Fantasies in Taiwan 179
   Weijung Chang

10. Girls Who Love Boys' Love: BL as Goods to Think with in Taiwan (with a Revised and Updated Coda) 195
    Fran Martin

Works Cited 221
Note on Contributors 246
Index 249

Acknowledgments

The editors wish to thank, most of all, the individual authors who have contributed their sharp, exploratory, and highly invested writing to this volume. We greatly respect the analysis, research, curiosity, and passion manifested by each. Being immersed ourselves within both academia and fandoms for years, the editors have taken great pleasure in teaching, researching, and participating in Chinese queer fan cultures. We also share a substantive appreciation for the queer fan discourses flowing digitally in and through mainland China, Hong Kong, and Taiwan and find the range of ideas, emotions, arguments, and enthusiasms articulated as urgent in the productivity of their mediated but still relatively open and contested expressions.

Writing about such desirous, polemical flows in Chinese-speaking fan communities in an academic volume has been a long-term yet always stimulating journey for us. Jing Jamie Zhao conceived the idea of an edited collection on queer fan cultures in mainland China, Hong Kong, and Taiwan and started the work of creating a team following her panel about queer Chinese media and cultures at the 2013 Society for Cinema and Media Studies conference in Seattle. Along the way, the coeditors and contributors of this book have developed a truly synergistic relationship and have worked together to create this volume, with all but one essay written specifically for this book (and the one previously published essay updated for this study). Along with other colleagues, different contributors also presented in panels together as the book was being assembled, for instance, at the 2015 AAS-in-Asia conference in Taipei and the 2015 Inter-Asia Cultural Studies conference in Surabaya. We are quite thankful for this discursive collaboration in and around the book. In addition, while preparing the manuscript and when seeking publishing possibilities in the early stages, we feel extremely grateful for the support, encouragement, and dialogue provided by a number of scholars in Chinese media cultural studies and Sinophone studies, such as Chris Berry, Shu-mei Shih, and John Erni. We would also like to thank the two anonymous readers for the Press for their astute comments.

For support throughout the preparation of this book, Maud Lavin thanks, at the School of the Art Institute, Dean of Faculty Lisa Wainwright, the departments of Visual and Critical Studies and Art History, Theory and Criticism, and her students. She is thankful for an SAIC Faculty Enrichment Grant, which helped fund research for her chapter of this study. In addition, she is grateful for a Senior Research Residency in the Cultural Studies Cluster at the Asia Research Institute, National University of Singapore—indispensable for providing research time and inspiration about issues of genders, sexualities, and East Asian cultural studies. For continued dialogue on these and related subjects, she thanks colleagues there and elsewhere, including Annie Bourneuf, Carolyn Brewer, Adam Cheung, David Getsy, Chua Beng Huat, Sun Jung, Kumiko Kawashima, Joan Kee, SooJin Lee, Lee Weng Choy, Qianhan Lin, Star Sijia Liu, Karen Morris, Terry Murphy, Zeenat Nagree, Margaret Olin, Shawn Michelle Smith, Sang-Yeon Loise Sung, and Xiaorui Zhu. And she is hugely grateful to her coeditors, Ling Yang and Jing Jamie Zhao.

Ling Yang is grateful for a research grant from the Sumitomo Foundation that helped fund the research for her two chapters and cover the reprint fees of Fran Martin's chapter. She thanks Koichi Iwabuchi and Eva Tsai for helping her obtain the grant. She is also grateful to Jessica Bauwens-Sugimoto, Jaqueline Berndt, Mark McLelland, Kazumi Nagaike, Fusami Ogi, Katsuhiko Suganuma, and James Welker for welcoming her into the academic circle of Japanese BL studies; and Tao Dongfeng and Naifei Ding for providing her much-needed encouragement and publishing support in the Chinese-speaking academic world. In addition, Yang feels deeply indebted to her research partner Yanrui Xu and all the BL creators and readers she and Yanrui have talked to over the years. Their passions and perseverance have inspired her to continue her "queer" research regardless of the circumstances. And above all, she is extremely thankful to her coeditors, Maud Lavin and Jing Jamie Zhao, who have helped her gain so much more than an extra line in her curriculum vitae.

Jing Jamie Zhao is thankful for the generous grants from the Chinese University of Hong Kong for her overseas academic activities. These have made possible her fruitful conference experiences and sharing of ideas about this book project with a good number of scholars globally. She is grateful for the tremendous time, patience, and help provided by Angela Wai-Ching Wong and Fran Martin in supervising her doctoral dissertation, a section of which is included in the book. She also extends gratitude to Howard Chiang, Tzu-hui Hung, Elana Levine, James Welker, Alvin Wong, and Audrey Yue for their encouragement and kind support of her research. She thanks her awesome coeditors, Maud Lavin and Ling Yang, and many other academic and personal friends for teaching her so much about being a decent, positive person and for standing by her in times of unexpected ups and downs in both her professional and private lives. Zhao's enduring appreciation goes to her partner, whose characteristic grace, generosity, and intelligence lighted her way through bramble and thistle over and over again.

Finally, *Queer Fan Cultures* is dedicated to people whom in different ways we love: Daiki Akama, Nana Bi, Bruce Black, Shuyun Huang, Audrey Lavin, Mengyan Sun, Jian Wang, Long Yang, Xuebing Yang, and Xiaoren Zhao.

The production of this volume was partly supported by the Fundamental Research Funds for the Central Universities (20720151016) administered by Xiamen University.

Note on Romanization and Chinese and Japanese Names

With the exception of Chapter 7, which uses Cantonese romanization, all of the chapters in this book use Hanyu pinyin to denote Chinese terms. Place names and personal names in Hong Kong and Taiwan are romanized according to local conventions. In romanized Japanese, macrons are put on long Japanese vowels except in the case of place names (e.g., Tokyo) and author names (e.g., Koichi Iwabuchi).

In both Chinese and Japanese languages, surnames precede given names. In this book, we use Western order for Chinese and Japanese names, i.e., given names precede surnames. There are some exceptions, however. In the case of Chinese names, the native order is preserved if the author or political or cultural figure is conventionally referred to as such in English (e.g., Li Yuchun). In the case of Japanese names, the native order is preserved if the names refer to historical figures (e.g., Katakura Kojūrō).

Introduction

Jing Jamie Zhao, Ling Yang, and Maud Lavin

Chinese-speaking popular cultures have never been so queer as in this digital, globalist age. In mainland China where entertainment media products with explicit homosexual themes have long been banned from public screening, its contemporary media industry is nonetheless eager to ride the wave of queer connotations and sentiments. In December 2015, *Go Princess Go!* (*Taizifei shengzhiji*, LeTV, 2015), a thirty-six-episode, lighthearted comedy peppered with gender flips (*xingbie fanzhuan*) and elements of BL (Boys' Love, a fan subculture narrating male homoeroticism) and GL (Girls' Love, a fan subculture narrating female homoeroticism) became one of the most popular web-based TV dramas in mainland China. The show had been viewed 2.4 billion times before it was pulled offline by government regulators for revision because of its explicitly sexual and indecent content in January 2016.[1] In Hong Kong and Taiwan, queer cultures not only have permeated offline consumerist societies, social media uses, and cyberspaces, but also have appeared in political movements.[2] In the 2014 Hong Kong Umbrella Movement (*Yusan yundong*, a prodemocracy political protest initiated by Hong Kong students), online BL fans and student protestors creatively paired two male student leaders, Alex Chow and Lester Shum, as gay lovers and produced a variety of fan art devoted to this couple.[3] Similarly, earlier in 2014, during the Sunflower Student Movement of Taiwan (*Taiyanghua xueyun*, a Taiwanese civic protest), two male student leaders, Chen Wei-ting and Lin Fei-fan, were also "rumored to be lovers."[4]

In response to this proliferation of queer representations, productions, fantasies, and desires, especially as manifested online, *Boys' Love, Cosplay, and Androgynous Idols: Queer Fan Cultures in Mainland China, Hong Kong, and Taiwan* (*QFC* hereafter) explores extended, diversified, digitized, and transculturally informed fan communities and practices that have been devoted to and that have cultivated various forms of queerness. The focus of this volume travels among fans of transnational androgynous celebrities, such as Hong Kong idol HOCC (Denise Wan-See Ho, see chapter 7), mainland Chinese superstar Li Yuchun (Chris Lee, see chapter 8), Taiwanese actress Joe Chen Chiao-En (chapter 6), and the American actress Katherine Moennig (chapter 4); the carnivalesque BL matchmaking of two Chinese-speaking male celebrities performing in CCTV's *Spring Festival Gala* (*Yangshi chunwan*, see chapter 5); the online and offline gendered performances of an all-male cosplay[5] group whose members mimic the girlish cuteness of Japanese ACG (anime,[6] comics, and games) characters and the Korean singing group Girls' Generation (chapter 2); mainland fanzines dedicated to the Japanese ACG series *Hetalia: Axis Powers* (chapter 3); fan-made videos (fanvids) starring a well-known Sinophonic transgender media character, Dongfang Bubai (Invincible Eastern, see chapter 6); transnational production and distribution networks of mainland *danmei* (the Chinese version of BL, see chapter 1) fandom; and the multidimensional Japaneseness of Taiwanese female BL fandoms (chapters 9 and 10).

In *QFC*'s investigations of such diverse Chinese-speaking fan communities, "queer" is employed as a productive analytical lens that "defines itself diacritically not against heterosexuality but against the normative,"[7] including any perspectival norms and ideals in both contemporary public cultural and scholarly discourses surrounding nation-states, linguistics, geopolitics, ethnicities, genders, and sexualities. Therefore, it serves as an umbrella term used in this volume to loosely refer to all kinds of nonnormative representations, viewing positions, identifications, structures of feelings, and ways of thinking. Accordingly, the range of queer fandoms *QFC* highlights includes explicitly homosexual-themed narratives and, beyond such categorization, a greatly diversified matrix of nonheteromarital, nonnormative sociocultural, sexual, and gender representations as well.

Despite the fact that queer fan practices have enjoyed a long local tradition in China,[8] contemporary Chinese-speaking queer fan cultures have also been shaped by the incessant and complex transregional, cross-cultural, and transnational cultural flows among East Asian cultures and between the East and West—as well as positionings vis-à-vis official culture and traditional norms. Most queer fantasies and narratives in Chinese-speaking fandoms are created either in the style of BL or GL. Both terms are borrowed directly from Japan and have their roots in Japanese manga (comics). In terms of transnational cultural flows and their influence, consider, for instance, that many Chinese-speaking queer fans playfully describe themselves as *zhai* (宅), *ji* (基), *fu* (腐), or a combination, meaning respectively staying at home all day and relying on the Internet to connect with the outside world; having close same-sex friends or same-sex desires; and harboring a strong interest in BL, GL, or both. The words *zhai* and *fu* derive, in that order, from the Japanese terms *otaku* (people with obsessive interests) and *fujoshi* (rotten women) and were introduced to the Chinese-speaking world by way of Taiwan. The former refers to obsessive ACG fans, mostly male, whereas the latter, passionate female BL fans. The word *ji* is the Cantonese transliteration of the English word "gay" and is now widely used in Mandarin-speaking regions to refer to homosociality and homoeroticism as well. This complex translingual mélange of fan identities gives a clear signal of an unabashed devotion to digital culture; to communicating via social media; to creating narratives that circulate digitally; to embracing the multiple participatory roles of fans in fandoms, particularly those involving queer sensibilities, codes, and socialities.

In response to these specificities of contemporary Chinese-speaking fan cultures, in analyses rooted in *QFC*'s major locations—mainland China, Hong Kong, and Taiwan—issues of cross-border consumption and borrowing of materials are traced by all of our contributors in relation to local contexts. Most of them also delineate fans' extensive use of digital technology and the uncertainty, fluidity, and performativity of subjectivity, identity, and desire in cyberspace. Since localized issues of censorship and different if closely related histories of gender and sexuality traditions are paramount in such considerations, *QFC*'s geographic organization helps to illuminate cultural differences among locations and the competing forces and factors influencing geocultural dissimilarities within Chinese-speaking queer fandoms, even at this time of global digital currents. To right an imbalance in the scholarly literature on queer East Asia, this volume is weighted toward an exploration of queer elements of mainland Chinese fandoms that have been less often written about than more visible, queer-influenced, public cultural aspects in Hong Kong and Taiwan.[9] Notably, because of the stringent censorship regime in mainland China, belonging through participation to queer fandoms involves some risk—and it arguably offers a strong alternative to public spaces marked as more normative and officially sanctioned.

Researching Chinese-Speaking Queer Fan Cultures

In analyzing contemporary Chinese-speaking fan cultures through a queer and transcultural perspective, *QFC* has engaged in a productive dialogue with a wide range of academic inquiries, filling gaps, contributing theoretical insights, and expanding horizons. The inception and organization of the volume have been greatly influenced by queer Asian studies, queer China studies, and queer Sinophone studies.[10] We share with those studies a common focus on nonnormative genders, sexualities, and desires; a complex understanding of the hybrid and heterogeneous nature of Chinese-speaking sociocultural practices and experiences; and a strong commitment to decenter Western gender and sexuality knowledge and theories. Yet, unlike those studies that "have tended to cluster around ethnographic approaches to specific sites of queer social life, on the one hand, and critical interpretations of queer-themed literature, films, and other media, on the other,"[11] *QFC* is oriented toward studies of digitized fan subcultures combining ethnographic approaches and other critical analyses, to both reflect the changing face of Chinese-speaking popular cultures and further broaden the scope of these existing fields.

QFC also bridges the gap between the well-established Anglo-American tradition of media fan research, the increased academic attention to celebrity fandoms in fan studies,[12] and the more recently emerged studies of transnational fandoms with Japanese origin, such as *otaku* culture and BL fandoms, in a concrete transcultural Chinese-speaking fannish context. Existing Western queer fandom studies, particularly the scholarship dedicated to slash/femslash (fan writing practices that explore male/female homoerotic romances), has flourished since the late 1980s.[13] Yet, this cluster of queer fan research in the main overlooks the existence of non-Western queer fandom and does not explain the contextual intricacies and particularities of diverse groups of global queer fans.[14] Meanwhile, contrary to the growing body of literature on the local, transnational, and cross-cultural consumptions of Japanese BL,[15] only a few recent English-language scholarly works have briefly covered BL/GL fandom and ACG fan practices in mainland China, Hong Kong, or Taiwan.[16] Through extensive and multimethodological research, our contributors proffer unique insights that make this volume both a disruptive force to any simplistic, if not ignorant, understandings of non-Western queer fandom and a significant alternative to the Anglo-American model of fandom studies. For instance, chapter 7 powerfully illustrates the differences between androgyny in Western contexts and the Sinophonic notion of neutrosexuality (neutral gender or sexual identities); while chapter 2 delimits a Chinese-specific transgender performance of an East Asian feminine cuteness. And chapters 9 and 10 demonstrate and contextualize the subjectively constructed Taiwanese fantasies surrounding "Japaneseness" in dissimilar ways.

QFC delineates, highlights, and complicates the existence of some disquieting ambivalence toward a wide array of gender, sexual, racial, sociocultural, and political identities within fannish spaces. Its essays bring particular pressure to bear on key issues of online fan negotiations with cultural strictures (chapters 4, 6, 7, and 8); media censorship (chapters 1, 5, and 10); political identities (chapters 3 and 8); and historical legacies (chapters 7 and 9), particularly in the People's Republic of China (PRC). Arguments emphasize the complexities and transgressiveness of these interfaces rather than easy polarities between general resistance and capitulation (chapters 2, 3, and 4). Some of our contributors also explore nondichotomous intricacies between grassroots production and top-down, profit-driven mass media industries (chapters 5 and 6). Thus, we see fandom itself as queer in essence, as it has positioned itself as a "heterotopia"[17]—a social and communal space that has been in constant exchange and contestation with mainstream society and cultures. Fan communities and networks in general afford fecund grassroots playgrounds for seeking of alternative "temporalities" and active "place-making practices" that are disruptive to and reinscripting of mainstream, hegemonic orders.[18]

Research involved in QFC mostly focuses on queer fannish fantasies and activities produced mainly by women for women. This gendering not only corresponds to the demographics of Chinese-speaking queer fandoms but also points to the key role of these sites as countering the evident gender hierarchy in the sweep of active fandoms in general. Such hierarchy has been integral to patriarchy and misogyny in fan cultures—as has long been recognized in previous fan studies.[19] While web-based Chinese-speaking queer fandoms engage a surprising range of participants of diverse genders and sexualities (for instance, see chapters 4, 7, and 8), they provide particularly valuable spaces for women—as well as others—to exercise agency, public communication, and creativity, partly as a result of the recent wave of feminist and lesbian, gay, bisexual, transgender, and queer (LGBTQ) movements and influences; the increasing power of women consumers; the relative gender leveling of digital technology; and conversely the enduring lack of power women—and minoritarian subjects—still experience in other publics in the regions. Hence, the question of how these fandoms might signify and appeal to women remains a key issue that we address throughout the volume. However, we are not claiming that these and other queer fandoms in general are exclusively female, as online (fannish) identity is always performative and fictional,[20] and the nonnormative images, gazes, identifications, and imaginaries in cyber fannish spaces have the power to disturb the more conventional aspects of the "heterosexual matrix"[21] by "dramatis[ing] incoherences in the allegedly stable relations between chromosomal sex, gender and sexual desire."[22] In fact, some of our essays (see chapters 2, 4, and 6) specifically examine the explicit play with cross-gender and cross-sexual-orientation identities greatly evident in the fandoms in question. Others (see chapters 4 and 7) implicitly suggest a renegotiation of certain virtual, imagined relations along homosocial lines, at time blurring, at times contesting rigid boundaries between fans who define themselves as LGBTQ people and those who do not.

Contextualizing Today's Chinese-Speaking Queer Fan Cultures

The Chinese-speaking entertainment media industry's high profiling of androgyny, homosociality, cross-dressing, and queerness has not only been met with an enthusiastic if controversial reception and extraordinary economic success but also in recent decades created a boom in Chinese queer fandoms.[23] Although *QFC* focuses on contemporary fandoms, particularly digital ones, there are pertinent historical precedents, of course.

In the realm of pop music, one can provide a long list of "suspected LGBT pop artists since the 1980s."[24] The late Hong Kong star Leslie Cheung Kwok Wing was a Chinese celebrity well known internationally for his androgynous persona, frequent cross-dressing media performances, and real-life bisexual relationships during the 1980s and 1990s. Further, the nonconformist gender performances and real-life romances of the Chinese–Hong Kong female singer Faye Wong has made her a Cantopop legend since the 1990s.[25] In the 1980s and 1990s Taiwanese music industry, a few tomboyish female singers, such as Jessey Lin and Eagle Pan, also experienced huge success. The Taiwanese female music group S.H.E., famous for its members' female masculinity and same-sex intimacies, has enjoyed a long and prosperous career since its debut in 2001.[26] In 2011, a self-identified *zhongxing* (neutrosexual) female music group MissTER made its debut in Taiwan and has since then gained significant popularity in Hong Kong and Taiwan. The group is composed of five tomboyish girls, some of whom are grassroots lesbian celebrities and have been out of the closet for years in cyberspace. In the early 2010s, the public coming-out of Denise Ho and Anthony Wong in Hong Kong and the team leader of MissTER Jin Dai in Taiwan further stimulated the growth of their queer stardom in Chinese-speaking regions.

Because of the PRC government's "no encouraging, no discouraging, and no promoting" attitude toward LGBTQ communities, few high-profile mainland pop stars have come out in public. Nevertheless, the visibility of queer gender performances and personae has risen remarkably in mainland China since the advent of globally formatted reality television. In 2005, the sudden surge in the number of androgynous female celebrities in one of the most influential and successful Chinese reality TV singing contests, *Super Girl* (*Chaoji nüsheng*, Hunan Satellite TV) helped the show gain more than 400 million viewers for its final competition episode that year[27]—not to mention the sudden proliferation of male homosocial and homoerotic images in its later copycat shows, *Happy Boy* (*Kuaile nansheng*, Hunan Satellite TV, 2007, 2010, 2013) and *My Hero* (*Jiayou! Hao nan'er*, Dragon TV, 2006–2007).

In the contemporary film industries of mainland China, Hong Kong, and Taiwan, directors with major queer-themed works showcase a diversity of ways to represent Chinese male homosexuality and fashion, female masculinity, homoeroticism, and lesbianism.[28] Even under mainland China's complex media censorship regulations, queerness has become a unique selling point. Although since 2008, the State Administration of Press, Publication, Radio, Film and Television in mainland China has categorized images of homosexuality in mass media as vulgar or obscene content that needs "to be cut or revised,"[29] the connotations of nonheterosexuality can still be seen in some mainland Chinese TV dramas and movies. The well-received Chinese TV series *Palace of Desire* (*Daming gongci*, Li Shaohong, CCTV8, 2000) and the Chinese New Year's blockbuster *If You Are the One* (*Feicheng wurao*, Feng Xiaogang, 2008, China), for example, both contain nonheterosexual characters. The Thai transsexual celebrity Rose became famous among Chinese viewers after starring in the 2012 Chinese New Year's film *Lost in Thailand* (*Renzai jiongtu zhi taijiong*, Xu Zheng, China), which generated RMB 1.26 billion (USD 230 million) in revenue and has been ranked as "the highest-grossing" Chinese-language domestic-released movie in history.[30] In addition, the most profitable film series produced by the mainland Chinese film industry, *Tiny Times* (*Xiao shidai*, Guo Jingming, 2013–2015, China),[31] is famous for its constant deployment and marketing of female and male homosociality and homosexuality to a predominantly female fan audience. One shot in the series features the two female leads kissing each other's lips as a sign of intimate same-sex friendship, while another shot shows a male character carrying another male character like a lover. While nonmainstream male masculinities and cross-dressing performances have often been enacted by comedians or in traditional opera characters on Chinese Central Television (CCTV), transgender celebrities and performances recently have also appeared in Mainland entertainment shows produced by provincial TV stations, such as *The Voice of China* (*Zhongguo haoshengyin*, Zhejiang TV, 2012–), *Your Face Sounds Familiar* (*Baibian dakaxiu*, Hunan Satellite TV, 2012–2014), *Day Day Up* (*Tiantian xiangshang*, Hunan Satellite TV, 2008–), and *Jinxing Show* (*Jinxing xiu*, Dragon TV, 2015–).

In Hong Kong media history, transgender subplots have rendered both the famous martial arts novel *The Smiling, Proud Wanderer* (*Xiao'ao jianghu*, Jin Yong, 1967–1969) and its adapted film series in the early 1990s (Tsui Hark, 1992–1993, Hong Kong) unprecedentedly successful. In the past decade, the Taiwanese TV industry has also witnessed a general trend of an enhanced presence of queer images. Adapted from the far-reaching Taiwanese queer novels written by Hsien-yung Pai, the TV shows *Crystal Boys* (*Niezi*, PTV, 2003) and *Love's Lone Flower* (*Gu lian hua*, CTS, 2005) have received great media and public attention. Some of the most popular Taiwanese TV talk shows, such as *Mala tianhougong* (Star TV, 2004–) and *Kangxi laile* (CtiTV, 2004–2016), have also featured transgender or gay hosts for more than a decade. One of the most popular Taiwanese variety TV shows, *Guess* (*Wocai wocai wocaicaicai*, CTV, 1996–2011), has frequently produced segments with transgender and nonheterosexual themes since 2007. In the first season of the TV show *Super Girl*'s Taiwanese counterpart, *Super Idol* (*Chaoji ouxiang*, SET, 2007–), the female contestant Jing Chang's notably androgynous persona drew overwhelming audience support and helped her eventually win the competition in 2008.

Furthermore, in the past several years, the information surrounding Thai queer entertainment has been imported and widely circulated within online Chinese-speaking fan networks. Because of their enormous public appeal among the Chinese-speaking audience, a few Thai celebrities who have starred in LGBTQ-themed movies or are famous for their transgender/transsexual appearances, such as Mario Maurer and Witwisit Hiranyawongkul featured in the teenage gay romance *Love of Siam* (*Chookiat sakveerakul*, 2007, Thailand), Sucharat Manaying and Suppanad Jittaleela featured in the teenage lesbian romance *Yes or No* (*Sarasawadee wongsompetch*, 2010, Thailand), and the butch lesbian singer and actress Zee Mattanawee Keenan, have been invited to perform in various TV shows and film festivals in mainland China, Hong Kong, and Taiwan.

In addition to this increasingly "queered" media milieu, Chinese-speaking queer fan cultures have also been profoundly shaped and diversified by the developments of the Internet and digital cultures. Both Hong Kong and Taiwan were connected to the Internet in 1991, while mainland China became a country with Internet access in 1994.[32] The Internet in Taiwan and in mainland China was initially used only for academic purposes. As a result, college students in these two regions became the privileged few who could explore online. In the early 1990s, some student fans took this opportunity to launch a manga and anime section on university bulletin boards. National Tsing Hua University, National Chiao Tung University, National Sun Yat-sen University, and National Taiwan University were among the first to set up university bulletin boards, and their manga and anime sections used to attract a great many users.[33] Since 1996, manga and anime sections also began to appear on the bulletin boards of prestigious mainland Chinese universities. The University of Science and Technology of China was the first to set up a "cartoon" section on its bulletin board, followed by Tsinghua University in Beijing, Shanghai Jiao Tong University, and Sun Yat-sen University in Guangzhou. In 1998, anime and manga fan clubs began to turn up at Peking University, Tsinghua University, and Renmin University.[34] With this preliminary establishment of online and offline fan networks, Chinese-speaking queer fandoms soon entered into a stage of rapid growth.

Around the early 2000s, many Chinese-speaking netizens started gaining easy access to unreleased and censored Western, especially American, queer-themed media, translated and redistributed via peer-to-peer (P2P) networks by Chinese fan translation (fansubbing) groups. Since then, Chinese fans' queer reading of Western celebrities and popular culture has been enjoying a growing diversity and complexity. High-profile Western media franchises like *Harry Potter*, *Sherlock Holmes*, and *The Avengers* series have all spurred a great amount of Chinese-speaking fan productivity.[35] The tropes, jargon, and conventions of Western slash fandom have also been imported via the Internet and begun to merge with those of the Japan-originated BL fandom in the Chinese-speaking cyberspace.

As Mark Duffett has observed, the spread of affordable broadband services offers fans "increased access to information, a greater speed of social interaction, and a new means of public performance."[36] The access to information is particularly important to queer fan cultures, as their fan objects are often deemed inappropriate or offensive by mainstream society. In the case of Mainland BL fandom, before the advent of the Internet, fans generally had very limited access to BL content. They had to take great trouble to go to particular trading places to purchase pirated print BL manga or BL anime CDs. Since the passion for BL was not a hobby they could discuss openly in school or at home, it was difficult for fans to meet and talk with like-minded fellow fans.[37] To enrich their knowledge about homosexuality, for instance, some heterosexual female BL fans would befriend gay male classmates and a few daring ones would even visit gay bars, but most could only resort to gay websites and gay porn circulated on the Internet. In addition to providing an anonymous and secure place for fans to search for the information they need, the Internet also enables fans to unleash their creativity and to build global fan communities. As a matter of fact, some queer fan cultures in mainland China, Hong Kong, and Taiwan have already carved out an interconnected and interdependent cyber, Chinese-speaking fannish world through common written languages, a shared set of fan lingo, and, most importantly, a collective passion for their fan objects.

Moreover, there are signs showing that this queer fan world is expanding to embrace or intersect with other non-Chinese-speaking locations in the Confucian cultural sphere, such as Vietnam and South Korea. The popularity of translated mainland Chinese BL novels in Vietnam has prompted the Vietnamese government to issue a string of orders to ban publications that contain homosexual content.[38] The hit Chinese historical TV drama *Nirvana in Fire* (*Langya Bang*, Beijing TV/Dragon TV, 2015), based on an online mainland BL novel, has also attracted many Korean BL fans after it was broadcast in South Korea. Some of them even traveled to Shanghai to share their fan works with Chinese fans at a Nirvana fan convention in April 2016.[39]

Chinese Fan Studies within Queer Sinophone Contexts

The English term "queer" has been reinvented in diverse Sinophonic LGBTQ minoritarian discourses to refer to *tongzhi* (gay), *guaitai* (weirdo), or *ku'er* (cool youth).[40] In turn, the English word "Chinese" has often been used globally to denote *zhongguo ren* (people with PRC nationality) or monolithically *huaren* (ethnic Chinese).[41] In contrast, we reappropriate and reposition both terms to refer to creative, significant, and intense diversification within regionally based fannish contexts. We do so to emphasize contemporary Chinese-speaking queer fan cultures' "multiple, contradictory, and fragmented" characteristics.[42] Inherent in this emphasis is an uncovering, too, of localized linguistic innovations (see chapters 2 and 9, for example).

Directly and indirectly *QFC* builds on the productive ground of Sinophone studies, the growing interdisciplinary academic field that takes pains to examine, as Shu-mei Shih has articulated, "Sinitic-language cultures on the margins of geopolitical nation-states and their hegemonic productions"[43] by means of "foregrounding the value of difficulty, difference, and heterogeneity."[44] In particular, Howard Chiang has argued that

> a non-hegemonic subversive definition of "Chineseness" should pay closer attention to the cultural differences between Sinitic-language communities on the margins of China (Taiwan, Hong Kong, etc.) and those within the People's Republic of China (PRC), rather than flattening out these unique cultural identifications with the bias of China-centrism.[45]

The ways performing Chineseness fueled by queer subjectivities are strategized enable us to decenter a univocal Chinese identity, tradition, and culture, and thus contribute to an understanding of the plurality, heterogeneity, multilinguistics, transregionality, and contextual specificity of Sinitic-language cultures and practices both within and outside continental China. These continuing debates over the meanings of China and Chineseness are immensely constructive for our analysis of marginalized (or even stigmatized) cultures, practices, and groups produced within, outside, and across regional borders of mainland China, Hong Kong, and Taiwan. They compel us to examine more closely the different political, legal, and cultural contexts that have profoundly intersected with (if often indirectly) the scale, activeness, and texture of Chinese queer communities and their related activities and gatherings.

In mainland China, homosexuality, which had been defined as a kind of hooliganism (*liumang zui*) since 1957, was decriminalized in 1997 and later depathologized in the official definition of mental diseases in 2001.[46] The most influential Mainland-based gay website, *Danlan*, was founded in late 2000.[47] In 2005, the first mainland Chinese queer women magazine, *Les+*, was also started in Beijing.[48] Many gay- and lesbian-oriented public spaces and organizations have also developed in a few major Mainland cities.[49] Yet the cultural influences of these queer media and communicative spaces have still been small in scale. In the meantime, the social and political atmosphere for mainland LGBTQ-related activities and groups has remained turbulent and precarious. Although the annual queer cultural and film festivals and gay parades in Beijing and Shanghai were launched as early as 2004, the police have often called off the events for unknown reasons.[50] Meanwhile, some negative prejudices toward gays and lesbians endure, as do the diverse hierarchies that stigmatize and marginalize bisexual and transsexual people within both mainland heteronormative and LGBTQ communities. On the contrary, Hong Kong and Taiwan seem to have more queer-friendly ambiences. Hong Kong legalized homosexuality in 1991—six years before the Mainland did so.[51] The Hong Kong Lesbian and Gay Film Festival has been held annually since 1989, while the pride parade and queer-related social movements in Hong Kong have also received massive support as well as certain levels of controversy within its own queer communities since 2000s.[52] Yet various religious and social groups have consistently objected to the Hong Kong government's promoting acceptance of homosexuality in the 2000s.[53] Taiwan has often been assumed to be a liberal and democratic state in terms of gender and sexual equality because of its multiparty political system and post–martial law stage (post-1987).[54] The annual gay parade in Taipei started in 2003. In 2014, it attracted more than 65,000 participants and thus became the largest social activity for gay rights and equality in Asia.[55] Yet it has also been found that the sex-negative traditions and other conservative social and political forces in Taiwan have been persistent in supporting "virtuous custom" (*shanliang fengsu*) through negating homosexuality and also prostitution.[56] A recent stark example of this conservatism would be that, in 2013, one Taiwanese female BL fan writer was arrested at comic fan event for producing sexually explicit content.[57]

Moreover, the different legislation concerning pornographic or obscene articles in mainland China and Hong Kong have forced the sexually transgressive queer fandoms in those two locales to mobilize remarkably different survival strategies and countertactics.[58] Sometimes the legal cost has been dangerously high. Significantly, in 2011, thirty-two young female BL writers were arrested by the police in Zhengzhou, China, on the charge of disseminating obscene articles.[59] Additionally, fan attitudes toward transnational queer cultural flows are also varied. Residing in the country that is the most friendly to Japanese culture in Asia, Taiwanese BL fans could access authorized Chinese translations of Japanese BL manga and openly profess their Japanophilia without fear of being censored. In mainland China, however, Japanese BL manga and novels can circulate only through piracy and with fan-made subtitles (fansubs), not only because they contain sexually explicit content but also because they are Japanese. Since Sino-Japanese ties deteriorated in the mid-1990s, the PRC government has systematically restricted the publication and broadcast of Japanese manga and anime. Chinese fans of Japanese popular culture may also be criticized for being unpatriotic by their peers.

Key Themes and Chapter Descriptions

QFC begins with a section of six chapters on queer fan cultures in mainland China. In quite different ways, each chapter deals directly or indirectly with the issue of government censorship and its impact on the development of queer fan cultures. Notably, in chapter 1, Ling Yang and Yanrui Xu examine the various tactics invented by Chinese *danmei* (BL) fans to evade censorship of sexually transgressive content and the building of a vast but vulnerable underground BL distribution network. Borrowing Hong Kong–based anthropologist Gordon Mathews's concept of "low-end globalization,"[60] they describe Chinese *danmei* fandom as "a form of low-end globalization that involves numerous semilegal or illegal transactions of information, works, goods, and money across the Taiwan Strait and in East Asia." Moreover, due to the intertwined, competing cultural, political, and economic factors in the mainland TV industry, some "queer-ish" TV content has been produced both despite and because of the strictures of this complex yet paradoxical censorship system. Both chapter 5 by Shuyan Zhou and chapter 6 by Egret Lulu Zhou discuss state regulations concerning TV production and reveal possible embedding of queer nuances in TV content—and show how queer connotations viewed through this lens could be considered, whether consciously or not, a sideways strategic step in the direction of gender and sexuality diversification while also avoiding direct confrontation with clear signs of homosexual and transgender identities in everyday life. These representations receive layered manipulations online that juxtaposed to one another can be seen as dancing closer to or away from officially approved gender and sexuality norms.

To say that these chapters and the fan practices they analyze represent an alternative to a polarized resistance/capitulation model of fandoms would be an understatement. Nor are official censorship practices clear and fixed in time in the PRC; thus, delving into specific moments of fan-official culture interfaces usefully reveals the complex fan mesh of reinscribing and reinterpreting official acts and their potentials. Hence, in chapter 2, Shih-chen Chao mentions the government's intervention in a popular reality television show that featured a transgender contestant; she then analyzes how cross-gender cosplay can be read as implicitly embracing yet explicitly distancing itself from such moments. Besides extensive censorship of queer content, the PRC government has also established elaborate restrictions of foreign media and cultural content, especially Japanese manga and anime and Western television shows. Chapter 3 by Ling Yang and chapter 4 by Jing Jamie Zhao engage with this aspect of censorship as they each explore how Chinese fans manage to access and reinterpret Japanese and American media products through unlicensed fansubs in cyberspace.

The mainland China section is arranged in an order that reflects the various strands of national, transnational, and transregional cultural traffic that have inspired and shaped the formation of local fandoms. The first three chapters investigate the dissemination and localization of queer fandoms, practices, and works originating in Japan. In chapter 1, "Chinese *Danmei* Fandom and Cultural Globalization from Below," the authors map out a broad picture of the development of Chinese BL fandom in the past two decades. To highlight the localization of the Japanese BL genre, they employ BL's Chinese name *danmei* throughout the chapter, even though the term BL is also widely used among Chinese fans as well. Their chapter focuses on three key aspects of Chinese *danmei* fandom: grassroots distribution networks, major fan "circles" or communities, and the rise of a women-dominated online public sphere. While capturing the ongoing convergence of the Japanese BL tradition and Western slash culture in Chinese *danmei* fandom and claiming that *danmei* has been turned into "a vibrant global cultural commons," they also point out that this commons is riddled with tensions and conflicts, especially when it is involved in real-world politics.

Cosplay in mainland China, too, can be used as a starting point to astutely analyze gendered and queered dimensions of Chinese fan cultures. Opening to large, mass culture issues of trans-Asian cultural translation along lines of genders and sexualities, chapter 2, "Cosplay, Cuteness, and *Weiniang*—The Queered *Ke'ai* of Male Cosplayers as 'Fake Girls'," specifically explores the localized work and reception of the China-based Alice Cos Group. The author asks, "In what way can 'cute' be precisely contextualized in East Asian cultures?" She investigates the boundaries that the Alice performers push and pull as they perform an intricate, ultracute, nonparodic mimesis of feminine Japanese manga characters and Korean girl pop stars, even while ducking identifications with transgender personae and same-sex practices. Queered disjunctures with gender and disconcerting reinscriptions with mainstream sexual identifications are staged hand in hand, under the veil of a *ke'ai* (cute) virtuosity.

Chapter 3, "'The World of Grand Union': Engendering Trans/nationalism via Boys' Love in Chinese Online *Hetalia* Fandom," examines the online Chinese fandom formed around a Japanese manga/anime series *Axis Powers Hetalia*, a lighthearted parody of world history based on nation anthropomorphism.

Originally published as a web comic in 2006, the series has enjoyed worldwide popularity and a considerable amount of controversy in South Korea and China for its alleged national stereotyping and whitewashing of Japan's aggression in World War II. Although China is only a minor character in the series, its visual representation is nevertheless intriguing enough for Chinese fans to churn out a whole slew of fan works. Through a critical analysis of diverse fan discourses and two canonical fan texts, this chapter inquiries about the intersections between gender politics and geopolitics, nationalism and transnationalism, and localization and globalization in the Chinese *Hetalia* fan world.

Apart from Japanese ACG culture, certain Chinese queer fandoms have also vigorously engaged with Western queer culture or, more accurately, imaginaries about it. Chapter 4, "Queering the Post-*L Word* Shane in the 'Garden of Eden': Chinese Fans' Gossip about Katherine Moennig," presents a critical analysis of Chinese fans' queer gossip discourse surrounding the American actress Katherine Moennig, most famous still for her breakthrough role as a butch lesbian character in the television series *The L Word* (Showtime, 2004–2009). Through a deconstructive reading of the gossip that imagines Moennig's real-life lesbian gender identities and homoerotic relationships in one of the largest cross-cultural fandoms in Chinese cyberspace, The Garden of Eden (Yidianyuan), the author reveals that, rather than simply assimilating or rejecting the normative understandings of the West as a civilized, queer-friendly haven and China as a backward, heterocentric nation, the fans' intricate fantasies about the Western queer world reflect their subjective, hybridized reappropriation and reinscription of the Chinese queer Occidentalist imaginations. Ultimately, she argues that the queer Occidentalism exemplified in this cross-cultural gossip functions as a survival strategy for queer fans to interrogate the depressing, heteropatriarchal realities in contemporary mainstream Chinese society.

The Chinese-speaking world is of course rich in its own fan reference objects and incredibly layered, contradictory, engrossing readings of them in online fandoms. Chapter 5, "From Online BL Fandom to the CCTV *Spring Festival Gala*: The Transforming Power of Online Carnival," recounts the "Looking for Leehom" saga, that is, the publicity journeys of and celebrity gossip about trans-Asian pop singer Wang Leehom and classical pianist Li Yundi: first, as fans playfully and romantically paired the two men in online narratives after watching their 2012 CCTV duo performance; second, as the two appeared to appropriate this BL framing for their own commercial benefit; third, as humor about their shipping (fannish pairing of media characters or celebrities)[61] even appeared on the usually heavily controlled CCTV *Spring Festival Gala*; fourth, into the denial of homosexuality by Wang, earning him the derisive moniker online of the "No. 1 Straight Guy in the Universe"; and last, to official and offline mass media uncomfortable attempts to address the situation. Throughout, the author Shuyan Zhou explores the fraught fan spaces and critiques the tendency of some digital-culture scholars to oversimplify such spaces as ones of carnival, developing instead a more nuanced approach that includes a consideration of carnival's conceptual limits.

Chapter 6, "Dongfang Bubai, Online Fandom, and Gender Politics of a Legendary Queer Icon in Post-Mao China," deftly analyzes the readings, rereadings, and gendered translations of the popular transgender character Dongfang Bubai (DFBB) as he/she has been interpreted by fans after the quite different incarnations in the modern Chinese writer Jin Yong's original Chinese novel *The Smiling, Proud Wanderer*; Hong Kong director Tsui Hark's film *Swordsman II*, where DFBB was played by the Taiwanese actress Brigitte Lin; and the mainland Chinese television producer-scriptwriter Yu Zheng's *Swordsman*, where DFBB is played as a "true woman" by the Taiwanese actress Joe Chen. The author Egret Lulu Zhou pays particular attention to fans' framing and reframing of DFBB and his/her loves, triumphs, defeats, and even self-mutilations variously as gay romance, heterosexual romance, or lesbian romance, but all through a queer lens. She also argues that fans' lesbian reading could coexist with homophobia and illustrates the notably awkward entanglements of queer- and nonqueer sentiments in this DFBB fandom.

The China section is followed by two chapters focusing on Hong Kong–based fandoms. Chapter 7, "Desiring Queer, Negotiating Normal: Denise Ho (HOCC) Fandom before and after the Coming-Out," analyzes the 2012 coming-out of Hong Kong lesbian star HOCC that has particular meanings for her Hong Kong fans who have over time ranged from speculating with titillation about her same-sex romances to masking any suggestion of these with heterosexual fiction or gossip about her. Through in-depth interviews and intricate cultural contextualization, Eva Cheuk Yin Li finds that before HOCC came out the ambivalence of her sexuality "was an important part of her stardom that allowed fans' playful speculation, evidenced by the vibrant queer fan culture." Yet, at times, HOCC fans remain self-disciplined by often culturally negotiating with "normal" ideals of female gender and sexuality during their queer readings. After HOCC's public coming-out, as Li reveals persuasively, "the tension between queer and normal has shifted from the heteronormative negotiation of a 'proper' female gender and accorded sexuality to the negotiation of a 'proper' lesbian embodiment" within her fandom.

Chapter 8, "Hong Kong–Based Fans of Mainland Idol Li Yuchun: Elective Belonging, Gender Ambiguity, and Rooted Cosmopolitanism," also explores fan responses to an androgynous female star of seemingly ambivalent sexuality—here mainland Chinese pop music phenomenon Li Yuchun—but from a different angle, focusing on how Mainland-born fans now residing in Hong Kong negotiate a sense of dual belonging with their affective fan articulations and activities. Maud Lavin raises questions about how Li's perceived cosmopolitanism and sexuality are used by a range of Hong Kong–based fans and followers.

Both Hong Kong chapters are rooted in its specific geocultural contexts and form some strong contrasts and connections to the mainland China chapters.

Introduction

For instance, due to the relatively more room for freedom of speech and social activism in Hong Kong, a well-known entertainment celebrity like HOCC is able to perform a high-profile public coming-out, whereas Wang Leehom and Li Yundi had to forcefully deny any same-sex interest within the mainland media cultural context when rumors about their homosexual relationship threatened to get out of control in Chinese cyberspace. Similarly, on the one hand, the ambivalent fan response to mainland gender-bending pop star Li Yuchun reflects the increasingly strained relationship between the Mainland and Hong Kong, most notably in the Umbrella Movement; and, on the other, the deep identifications of mainland fans of Li Yuchun living in Hong Kong speak to a strategic use of the idol's androgynous gendering and its cosmopolitan connotations to negotiate everyday, affective life in Hong Kong.

Differences aside, the Hong Kong chapters and mainland China chapters also share some common themes. Chapter 8's concern of "the use of mass cultural consumption to negotiate border crossing and elective belonging in ways that are primarily separate from identification with local or national governments" is echoed by the discussion in chapter 3 of how Chinese *Hetalia* fans use this Japanese manga series to negotiate the tension between an imperialistic, backward-looking nationalism and a more forward-looking cosmopolitanism. Moreover, the two Hong Kong chapters, as well as the mainland China chapters 2, 4, and 6, all delve into the complexities of queer readings and performativities, and the multifaceted negotiations about genders and sexualities, and between queerness and normativity, in fan communities.

The cross-cultural and gender/sexuality themes continue as the book's focus moves to Taiwan with two closely related chapters on Taiwanese BL fandom and its engagement with Japan and Japaneseness. In chapter 10, "Girls Who Love Boys' Love: BL as Goods to Think with in Taiwan (with a Revised and Updated Coda)," Fran Martin revisits her substantive 2005 study of the BL scene in Taiwan. She traces the history of Taiwanese fans' involvement with Japanese BL manga and asks in essence what BL does for Taiwanese fans. Utilizing the idea of "worlding," Martin argues that Taiwanese fans have created two worlds with BL texts: "an imaginative geography of a 'Japan' that is characterized by sex-gender ambiguity/fluidity/nonconformity," and "a social subworld," or "community of readers, fans, and creators of BL narratives" where complex debates concerning gender and sexuality have been carried out. The chapter concludes with a brief reconsideration of the potential impacts of Internet regulation and censorship on the flourishing transnational worlds of BL fandom.

In chapter 9, "Exploring the Significance of 'Japaneseness': A Case Study of *Fujoshi*'s BL Fantasies in Taiwan," Weijung Chang explores the culture of Taiwanese *fujoshi* (female BL fans) to situate their affective investment in Japan and Japaneseness in the unique Japanophilic context of postcolonial Taiwan. Through looking back at the historical relationship between Taiwan and Japan and the lingering influence of Japan's colonial legacy in Taiwan, the author points out that Japan is not merely a distant fantasy world to Taiwanese *fujoshi* but "a hybrid based on actual experiences with Japanese residents in Taiwan and imaginary concepts of Japan proper." Thus, Taiwanese *fujoshi* are constantly negotiating the contradictory image of Japan as something both familiar and foreign. She also examines the various ways Taiwanese *fujoshi* integrate elements of Japaneseness into their everyday life and how those elements enhance their pleasures in BL fantasy.

Both Taiwan chapters speak directly to the three BL chapters (1, 3, and 5) in the mainland China section. As one of the most prominent forms of queer fandom in the Chinese-speaking world, BL has drawn dedicated followers in all three regions, particularly in Taiwan and mainland China. Yet Taiwanese and mainland BL fandoms have at least two remarkable differences. First, the consumption of Japanese BL manga and novels carries a special weight in Taiwanese BL fandom due to the general receptiveness of Japanese pop culture in Taiwan. In contrast, mainland BL fandom puts more emphasis on the production and consumption of PRC-original BL works. Second, while both mainland and Taiwanese BL fans have used BL as a transformative tool in discourses on genders and sexualities, mainland BL fans have also mobilized BL to build a public space that engages in alternative political expressions. Furthermore, Taiwanese *fujoshi*'s Japanophilia resonates well with the tactical use of Occidentalism in the postcolonial based queer fandom of Western celebrities and media discussed in chapter 4. The self-conflicting longings, pleasures, and hopes involved in the imagination of an idealized other remind us of the strategized "utopian dimension" of fandom and popular culture in general.[62]

Conclusion

QFC's essays analyze local and transcultural consumption and reinterpretations of queer cultural flows despite and in negotiation with different national censorship practices and varied gender, sexuality, and local category-trespassing identifications and belongings. And, in a larger sense, by presenting these ten pieces analyzing queer fandom contribution, we have highlighted the multivalence, plurality, and paradoxes of gender and sexual identities within Chinese-speaking, queer, fannish sociocultural contexts. In conclusion, we would like to sketch out a few promising areas of Chinese-speaking queer fan cultures for future research.

First, of course, is the participation of male fans in BL, GL, ACG, cosplay, and celebrity fandoms, such as the gay male fandom surrounding music diva Faye Wong in Hong Kong, Taiwan, and Singapore.[63] How do male fans, straight or nonstraight, engage in queer fantasies, narratives, and practices? How do they socialize with female fans in the same fandoms? Have queer fandoms fostered a more egalitarian style of communication between genders and more positive group dynamics given the deep-rooted misogyny common in Chinese-speaking societies? How do the reading strategies of Chinese-speaking queer male fans resemble or differ from heterosexual male readers of BL, or *fudanshi* (rotten men), in Japan?[64]

Second, the complexity of gender and sexual identities of Chinese-speaking BL fans has been an issue that has aroused considerable interest among researchers.[65] Yet, instead of focusing on questions such as why heterosexual women are interested in male homosexuality, as if sexual identity was somehow fixed and unchangeable, it is probably more fruitful, like Fran Martin's chapter in this volume, to explore how fans navigate in the strange new world opened up by queer fandoms; how they play and negotiate with various nonnormative desires, identifications, and belongings; how they imagine, defend, and redraw their subjective gender and sexual boundaries.

Third, lesbian BL researcher Akiko Mizoguchi has spoken about a "yaoi (another term denoting BL in Japan) sexual orientation," pointing out that female *yaoi* fans "consider themselves a sort of sexual minority."[66] Similarly, Japanese psychiatrist Tamaki Saito has used the term "otaku sexuality" to describe male *otaku*'s attachment to fictional female characters, which is satisfying enough to replace emotional and sexual relationships with real persons.[67] How can we theorize this multiplication of sexuality imaginatively generated in conjunction with popular cultural practices in East Asia? Is it possible to add *fujoshi* and *otaku* to the now-conventional list of LGBTQ to refer to new forms of queer sexuality that challenge our traditional notions of sexuality, media consumption, as well as the dichotomy between fantasy and reality?

Fourth, the queer transcultural flows examined in *QFC* largely originate from Japan and the United States, two influential centers of global popular culture. Yet, as increasingly more non-Western queer celebrities and media products have gained followers in the Chinese-speaking world through the Internet and social media, as more multilingual and multinational digital platforms for fan production and networking have been established, it is necessary for researchers to trace interactions of Chinese-speaking fans with queer fans and fan objects from South Korea, Southeast Asia, and other non-Western geographical locations to further dismantle the East/West and Chinese/non-Chinese dichotomies and related hierarchies sustained by Euro-American and China centrisms as regards cultural representations of genders and sexualities.

In short, we would like to use *QFC* to invite and encourage further research to explore any queering of or queered frustrations, promises, pleasures, confrontations, and entanglements that result from and deconstruct all kinds of binarisms and normative ideals about identities and subjectivities within fannish participatory spaces and affective communities in the Chinese-speaking world and elsewhere.

Notes

1. *"Taizifei shengzhiji* xiaxian le!" [*Go Princess Go!* Taken offline!], *Shandong shangbao* [Shandong Business Daily], January 21, 2016, accessed April 21, 2016, http://news.163.com/16/0121/14/BDS1BL3R00014Q4P.html.
2. Vera Mackie and Mark McLelland, "Introduction: Framing Sexuality Studies in East Asia," in *Routledge Handbook of Sexuality Studies in East Asia*, ed. Mark McLelland and Vera Mackie (New York: Routledge, 2014), 1–17.
3. Maud Lavin and Xiaorui Zhu, "Alexter: Boys' Love Meets Hong Kong Activism," *fnewsmagazine*, November 17, 2014, accessed July 20, 2015, http://fnewsmagazine.com/2014/11/alexter-boys-love-meets-hong-kong-activism/.
4. "Alexter," *Umbrella Terms*, accessed July 21, 2015, http://www.umbrellaterms.hk/main/blog/keyword-alexter.
5. Cosplay is a fan subculture during which fan-performers wear costumes to impersonate media characters or celebrities. For a detailed definition, see Nicolle Lamerichs, "Stranger Than Fiction: Fan Identity in Cosplay," *Transformative Works and Cultures* 7 (2011), accessed April 1, 2016, *http://journal.transformativeworks.org/index.php/twc/article/view/246/230*.
6. *Anime* refers to animated media.
7. Andrew Parker, "Foucault's Tongues," *Mediations* 18.2 (1994): 80.
8. For more details, see Andrea S. Goldman, *Opera and the City: The Politics of Culture in Beijing, 1770–1900* (Stanford, CA: Stanford University Press, 2012); and Wu Cuncun, *Homoerotic Sensibilities in Late Imperial China* (New York: RoutledgeCurzon, 2004).
9. Significantly, there is a substantial landmark scholarship on homoeroticism-related issues in Mainland China, such as Bret Hinsch, *Passions of the Cut Sleeve: The Male Homosexual Tradition in China* (Los Angeles: University of California Press, 1990); Loretta Wing Wah Ho, *Gay and Lesbian Subculture in Urban China* (New York: Routledge, 2010); and Lucetta Yip Lo Kam, *Shanghai Lalas: Female* Tongzhi *Communities and Politics in Urban China* (Hong Kong: Hong Kong University Press, 2012); Wenqing Kang, *Obsession: Male Same-Sex Relations in China, 1900–1950* (Hong Kong: Hong Kong University Press, 2009); Tze-Lan D. Sang, *The Emerging Lesbian: Female Same-Sex Desire in Modern China* (Chicago: University of Chicago Press, 2003). However, this series of writings tends not to focus on fan studies or in-depth on digital culture and queerness in general. Our volume builds on this existing literature in ways that both unveil the variety and complexity of queer dimensions of fannish practices within contemporary mainland Chinese popular cultural ambience and divulge the historicity, futurity, and transformativity of mainland Chinese queer-related media cultures in a globalized world. For Hong Kong and Taiwan, there has been a broader scholarly and journalistic discourse on localized homosexual-themed cultures; and the cultures themselves enjoy more visibility than do their equivalents in mainland China. Influential texts include Hans Tao-Ming Huang, *Queer Politics and Sexual Modernity in Taiwan* (Hong Kong: Hong Kong University Press, 2011); Helen Hok-Sze Leung, *Undercurrents: Queer Culture and Postcolonial Hong Kong* (Vancouver: University of British Columbia Press, 2008); Song Hwee Lim, *Celluloid Comrades: Representations of Male Homosexuality in Contemporary Chinese Cinemas* (Honolulu: Hawai'i University Press, 2006); Fran Martin, *Situating Sexualities: Queer Representation in Taiwanese Fiction, Film and Public Culture* (Hong Kong: Hong Kong University Press, 2003); and Denise Tse-Shang Tang, *Conditional Spaces: Hong Kong Lesbian Desires and Everyday Life* (Hong Kong: Hong Kong University Press, 2011). Some of this body of literature

has explicated the multiplication of Hong Kong and Taiwanese queer politics, movements, and visual and literary arts along with the increasing popularity of Internet use and digital media in these two regions. The contributions to our volume further this previous scholarship by focusing specifically on Hong Kong and Taiwanese queer fan cultures and activities.

10. For example, see Howard Chiang, ed., *Transgender China* (New York: Palgrave Macmillan, 2012); Howard Chiang, "(De)Provincializing China: Queer Historicism and Sinophone Postcolonial Critique," in *Queer Sinophone Cultures*, ed. Howard Chiang and Ari Larissa Heinrich (New York: Routledge, 2014), 19–51; Petrus Liu, "Why Does Queer Theory Need China?" *positions: East Asia Cultures Critique* 18.2 (2010): 291–320; Audrey Yue, "Queer Asian Cinema and Media Studies: From Hybridity to Critical Regionality," *Cinema Journal* 53.2 (2014): 145–51. For a detailed summary on this topic, see Fran Martin et al., introduction to *AsiaPacifiQueer: Rethinking Genders and Sexualities*, ed. Fran Martin et al. (Urbana: University of Illinois Press, 2008), 1–27; and Fran Martin, "Transnational Queer Sinophone Cultures," in *Routledge Handbook of Sexuality Studies in East Asia*, ed. Mark McLelland and Vera Mackie (New York: Routledge, 2014), 35–48.

11. Martin, "Transnational," 45.

12. Mark Duffett, "Celebrity: The Return of the Repressed in Fan Studies?" in *The Ashgate Research Companion to Fan Cultures*, ed. Linda Duits and Koos Zwaan (Farnham, UK: Ashgate, 2014), 163–80.

13. See Camille Bacon-Smith, *Enterprising Women: Television Fandom and the Creation of Popular Myth* (Philadelphia: University of Pennsylvania Press, 1992), 228–81; Henry Jenkins, *Textual Poachers: Television Fans and Participatory Culture* (New York: Routledge, 1992), 190–227; Sara Gwenllian Jones, "Histories, Fictions, and Xena: Warrior Princess," *Television & New Media* 1.4 (2000): 415; Julie Levin Russo, "Textual Orientation: Queer Female Fandom Online," in *The Routledge Companion to Media & Gender*, ed. Cynthia Carter, Linda Steiner, and Lisa McLaughlin (New York: Routledge, 2014), 452.

14. Some foundational works are Bacon-Smith, *Enterprising Women*; Jenkins, *Textual Poachers*; Constance Penley, "Feminism, Psychoanalysis, and the Study of Popular Culture," in *Cultural Studies*, ed. Lawrence Grossberg, Cary Nelson, and Paula A. Treichler (New York: Routledge, 1992), 479–500; Joanna Russ, ed., *Magic Mommas, Trembling Sisters, Puritans & Perverts: Feminist Essays* (New York: Crossing Press, 1985).

15. Some major works include Patrick W. Galbraith, *The Otaku Encyclopedia: An Insider's Guide to the Subculture of Cool Japan* (New York: Kodansha International, 2009); Mizuko Ito, Daisuke Okabe, and Izumi Tsuji, eds., *Fandom Unbound: Otaku Culture in a Connected World* (New Haven: Yale University Press, 2012); Antonia Levi, Mark McHarry, and Dru Pagliassotti, eds., *Boys' Love Manga: Essays on the Sexual Ambiguity and Cross-Cultural Fandom of the Genre* (Jefferson, NC: McFarland, 2010); Mark McLelland et al., eds., *Boys Love, Manga, and Beyond: History, Culture, and Community in Japan* (Jackson: University of Mississippi Press, 2015); Timothy Perper and Martha Cornog, eds., *Mangatopia: Essays on Manga and Anime in the Modern World* (Santa Barbara, CA: Libraries Unlimited, 2011).

16. See, for example, Jin Feng, *Romancing the Internet: Producing and Consuming Chinese Web Romance* (Boston: Brill, 2013); Katrien Jacobs, *The Afterglow of Women's Pornography in Post-digital China* (New York: Palgrave Macmillan, 2015); Fran Martin and Larissa Heinrich, eds., *Embodied Modernities: Corporeality, Representation, and Chinese Cultures* (Honolulu: University of Hawai'i Press, 2006); Yanrui Xu and Ling Yang, "Forbidden

Love: Incest, Generational Conflict, and the Erotics of Power in Chinese BL Fiction," *Journal of Graphic Novels and Comics* 4.1 (2013): 30–43; Ling Yang and Hongwei Bao, "Queerly Intimate: Friends, Fans and Affective Communication in a *Super Girl* Fan Fiction Community," *Cultural Studies* 26.6 (2012): 842–71.

17. Rhiannon Bury, *Cyberspaces of Their Own: Female Fandoms Online* (New York: Peter Lang, 2005).
18. Jack Halberstam, *In a Queer Time and Place: Transgender Bodies, Subcultural Lives* (New York: New York University Press, 2005), 6.
19. See, for example, Bacon-Smith, *Enterprising Women*; Jenkins, *Textual Poachers*; and Andrea Wood, "'Straight' Women, Queer Texts: Boy-Love Manga and the Rise of a Global Counterpublic," *Women's Studies Quarterly* 34.1/2 (2006): 394–414.
20. For a more detailed discussion on this point, see Karen Hellekson and Kristina Busse, eds., *Fan Fiction and Fan Communities in the Age of the Internet* (Jefferson, NC: McFarland, 2006).
21. Judith Butler, *Gender Trouble: Feminism and the Subversion of Identity* (New York: Routledge, 1990).
22. Annamarie Jagose, *Queer Theory: An Introduction* (New York: New York University Press, 1996), 3.
23. For related discussion, see Eva Cheuk-Yin Li, "Approaching Transnational Chinese Queer Stardom as Zhongxing ('Neutral Sex/Gender') Sensibility," *East Asian Journal of Popular Culture* 1.1 (2015): 75–95.
24. Qian Wang, "Queerness, Entertainment, and Politics: Queer Performance and Performativity in Chinese Pop," in *Queer/Tongzhi China: New Perspectives on Research, Activism and Media Cultures*, ed. Elisabeth L. Engebretsen and William F. Schroeder (with Hongwei Bao) (Copenhagen: NIAS Press, 2015), 155.
25. Anthony Fung, "Faye and the Fandom of a Chinese Diva," *Popular Communication: International Journal of Media and Culture* 7.4 (2009): 252–66.
26. "S.H.E.," Baidu Baike, accessed July 20, 2015, http://baike.baidu.com/view/3187.htm?fromtitle=SHE&fromid=10713083&type=syn#ref_[1]_3187.
27. Audrey Yue and Haiqing Yu, "China's Super Girl: Mobile Youth Cultures and New Sexualities," in *Youth, Media and Culture in the Asia Pacific Region*, ed. Usha M. Rodrigues and Belinda Smaill (Newcastle: Cambridge Scholars Publishing, 2008), 118; Lucetta Yip Lo Kam, "Desiring T, Desiring Self: 'T-Style' Pop Singers and Lesbian Culture in China," *Journal of Lesbian Studies* 18.3 (2014): 252–65.
28. For more details, see Chris Berry, "*East Palace, West Palace*: Staging Gay Life in China," *Jump Cut: A Review of Contemporary Media* 42 (1998): 84–89; Chris Berry, "*Wedding Banquet*: A Family (Melodrama) Affair," in *Chinese Films in Focus: 24 New Takes*, ed. Chris Berry (London: British Film Institute, 2003), 183–90; Chris Berry, "The Sacred, the Profane, and the Domestic in Cui Zi'en's Cinema," *positions: East Asia Cultures Critique* 12.1 (2004): 195–201; Lim, *Celluloid Comrades*; Martin, *Situating Sexualities*; Liang Shi, *Chinese Lesbian Cinema: Mirror Rubbing, Lala, and Les* (Lanham: Lexington Books, 2015); Alvin Ka Hin Wong, "From the Transnational to the Sinophone: Lesbian Representations in Chinese-Language Films," *Journal of Lesbian Studies* 16.3 (2012): 307–22; Audrey Yue, "What's So Queer about *Happy Together*? A.k.a. Queer (N)Asian: Interface, Mobility, Belonging," *Inter-Asia Cultural Studies Journal* 1.2 (2000): 251–64.
29. Shi, *Chinese Lesbian*, 45.
30. May Nimfa Idea, "*Lost in Thailand* Filmmakers Brainstorm with Audience to Ensure Movie's Success," *yibada*, June 18, 2015, accessed March 10, 2016, http://en.yibada.

com/articles/39365/20150618/lost-in-thailand-lost-in-hong-kong-highest-grossing-films-in-china-filmmakers-in-china-best-comedy-movie-in-china.htm.

31. Clifford Coonan, "China Box Office: 'Tiny Times 4.0' Lead as Local Youth Flicks Dominate," *Hollywood Reporter*, July 13, 2015, accessed July 15, 2015, http://www.hollywoodreporter.com/news/china-box-office-tiny-times-808489.

32. Xindong Fang et al., "Zhongguo hulianwang ershinian: Sanci langchao he sanda chuangxin [2]," [Twenty years of China's internet: Three waves and three innovations (2)], *People*, April 21, 2014, accessed July 20, 2015, http://media.people.com.cn/n/2014/0421/c40606-24922639-2.html.

33. Shahulu Tongmeng, *Taiwan azhai qishilu* [Taiwan *otaku* apocalypse], *lightnovel.cn*, September 8, 2010, accessed July 20, 2015, http://www.lightnovel.cn/thread-214503-1-1.html.

34. "Zhongguo ACG quan de fazhan lishi shi zenyang de, younaxie zhongyao wangzhan?" [What's the development history of Chinese ACG circle, are there any important websites?], *Zhihu*, accessed July 20, 2015, http://www.zhihu.com/question/22561605.

35. "Gay Love Theory as Fans Relish Sherlock in China," *BBC*, January 2, 2014, accessed July 24, 2015, http://www.bbc.com/news/blogs-china-blog-25550426; John Wei, "Queer Encounters between Iron Man and Chinese Boys' Love Fandom," *Transformative Works and Cultures* 17 (2014), accessed July 20, 2015, http://journal.transformativeworks.org/index.php/twc/article/view/561/458.

36. Mark Duffett, *Understanding Fandom: An Introduction to the Study of Media Fan Culture* (New York: Bloomsbury Academic, 2013), 236.

37. Yuxi Yang and Boyin Liu, "Quanmeiti shidai de miwenhua yanjiu—yi danmei miqun weili" [Fan cultural studies in an age of digital media—using *danmei* fandom as an example], *Xinwen aihaozhe* [Journalism Lover] 3 (2012): 15–16.

38. "Yuenan fengsha wailai yanqing *danmei* xiaoshuo, zhongguo wangluo wenxue bizhong za" [Vietnam bans foreign romance and *danmei* novels, most come from Chinese internet literature], *Jinghua shibao* [Beijing Times], May 27, 2015, accessed May 1, 2016, http://culture.ifeng.com/a/20150527/43847161_0.shtml.

39. For news coverage of the popularity of the show in South Korea, see Vittorio Hernandez, "Chinese Drama 'Nirvana in Fire' Catches Interest of South Korean TV Viewers," *yibada*, April 13, 2016, accessed May 8, 2016, http://en.yibada.com/articles/116157/20160413/chinese-drama-nirvana-in-fire-catches-interest-of-south-korean-tv-viewers.htm. For information of the participation of Korean fans at the Shanghai fan convention, see the convention's official Weibo account at http://weibo.com/u/5763841308?refer_flag=1001030201_&is_all=1.

40. For detailed discussions on Sinophonic appropriations of the English term *queer*, see Hongwei Bao, "'Queer Comrades': Transnational Popular Culture, Queer Sociality, and Socialist Legacy," *English Language Notes* 49.1 (2011): 131–37; Song Hwee Lim, "How to Be Queer in Taiwan: Translation, Appropriation, and the Construction of a Queer Identity in Taiwan," in *AsiaPacifiQueer: Rethinking Genders and Sexualities*, ed. Fran Martin, Peter A. Jackson, Mark McLelland, and Audrey Yue (Urbana: University of Illinois Press, 2008), 235–50; and Martin, *Situating Sexualities*, 32–33.

41. For a detailed discussion on the English term *Chinese*, see Martin, "Transnational," 35–48.

42. Martin, "Transnational," 35.

43. Shu-mei Shih, "The Concept of the Sinophone," *PMLA* 126.3 (2011): 710.

44. Shu-mei Shih, *Visuality and Identity: Sinophone Articulations across the Pacific* (Berkeley: University of California Press, 2007), 5.
45. Chiang, "(De)Provincializing," 31.
46. Lisa Rofel, "Grassroots Activism: Non-normative Sexual Politics in Post-socialist China," in *Unequal China: The Political Economy and Cultural Politics of Inequality*, ed. Wanning Sun and Yingjie Guo (New York: Routledge, 2013), 154.
47. The website is available at http://www.danlan.org/about.htm.
48. Kam, *Shanghai Lalas*, 97.
49. See Kam, *Shanghai Lalas*; Elisabeth Lund Engebretsen, *Queer Women in Urban China: An Ethnography* (New York: Routledge, 2014).
50. "Tongxinglianjie zao jingjingfang tuxi fengbi" [The Gay Festival was cracked down on and closed by the Beijing police], *Hong Kong Commercial Daily*, December 27, 2005, accessed July 20, 2015, http://3g.xici.net/d33726324.htm.
51. Travis S. K. Kong, "A Fading *Tongzhi* Heterotopia: Hong Kong Older Gay Men's Use of Spaces," *Sexualities* 15.8 (2012): 908. Also, for a more detailed discussion related to this topic, see Lim, *Celluloid Comrades*, 37.
52. Travis S. K. Kong, Sky H. L. Lau, and Eva C. Y. Li, "The Fourth Wave?" A Critical Reflection on the *Tongzhi* Movement in Hong Kong," in *Routledge Handbook of Sexuality Studies in East Asia*, ed. Mark McLelland and Vera Mackie (New York: Routledge, 2014), 188–202.
53. Day Wong, "Rethinking the Coming Home Alternative: Hybridization and Coming Out Politics in Hong Kong's Anti-Homophobia Parades," *Inter-Asia Cultural Studies* 8.4 (2007): 608.
54. Petrus Liu, "Queer Marxism in Taiwan," *Inter-Asia Cultural Studies* 8.4 (2007): 517–39.
55. "Taiwan tongzhi youxing" [Taiwan Gay Parade], *Wikipedia*, last modified October 27, 2014, https://zh.wikipedia.org/wiki/%E5%8F%B0%E7%81%A3%E5%90%8C%E5%BF%97%E9%81%8A%E8%A1%8C.
56. Huang, *Queer Politics*.
57. Daai DQ, "[Erciyuan] gongkai jihu wuma 18/jin tongrenzhi Taiwan tongren zuozhe beibu" [Two-dimension publicizing almost uncensored 18/forbidden fanzines taiwanese author was arrested], *tgbus*, August 22, 2013, accessed July 20, 2015, http://bbs.tgbus.com/thread-5196325-1-1.html.
58. See Mei Ning Yan, "Regulating Online Pornography in Mainland China and Hong Kong," in *Routledge Handbook of Sexuality Studies in East Asia*, ed. Mark McLelland and Vera Mackie (London: Routledge, 2015): 387–401; Ting Liu, "Conflicting Discourses on Boys' Love and Subcultural Tactics in Mainland China and Hong Kong," *Intersections: Gender and Sexuality in Asia and the Pacific* 20 (2009), accessed October 22, 2014, http://intersections.anu.edu.au/issue20/liu.htm.
59. Erika Junhui Yi, "Reflection on Chinese Boys' Love Fans: An Insider's View," *Transformative Works and Cultures* 12 (2013). doi:10.3983/twc.2013.0424.
60. Gordon Mathews, *Ghetto at the Center of the World: Chungking Mansions, Hong Kong* (Chicago: University of Chicago Press, 2011).
61. For a detailed definition of this term, see Nicola Balkind, *Fan Phenomena: "The Hunger Games"* (Chicago: University of Chicago Press, 2014), 133.
62. Here our discussion links productively with a lineage in fan studies begun movingly discussed by Henry Jenkins. See Jenkins, *Textual Poachers*, 281–82.

63. Shzr Ee Tan, "Beyond the 'Fragile Woman': Identity, Modernity, and Musical Gay Icons in Overseas Chinese Communities," in *Popular Culture in Asia: Memory, City, Celebrity*, ed. Lorna Fitzsimmons and John A. Lent (Basingstoke, UK: Palgrave Macmillan, 2013), 183–205.

64. Kazumi Nagaike, "Do Heterosexual Men Dream of Homosexual Men? BL *Fudanshi* and Discourse on Male Feminization," in *Boys Love, Manga, and Beyond: History, Culture, and Community in Japan*, ed. Mark McLelland et al. (Jackson: University Press of Mississippi, 2015), 189–209.

65. See, for example, Yin-Huei Chang, "Qiangwei chanrao shizijia: BL yuetingren wenhua yanjiu" [Crucifix entwined with roses: A cultural study of BL audience] (MA thesis, National Taiwan University, 2007); Yannan Li, "Japanese Boy-Love Manga and the Global Fandom: A Case Study of Chinese Female Readers" (MA thesis, Indiana University, 2009); Weibo Wang, "Xinlixue shiye xia de xinxing yawenhua qunti—zhongguo 'tongrennü' xianzhuang jiqi chansheng de shehui xinli genyuan tanxi" [A psychological perspective of an emerging subcultural group: Exploring the socio-psychological causes of Chinese "fangirls"] (MA thesis, Xuzhou Normal University, 2011).

66. Akiko Mizoguchi, "Theorizing Comics/Manga Genre as a Productive Forum: *Yaoi* and Beyond," in *Comics Worlds and the World of Comics: Towards Scholarship on a Global Scale*, ed. Jaqueline Berndt (Kyoto: International Manga Research Centre, Kyoto Seika University, 2010), 155–56, accessed April 21, 2016, http://imrc.jp/lecture/2009/12/comics-in-the-world.html.

67. Patrick W. Galbraith, *The Moe Manifesto: An Insider's Look at the Worlds of Manga, Anime, and Gaming* (Singapore: Tuttle Publishing, 2014), 179–84.

I.

Mainland China

1
Chinese *Danmei* Fandom and Cultural Globalization from Below

Ling Yang and Yanrui Xu

Introduction

Danmei[1] (耽美), or Boys' Love (BL), is a genre of male-male romance created by and for women and sexual minorities. It comes in a variety of formats: fiction, manga, anime, games, audio drama, MV, songs, and cosplay. First appearing in Japanese girls' comics in the 1970s, the genre has gained tremendous popularity in East Asia and worldwide via the spread of Japanese ACG (anime, comics, and games) culture. As a particular mind-set and emotional structure, rather than a specific media text, BL can be linked to numerous forms of popular culture from many parts of the world. In China, *danmei* is no longer solely associated with Japanese popular culture. Instead, it has successfully merged with a diverse range of local and global media and celebrity cultures, and developed into a transnational, all-inclusive, and female-dominated meta-fan culture. By tracing the trajectory of Chinese *danmei* fandom in the past two decades, this paper explores the possibility of *danmei* as a model of grassroots globalization that subverts heterosexual normativity,[2] fosters alternative social and economic networks, and generates a convergence of cultural and media flows from both the East and the West.

The data for this chapter are drawn from our own BL/GL[3] fan experiences (ten years for Xu, seven years for Yang), online ethnography of BL websites, face-to-face and online interviews with BL fans, and field research of BL distribution networks. We interviewed twenty-seven *danmei* fans, including one Taiwanese *danmei* publisher, eight professional and amateur *danmei* creators, and eighteen *danmei* readers, from January 2014 to September 2014. The interviews lasted from one hour to ten hours, depending on the willingness of the interviewees. We also visited comic markets, magazine wholesalers, and BL bookstores in Taipei, Shanghai, Beijing, Guangzhou, Wuhan, and Changsha from August 2013 to August 2014.

Inspired by Mizuko Ito's three-pronged conceptual framework in discussing transnational *otaku* culture,[4] we approach the ongoing "gloBLisation"[5] from three different aspects: the online and offline infrastructures that enable the commercial and noncommercial transnational distribution of *danmei* works, *danmei* circles devoted to different types of *danmei* creations and fan objects but connected by their common homoerotic imagination, and the emergence of an online transnational Chinese public sphere where women from Chinese diasporas around the world could discuss and debate all kinds of fannish, feminine, and political topics. We are interested in finding out how a transnational fandom like *danmei* can flourish in a repressive environment, how it seizes various resources to nourish itself and negotiates with various forces for a space of its own, how it intersects with other media flows and cultural movements, and how its global reach facilitates the understanding between self and other. We seek to use the example of *danmei* fandom to challenge the masculinized, top-down model of thinking about transnational cultural flows that overemphasizes national origin, the industrial player, the official economy, and the competition for soft power at the expense of other glocalized, noninstitutionalized, nonprofit, noncompetitive ways of cultural exchange.

Infrastructures: The High Tech and Low End of Cultural Globalization

Danmei was first introduced to China in the early 1990s when a large quantity of pirated Japanese manga, including BL manga, flooded the Chinese market. Because of its dual association with homosexuality and pornography, the genre remains to this day a vulnerable target of state censorship.[6] Like the dissemination of Japanese anime in the United States that has been pulled "through the energies of enthusiastic fans," rather than pushed by the cultural industries,[7] the exponential growth of *danmei* in China is also driven by fan demand. Through utilizing new media technologies, exploiting regulatory loopholes, and evading or flouting the restraints of censorship, a spectrum of actors, including fan communities, small businesses, and big corporations, has been able to construct a transnational distribution network that encompasses both digital and print media, retail and wholesale channels, as well as face-to-face trading.

The emergence of Chinese *danmei* culture is closely linked to the development of the Internet, which has played a crucial role in the formation of fan identity, the building of fan community, and the production and circulation of original and derivative *danmei* works. The anonymity of the Internet also provides a relatively safe space for fans to "come out" and share their hobby with fellow fans. Early *danmei* forums and websites were usually run by students, who had neither money nor experience, and often suffered from funding shortage and unstable servers.[8] After the rise of big commercial websites like Jinjiang Literature City (jjwxc.net, 2003–), Liancheng Read (lcread.com, 2007–), and Danmei Chinese Web (52blgl.com, 2008–), those self-owned noncommercial websites gradually went into decline. Among the commercial websites, Jinjiang is undoubtedly the most influential. With 7 million registered users and 50,000 contracted writers, the website has published more than 500,000 titles, covering a large variety of literary genres, such as original heterosexual romance, BL, GL, and all types of fan fiction, but it is mostly known for its high-quality original *danmei* works.[9]

Compared to the proliferation of *danmei* novels, original *danmei* manga series are still quite rare in the Chinese-speaking world because of the lack of legal distribution platforms and the extremely high investment of time and effort on the part of artists. An experienced writer can finish a novel within two or three months. But it would take years for an artist to complete a manga adaptation of a novel or create her own manga series. On U17.com (2006–), the biggest original manga website in China and the manga version of Jinjiang, one can find only a few hundred completed or recently updated titles in its *danmei* section. Since U17 bans the display of naked body, let alone private parts, *danmei* artists who choose to publish their works on the website have to pay more attention to storylines and drawing styles to attract readers.

Apart from commercial websites, Baidu Post Bar, the biggest Chinese communication platform provided by the search engine company Baidu, offers ample space for *danmei* fans to set up open-access "bars" or forums at no cost. The Baidu "*Fujoshi*[10] Bar," "BL Bar," and "Events Recording Bar" all boast more than 500,000 registered users. Since 2010, many *danmei* writers, artists, and publishers have used Sina Microblog, a hybrid of Twitter and Facebook, to share their life experience, connect with their fan base, and announce publication information. Fans also use social networking services to circulate *danmei* jokes, gay rumors, and LGBT activity news. In 2010, Sina Microblog organized its first micro fiction competition, and *danmei* turned out to be the most popular genre in the competition. In the past two years, Lofter.com, a Tumblr-like light blogging platform has caught on among *danmei* fanfic writers, who enjoy the more exclusive and artistic atmosphere there. Unlike commercial writers, fanfic writers are more interested in finding like-minded peers and sharing work with them than getting a lot of broad public attention.

Although it is much more difficult to publish *danmei* in print than online because of the tight control of the publishing industry,[11] print *danmei* magazines have been published in China through fake or borrowed publication permits since 1999. Early *danmei* magazines like *Danmei Season* (*Danmei jijie*) and *Adonis* (*Adonisi*) aimed to introduce the best and most popular Japanese BL works to Chinese fans. In 2005, a new *danmei* monthly *Perfect Sky* (*Feitian*) was launched to promote original *danmei* fiction written by domestic writers. After the demise of a string of illegal BL magazines, the first legal BL magazine, *Tianman BLue* (*Tianman lanse*), hit the market in September 2013. The monthly not only has an official permit for running publications, a much coveted asset in Chinese publishing industry, but is produced by Guangzhou Tianwen Kadokawa Animation and Manga Company, a company whose coinvestors are the state-run Zhongnan Publishing and Media Group and the Hong Kong branch of Kadokawa

Corporation. Yet, except cleverly highlighting the letters "BL" in the magazine name, the publisher cautiously avoids any direct link to *danmei*. The submission guidelines of the magazine also rule out any explicit content so that contributors can only play around with ambiguous homoerotic feelings between male characters. As a legal magazine, *BLue* is able to enjoy broad exposure and extensive distribution channels. In our field research in Wuhan, Changsha, and Guangzhou, we saw posters of the magazine displayed conspicuously at retailers and wholesale markets. The legalization of a single *danmei* magazine, however, does not mean that the Chinese government has started to show more tolerance toward BL content. In fact, right after the first issue of *BLue* was released, two *danmei* magazines of original and translated Japanese BL content, *Boyfriend* (*Nanpengyou*) and *BOLO* (*Bolozhi*), were prosecuted and forced to cease operation.

The boom of the comic market (*tongrenzhan*) since 2011 has brought new opportunities for *danmei* producers to bypass official publishers and market their self-published original works (*gerenzhi*) or fanzines/*dōjinshi* (*tongrenzhi*) directly to readers. In 2013, about 110 fan-oriented comic markets were held in thirty cities across China.[12] Big comic markets could easily draw more than 10,000 participants in one day. Although not fully legal in China, self-publishing is far more profitable than commercial publishing. According to Feng Nong, China's leading *danmei* writer, a self-published title would break even once it has sold 300 copies. A commercially published author usually earns only 8 per cent of the sales as royalties, but a self-published author can pocket 50 per cent of sales revenue and does not have to pay tax. That is to say, an author can earn more from selling 1,000 self-published copies than from selling 5,000 commercial copies.[13] In the carnival atmosphere of comic markets, fan participants are often in the mood for spending. Hence, it is not difficult for a well-known *danmei* artist or writer to sell 500 copies in two to three hours at a book-signing event. With due caution, it is also possible to sell explicit *danmei* works at comic markets.[14]

To dodge censorship at home, some Chinese *danmei* writers have chosen to publish their works in Taiwan, where the publishing and viewing of sexually explicit content is legal for adults over eighteen years old.[15] Since the first half of the 2000s, small, fan-managed, BL-oriented Taiwanese publishing houses have actively acquired manuscripts from mainland BL writers as a way to reduce costs and increase sales.[16] Over the years, mainland writers have become the major content creators for the Taiwanese BL publishing industry. In January 2014, we visited Yaoi Society, a library and rental store specializing in BL manga and novel in Taipei. By our own estimate, at least half of the 10,000 or so BL volumes collected by the society are written by mainland writers. The published-in-Taiwan works are often sold back to mainland readers via the Internet. Yet those Taiwanese editions generally use a vertical page layout that is difficult to read for mainland readers, and they are usually twice or even three times more expensive than mainland books, meaning only the most loyal fans purchase them. Besides, published-in-Taiwan books also need to be approved by the Chinese government before sale. One of Feng Nong's friends used to be engaged in the selling of Taiwanese *danmei* books, as she wanted to help mainland authors to earn more royalties. Later the seller was arrested and sentenced to two years in prison on the charge of running an "illegal business operation."[17]

Chinese writers and readers have also made use of Taiwanese literature websites like myfreshnet.com (2000–2014) to publish and read explicit BL works. A survey conducted by Ting Liu shows that as early as 2008, Chinese *danmei* writers already outnumbered Taiwanese *danmei* writers by two to one on Taiwanese websites.[18] Like Jinjiang, Fresh Net has implemented a pay-per-view system that charges readers a small fee to access certain VIP chapters published on its website. The revenue generated from readers' payments is then split between the website and the writers. Although mainland users often experience difficulty logging in and opening the web pages, Fresh Net's sizable reader base (1.5 million registered users) and greater freedom of expression still attracted many mainland professional *danmei* writers until it developed financial trouble and fell behind with remuneration to writers in early 2014.[19] The website later stopped updating its content and no longer exists today. In the summer of 2014, notable Taiwanese BL publisher Longma Book established a new online literary website that largely caters to mainland BL fans.

In his study of South Asian and African traders in Hong Kong and China, Gordon Mathews uses the term "low-end globalization" to refer to a type of "globalization from below."[20] Unlike the "high-end globalization" represented by multinational corporations operating more or less within the boundary of law and championed by nation-states, low-end globalization typically involves small businesses and individual traders operating under the radar of the law without the protection of states. In many ways, *danmei* is also a form of low-end globalization that involves numerous semilegal or illegal transactions of information, works, goods, and money across the Taiwan Strait and in East Asia, even though it also thrives on the Internet and through other advanced communication technologies. But unlike those developing-country traders who are motivated mainly by financial gain, the informal economy of *danmei* is "an imbricated commercial/gift culture that is in itself heterogeneous."[21] In this thick mesh of nonprofit fan communities, semicommercial fan producers, corporate-owned but fan-managed commercial websites and magazines, and semilegal family wholesalers and retailers, Chua Beng Huat's sweeping claim that the affective labor of fan consumers will always wind up being exploited by the cultural industries no longer holds water,[22] as all the participants in this network are the targets of endless antiporn, anti-illegal-publication, and antipiracy campaigns of the nation-state. When big corporations try to cash in on the huge *danmei* market, they bear the same risk of playing in the legal grey zone as small players.

In our interviews with *danmei* fans, we find that a significant portion seldom spends money on their hobby. They merely download free *danmei* novels, generally in the .txt format, from e-library or file hosting services on the Internet.

Those resources are provided either by individual fans or the controversial "novel sweeping groups" (*saowen zu*). Organized by fan volunteers, those groups regularly collect, cull, and publicize BL novels, manga, dramas, songs, and gay videos for free, without any authorization from the copyright owners. Some *danmei* writers also insist on creating *danmei* stories for free and claim that only free works are the best works. Even among professional *danmei* writers, money is not their primary concern; otherwise, they would have already switched to heterosexual romance, which would bring them more financial rewards through official print publication and the opportunity of television, film, and manga adaptations.

Circles: Organizational Divergence and Cultural Convergence

Currently, Chinese *danmei* fandom is made up of three prominent circles: the original[23] *danmei* circle (*yuandan quan*) that focuses on the production, consumption, and adaptation of original Chinese-language *danmei* novels; the Japanese circle (*rixi quan*) dedicated to the translation of Japanese BL works and the fan re-creation of Japanese ACG series; and the Euro-American circle (*oumei quan*) devoted to the production and translation of slash fanfic of Euro-American media products. Each of the three circles has its unique features. The original *danmei* circle is the largest and most commercialized; the Japanese circle, the oldest and most multifarious; the Euro-American circle, the fastest growing and most anti-commercial. Fans of Chinese, Japanese, Korean, and Euro-American pop stars and sports celebrities have also set up their own real person *danmei*/slash fanfic circles, but generally with less influence and smaller reach than the aforementioned three circles. It is worth noting however, that there is no hard-and-fast boundary between all these fan circles. While some BL fans might have fixed attachments to certain formats, genres, or fan objects, most are nomadic, constantly moving from one circle to another, bringing fan knowledge of previous circles to new ones. Such cultural cross-fertilization has greatly enriched the development of Chinese *danmei* culture, making it a vibrant global cultural commons.

Since *danmei* originated in Japan, many first-generation Chinese *danmei* fans had devoted their time and efforts to the translation and dissemination of Japanese BL manga and novels. Yet with the rapid growth of indigenous *danmei* fiction, Japanese BL fiction with its so frequent high school or work office backgrounds has gradually fallen out of favor with Chinese readers. Today, the majority of Chinese fans are drawn to the Japanese circle by its unique BL-oriented ACG products. They turn to commercial manga websites like Rotten Manga (mh.fumanhua.com, 2007–) to browse original Japanese BL manga series, Zerodm.tv (2008–) for Japanese BL anime, and Otomedream.com (2001–) for Japanese BL dramas and games. Besides the consumption of Japanese BL content, Chinese fans have also engaged in the re-creation of Japanese ACG series themselves.

On Baidu Post Bar alone, there are more than 6,000 bars centered on the pairing up, or "shipping," of male Japanese manga and anime characters, which in turn has generated numerous fanfics, fan art, and fan videos. The well-known Japanese online artist community Pixiv.net (2007–) is also popular among Chinese BL artists and ACG fans in general, as they can get in touch with top Japanese BL artists on the website, as well as showcase their own works to an international audience. Because of the rapid increase of new users from China, Pixiv.net has even launched a simplified Chinese user interface.

While some members in the Japanese circle have built a business model based on multiple copyright infringements, others stick to their noncommercial and nonprofit principles. Rotten Manga is a prime example of piracy. Through unauthorized use of fan scanlation, that is, scanning and translation, and licensed Taiwanese translation, the website has accumulated more than 3,000 completed or ongoing Japanese BL manga titles. Readers can access those works for free without logging in, but they have to put up with the advertisements on the site. To prevent the commercial use of fan translation, many nonprofit fan communities have set up strict registration systems. For instance, registrations for Otomedream are manually reviewed by the administrators, and some fans have been denied membership several times before they are finally allowed to join the forum. Even after they become full members of the forum, they are still required to pay a certain amount of virtual currency to access fan-translated content.

The aesthetics and conventions of Japanese BL help lay the foundation of Chinese *danmei*. One defining feature of Japanese BL is the dyad of *seme* (*gong* in Chinese, literally, the attacker, similar to the top in self-defined gay relationships with labeled positions) and *uke* (*shou*, literally, the receiver/bottom). In BL-style male-male relationships, one partner must be the *seme*, the other, the *uke*, and the assignment of the roles is usually fixed and nonreversible. For instance, the pairing of Levi/Eren from the hit Japanese manga and anime series *Attack on Titan* (2009–) is far more popular than that of Eren/Levi in China, meaning that most Chinese fans prefer Levi, rather than Eren, to play the role of *seme*. Another feature of Japanese BL is the emphasis on the beautiful appearance of the male couple. In BL manga, especially, both the *seme* and the *uke* look young and handsome, and the *uke* is often depicted as an effeminate young boy, physically shorter and weaker than the *seme*. Japanese BL also invents an extensive categorization of the character traits of *seme* and *uke*. The pairing of personalities can lead to a variety of *seme/uke* combinations, and different combinations can arouse different expectations and pleasures in readers.[24]

Since Chinese fans started to create their own indigenous *danmei* stories in the late 1990s, Jinjiang has emerged as the key site for the original *danmei* circle. While co-opted by China's flourishing web literature industry, the website retains the flavor of a noncommercial fan community. It consists of two main subsites: the "Green Jinjiang" (so named because of the background color of the site), where writers can charge readers viewing fees, and the "Pink Jinjiang," where users can share their works and chat about various topics for free. To foster interaction between readers and writers, the Green Jinjiang also designs a space for readers to leave comments after reading every chapter, and Jinjiang readers are known to be more willing to communicate with writers than readers of other commercial websites.[25] Compared to the "silly, simple, and sweet" heterosexual romance prevalent on other women-oriented literature websites, Jinjiang *danmei* writers are more inclined to experiment with diverse styles and themes and have incorporated elements of science fiction, sports, and other traditionally "unfeminine" genres into their writings.[26] Their creativity has turned Jinjiang into the trendsetter for the whole web literature industry.

In recent years, the global popularity of the BBC television series *Sherlock* (2010–) and the Marvel Cinematic Universe films has greatly stimulated the expansion of the Euro-American circle in China. From 2010 to 2014, members of Suiyuanju (mtslash.org, 2005–), the largest online forum in the circle, soared from 10,000 to more than 270,000. While primarily dedicated to the publishing of slash fanfic of Anglo-American movies and television series, Suiyuanju also hosts a lively discussion board that often engages with issues of women's rights and gender politics. For example, in 2014 a gay *danmei* fan initiated a thread wondering why the role of *seme* and *uke* cannot be reversed in BL, as it is clearly different from real-life gay relationships.[27] The thread soon turns into a comparative analysis of the gender implications of BL and slash, as fans realize that there is no equivalent concept of *seme* and *uke* in slash.

Besides Suiyuanju, fans of Euro-American circle have also frequented non-Chinese fan sites like LiveJournal, Tumblr, and AO3 (archiveofourown.org, 2009–). The latter is a noncommercial, nonprofit fan-works hosting place with more than 1.3 million works and 410,000 registered users from all over the world. All the works on AO3 can be read and downloaded free of charge, and there are no advertisements on the site.[28] While the majority of the works are written in English, there are also works written in a dozen other languages, including Chinese. One of our interviewees, a first-year graduate student majoring in French language and literature, told Yang that she has been a registered member of AO3 since 2013. She is a fan of the Cold War spy film *Tinker Tailor Soldier Spy* (2011), but there are very few Chinese fanfics about this work. She was thrilled to find a small fandom of this film on AO3, where she has come across fanfics of entirely different styles from Chinese ones. Aided by Google Translator, she is able to communicate with international fans in Portuguese, Italian, Russian, and Czech. The following is an excerpt of her e-mail to Yang about her AO3 experience:

> Upon crossing the language barriers, one can gradually find out that regardless of languages, those fanfics are all expressions of love for the same fandom/cp [character pairing, original English]. At that moment, one can feel the subtle cross-cultural resonation, akin to what the Chinese idiom "harmony without sameness" [*he er butong*] has meant.[29]

The above self-reflection on transcultural fan activities seems to echo nicely Chin and Morimoto's observation that "fans become fans of bordering-crossing texts or objects not necessarily because of *where* they are produced, but because they may recognise a subjective moment of affinity regardless of origin."[30] However, the issue of the nation-state still looms large in the cultural landscape of *danmei*, not only because individual fans are unequally endowed with the ability to transcend national, cultural, and linguistic barriers in their pursuits of fan objects, but because Chinese *danmei* fandom as a whole has to deal with government censorship on a daily basis. In the following section, we will take the anonymous *danmei* forum Xianqing as an example to explore how fans' affective investments are intertwined with and complicated by their national and political affiliations in a transnational Chinese public sphere generated by the production and consumption of *danmei*.

Space: A Nationalistic Transnational Chinese Sphere

Established by Jinjiang Literature City in 2003, Xianqing has developed into the most renowned *danmei* discussion forum in the Chinese-speaking world in the past decade. It welcomes all sorts of information, fantasy, and gossip related but not limited to *danmei* and draws tens of thousands of hardcore *danmei* fans daily. Typical discussion topics include reviews and recommendations of *danmei*-related works, sharing of writing experiences, shipping of celebrities or fictional characters, current events around the world, interesting historical tidbits, and the realities of LGBT life. Everyday topics like jobs, relationships, and food are also favored by many participants.

To avoid government censorship and uninitiated outsiders, the discussion on Xianqing is heavily laden with *danmei* jargon and special code words invented by Xianqing users. Unless one has spent a considerable amount of time immersed in the forum, one would be unable to fully decipher the content of discussion, let alone join the conversation. The rule of anonymous posting has further fostered an acerbic style of communication on the forum. Although Xianqing users address one another as "girl" (*guniang*) by default, few hold refined manners or feminine coyness in high regard. Instead, those female fans admire toughness, audacity, eloquence, and humor, qualities that are generally associated with men, rather than women, in Chinese society and speak freely about masculine-designated topics like sex, sports, politics, and the military. As a result, Xianqing is known for its endless arguments and squabbles among users, which is exactly the opposite image of the "harmonious society" promoted by the state.

Another notable feature of Xianqing is its large number of overseas users. As Guobin Yang has pointed out, Chinese Internet culture has always had a transnational dimension because the social history of the Chinese Internet began among overseas Chinese students and scholars in the late 1980s. Besides, early Internet users in China had to rely on Chinese-language sites outside China "due to the scarcity of content in domestic Web sites."[31] However, the direction of the information flow has gradually changed in recent years, especially in the field of web literature. Statistics released by Jinjiang show that the website has a high concentration of metropolitan and international users, with 67 per cent of users coming from top Asian cities like Shanghai, Beijing, Taipei, Hong Kong, and Guangzhou, 25 per cent from the United States, Canada, Australia, and other foreign countries.[32] Although Taiwanese and Hong Kong BL fans are not highly visible on Xianqing for reasons we will soon discuss, there is a conspicuous presence of Chinese diaspora participants living in North America, Australia, and Europe, and they have been jokingly called the "Party of Time Difference" (*shicha dang*) on Xianqing. Those overseas fans tend to be either first-generation Chinese immigrants or Chinese students studying overseas.

While Xianqing could be described as a "transnational Chinese cultural sphere" that uses Chinese as the dominant language of communication with participants consisting of ethnic Chinese around the world,[33] some of its contributors have demonstrated a strong nationalistic and progovernment stance in discussing political issues, particularly issues concerning national unity. They would vehemently lash out at any act or speech that is suspected to diminish the authority of the party leaders, the nation-state, and traditional culture, rendering peaceful dialogues between different political views rather difficult on the forum. As a result, native Taiwanese and Hong Kong users and prodemocracy Chinese users often dare not to speak out in Xianqing's political discussions. The four consecutive threads about the 2014 prodemocracy movement in Hong Kong give us a glimpse of how the ethos of nationalism is played out in this transnational public sphere.

On the afternoon of September 30, 2014, a fan posted a short message on Xianqing saying that his or her friend was planning to leave Hong Kong because the student demonstration was suppressed and the situation was quite chaotic. The fan ended the post with a question, "Does anyone know what's going on in Hong Kong?"[34] Within twenty-four hours, the post had evolved into one of the hottest threads on Xianqing with more than 82,000 hits and about 3,000 replies. Yet, except for a couple of posts that tried to explain the goal of the Occupy Central movement, the response in the thread was overwhelmingly negative and scornful, as most discussants held that the student protests were instigated by hostile Western forces and would destabilize Hong Kong's economy, which is exactly the same excuse the Chinese government used to suppress the democratic movement in 1989.

To be fair, Xianqing's sneering attitudes toward Hong Kongers are by no means exceptional or excessive among Chinese citizens, especially in light of the escalating tension between local residents in Hong Kong and mainland Chinese in recent years.[35] Compared to those Mainlanders who had no clue about the political turmoil in Hong Kong because of media censorship, Xianqing participants could even be praised for their passion for politics, even though they are inclined to support the government rather than the students. Most of the information about the protests was supplied by overseas fans who have access to Facebook, Twitter, local newspapers in Hong Kong, and Western media. Unfortunately, those fans mainly circulated news and images of the anti-Occupy protests in Hong Kong in the attempt to prove that the prodemocracy movement is a terrible mistake.

China scholars have offered a number of different theories about the cause of rampant nationalism on the Chinese Internet. Shubo Li attributes the phenomenon to Chinese government efforts to dismantle the online public space "until the folk discourse is no longer able to carry deliberative discussions on public matters apart from unreflective nationalism and popular prejudices."[36] Yang and Zheng emphasize the psychological aspect of youth nationalism. They argue that there is a "psychological gap" or "imbalance" between youth's "expectation of China's international status and the actual prestige accorded to China by the West." Growing up in an era of unprecedented economic growth in China, the new generation of youth tends to believe that China deserves more respect from the international community for its enhanced national strength. When this expectation is not met, nationalistic sentiments are stirred up.[37]

Indeed, we can apply both explanations to the case of Xianqing. There used to be many heated political debates on Xianqing around 2006. A *danmei* writer named Han Yi was known for her criticism of nationalism at that time, and her views had attracted both supporters and detractors. Since 2008, however, with the tightening of Internet censorship, public opinion on the forum has been carefully monitored to toe the party line, and critical voices have therefore become increasingly rare. Nevertheless, we also detect genuine frustrations and resentments about the ubiquitous China-bashing in the West among Xianqing participants, like the following reply posted by a student studying in Australia in response to the discussion of the media coverage of the Occupy Central movement in the West:

> It's so annoying. This Sunday, there was an interview with Hong Kongers; Monday, with Tibetan separatists; Tuesday, with Xinjiang separatists. Really, really annoying! This damned kangaroo [Australia] on one hand depends on us for living and on the other hand speaks ill of China every day. I've had numerous debates with my landlord. But this old guy has been thoroughly brainwashed. He always has that attitude "I've got democracy so I'm holier than you and you're from a despotic country therefore you know nothing." A while ago, he kept rambling when watching a program about Xinjiang separatists. I was so mad that I retorted back: "You guys have no democracy at all. In real democracy, all of you would go back to U.K. and give the country back to aboriginal Australians." Finally he was speechless.[38]

Obviously, this girl has taken the criticism of China as a personal attack because the national image is closely linked to her own self-image. Faced with the huge perception gap between her image of China (a rising great power) and how the outside world sees China (a repressive authoritarian state), she resorts to nationalistic mentality as a defense mechanism.

This strong adherence to national identity could be a source of tension and conflict in the transnational *danmei* fandom. Not long after the Hong Kong protests began, a Chinese *danmei* writer posted a casual insulting comment about the protests in her Microblog account. Her Taiwanese sales agent, a local *tongrenzhi* group that happened to be sympathizers of Hong Kong student protestors, saw the comment and immediately decided to terminate cooperation with her. With the establishment of Internet *tongrenzhi* sales networks like Tianchuang Lianmeng (doujin.bgm.tv) in 2008, Chinese BL authors can sell their works to the whole Chinese-speaking world through local fan-agents who promote their works in overseas comic markets. This kind of informal transnational distribution channel relies on the mutual trust forged in the fan circles, rather than through legal contracts, for smooth operation. Yet the incident described here seems to indicate that the bond between fans might well be eroded or overridden by national and political affiliations.

Because of the colonial history and economic and political competition in the region, the nationalistic response to transnational cultural traffic has been a key concern in studies of East Asian popular culture.[39] Research on transnational fandoms in East Asia tends to present fandoms as always standing behind their fan objects in a time of crisis and resisting directly and indirectly the parochial patriotism of the nonfan publics.[40] Yet our study of Chinese *danmei* fandom shows that fans of transnational pop culture are not necessarily more liberal about national politics than nonfans and that "pop cosmopolitanism"[41] and nationalism can actually go hand in hand. While forums like Xianqing do provide a sexually progressive and politically engaging public space for the open discussion of nonnormative sexualities, as well as gender and political issues,[42] the problem is that the content and nature of this public space has been severely circumscribed by government regulations.

Conclusion: Beyond the *Seme* Standpoint

This chapter analyzes the platforms and communities of Chinese *danmei* fandom, along with the transnational public sphere generated by the fandom in order to illuminate the operating mechanism of grassroots transnational cultural flows. While the production, distribution, and consumption of *danmei* content mainly depend on the Internet and other state-of-the-art communication technologies, traditional print media and physical infrastructures like comic markets are also indispensable to the healthy survival of the fandom. As a form of low-end globalization that operates in an unconducive legal environment, Chinese *danmei* production has concentrated in areas that require less training and capital like fiction, audio drama, and cosplay, rather than the time-and-capital-intensive manga and anime.

Through two decades of fan dissemination, the genre has spawned three major fan circles and many other minor circles. While the original *danmei* circle has now formed the backbone of Chinese *danmei*, the Japanese circle continues to play an irreplaceable role in the fandom. The recent rise of Euro-American circle has further brought in a new cluster of slashing materials, a new set of jargon, tropes, and aesthetics,[43] and, more importantly, a stronger awareness of the global spread of female-oriented homoerotic imagination to Chinese *danmei* fandom. The constant intersecting and merging of the three circles have made *danmei* a significant cultural force to be reckoned with in China, as evidenced by the fact that more and more media productions find it necessary to pander to "fan girls' interests in homosexual relationships."[44]

In addition to offering a venue for fannish interaction, large online *danmei* forums like Xianqing have also become a unique transnational public space for women to gather and share their social concerns. Emboldened by the taboo-breaking spirit of *danmei* and protected by anonymity, Xianqing users have developed a strong insider culture and a particularly aggressive mode of communication, similar to the communication style of Japanese megaforum 2channel that has been summarized as "intimate but harsh; the harshness is itself a kind of intimacy."[45] While the strategic deployment of female aggressiveness could be constructive to "an empowered, representative, and agonistic democracy,"[46] it can also lead to virulent nationalism and political conservatism in an undemocratic national context. In other words, *danmei* fans in the Chinese-speaking world may be united by their common fan interest, but they are also divided by political beliefs and national identities.

The general line of inquiry into transnational cultural flows in East Asia is to find out how and why the cultural production of a particular nation, such as Japanese TV dramas or the Korean Wave, is received in locales outside that nation.[47] And the more places this national cultural traffic can reach, the more soft power the nation is supposed to have.[48] The media and popular content in focus is usually produced by the cultural industries and contributes to the blending of "nationalistic *nation-building*" and "capitalist *nation-branding*."[49] In this chapter, we would like to call for more attention to the fan-led cultural globalization from below, where the competition for overseas markets is far less important than the capacity to access the best which has been thought and said in the fandom, to twist Matthew Arnold's well-known quote a little bit,[50] and to enhance the affective pleasure of oneself and fellow fans. In our views, the obsession about penetrating one's cultural power into another pertains very much to the standpoint of the *seme*, to use the BL lingo, and references little to the interests and needs of the *uke*. While in the BL world, the *seme* and *uke* are fundamentally equal, albeit playing different roles in the sexual economy, it is rather strange that in the global cultural economy the *seme* is considered superior to the *uke*, as if the quest for "soft" power were the sole purpose of cultural intercourse. While it is unclear whether the Japanese government would take pride in the global spread of BL culture and view it as a vindication of Japanese soft power, Chinese fans definitely do not perceive *danmei* merely as the manifestation of Japanese cultural influence because the genre has been blended with popular content from diverse source countries. In fact, we would like to envision Chinese *danmei* as occupying the position of a promiscuous *uke*, "a sea that receives all rivers" (*haina baichuan*),[51] for it has pulled together a large variety of cultural resources across time and place, including the indigenous homosexual tradition, feminist and LGBT perspectives, Japanese ACG culture, the Korean Wave, Western slash culture, and global sports culture. It is precisely this ability to receive and connect that helps *danmei* evolve from a small underground fandom into an open and influential cultural movement.

Acknowledgments

This research was supported by a grant for Japan-related research projects from the Sumitomo Foundation (Reg. No.: 128017). An earlier version of the chapter was presented at "Asian Cultural and Media Studies Now" held at Monash University on November 6, 2014. We would like to thank Koichi Iwabuchi for inviting us to this stimulating conference, Audrey Yue for her insightful comments and probing questions, and many other conference participants for their interest and encouragement.

Notes

1. *Danmei* (耽美), literally "addicted to beauty," is the most common name for BL in China. It is borrowed from the Japanese word *tanbi*, which looks very much like an original Chinese term to Chinese speakers. In this paper, we use the term *danmei* when we want to highlight the differences between Chinese BL fandom and its Japanese counterpart. While Chinese fans often use *danmei* and BL interchangeably, the younger generation of Taiwanese fans seems to prefer BL to *danmei*.
2. For detailed discussions of the gender and sexual transgressiveness of *danmei* genre, see Yanrui Xu and Ling Yang, "Forbidden Love: Incest, Generational Conflict, and the Erotics of Power in Chinese BL Fiction," *Journal of Graphic Novels and Comics* 4.1 (2013): 30–43; "Zhongguo danmei (BL) xiaoshuo zhong de qingyu shuxie yu xing/bie zhengzhi," [Erotic desires and gender/sexuality politics in Chinese boys' love (BL) fiction], *Taiwan shehui yanjiu jikan* [Taiwan: A radical quarterly in social studies] 100 (2015): 91–121; Ke Ning, "Zhongguo danmei xiaoshuo zhong de nanxing tongshehui guanxi yu nanxing qizhi" [Male homosocial bonding and masculinity in Chinese *danmei* fiction] (PhD diss., Nankai University, 2014).
3. GL is the abbreviation of "Girls' Love," meaning same-sex relationships between women.
4. Mizuko Ito, introduction to *Fandom Unbound: Otaku Culture in a Connected World*, ed. Mizuko Ito, Daisuke Okabe, and Izumi Tsuji (New Haven: Yale University Press, 2012), xi–xxxi.
5. Dru Pagliassotti, "GloBLisation and Hybridisation: Publishers' Strategies for Bringing Boys' Love to the United States," *Intersections: Gender and Sexuality in Asia and the*

Pacific 20 (2009), accessed October 22, 2014, http://intersections.anu.edu.au/issue20/pagliassotti.htm.
6. For a detailed study of the external censorship and internal regulations of *danmei* fandom, see Ling Yang and Yanrui Xu, "'The Love That Dare Not Speak Its Name': The Fate of Chinese *Danmei* Communities in the 2014 Anti-porn Campaign," in *The End of Cool Japan: Ethical, Legal, and Cultural Challenges to Japanese Popular Culture*, ed. Mark McLelland (London: Routledge, 2016), 163–83.
7. Sean Leonard, "Progress against the Law: Animation and Fandom, with the Key to the Globalization of Culture," *International Journal of Cultural Studies* 8.3 (2005): 282.
8. Di Wu, "Yiru danmei shensihai—wo de geren 'danmei tongren' shi" [Once entering *danmei*, it is as deep as sea—my personal *"danmei/*fanfic" history], in *Wangluo wenxue pinglun diyiji* [Web literature review] vol. 1, ed. Guangdong Provincial Writers' Association and Guangdong Web Literature Institute (Guangzhou: Huacheng chubanshe, 2011), 155.
9. "Guanyu Jinjiang" [About Jinjiang], Jinjiang Literature City, accessed October 22, 2014, http://www.jjwxc.net/aboutus/.
10. In Japan, female BL fans refer to themselves as *fujoshi*, literally "rotten women." This self-deprecating term was later adopted by Chinese *danmei* fans and written as 腐女 in Chinese. In both Japanese and Chinese languages, the word *fujoshi* is a pun on the word 婦女 (woman). For a study of the origin and use of the term in Japan, see Midori Suzuki, "The Possibilities of Research on *Fujoshi* in Japan," *Transformative Works and Cultures* 12 (2013), doi:10.3983/twc.2013.0462.
11. In China, all print publications must first obtain a "book number" or "periodical number" from the state before going to print. Otherwise, the publication is deemed illegal. Since BL's focus on same-sex love is regarded as "unhealthy" and "vulgar" by mainstream society, few official publishers dare to risk publishing unabridged BL works or magazines. For more information about the publishing industry in China, see Xiaoyan Huang, "From Survival to Profit: A Canadian Book Publishers' Guide to China, the World's Largest Market" (MA thesis, Simon Fraser University, 2005).
12. acg.178.com, "Tongrenzhan" [Comic markets], accessed January 20, 2016, http://acg.178.com/list/88652054089.html.
13. Feng Nong, personal interview, February 28, 2014.
14. There is no ratings system for cultural products in China. But some fans would put an "R18" label on their explicit fan works. We once purchased a number of erotic *tongrenzhi* at a large-scale comic market in Shanghai in 2013. The girl vendor checked our appearance, made sure that we were over eighteen years old and sold the books to us readily.
15. See Fran Martin's chapter in this volume.
16. Chih-Lan Tsai, "Nüxing huanxiang guodu zhong de chuncui aiqing—lun Taiwan BL xiaoshuo" [The pure love in the kingdom of women's fantasy—on BL novels in Taiwan] (MA thesis, National Taiwan Normal University, 2011), 51–52.
17. Feng Nong, personal interview.
18. Ting Liu, "Conflicting Discourses on Boys' Love and Subcultural Tactics in Mainland China and Hong Kong," *Intersections: Gender and Sexuality in Asia and the Pacific* 20 (2009), accessed October 22, 2014, http://intersections.anu.edu.au/issue20/liu.htm.
19. otsutohana, "Yirenbei deng zuojia lianhe zhuitao tuoqian gaofei" [Yirenbei and other writers jointly demand their lagged-behind remunerations], accessed October 22, 2014, http://tieba.baidu.com/p/2973080918?pn=1.

20. Gordon Mathews, *Ghetto at the Center of the World: Chungking Mansions, Hong Kong* (Chicago: University of Chicago Press, 2011); Gordon Mathews and Yang Yang, "How Africans Pursue Low-End Globalization in Hong Kong and Mainland China," *Journal of Current Chinese Affairs* 41.2 (2012): 95–120.
21. John Wei, "Queer Encounters between Iron Man and Chinese Boys' Love Fandom," *Transformative Works and Cultures* 17 (2014), accessed October 22, 2014, http://journal.transformativeworks.org/index.php/twc/article/view/561/458.
22. Chua Beng Huat, *Structure, Audience and Soft Power in East Asian Pop Culture* (Hong Kong: Hong Kong University Press, 2012), 117.
23. The word "original" here means original productions, as opposed to derivative fan productions. It does not imply that the circle was established earlier than other circles.
24. For more information about BL characters types in Japan and their effects on *fujoshi*, see Patrick W. Galbraith, "Moe: Exploring Virtual Potential in Post-millennial Japan," in *Researching Twenty-First Century Japan: New Directions and Approaches for the Electronic Age*, ed. Timothy Iles and Peter C. D. Matanle (Lanham, MA: Lexington Books, 2012), 359.
25. For a detailed study of the web features and interaction between writers and readers on the Green Jinjiang, see Jin Feng, *Romancing the Internet: Producing and Consuming Chinese Web Romance* (Boston: Brill, 2013), 53–68.
26. Ling Yang and Yanrui Xu, "Queer Texts, Gendered Imagination, and Popular Feminism in Chinese Web Literature," in *Queer/Tongzhi China: New Perspectives on Research, Activism, and Media Cultures*, eds. Elisabeth L. Engebretsen and William F. Shroeder (with Hongwei Bao) (Copenhagen: NIAS Press, 2015), 131–52.
27. yuezhifeng. "Weihe huiyou CP buke ni de xinli?" [Why does the psychology that character pairings cannot be reversed exist], accessed December 2, 2016, http://www.mtslash.org/forum.php?mod=viewthread&tid=119166&highlight=CP%B2%BB%BF%C9%C4%E6.
28. https://archiveofourown.org/, accessed December 22, 2014. AO3 was created by the Organization for Transformative Works (OTW), which also publishes the peer-reviewed fan studies journal *Transformative Works and Cultures*. For a brief discussion of the politics of the AO3 project, see Alexis Lothian, "An Archive of One's Own: Subcultural Creativity and the Politics of Conservation," *Transformative Works and Cultures* 6 (2011), accessed January 20, 2016, http://journal.transformativeworks.org/index.php/twc/article/view/267/197.
29. Claud Z, e-mail communication with author, September 12, 2014.
30. Bertha Chin and Lori Hitchcock Morimoto, "Towards a Theory of Transcultural Fandom," *Participations: Journal of Audience and Reception Studies* 10.1 (2013): 99, emphasis in the original.
31. Guobin Yang, *The Power of the Internet in China: Citizens Activism Online* (New York: Columbia University Press, 2009), 187–88.
32. "Guanyu Jinjiang."
33. Guobin Yang, "The Internet and the Rise of a Transnational Chinese Cultural Sphere," *Media, Culture & Society* 25.4 (2003): 470.
34. "You meiyou ren zhidao xianggang fasheng shenme shi le?" [Does anyone know what's going on in Hong Kong], accessed October 22, 2014, http://bbs.jjwxc.net/showmsg.php?board=3&boardpagemsg=1&id=735974&page=0.
35. David Wertime, "In China, Shrugs and Sneers for Hong Kong Protesters," *Foreign Policy*, October 2, 2014, accessed October 22, 2014, http://www.foreignpolicy.com/

articles/2014/10/01/in_chinese_mainland_shrugs_and_sneers_for_hong_kong_protesters. And on Hong Kong residents' prejudices against Mainlanders, see Maud Lavin's essay in this volume.

36. Shubo Li, "The Online Public Space and Popular Ethos in China," *Media, Culture & Society* 32.1 (2010): 75.
37. Lijun Yang and Yongnian Zheng, "*Fen Qings* (Angry Youth) in Contemporary China," *Journal of Contemporary China* 21.76 (2012): 652.
38. "Qiuhou sanbu erhaolou: ganle baihuashecao shui, laishi haizuo zhongguoren" [The second building about Autumn strolling: bottoms up Laoshan oldenlandia mineral water, let's still be Chinese in our next lives], October 2, 2014 (12:07:23), accessed July 5, 2015, http://bbs.jjwxc.net/showmsg.php?board=3&boardpagemsg=1&id=736150&page=3.
39. See, for example, Chris Berry, Nicola Liscutin, and Jonathan D. Mackintosh, eds., *Cultural Studies and Cultural Industries in Northeast Asia: What a Difference a Region Makes* (Hong Kong: Hong Kong University Press, 2009); Chua Beng Huat and Koichi Iwabuchi, eds., *East Asian Pop Culture: Analysing the Korean Wave* (Hong Kong: Hong Kong University Press, 2008).
40. Chua, *Structure, Audience and Soft Power*, 110–12; Eva Tsai, "Existing in the Age of Innocence: Pop Stars, Publics, and Politics in Asia," in Chua and Iwabuchi, *East Asian Pop Culture: Analyzing the Korean Wave*, 217–42.
41. Henry Jenkins, Sam Ford, and Joshua Green, *Spreadable Media: Creating Value and Meaning in a Networked Culture* (New York: New York University Press, 2013), 275–78.
42. For further elaboration of this point, see Ling Yang and Yanrui Xu, "*Danmei*, Xianqing, and the Making of a Queer Online Public Sphere in China," *Communication and the Public* 1.2 (2016): 251–56.
43. John Wei, "Queer Encounters."
44. Erika Junhui Yi, "Reflection on Chinese Boys' Love Fans: An Insider's View," *Transformative Works and Cultures* 12 (2013), doi:10.3983/twc.2013.0424.
45. Akihiro Kitada, "Japan's Cynical Nationalism," in *Fandom Unbound: Otaku Culture in a Connected World*, ed. Mizuko Ito, Daisuke Okabe, and Izumi Tsuji (New Haven: Yale University Press, 2012), 70.
46. Maud Lavin, *Push Comes to Shove: New Images of Aggressive Women* (Cambridge, MA: MIT Press, 2010), 250.
47. Koichi Iwabuchi, *Recentering Globalization: Popular Culture and Japanese Transnationalism* (Durham, NC: Duke University Press, 2002); Koichi Iwabuchi, *Feeling Asian Modernities: Transnational Consumption of Japanese TV Dramas* (Hong Kong: Hong Kong University Press, 2004); Chua and Iwabuchi, *East Asian Pop Culture*.
48. Chua, *Structure, Audience and Soft Power*.
49. Shuling Huang, "Nation-Branding and Transnational Consumption: Japan-Mania and the Korean Wave in Taiwan," *Media, Culture & Society* 33.1 (2011): 15, emphasis in the original.
50. The original quote is, "culture being a pursuit of our total perfection by means of getting to know, on all the matters which most concern us, the best which has been thought and said in the world." Matthew Arnold, *Culture and Anarchy*, ed. with an introduction by J. Dover Wilson (Cambridge: Cambridge University Press, 1960), 6.
51. This is a famous Chinese idiom that comes from the writings of the Taoist philosopher Zhuangzi (369–286 BCE).

2
Cosplay, Cuteness, and *Weiniang*

The Queered Ke'ai *of Male Cosplayers as "Fake Girls"*

Shih-chen Chao

Introduction

This chapter examines and queries the phenomenon of *weiniang* (fake girl), using an all-male cosplay group named AC Ailisi Weiniang Tuan (AC Alice Fake Girl Group, Alice Cos Group hereafter) as the case study. The members of Alice Cos Group are young men in their twenties who are well-known for cosplaying female roles from Japanese animation and manga and Korean female pop groups, and for mimetically reflecting femininity—not in a parodic way—in cosplay/comic conventions as well as on TV shows. The very essence of youthful femininity in today's China lies in performing *ke'ai* (cuteness). In the case of Alice Cos Group, the members commonly demonstrate success in incorporating the cultural fantasy of *ke'ai* while performing femininity when they cosplay various female roles in public spaces. I will start with a brief overview of the notions of cosplaying and of gender performance (as opposed to performativity, which is a constant reinhabiting and usually reaffirming of normative gender roles in individual daily lives)[1] and the ways these concepts link back to the growing popularity of the *weiniang* phenomenon in mainland China. Using Alice Cos Group as exemplary, I will then examine the group's Internet persona through its online fan clubs and Weibo (the Chinese version of Twitter) messages. This examination leads to the concluding analysis of the group's heavy exercise of the cultural fantasy of *ke'ai*. My analysis explicates *ke'ai* from the origin of cuteness, which is a babyish cuteness. I also examine the way in which cuteness is developed into the concept of the virgin/whore facial features and body image with a *sajiao* (coquettishness) undertone in the context of today's China. This chapter argues that the group performs both queerness and *ke'ai* to successfully deliver a theatrical performance of gender that presents an intriguing inconsistency between socially anticipated "proper" gender expressions and assigned gender in today's China. By incorporating the cultural fantasy of a feminized *ke'ai*, the male group transforms normative codes of a gendered performance by presenting *ke'ai*-oriented femininity on its members' biologically male bodies. In doing so, the group achieves a theatrical queerness whereby this performed *ke'ai* femininity contributes to queer spaces within the mainstream heteronormative environment in China.

Cosplaying, Cross-dressing, and *Weiniang*

Cosplay (or costume play) began as a kind of cross-cultural collaboration between the United States and Japan in the early 1980s when a Japanese game designer visited a convention in the United States. Afterward he was inspired by the costumed fans at the convention and wrote about the experience to encourage Japanese fans to follow suit.[2] Nowadays cosplay has become a globalized fan-oriented phenomenon,[3] with fans attending conventions and impersonating their favorite fictional characters depicted in anime, comics (manga), and games (ACG hereafter). In particular, cosplay has offered many young people across East Asia an opportunity to act out their fantasies in public spaces that are different from ones they usually inhabit. Nevertheless, cosplay is not just about bearing a resemblance to fictional characters from ACG, since it also highly engages with the notion of performance or to perform. By "to perform" in this chapter, I mean specifically to take an action to entertain an audience, rather than simply do or execute. Good cosplayers, sporting their costumes, props, and performing skills in a public space, such as ACG conventions, can breathe life into any fictional character they assume, transforming the originally 2-D characters into a 3-D presentation. Meanwhile, cosplay, as a role-playing game for enthusiastic fans of ACG, is also "fraught with the negotiations and representations of power and gender."[4] That is, although cosplay seems to be merely a subculture where young ACG fans participate in conventions to express their love for the fictional roles they identify with, in fact cosplay can serve as a means to revisit and negotiate heteronormative discourse often to achieve more gender fluidity, for example, by imitating the opposite gender of a cosplayer's assigned one.

Such a performance is known as cross-play in the realm of cosplay. There are MTF (male to female) cross-play performances and FTM (female to male) cross-play ones. For instance, a female cosplayer can choose to assume Naruto, the leading male character from the Japanese manga *Naruto*; likewise, a male cosplayer is welcome to assume Usagi Tsukino, the leading female character from the Japanese manga *Sailor Moon*. Walking into an ACG convention, it is not difficult to spot a skit being performed by female cosplayers as some of them assume male characters publicly making a pass at other female cosplayers who assume female characters from a piece of popular ACG work. The cross-play phenomenon in cosplay led Thorn to argue that cosplay "often entails cross-dressing," which instigates "multilayered heterosexual and homosexual tensions."[5] Cross-play is more common among female cosplayers. Take two rather popular cosplayer websites, Cosplay[6] and Worldcosplayer,[7] where female cosplayers significantly outnumber male cosplayers. The same situation is generally reflected in ACG conventions in East Asia.

The phenomenon of male cosplayers cross-dressing as female ACG characters has become more visible in recent years in public spaces and, increasingly, over the Internet. In Japan, a new phrase, *otoko no ko* (male daughter), is derived from *otoko no ko* (male child). This phrase is used to refer to those males who cross-play girls so perfectly with their skills that audiences easily take them for being inherently feminine.[8] An *otoko no ko* maids café opened in 2009, based in Akihabara, Tokyo, a place well known for being an ACG fan sanctuary. The main feature is all of its attendants are young boys cross-dressing as young female maids serving beverages and food.[9] One crucial means by which male daughters cross-play female characters successfully is to act cute or *kawaii* (cute/adorable).[10] They usually cosplay the ACG roles known for being femininely *kawaii* in a public space. The typical physical features of being femininely *kawaii* include big eyes, thick and long eyelashes, long hair, a small face with a pointed chin, and slim build, often adorned by a Lolita-style dress with lace and ruffles. Those features are employed to stress the notions of youth, naïveté, and innocence, which help to elicit a perception of infantile fragility and harmlessness in the audience. The physical features reflect the literal meaning of *kawaii*—cute, charming, darling, and ostentatiously adorable.[11]

As the notion of male daughters travels outside Japan into Chinese-speaking regions, an equivalent term, *weiniang* (fake girl),[12] has been coined to describe the Chinese counterpart of the male daughters phenomenon. Because of pressure from offline, traditional heteronormative social discourse, the *weiniang* phenomenon largely exists online. In Baidu Post Bar (Baidu tieba), arguably the largest Chinese online community offering virtual spaces to different fan groups, there are groups devoted to the discussion and sharing of the *weiniang* phenomenon. Weiniang ba[13] currently has more than 5 million entries and numerous photographs. The messages are similar to the Twitter style—short text entries with photos. Most of the photos uploaded to the bar feature young boys dressed up as *weiniang*.

Although most of the *weiniang* remain online, some of them have begun to receive more visibility through mass media. Several *weiniang* cosplayers are so well known that they have gained celebrity status, not only among cosplayers but also outside cosplay fandom through exposure on mass media. Liu Zhu is one example. In 2010, he participated in a talent show produced by Hunan Satellite Television Station named *Kuaile nansheng* (Happy male voice), presenting himself to the audience in a way traditionally regarded as feminine—long dress, long hair, and makeup. When he first came on stage, his performance was interrupted several times by one of the judges who questioned Liu about his ambiguous gender identity, demanding the gender issue be clarified.[14] Despite the controversy, Liu achieved celebrity status afterward. Another case in point is the *weiniang* performer Xiao Can, one of the ninety-nine contestants on season five of the talent show *Zhongguo daren xiu* (China's got talent) hosted by Shanghai Dragon TV. He was ranked as the fourteenth–most popular contestant based on Internet voting.[15] After the episode in which Xiao Can showcased his talent in January 2014, the mass media crowned him with the title of "the most beautiful *weiniang*" in China.[16] In considering the reception of Xiao Can's performance, on the one hand, there are netizens and other viewers who heavily condemn this behavior; on the other hand, the popularity of such *weiniang*s as well as the media exposure and attention they are given show that *weiniang* is a growing phenomenon. Overall, it has been accepted by many people who do not frown upon the phenomenon, demonstrating increased tolerance toward cross-dressing and cross-gender performances in China.

The Alice Cos Group: Presentation of Girlishness and Performing Cuteness

The Alice Cos Group exemplifies such an all-male, fan-oriented, and now more commercialized *weiniang* group in China. It was formed on October 1, 2009, in Wuhan, the capital city of Hubei Province as well as one of the most populous cities in China. Members of the group are on average twenty-one years old and come from different backgrounds—some of them are students, others young professionals. The group's members are well known for their high-quality presentation of cosplayed female ACG roles and of female pop singers. They present themselves as girls so credibly that in one of their earliest public appearances it was arranged for someone to run across the stage holding up a big poster that stated "They are Men!" to clarify that the group members are biologically male. Arguably the first group of its kind in China enthusiastically promoting the notion of *weiniang* through media exposure, the group has been severely criticized for its cross-playing.[17] Despite such social criticism, the group still carries on, now well past celebrating its fifth anniversary. Currently, its public relations agent is a group member who uses the stage name of Coser Xiaolu. The other core members include Haoge, Muying, Putu, Quan Xiaoyao, Tang Bomao, Xiaofeng, Xiaohua, and Xiaolin. To ensure each member's excellent portrayal of a female persona, the group applies a strict standard for appearance and physical build when new members are recruited. For instance, a potential member has to have "pretty/soft" facial features; his height is ideally between 162 and 175 centimeters, with small shoulders and a slim build. In addition, good physical coordination is highly desirable because the group's public performances all include choreography.[18] To be a professional *weiniang*, having relatively fair skin and thin, long legs are also highly desirable qualities.[19] In a Weibo entry where the group recruits new members, it states that it is looking for young men who are interested in cosplaying *weiniang* and in dancing, who have a slender build and an outgoing personality, and, most importantly, who are cute.[20]

Although it started from the notion of amateur cosplaying, the group is now more than just an amateur cosplay group—its members see cosplaying *weiniang* as a professional activity. They charge a fee[21] for public appearances on different occasions, and they are usually fully booked for their public performances. Not only do they have official channels on popular social media such as Weibo, Youku (the Chinese version of YouTube), and Baidu Post Bar, they also run a virtual store on Taobao (the Chinese version of eBay)[22] selling their autographed photos/posters and other cosplay-related items. Apart from regularly attending various cosplay conventions and promoting themselves online, the group has also been invited onto several television shows for interviews and to showcase their cosplaying skills.[23] As one of the most successful Chinese male-cosplaying-female groups visible across different media platforms, it presents interesting features of the fan-oriented cosplaying trend and of queered cuteness in Chinese-speaking regions.

Figure 2.1
A screenshot taken from the Alice Cos Group's official Weibo account at http://weibo.com/alice520cosplay on August 12, 2014. The members are emulating the Japanese pop group AKB48 in this screenshot.

Figure 2.2

A screenshot taken from the Alice Cos Group's official Weibo account at www.weibo.com/alice520cosplayer#rnd1407792602992 on August 10, 2014. A list of the Alice Cos Group's public ACG performances is being advertised. All of the members cosplay Japanese anime/manga characters in this screenshot, except the member at the bottom right corner emulating the Japanese idol group AKB48.

Figure 2.3

A screenshot taken from the Alice Cos Group's official Weibo account at http://www.weibo.com/p/1005052139358713/album?from=profile_right#wbphoto_nav on August 10, 2014. The Alice Cos Group members are demonstrating their outfits and looks, referring to themselves as "Candy Girls."

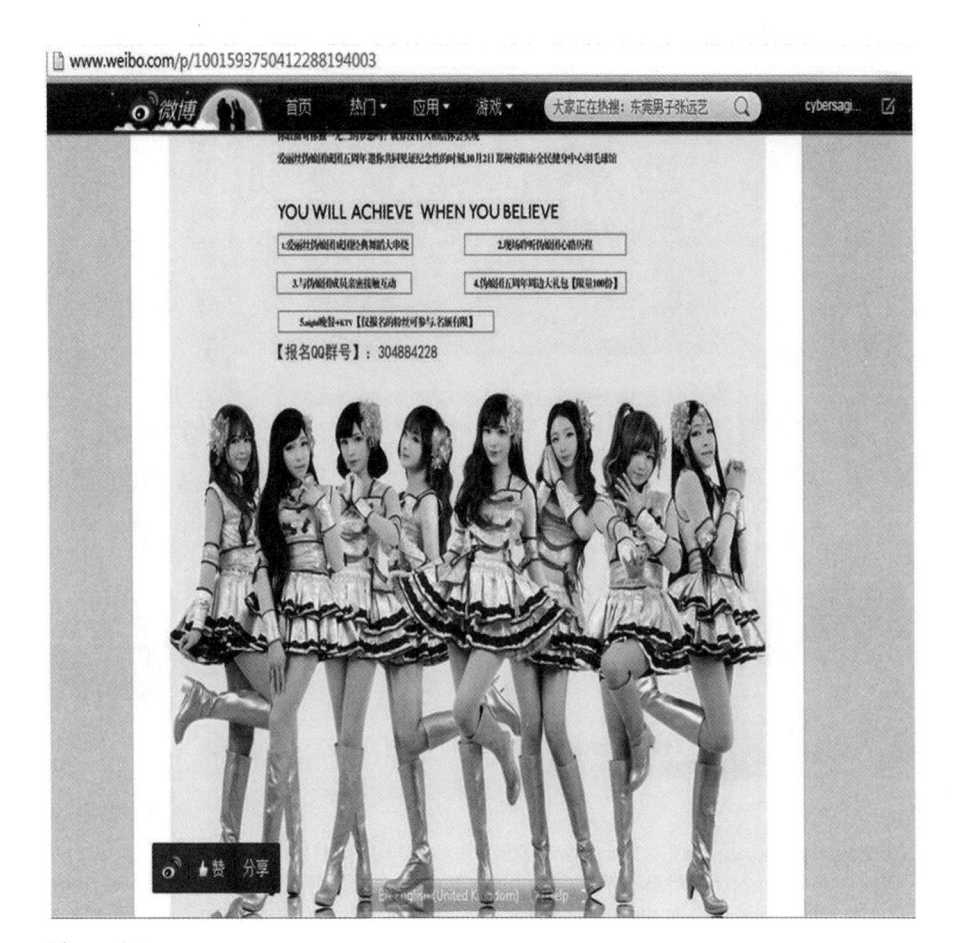

Figure 2.4

A screenshot taken from the Alice Cos Group's official Weibo account at http://www.weibo.com/p/1001593750412288194003 on September 7, 2014. The Alice Cos Group is allegedly emulating the Korean pop group Girls' Generation to celebrate their fifth anniversary.

Figure 2.5

A screenshot taken from the Alice Cos Group's official Weibo account at http://www.weibo.com/p/1005052139358713/home?from=page_100505&mod=TAB#place on February 14, 2015. The members describe this as their latest cosplay project for Chinese New Year 2015 at http://www.weibo.com/p/1001593807262534696970. As shown in the screenshot, the members dress in bright shining outfits, emulating female characters from a Japanese animation *Love Live!* Two more new members, Qimeng and Yinnai, were recruited for this project.

In photographs, microblogging messages, and videos showcasing their live performances at ACG conventions across the country or on TV shows, the group has repeatedly reinforced and implemented a cultural fantasy of cuteness in its public images. As the screenshots 1–5 taken from its official Weibo site show, the group is strongly committed to a sense of "girlish cuteness." The attributes of girlish cuteness are commonly presented as having innocent, cute facial features but with sexualized body images. So the members' facial features include fair skin; long eyelashes; big, watery eyes; shiny lips; small, oval faces with sharp, pointed chins; and thick hair fringes, whereas their sexualized body images are epitomized by showcasing parts of their bodies and their slim builds that reflect the recruitment standards previously described. The members' outfits are usually in bright colors, with tutu miniskirts to expose their long legs, and these come with "girlish" decorations such as floral and feather barrettes, ruffles, and ribbons commonly seen in the little girls' clothing section of stores (unless they are cosplaying particular ACG characters whose physical features show none of the above-mentioned attire characteristics).

The body language and the postures expressed by the group members suggest a strong sense of *sajiao*. *Sajiao* is a common behavior among many young Chinese women.[24] It was originally used to refer to children behaving in a cute and soft way to gain favors from an adult. However, this behavior can be observed today among many young Chinese women as well. As evident in all of the illustrated screenshots, the members' hands are usually placed gently and close to their torsos to avoid any sense of confrontation or intimidation and to generate an ambiance of tenderness or compliance. Some members have their palms softly placed against their cheeks or their fingers playfully pointed to their chins; others have their palms crossed and tenderly placed against their chests, or they put their hands closer to their faces in a coquettish way. In addition, the members tend to tilt their heads to one side, looking directly at the camera in a docile, charming fashion. They neither stare at nor glare into the camera when photographed; they gaze at the camera lovingly and gently. These girlish postures are often seen in the group's promotional photographs.

On the group's official channel on Youku, ninety-two videos had already been uploaded by October 5, 2014. In the repertoire of videos, the above-mentioned girlish features of the performers' appearances are clearly presented. They wear makeup and wigs with heavy fringes to make their faces smaller and more adorable, and they are usually dressed in short skirts to show their long, slender legs. While the majority of the videos were taken when the group was invited to attend ACG conventions and at its offstage choreography rehearsals, recently there have also been more videos of the group's TV appearances, which suggests that it has become more recognizable outside of the ACG fandom. During its public appearances as seen in the videos, the group usually chooses to either cosplay female characters from popular Japanese anime/manga and Japanese female pop groups or Korean female pop groups. Cosplaying Chinese historic/fictional female characters is sometimes chosen, but rarely. Between the Japanese style and the Korean style, the group does not seem to have a strong preference. The frequency of the group members cosplaying female Japanese anime/manga characters and pop groups is roughly equivalent to the frequency of them cosplaying performers in the Korean female pop singing group Girls' Generation, judging from these ninety-two videos. This might suggest that the group comes under the influence of both Japanese anime/manga and Korean pop styles in presenting itself as *weiniang*.

Regardless of which style it presents, girlish cuteness is the key to the group's public image. In the top three most popular videos as of October 5, 2014, on their Youku channel, the group imitates the styles of the K-pop group Girls' Generation, the J-pop group AKB 48, and the Japanese anime/manga *Sailor Moon*. In these three videos, the members commonly dance to the music in colorful, shining outfits and short tutu skirts, while making cute gestures to the music and smiling tenderly, innocently into the cameras. Accepting their different styles, their viewers, most of whom are female,[25] are supportive and approving of their performances. In one video when the group cosplayers go onstage dressed in Victorian maid costumes (a miniskirt version) and headpieces in the form of fluffy cat ears, a girl screams, "Wow! So slender!" in a positive tone when she sees them on stage.[26] In another video, when one of the members dances to the music cosplaying the character Sailor Mercury from *Sailor Moon*, some female audience members exclaim in the background, "Wow! So cute, they are so cute! How can boys be so cute?"[27]

While the group successfully associates its public image with the notion of "girlish cuteness," the notion is further enhanced by the group's proactive self-promotion on social media. Currently, there are two official Weibo pages pertaining to the group: its first official Weibo page[28] and a much more recently set up Weibo page, AC Alice Fake Girl Group National Fan Club (AC Ailisi weiniang tuan quanguo houyuan hui).[29] It uses these two channels as the main base to publicize its scheduled performances and to share its photographs. Frequently, its fans also post photographs and videos to the time lines on these two Weibo pages, sharing their excitement with other fans about their personal encounters with group members with positive compliments such as, "Such cute boys, cuter than me, I feel ashamed of being a woman!"[30] "Oh! I saw a goddess today! The goddess was so beautiful! I am the one who looks like a guy in the photo when I stand next to him!"[31] "Alice Cos Group members are so pretty, *kawaii*! Cute!"[32] and "My heart was jumping out of my chest! They are so pretty! I am so touched to see their live performance!"[33] Comments from fans about feeling thrilled to see the group in person, about its members being cute, and about making them feel *meng* (bud, sprout; also, as derived from Japanese anime/manga popular culture, a loving feeling toward a cute object or a person) toward its members are quite common. It is worth noting that most comments previously mentioned are made by female ACG fans who have always seem to hold more of a positive and encouraging attitude than male fans toward gender fluidity and queerness. For example, the phenomenon of *funü* (rotten women) is fairly common in the ACG world in the Chinese-speaking regions. "Rotten women" is an ACG loan phrase from Japan *fujoshi*, referring to the straight female ACG fans who are fascinated with narratives involving two or more good-looking male characters. The narratives mainly include bromance (such as in the US sci-fi/fantasy drama *Supernatural*) in which there is no romantic/sexual relation between the male characters, but room is left for ACG fans to exercise their imagination about what could happen between them, thus related to but also in contrast with BL (Boys' Love), whereby there is a romantic/sexual relation to varying degrees between the male characters. Many rotten girls will go so far as to produce slash fan fiction based on non-bromance, non-BL narratives to explore queerness.[34]

Cultural influence among East Asian regions in the form of having loanwords from Japan in modern Chinese has been a regular practice since the 1900s.[35] An influx of at least hundreds of Japanese loanwords has flown into modern Chinese language.[36] This practice is no exception—if not even more common than in other areas—in Chinese popular culture and queer culture. The Chinese word *meng* exemplifies such a cultural/language influence, as it developed from the Japanese word *moeru* (萌える) with the literal meaning referring to a plant sprouting. It is suggested that the word *moeru* (燃える, to burn) was originally used by Japanese ACG fans to express their loving feelings toward their favorite ACG characters and works. Through a typing error in an online discussion forum, some fans mistyped "to burn" as "to sprout." Since then "to sprout" has been used in an ACG context very often. Nowadays in the ACG fan world when someone sees a *kawaii* character and feels infatuated with the character, he or she describes the loving feelings toward the character as like a plant sprouting.[37] In the Chinese-speaking context of ACG fan culture, the meaning of *meng* also connotes the Japanese word *moe*. It is used frequently as both a verb and an adjective to refer to the loving feelings toward someone or something mainly due to lovability or cuteness. It is worth noting that most of the positive comments about the group members, judging from the photos they share or the tone of the language used in the text, suggest that those comments were left by female fans who confirm that they feel *meng* after seeing an Alice Cos Group performance. The performance of biologically male cosplayers in feminine roles seems to be more accepted and welcomed among female fans.

As well as these two official Weibo pages, all the members have their individual Weibo channels where they continue assuming the identities of *weiniang* to promote their girlish cuteness and the group. The messages on the individual Weibo sites can be roughly categorized as follows: promotion of the scheduled public activities, sharing selfie photographs and pictures from private photo sessions, and articulating personal feelings about cosplaying *weiniang*. Occasionally, there are some messages about what could be roughly categorized as "traditionally male-oriented" topics such as joining sport activities and playing online games, but these are infrequent. Haoge, for instance, currently has more than 100,000 fans following him on Weibo, making him the most popular Alice Cos Group member. He had published 343 Weibo entries up to October 5, 2014. At the top of his personal Weibo site there is a photograph of him wearing a tight, shiny, silver minidress demonstrating his sexy body curves and beautiful long legs, with long, curly hair, and a thick fringe. A slogan running across the top left corner says *Meili wu guojie, Meili wu xingbie* (Being beautiful is borderless, being beautiful is genderless). In another message posted on August 31, 2014, he claims that since he regards himself a real man he dared to challenge himself to do what most men dared not—the message was accompanied by a series of photographs in which Haoge is in a Japanese high school girl's tight swimming suit showing off his long legs and slim shape cosplaying Japanese anime/manga female characters with different backgrounds, one of which shows Haoge smiling tenderly while sitting on a pink Hello Kitty carpet.[38]

Haoge's choice of the word "beautiful" in his Weibo slogan, along with his claim of "being a real man" are interesting. First of all, the Chinese phrase *meili* can be associated with both genders (such as *meinü*, "beautiful woman," and *meinanzi*, "beautiful man"). Using the adjective *meili*, Haoge's message insinuates that beauty is a genderless notion that can be applied to both male and female. For Haoge, he chooses to perform the notion of beauty in a more feminine style on a biologically male body. Second, as Haoge mentions that a real man would dare to challenge himself, including putting on a girl's tight swimming suit for a photo shoot, Haoge tries to reassert his "masculinity" by associating it with his bravery in performing "femininity." Being brave is a feature associated with normative masculinity. Kam Louie argues that instead of the yin/yang archetype, Chinese masculinity is structured by *wen/wu* archetypes, where *wen* refers to gentleman-scholar traits such as intellectual prowess, and *wu* refers to martial masculinity characteristics such as bravery. Kam describes *wen* as "cultural attainment" and contrastingly *wu* as "martial valour."[39] The tension between *wen* and *wu* and the extent to which both elements are presented change dynamically to constitute Chinese masculinity in different historical settings.[40] In Haoge's case, he stretches the element of *wu* by presenting enormous courage in the means of publicly performing femininity on a biologically male body since the majority of Chinese men dare not do so. Having done so, Haoge makes himself a more daring, courageous male as he turns the notion of male-performed hyperfemininity into a greater display of masculine bravery. Haoge's claim of masculinity and his performed femininity point to the possibility of performing *ke'ai*-oriented theatrical queerness in today's China.

Weibo messages from other members of the group are not much different from those posted by Haoge. Xiaohua, the founder of the group, had published 1,097 Weibo entries and had 14,885 fans following him up to October 5, 2014. Compared with Haoge, who occasionally writes about national/public affairs, Xiaohua's messages very much concentrate on his experience as a *weiniang* and are accompanied by group promotion photographs or public performance videos, and occasionally about his personal life (such as considering using a whitening lotion to make his skin tone fairer, on June 19, 2012).[41] Xiaohua also mentions other topics related to the group, and these help to elucidate his motivation for establishing a cosplay group as such. In one Weibo message posted on August 29, 2011, Xiaohua stated that the reason he started the group was purely because he enjoys the idea of cosplaying *weiniang* through the group's activities. However, he was upset about some incorrect comments by the mass media claiming that the group members had compared themselves to Mei Lanfang (1894–1961), the highly respected Peking Opera artist who was famous for performing female roles on stage. According to Xiaohua, there was no notion of having any linkage to Mei Lanfang when the group was started.[42] In another message posted on April 11, 2012, Xiaohua complains that the media misunderstood the group by assuming that the group members practiced cross-dressing in their everyday lives offstage, and that some media jumped on any opportunity to criticize the group for being morally corrupt. In particular, Xiaohua differentiates the group members from Liu Zhu, the other well-known *weiniang*, who, as mentioned, had become a grassroots celebrity while presenting himself in a feminine fashion on a talent show produced by Hunan Satellite TV station. The group believes that that Liu had gone over the top of the connotation of *weiniang* because of Liu's cross-dressing behavior as an everyday life practice, offstage as well as on.[43]

Interestingly in the case of Liu, he has specified that he is not happy about being referred to as a *weiniang* after he became a grassroots celebrity. He stated in one interview that he did not prefer to be understood as a *weiniang* since his propensity toward being feminine is gradual and natural. He envies beautiful women, and he has four to five close female friends with whom he goes shopping or has "girl talk" with regularly. He is not like those *weiniang* who intentionally dress up in a feminine style and deliberately imitate femininity in a specific context.[44] Judging from this interview, Liu could be considered transgender or transsexual. As for the group members, they very likely do not want to be misunderstood as a transgender/transsexual group. In an interview, the members explained that intentionally dressing up like a girl is only a theatrical performance they enjoy because of their passion for the ACG subculture, in which cosplay has an important role. In the same interview, they indicate that some members have girlfriends and explicate that they are "ordinary people" (*putong ren*) when they are offstage.[45] Haoge, similarly in another interview, points out that he is "normal" when he is offstage. He does not dress up in a traditionally feminine style unless it is for cosplaying. He also stresses that many people know that he has a girlfriend.[46]

Moreover, Liu's public appearance and fame drew the attention of the State Administration of Press, Publication, Radio, Film and Television (SAPPRFT) in China. It is alleged that the SAPPRFT ordered that Liu be prohibited to enter the next round of the talent show, disregarding his music talent, because of Liu's ambiguous gender identity. Liu's gender expression and behavior deviate from the state-promulgated gender norms. Consequently, he was denied further success on the talent show as he failed to make it to the next round of the competition. In an interview following, Liu pointed out that he had already heard the rumors that he would not be allowed to enter the semifinal due to his gender identity. Meanwhile, Liu expressed discontent about why his gender expression was not approved.[47] Therefore, it is likely that the group members would also be concerned about the future development of *weiniang* performance should they be prohibited by the state and misunderstood by the general public with respect to their gender identities. They each only employ a nonnormative gender expression that is obviously inconsistent with their assigned one for the purpose of theatrical cosplay. Meanwhile, they constantly emphasize within mainstream communicative spaces that as cis males they do not have any gender identity issues in their offstage real lives. In this regard, the group does not seem to be interested in radically challenging real-world heteronormativity. To some extent, in contrast to Liu's radically transgressive gender-bending persona, some of the group members even support certain gender norms and conventional ideals. Nevertheless, what the group showcases is an intricate, self-contradictory, queer performative possibility through which both normative and nonnormative gender identities can be perfectly reified, theatrically performed, and, in the meantime, mutually switchable on the bodies of the same cis-male performers. Seen in this light, their sophisticated gendered negotiations with queer theatricality and daily heteronormativity open up promising spaces for the sustained existence and survival of nonnormatively gendered expressions, performances, and groups within mainstream, heterocentric Chinese media and cultural environments.

Queered *Ke'ai* of the Alice Cos Group's *Weiniang*: An Act of Double Performativity

The group's way of presenting and behaving with girlish cuteness is quite definitive. However, as the word "cute" serves as an umbrella term for the translation purpose of referring to similar features present in different cultures, in what way can "cute" be precisely contextualized in East Asian cultures? To answer this question, this section examines the cultural fantasy of cuteness by first focusing on the origin and fundamental elements of cuteness.

A babyish, infantile cuteness is universal, and it helps to explicate why human beings find infantile creatures appealing. A series of cute studies has been conducted to contextualize the notion of cuteness from a psychological and evolutionary perspective. Konrad Lorenz was a pioneer scientifically theorizing babyish cuteness to examine the correlation between cuteness and attractiveness. Konrad Lorenz sees cuteness as part of a *Kindchenschema* (baby schema). He argues that an innate release mechanism of caring is triggered when adults see a living creature with babyish features such as a large head, large and low-lying eyes, protruding forehead, round cheeks and body shape, which is why humans usually find babies to be cute.[48] John Morreall claims that human babies are the primary example from which the sense of cuteness derives: cuteness has "the disposition to elicit from adults a response of wanting to hold, cuddle, and care."[49] This babyish cuteness is used commercially today as a marketing strategy in many areas around the world. The commercial notion of cuteness is illustrated in Stephen Jay Gould's analysis of Mickey Mouse's biological "evolution." Using cuteness as a marketing strategy, Gould points out that Disney intentionally makes Mickey Mouse more lovable through his babyish cuteness (big eyes, a relatively larger head, and a smaller, shorter torso), and that his public image has evolved from a mouse with beanie eyes and a sharp nose into an adorable creature with large eyes and a small nose over the course of half a century.[50] The commercial success of employing cuteness inspires more businesses to do so. For instance, Italian artist Simon Legno (1977–) and his business partner created a brand named Tokidoki, which is well known for its cute, bright, and Japanese-themed graffiti style in which many cute creatures with large heads and sparkling eyes are featured. Tokidoki is now a fairly popular brand among young people globally. Last but not least, the ubiquitous pink Hello Kitty has conquered the world exercising her mouthless cuteness as an ultimate form of charisma on consumers of all ages. Cuteness, associated with infants and babies, poses a sharp contrast to aging and maturity. Not only can cuteness be contextualized as an infantile characteristic to successfully instigate a sense of caring within others, but it also strongly connotes the idea of youth, which in turn connotes innocence and naïveté. The quality of cuteness is naturally appealing to human beings, and a recent study substantiates this appeal. The study focuses on "cute aggression," concluding that the cuter a living creature is the more people will want to cuddle it tightly or squeeze it, because people simply cannot resist something if it is too cute.[51] As the idea of cuteness becomes popular and has proven hard to resist by many people, it is consumed in diverse forms. Some would choose to dress in pink like Hello Kitty; others would decorate their living space with accessories, such as their rooms or their backpacks, in the form of cute fluffy animals and cute ACG figures. The consumption of cuteness can even mean for some the fantasy of becoming a commoditized cultural object to embody as they experience everyday life.

Today, cuteness is further carried out in different cultural contexts. The ramifications of cuteness are largely reflected through popular culture and mass consumerism, especially in East Asia, where the notion of "something too cute to resist" is very marketable. Less maturity, or neotenized features to indicate youth as attractiveness, has been infiltrated into contemporary East Asian cultures commercially, being woven into the everyday life of numerous young people. Two of China's neighboring countries, Japan and South Korea, heavily exercise cuteness in their popular cultures and successfully export their soft power to the world.

The Japanese obsessive consumption of the idea of *kawaii* is well known to the world and frequently researched. *Kawaii* is more than just looking and behaving cute, it is also a way of life, a means for some to resist male-dominated Japanese tradition and work ethic.[52] *Kawaii* has now become a distinctive feature of postwar Japanese consumer culture in which the notion is applied widely to objects and persons, from Hello Kitty to big, starry-eyed ACG characters to pop idol groups. *Kawaii* initially started as an escape from the traditional Japanese culture of self-discipline and responsibility among young people,[53] but Japanese business soon detected the potential market for it and started incorporating *kawaii* features into everyday commercial practice. The primary qualities of *kawaii*, as Sharon Kinsella defines, are "essential[ly] childlike," and "celebrat[ing] sweet, adorable, innocent, pure, simple, genuine, gentle, vulnerable, weak, and inexperienced social behaviour and physical appearances."[54] Anne Allison sees the quality as more associated with the notion of *yasashii* (gentleness).[55] Examining the making of an idol in contemporary Japan, Hiroshi Aoyagi sees cute as encompassing "pretty looks" and behaving "in a sweet, meek, and adorable way."[56] Despite implying characteristics such as childlikeness, innocence, and purity, *kawaii*, according to Christine R. Yano, has its sexual implications. The extent to which *kawaii* is associated with female sexuality varies, yet it "always carries the potential for sexuality, even when not overtly sexualized."[57] So *kawaii*, despite having been asexual to begin with,[58] now connotes innocence and purity but also sexuality. In other words, encompassing the quality of being infantile, childlike, and adorable (which corresponds to the previously mentioned baby schema), Japanese *kawaii* carries an undertone of feminine sexuality. The mixed quality of childlike innocence and feminine sexuality can be observed in the group's screenshots as they cosplay Japanese anime/manga characters and members of pop idol groups. The commonality between their image in the screen shots and Japanese *kawaii* exists in the sense of looking sweet, adorable, purely innocent, of appearing gentle, and of implying a sense of sexuality when they show off their long legs and their slim bodies.

South Korea, according to Chuyun Oh, is where cuteness is prioritized over sexiness in women as the "society's fascination with adorable, cute and child-like femininity."[59] Using the extremely popular female pop-group Girls' Generation as an example (as mentioned, this is a female pop group that the Alice Cos Group emulates frequently), Oh points out that the "mandatory cuteness" reflected in the K-pop industry involves the notion of "a young-looking baby face and glamorous body," which implies an ideal femininity of "an innocent but seductive 'virgin-whore' identity."[60] In addition, "acting like a kid with girly, cute attitudes" and presenting "a girlish and childlike persona through particular voices and movements" are also indispensable elements of the Korean mandatory cuteness.[61] This type of cuteness has become a model for many young Korean women to follow and also serves as a fundamental element of Korean pop.[62] Michael Fuhr further points out that the voice quality of Girls' Generation reveals a strong notion of *"aegyo* cuteness" in which "baby talking, tweety-bird-like speaking, and girlish squeaking and giggling all belong to the vocal repertoire of *'aegyo* cuteness.'"[63] The *aegyo* cuteness in the voice, together with the frequently seen cute facial expressions and gestures such as "wide eyes, mouth agape, a pneumatic pout, finger-on-cheek, and palm-on-cheek," confirm the highly desirable cuteness with an undercurrent of sexuality in a woman in South Korea.[64] Associating the notion of Korean *aegyo* back to the group members' screenshot when they cosplay Girls' Generation, once again a sense of commonality is there. The members demonstrate adorable femininity, with cute facial expression and gestures, and their slim body image and short skirts give out a sense of sexuality.

While *kawaii* and *aegyo* qualities have their cultural distinctiveness under the umbrella translation "cute," the commonality both Japanese *kawaii* and Korean *aegyo* impose on femininity is the notion of the virgin/whore identity. This virgin/whore identity is incorporated into the reformation of contemporary *ke'ai* (cute/likable/lovable) as applied to young women in mainland China. *Ke'ai*, being generally understood as the notion of "to be likable/lovable" in its original semantic sense,[65] now is shifting toward the influx of culturally mixed trends leading toward a popular notion among young Chinese women that they must present themselves with the combination of innocent but sexualized femininity to be likable/lovable in keeping with a combined virgin/whore image. Vast numbers of Chinese girls seek to make themselves look like a sexy doll in their selfie photos—facial features of exceptionally big, watery eyes with unusually large pupils (wearing black-colored contact lenses to make their pupils appear larger) and thick, long eyelashes; a small face with an extremely pointed chin, mostly with a heavy hair fringe; and body features showing off a slim build, fair skin, long legs, and big breasts. The dual quality of innocence and seduction is invariably accentuated in selfie photos shared online. Usually, they willingly show their cleavage—popularly known as the "career line" in the Chinese-speaking regions[66]—or their long legs. They look naïve, innocent, and gentle, yet their body image suggests that of a sexually mature and seductive female. In 2011, discussions around a young Chinese woman's selfie photos topped the search chart in South Korea because she looked exactly like an inflatable sex doll. Her appearance in the photographs presented all the features listed above.[67] Numerous Chinese girls replicated the same appearance formula in their selfie photos either by using heavy makeup or image-editing software. The group's screenshots attest to the formula of the virgin/whore identity. Its imitation of the Japanese pop idol group AKB48 and of the South Korean girls' pop group Girls' Generation also substantiate the Japanese and South Korean influences on the formation of *ke'ai* in today's China.

Although, at the present stage, it is a challenge to determine the extent to which and the ways in which *kawaii* and *aegyo* impact the formation of modern-day *ke'ai*, it is highly doubtful that *ke'ai* can be said to be just a simple replication of *kawaii* or *aegyo*. In an examination of the *feizhuliu* (nonmainstream) subculture online, Qiu Zitong argues that *sajiao* adds a Chinese touch to the formation of the *feizhuliu* subculture as *ke'ai* draws heavily from Japanese and Korean popular culture.[68] Yet, the unique feature of Chinese *sajiao*, that *ke'ai* accentuates *sajiao* as a way of shaping many young Chinese women's sexual subjectivity and femininity, should be further elaborated. For instance, *jiaomei ke'ai* (coquettish / sexually charming / sweet and cute), one frequently used Chinese phrase to describe women, incorporates the notion of *sajiao* for women to get advantages from men in a patriarchal context. Chinese *sajiao*, in this sense, is a performative act for a woman to intentionally make herself seemingly infantile, subordinate, and helpless to gain favor from men. The performative act includes "stomping her foot, whining cutely, pouting her lips and making eyes at"[69] her targeted subject and speaking by "prolong[ing] the pronunciation of vowels and soften[ing] the pronunciation of consonants."[70] Using *sajiao* as a subjective means to make her male companion feel superior and needed, a young Chinese woman can obtain favors from him to suit her own needs. Seemingly, *sajiao*, together with virgin/whore face and body images, constitutes the today's Chinese *ke'ai* that many young Chinese women see as the principle dictated to them about their image and behavior. It is worth recalling in this context that the notion of gender, according to Judith Butler, is both an involuntary act and subjective performance, not innate but performative.[71] As she elaborates, gender "proves to be performative—that is, constituting the identity it is purposed to be. In this sense, gender is always a doing."[72] The notion of gender performativity, in this sense, describes how the reiterated and ritualized bodily acts (of young Chinese women) respond to patriarchal dictates of conventionally gendered attributes, such as physical appearance, behavior, and dress style.[73]

With *ke'ai* being performed on a collective level, it is now a socially accepted and even anticipated femininity code in contemporary Chinese society. Referring to this code also serves as the strategy for the group to transgress gender difference during performing *weiniang*. The group captures and expresses the essence of *ke'ai* to the point that hardly any of its audience realizes that the group members are biologically male when they see an Alice Cos Group performance unless further elucidation is given. To the group members, to act more *ke'ai* than real women is a way to reassuringly assert their ability to perform normative or even exaggerated femininity. This reassurance sometimes can also serve as both a productive marketing strategy and the main way to sustain the group's performance career.

Moreover, to be *weiniang*—performing femininity on a biologically male body—is often deemed unacceptable and discouraged if not forbidden by the heteropatriarchal normative gender system. By taking on cross-dressing practices in public spaces, *weiniang* cross-players weave queerness into ACG conventions held in mainstream, heterocentric public spaces. This kind of *weiniang* performance further queers the Alice Cos Group. This form of queerness can be understood as "whatever is at odds with the normal, the legitimate, the dominant" and "demarcates not a positivity but a positionality *vis-à-vis* the normative."[74] This queer dimension allows the group to negotiate with and disturb the heteronormative dictation of uniformity between socially accepted gender expressions and assigned gender roles. In doing so, the group members use their biologically male bodies as a collective venue on which normative cute femininity is repetitively and consciously acted out. In this regard, the group presents a queered *ke'ai* that well illustrates the performative nature of gender and sexuality.

Conclusion

The Alice Cos Group has successfully established fame inside and outside of the cosplayers' fandom mainly due to its deviation from and challenge to gender norms in today's China. Both consuming existing notions of *weiniang* and further exploring them, the Alice Cos Group members present themselves to the general public by dressing up in a cute, girly way, posing in a *sajiao* fashion and accentuating virgin/whore facial features and body image, and an implied heterofeminine sexuality. Such a presentation successfully captures the features of *ke'ai*, which has become part of the gender performativity of many young Chinese women. While much of the *weiniang* phenomenon still resides in a virtual, online world, the group also consciously performs *ke'ai* on public occasions not only at cosplay conventions but also on provincial TV programs to promote an alternative gender performance message obviously deviating from the general, heteronormative narrative in China.[75] In addition, by openly performing *ke'ai*, a quality constituting modern day femininity, on male bodies in a theatrical queer (as in nonnormative) setting, the group delivers what I have analyzed as queered *ke'ai*, a double act of performing *ke'ai* and queerness in one well-designed package. The group's public performance of gender expressions that are inconsistent with the members' assigned gender shows such inconsistency has become more viable and accepted by the general public. Such gender performances in public spaces serve as implicit, deviant challenges to real-world heteronormative discourse in today's China.

Notes

1. Judith Butler, *Gender Trouble: Feminism and the Subversion of Identity; with an Introduction by the Author*, second edition (New York: Routledge, 2006).
2. Teresa Winge, "Costuming the Imagination: Origins of Anime and Manga," in *Mechademia 1: Emerging Worlds of Anime and Manga*, ed. Frenchy Lunning (Minneapolis: University of Minnesota Press, 2006), 66–67.
3. See Jen Gunnels, "'A Jedi Like My Father before Me': Social Identity and the New York Comic Con," *Transformative Works and Cultures* 3 (2009), accessed August 9, 2014, http://journal.transformativeworks.org/index.php/twc/article/view/161/110; Jin-Shiow Chen, "A Study of Fan Culture: Adolescent Experiences with Animé/Manga *Doujinshi* and Cosplay in Taiwan," *Visual Arts Research* 33.1 (2007): 14–24; Nicolle Lamerichs, "Stranger Than Fiction: Fan Identity in Cosplay," *Transformative Works and Cultures* 7 (2011), accessed August 9, 2014, http://journal.transformativeworks.org/index.php/twc/article/view/246/230; Nicolle Lamerichs, "The Cultural Dynamic of *Dojinshi* and Cosplay: Local Anime Fandom in Japan, USA and Europe," *Participations* 10.1 (2013): 154–76.

4. Frenchy Lunning, "Cosplay, Drag, and the Performance of Abjection," in *Mangatopia: Essay on Manga and Anime in the Modern World*, ed. Timothy Perper and Marthan Cornog (Santa Barbara, CA: Libraries Unlimited, 2011), 75.
5. Matthew Thorn, "Girls and Women Getting Out of Hand: The Pleasure and Politics of Japan's Amateur Comics Community," in *Fanning the Flame: Fans and Consume Culture in Contemporary Japan*, ed. William W. Kelly (New York: State University of New York, 2004), 176.
6. The website is available here: www.cosplay.com.
7. The website is available here: https://worldcosplay.net.
8. Brian Ashcraft, "What Is Japan's Fetish This Week—Male Daughters," last modified May 26, 2011, accessed September 8, 2014, http://kotaku.com/5804979/what-is-japans-fetish-this-week-male-daughters.
9. The website of the *otoko no ko* maids café is available here: http://newtype.ms. Visitors can see the café advertises its business using the Japanese Kanji *otoko no ko* (male daughters) to elucidate the underlying gender-bending theme of the café.
10. *Kawaii* is the Japanese word for cuteness.
11. *Oxford English Dictionary*, s.v. "Kawaii," accessed September 8, 2014, http://www.oed.com/view/Entry/276314?redirectedFrom=kawaii#eid.
12. *Niang* in Chinese language refers to a mother, not a young girl. Obviously the notion of using *niang* to refer to young girls is a loan from Japanese Kanji.
13. Weiniang Ba (Weiniang Bar) is available here: http://tieba.baidu.com/f?ie=utf-8&kw=%E4%BC%AA%E5%A8%98, accessed September 10, 2014. As of February 2, 2015, there were 5,300,089 posted messages in the post bar, the number of bar participants was 95,096. Though this bar did not specify when it officially started, the earliest message posted gave a clue to the question—it was posted on February 19, 2008. http://tieba.baidu.com/p/326447103, accessed February 2, 2015.
14. "Weiniang Liu Zhu potianhuang huo wangyou liting, Anni Meigui yiyin yalida gaikou" [Weiniang Liu Zhu received unprecedented support from Chinese netizens, Anni Meigui allegedly changed her attitude against Liu's gender identity to wish Liu the best due to pressure from netizens], *Hunan TV News*, last modified May 4, 2010, accessed February 13, 2015, http://ent.hunantv.com/z/20100504/639208.html.
15. The ranking information can be found at http://daren.dragontv.cn/4/player/sort.php?order=vote&page=1, accessed August 9, 2014. This website has been archived. The snapshots of the website can be viewed at *http://archive.is/lfmRX*, accessed December 2, 2016.
16. Photographs of him presenting himself as a *weiniang* can be viewed on his Weibo, https://weibo.com/u/1837937193, accessed September 12, 2014.
17. "Wuhan gaoxiao xian weiniangtuan, chengli yinian tuanyuan jin erbairen" [Weiniang group founded in a Wuhan University, nearly 200 members recruited since its commencement], *Chinese Radio International*, last modified October 19, 2010, accessed August 22, 2014, http://big5.cri.cn/gate/big5/gb.cri.cn/27564/2010/10/19/114s3025760.htm. Criticisms have been posted on their Weibo pages accusing them of being morally corrupt.
18. "Taishang banxiang liang taixia hen yemen, weiniangtuan wuju feiyi zhuimeng" [Beautiful girls on stage masculine guys off stage, Weiniang tuan members are not afraid to pursue their dreams despite public criticisms], *Hubei Xinhua Net*, last modified July 7, 2011, accessed August 22, 2014, http://big5.xinhuanet.com/gate/big5/www.hb.xinhua.org/newscenter/2011-07/07/content_23185585.htm.

19. "Cross-Dressing *Weiniang* a Hit at ChinaJoy," *Shanghai Daily*, last modified July 30, 2012, accessed September 12, 2014, http://www.china.org.cn/china/2012-07/30/content_26058971.htm.
20. The recruitment is advertised on Alice Cos Group's official Weibo channel, http://www.weibo.com/2139358713/AzRBWEuKC?mod=weibotime#_rnd1412800596437, accessed September 13, 2014.
21. "Wuhan gaoxiao nansheng zu 'weiniangtuan' shangyan buduan, chuchangfei meici meiren wubaiyuan," [University males students based in Wuhan City started a Weiniang cosplayer group and have received constant invitation for public performance, five hundred RMB per Weiniang per performance], *Xinhua Net*, last modified April 10, 2012, accessed May 12, 2015, http://news.xinhuanet.com/photo/2012-04/10/c_122953786.htm. The performance fee has not been disclosed by any Alice Cos Group member on their Weibo. Therefore, this piece of news is the only source regarding their performance fee; however, it is very likely that it has risen with their growing popularity.
22. Their official virtual store on Taobao is available here: https://ac2009.taobao.com, accessed September 13, 2014.
23. For instance, they have appeared on Hunan Satellite TV, Jiangsu TV, and Shanghai Dragon TV. Footage of members being interviewed can be found at the Alice Cos Group's official video-streaming channel, http://www.youku.com/playlist_show/id_6608355.html.
24. See "Chinese Women and Sa Jiao," *China Daily*, last modified April 14, 2014, accessed February 4, 2015, http://www.chinadaily.com.cn/opinion/2014-04/14/content_17431563.htm; Tiara Lin, "Men Succumb to Women's Sajiao Spell," *Global Times*, last modified January 17, 2013, accessed February 4, 2015, http://www.globaltimes.cn/content/756586.shtml.
25. There is no clear indication of the Alice Cos Group's audience gender makeup. Judging by the tone and language usage of the messages left on the Alice Cos Group's Weibo, along with the photos the participants share, I would argue that most of ACG's audiences are female anime, comic, and game fans.
26. The video is available here: http://v.youku.com/v_show/id_XNTkxNTU5NTAw.html at 00:30, accessed September 15, 2014.
27. The video is available here: http://v.youku.com/v_show/id_XNTU5NDU1NTE2.html at 00:35, accessed September 15, 2014.
28. The page is available here: http://weibo.com/alice520cosplay.
29. The page is available here: http://weibo.com/u/3932434256.
30. See http://www.weibo.com/2139358713/B2p8H1QcD?mod=weibotime, accessed September 17, 2014.
31. See http://www.weibo.com/2139358713/Bqc3uzcJM?mod=weibotime, accessed September 17, 2014.
32. See http://www.weibo.com/2139358713/AAd8V971K?mod=weibotime, accessed September 20, 2014.
33. See http://www.weibo.com/2139358713/ApBAxxENZ?mod=weibotime#_rnd1412883018420, accessed September 20, 2014.
34. There has been much study on the rotten girl phenomenon in the Greater Chinese Regions. For example, see Chris Berry, "The Chinese Side of the Mountain," *Film Quarterly* 60.3 (2007): 32–37; Jin Feng, "'Addicted to Beauty': Consuming and Producing Web-Based Chinese *Danmei* Fiction at Jinjiang," *Modern Chinese Literature*

and Culture 21.2 (2009): 1–41; Yanrui Xu and Ling Yang, "Forbidden Love: Incest, Generational Conflict, and the Erotics of Power in Chinese BL Fiction," *Journal of Graphic Novels and Comics* 4.1 (2013): 30–43; Shih-chen Chao, "Grotesque Eroticism in the Danmei Genre: The Case of Lucifer's Club in Chinese Cyberspace," *Porn Studies* 3.1 (2016): 65–76.

35. Lydia H. Liu presented a thorough list of Japanese words and phrases composed in Japanese Kanji to represent western ideas. The words and phrase were later introduced into modern Chinese language to present those ideas as well. Lydia H. Liu, "Appendix B: Sino-Japanese-European Loanwords in Modern Chinese," and "Appendix C: Sino-Japanese Loanwords in Modern Chinese," in *Translingual Practice: Literature, National Culture, and Translated Modernity China, 1900–1937* (Stanford, CA: Stanford University Press, 1995), 284–98, 299–342.

36. Insup Taylor and M. Martin Taylor, "Spoken Chinese," in *Writing and Literacy in Chinese, Korean and Japanese*, revised edition (Philadelphia, PA: John Benjamins Publishing Co., 2014), 31–32.

37. Luke Sharp, "Maid Meets Mammal: The 'Animalized' Body of the Cosplay Maid Character in Japan," *Intertexts* 15.1 (Spring 2011): 65–67.

38. See http://www.weibo.com/2141792331/BkSzvcTJZ?from=page_1005052141792331_profile&wvr=6&mod=weibotime&type=comment#_rnd1423921611245, accessed September 18, 2014.

39. Kam Louie, *Theorising Chinese Masculinity: Society and Gender in China* (Cambridge, Cambridge University Press, 2002), 4.

40. Ibid.

41. See http://www.weibo.com/1767918494/yozTXwLTw?mod=weibotime, accessed September 20, 2014.

42. See http://www.weibo.com/1767918494/xlKPPaIwp?mod=weibotime, accessed September 24, 2014. The whole message Xiaohua left on Weibo is: "On that day when we gathered together, I watched Quan Xiaoyao teaching Alice Cos Group members Xiaolu and Tang Bomao choreography to the song 'Go Go Summer' again and again. As he counted beats louder and louder, I couldn't help recalling the time when the Alice Cos Group was just started. We had no professional make-up artists, no professional camera facilities, not knowing any professional tailors to make cosplay attires, no professional choreographers, no backup members. The reason why we do what we do is because we enjoy the hobby, nothing else. Nevertheless, our efforts were returned with the twisted message made up by the mass media as they untruthfully state that we intended to compare ourselves—a group of university male students dressing up as girls—to Mei Lanfang, putting ourselves on a par with the well-respected artist. It is all a ridiculous hype by the mass media!" (my translation). Based on this message, it is clear that Xiaohua was upset about the mass media trying to put words in their mouths, but he did not point out if it ever occurred to him that the Alice Cos Group would be a modern-day legacy of Mei Lanfang's cross-dressing performance in any regard.

43. See http://www.Weibo.com/1767918494/ye6o0w1da?mod=Weibotime, accessed September 25, 2014.

44. "Liu Zhu: Bu xihuan beijiao 'weiniang,' yu nanshi shihao bu toulu xingbie" [Liu Zhu: Dislikes the idea of being addressed as a Weiniang, refuses to disclose his sexual identity when men express interest in him], *China Daily*, last modified May 10, 2010, accessed February 4, 2015, http://ent.chinadaily.com.cn/2010-05/10/content_13703610.htm.

45. "Taishang banxiang liang taixia hen yemen, weiniangtuan wuju feyi zhuimeng" [Beautiful girls on stage masculine guys off stage, Weiniang tuan members are not afraid to pursue their dreams despite public criticisms], *Hubei Xinhua Net*, last modified July 7, 2011, accessed August 22, 2014, http://big5.xinhuanet.com/gate/big5/www.hb.xinhua.org/newscenter/2011-07/07/content_23185585.htm.
46. "Jiaomei ruwo, weiniang de qianshi jinsheng" [Me, coquettish—the before life and present life of a *Weiniang*], *V Fashion Show*, accessed February 14, 2015, http://hb.sina.com.cn/zt/showtime22/index.shtml.
47. "Chuan guangdian zongju fajinggao, 'weiniang' Liu Zhu jiangbei taotai" [State administration allegedly issued a warning, *weiniang* Liu Zhu would be forbidden to enter the next round of the talent show], *Yunnan Xinhua News*, last modified May 22, 2010, accessed February 4, 2015, http://big5.xinhuanet.com/gate/big5/www.yn.xinhua.org/video/2010-05/22/content_19857068.htm.
48. Konrad Lorenz, *Studies in Animal and Human Behavior*, vol. 2, trans. Robert Martin (Cambridge, MA: Harvard University Press, 1971), 154.
49. John Morreall, "Cuteness," *British Journal of Aesthetics* 31.1 (January 1991): 40.
50. Stephen Jay Gould, "A Biological Homage to Mickey Mouse," accessed August 27, 2014, http://faculty.uca.edu/benw/biol4415/papers/Mickey.pdf.
51. Carrie Arnold, "Cuteness Inspires Aggression," *Scientific American Mind* 24 (July/August 2013): 18, accessed October 5, 2014, http://www.nature.com/scientificamericanmind/journal/v24/n3/pdf/scientificamericanmind0713-18b.pdf.
52. A number of researchers have focused on the analysis of Japanese *kawaii*. For instance, see Sharon Kinsella, "Cuties in Japan," in *Women, Media and Consumption in Japan*, ed. Lise Skove and Brian Morean (Richmond: Curzon, 1995), 220–54; Christine R. Yano, "Wink on Pink: Interpreting Japanese Cute as It Grabs the Global Headlines," *Journal of Asian Studies* 68.3 (2009): 681–88.
53. Kinsella, "Cuties in Japan," 251–52.
54. Ibid., 220.
55. Anne Allison, "Portable Monsters and Commodity Cuteness: Pokémon as Japan's New Global Power," *Postcolonial Studies* 6 (2003): 381–95.
56. Hiroshi Aoyagi, *Islands of Eight Million Smiles: Idol Performance and Symbolic Production in Contemporary Japan* (Cambridge, MA: Harvard University Press, 2005), 73.
57. Christine R. Yano, "Kitty Litter: Japanese Cute at Home and Abroad," in *Toys, Games, and Media*, ed. Jeffrey Goldstein, David Buckingham, and Giles Brougère (Mahwah, NJ: Lawrence Erlbaum Associates, 2004), 60.
58. Larissa Hjorth, *Mobile Media in the Asian-Pacific: Gender and the Art of Being Mobile* (New York: Routledge, 2009), 96.
59. Chuyun Oh, "The Politics of the Dancing Body: Racialized and Gendered Femininity in Korean Pop," in *The Korean Wave: Korean Popular Culture in the Global Context*, ed. Yasue Kuwahara (New York: Palgrave Macmillan, 2014), 63.
60. Ibid., 63, 61.
61. Ibid., 63.
62. Youna Kim, "The Korean Wave: Korean Media Go Global," in *Korean Media in a Digital Cosmopolitan World* (New York: Routledge, 2013), 20. Kim indicates that K-pop female idols always emphasize the cute and the innocent.
63. Michael Fuhr, "Voicing Body, Voicing Seoul," in *Vocal Music and Contemporary Identities: Unlimited Voices in East Asia and the West*, ed. Christian Utz and Frederick

Lau (New York: Routledge, 2013), 278–79. Fuhr defines *aegyo* as someone "behaving in a coquettish manner."

64. Ibid., 278–79.
65. *Online Revised Chinese Dictionary*, s.v. "Ke'ai," last accessed February 4, 2015, http://dict.revised.moe.edu.tw/cgi-bin/cbdic/gsweb.cgi?o=dcbdic&searchid=Z00000076225. This online dictionary is provided by Taiwanese Minister of Education.
66. Yiu Fai Chow and Jeroen de Kloet, *Sonic Multiplicities: Hong Kong Pop and the Global Circulation of Sound and Image* (Bristol, UK: Intellectual, 2013), 156.
67. Fauna, "Wang Jiayun: Chinese Blow-Up Doll Becomes Famous in Korea," *ChinaSMACK*, last modified February 23, 2011, accessed October 7, 2014, http://www.chinasmack.com/2011/pictures/wang-jiayun-chinese-blow-up-doll-becomes-famous-in-korea.html.
68. Qiu Zitong, "Cuteness as a Subtle Strategy: Urban Female Youth and the Online *Feizhuliu* Culture in Contemporary China," *Cultural Studies* 23.2 (2013): 226.
69. Jessica A. Larson-Wang, "What Are You, Five? Chinese Women and *Sa Jiao*," last modified December 21, 2012, accessed October 27, 2014, http://www.echinacities.com/news/What-are-You-Five-Chinese-Women-and-Sa-Jiao.
70. James W. Neuliep, *Intercultural Communication: A Contextual Approach*, sixth edition (Los Angeles: Sage, 2015), 269.
71. The extension of Butler's notion of gender performativity will be explored further when analyzing Alice Cos Group as a *weiniang* phenomenon later in the chapter.
72. Butler, *Gender Trouble*, 34.
73. Ibid.
74. David M. Halperin, *Saint Foucault: Towards a Gay Hagiography* (New York: Oxford University Press, 1995), 62.
75. Although the gender performance of the group brings to mind the rich and complex "gender b(l)ending" tradition in the history of Chinese theater, the group is clearly informed by the popular, contemporary Japan-originated ACG culture, rather than traditional Chinese opera. For a thorough investigation of the issue of cross-dressing and gender play in Chinese opera, see Siu Leung Li, *Cross-Dressing in Chinese Opera* (Hong Kong: Hong Kong University Press, 2003).

3
"The World of Grand Union"

Engendering Trans/nationalism via Boys' Love in Chinese Online Hetalia *Fandom*

Ling Yang

Hetalia: Axis Powers (2006–), also known as *Axis Powers: Hetalia*, or APH, is a Japanese manga and anime series that has achieved global popularity in recent years.[1] It presents an allegorical interpretation of world history by using cute little boys and, occasionally, girls with distinct human forms and names to personify countries and a set of domestic tropes to allude to world "affairs" in the double sense of the word. In *Hetalia* vocabulary, cohabitation refers to military invasion, marriage implies formal annexation, poor health signifies political and economic instability, and so forth. Through this radical mapping of the private, intimate sphere onto the public sphere, *Hetalia* manages to render distant, tedious historical facts vividly alive and relatable for fans, and facilitates their attachment to the country characters. So far about fifty countries and regions have made their appearances in the series, and China is one of them. Although China gets mentioned in passing most of the time, its representation in *Hetalia* nonetheless provides Chinese fans an emotional focal point to construct their own images of China, to reflect on China's convoluted history, and to imagine its current standing and future direction in the world.

Most of the Chinese *Hetalia* fan works are framed as narratives of Boys' Love (BL), a genre of male-male same-sex stories. While BL is often read as women's "fantasy," "romance," or "pornography" by Japanese and English-speaking scholars,[2] in the Chinese language, the genre also has a complicated semantic link with politics in its narrow sense, that is, the art of government. In *The Book of Rites* (*Liji*), Confucius (551–479 BCE) envisions a utopian world of "grand union" (*datong*) where people live in permanent peace, justice, and harmony. Enthusiastic BL fan girls, so-called *tongrennü*,[3] have jokingly borrowed the Confucian idea to articulate their own dreamland where the whole world is conceptualized and interpreted through the same-sex relationship (*tongxinglian*) between *seme* (top) and *uke* (bottom). The lyrics of a self-parody song about the life of *tongrennü* read: "We need far more successors in order to realize the invincible BL world of grand union, for the revolution has not yet succeeded."[4] These lines are not only a witty pun on the Confucian utopia but also a sly mockery of the well-known deathbed quote from Dr. Sun Yat-sen (1866–1925), the founding father of Republican China: "The revolution has not yet succeeded; comrades must strive further." In this song, *tongrennü* are conceived as mind-game guerrillas who are engaged in an unfinished struggle toward a homosexual utopia, a task no less arduous than any political revolution. With its motto of "love and peace" and a large variety of male country characters, *Hetalia* seems to be a perfect embodiment of both the original Confucian spirit and the current homoerotic extension. It has thus inspired many Chinese fans to play with the pairing up of countries and tease out the *seme/uke* dynamics in international relations.

Although *Hetalia* reached the peak of its popularity in China in 2009 and 2010 and since then has entered a phase of decline, it continues to draw a sizable fandom, and its influence on Chinese popular culture is far from over. In this chapter, I will provide an account of *Hetalia*'s circulation in China, especially how it is appropriated and recreated by Chinese fans. I will explore what happens when BL meets nation, when "queer nation" develops into "queer trans/nationalism," when gender politics intersects with geopolitics. If any nation is, as Benedict Anderson has famously argued, "an imagined political community,"[5] it is then necessary to find out how this imagining process is socially and historically conditioned, and laden with gender implications. Current research on the genre of BL and its cross-national fandoms tends to focus on issues of sexuality, sexual orientation, and gender politics.[6] While those issues certainly constitute the most salient aspects of BL, they do not exhaust the interpretive potential of the genre. The *Hetalia* boom in China shows that BL not only can function as a tool to reshape configurations of gender and sexuality, it can also be employed by young women and others as a vehicle for political expression.

Online *Hetalia* Fandom: Popularity and Controversy

Like many Japanese manga and anime titles currently popular in China, *Hetalia* has never been published or broadcast through official channels. Instead, it is disseminated mainly through Internet fan sites, manga websites, and video streaming sites. Pirated print copies of manga can also be bought from online and offline ACG shops. There are two major online *Hetalia* fan communities in China: the Love and Peace Bulletin Board System (hereafter abbreviated as LP) and Baidu *Hetalia* Post Bar (*Hetalia* Bar for short). Both were established in July 2008, four months after the first *Hetalia tankōbon*[7] came out in Japan. LP and *Hetalia* Bar represent two different organizational styles in the Chinese online fan community. LP is an independent and closed forum with elaborate rules and disciplines. To access LP, newcomers have to register with an invitation code from existing members of the forum or wait for the randomly selected "open registration" days. LP used to have about 10,000 members during its heyday in 2010. Since then, however, the forum has suffered from technical problems and a loss of active membership and finally ceased operation around 2012. *Hetalia* Bar, by contrast, is an open-access and easy-to-use forum under the aegis of Baidu Post Bar. Anyone can lurk in the bar and browse through all the entries posted there. One can also post a comment or thread after a simple user registration. Owing to its stable operation, the number of registered members of *Hetalia* Bar increased from 7,000 in 2010 to 121,000 in January 2016.

Both LP and *Hetalia* Bar have implemented an "APH netiquette" in their administration. The netiquette was first proposed by Kuruma, a Taiwanese ACG fan living in Japan, to address the potential trouble related to the dissemination of *Hetalia* in Taiwan.[8] Recognizing that many people could be offended by the humorous parody of World War II history and the national stereotypes involved in country anthropomorphism, Kuruma suggests several preventive measures to avoid misunderstanding and controversy. The most important measure is for fans to use each country's human name or nickname instead of official name at public websites, or use symbols of "/" and "." between the Chinese characters of each country name to bypass search engines. For instance, fans should use "意/大/利" or "意.大.利" when mentioning Italy in Chinese.

Despite fan efforts to keep a low profile for *Hetalia*, the proliferation of self-published *Hetalia tongrenzhi*, or fanzines, shows that the series has already won a cult following. As of October 28, 2010, Tianchuang Lianmeng, an online information clearinghouse for Chinese-language *tongrenzhi*, listed 1,090 *Hetalia* fanzine titles in its database, which amounted to one fifth of the total number of fanzines (5,432) registered there. The boom of *Hetalia tongrenzhi* is partly indebted to the textual features of the original series, which focuses not on developing a complete narrative but on presenting "the characters and settings" that make up its "worldview."[9] The "extremely loose" "emplotment, setting, and psychological characterization" provide ample spaces and stimuli for fan imagination and re-creation.[10] The fan-friendly attitude of Hidekaz Himaruya,[11] the author of *Hetalia*, has also greatly encouraged fan works. Himaruya has posted a large amount of *Hetalia*-related materials on his personal blog and allowed users to freely appropriate those materials for re-creations.[12]

To facilitate the trading of *tongrenzhi*, *Hetalia* fans have organized APO (APH Only) events across the country. I attended one such event in Hangzhou, the affluent capital of Zhejiang Province, in August 2010, and another in Guangzhou in August 2014. The first was organized by five high school girls and drew a crowd of 200 fans, all female. The Guangzhou event was held at a spacious venue intended for fashion shows and drew about 400 fans, among whom I saw only one male organizer and two male cosplayers.[13] Most of the participants at the two events appeared to be secondary school or college students. At both events, fans sold and purchased *tongrenzhi* and spin-offs, participated in games and contests of fan knowledge, and cosplayed their favorite nation characters. *Hetalia* fans' penchant for cosplay has given rise to a niche market for *Hetalia* costumes and flags.

In February 2009, after the first episode of animated *Hetalia* was available on Tudou, an online streaming site in China, an excited fan posted many *Hetalia* pictures and scanlations at Tianya, a well-known BBS in China.[14] The thread lived on till the end the year, eventually receiving over 240,000 hits and more than 2,000 replies. Surprisingly, except for a few hate messages, the public discussion of *Hetalia* was quite peaceful as a whole. Disgruntled discussants were reminded to keep an open mind, not to sink to the level of South Koreans, a reference to the South Korean protest of *Hetalia* in January 2009 and the subsequent cancellation of the scheduled broadcast of the anime version of the series on a Japanese TV station.[15] The incident was viewed by many Chinese fans as an unfortunate overreaction. The Chinese audience's general tolerance of *Hetalia* seems to be well grounded. Although positioning itself as an irreverent, lighthearted historical parody, this Japanese series nonetheless remains "politically correct" on the single most important issue in Sino-Japanese history—Japan's aggression against China from 1894 to 1945—in the eyes of Chinese people. The manga version of *Hetalia* alludes to the wrongs Japan did to China by depicting Japan stabbing China in the back at one point and leaving a permanent scar. This historical detail, however, is not shown in the anime adaptation.

In response to the public concern of the series' potential whitewashing of Japanese aggression in history, one fan posted in the Tianya thread:

> I haven't forgotten history, yet as an anime and manga fan, I support this series. I think it's very cute; Yao-san[16] is very cute. I have always wanted to personify China, but the Chinese government forbids any politicization of manga.[17] Up till now China's manga market is too narrowly-defined. Now finally there is a little character for fans to work on and we surely are going to make good use it. The power of fan circles in China is really strong!!![18]

Anime and manga are often looked down upon as childish forms of entertainment, "created to escape from the pressures of the real world."[19] *Hetalia*'s success in China, however, shows that anime and manga actually lead fans back to the real world to see it in a fresh light. Chinese fans like to share their stories with fellow fans about how they have been changed by *Hetalia*, how they have started to have a strong interest in world geography and history, and how they have become addicted to news programs and current events. *Hetalia*'s transnational popularity also provides a platform for fans of various nationalities to mingle and exchange ideas. Bilingual Chinese fans have engaged in authorized translation of fan works produced in English and Japanese. They have also supplied English subtitles for their own works so as to share them with fans from other parts of the world. For some fans, this grassroots transcultural practice is far more interesting than the simple consumption of the original Japanese series. More importantly, the series has opened up an alternative space for fans to discover and explore multiple angles of history and to articulate their own understanding of world history and world order.

Seme or Uke? Two Contested Images of China

Hetalia portrays the character of China (hereafter referred to by its human name Yao, to avoid confusion) as a youthful-looking 4,000-year-old immortal and the elder brother to other East Asian nations. He is peaceful, feminine, wears a girlish ponytail, and is played by a voice actress in the anime. While many Chinese fans appreciate *Hetalia*'s acknowledgement of China's longstanding historical and cultural influence in East Asia, some also feel uncomfortable with Yao's "Virgin-Mary-flat-chest-*uke*"[20] role in the world community. Yao's femininity is thrown into sharp relief when he is standing side by side with four of the Western Allied Forces members. Among this group of five, he is obviously the shortest and slimmest in stature. He is not only seen as effeminate but also inconsequential, as no one seems to take him very seriously, not even his own brothers and sisters. In episode 20 of the *World Series*, Yao is so fed up with being bossed around by the United States and the UK that he violently pounds his head on the wall in a fit of rage. Yet it would be too hasty to claim that *Hetalia* exemplifies the Orientalist discourse that feminizes the Orient/China or Occidentalism with its fixation on the West,[21] for the dichotomy of *seme*/*uke*, or masculine/feminine, aggressive/passive, does not operate in the same way in the BL world as it does in the "straight" world. To get a glimpse of how far apart the two worlds can be, we can compare *Hetalia* with stories of Youngster C (C qingnian).

When Himaruya started his anthropomorphic web comic back in 2006, some Chinese BL fans were also creating their own BL-style allegories of world politics at Xianqing, a popular online BL forum.[22] After humanizing and coupling dynasties and cities in China, those fans turned their eyes to countries and began to entertain each other by telling the stories of Youngster C, a code name for China. From December 2006 to December 2007, there were altogether ten threads dedicated to the Youngster C stories.[23] In those folk stories, Youngster C is consistently characterized as a scheming *seme* who uses his extraordinary beauty and refined manners to outsmart his rivals. Representing postreform China since the late 1970s, Youngster C's manipulative behaviors are justified by his strong desire to avenge the humiliations his ancestors suffered. Other main characters include Master A (the United States), Youngster C's archenemy, an arrogant and domineering thug who is inclined to take others as his "mistresses," and Little J (Japan), a rich yet ugly youth who is eager to assert some power based on his wallet but in the end is always reduced to being Master A's submissive "mistress."

In one story told in April 2007, Youngster C is planning to hold a meeting with some big guys from Africa, an allusion to the Beijing Summit of the Forum on China-Africa Cooperation. Master A decides to play Little F (France) off against Youngster C by warning Little F that his interests in Africa would be undermined by Youngster C's expansion of influence in that region. Aware of

Master A's malicious intention, Youngster C visits Little F and flirts with him, knowing that the latter is infatuated with Oriental beauty. Little F soon falls under the charm of Youngster C and is convinced that what Youngster C has done is for the benefit of both of them. There are obvious parallels in themes and characterizations between Youngster C's stories and *Hetalia*, even though they seem to be independent works. For example, in episode 20 of *Hetalia World Series*, France is depicted as drooling over China in his dream and murmuring "kawaii" (cute). After *Hetalia* caught on in China, however, Youngster C merely becomes a nickname for Yao, not vice versa.

A number of factors might have contributed to fans' preference for the imported Yao over the indigenous Youngster C. First of all, Youngster C's stories are told only in words because his creators claim that he is too holy to be represented visually. In contrast, *Hetalia* is a Japanese *moe*-style visual work, designed to appeal to manga and anime fans. Second, Youngster C's stories conflate the country of China with the Chinese government and exhibit a strong progovernment stance. As one *Hetalia* fan commented, Youngster C is the personification of the incumbent Chinese government, rather than the country of China, and country, being the totality of territory and people, should not be confused with the government. By assigning each country a "boss" to symbolize the government, *Hetalia* is clearly more thoughtful in this regard.[24] Last but not the least, a *uke* protagonist is usually more popular than a *seme* one among Chinese BL fans, because the BL world is ruled by the *uke*, not the *seme*. A general "principle" of BL dictates that "if you love him, let him be a *uke*," which means that fans get more pleasure out of the fantasy game if they let their favorite characters play the role of *uke* in artistic creations.

In their defense of the *uke* Yao, *Hetalia* fans have uncannily fused their preference for *uke* over *seme* in the BL world with a critique of indiscriminate worship of might in realpolitik, as if to suggest that gender politics are inherently connected with geopolitics and the subversion of the patriarchal gender norm of the superiority of masculinity over femininity will also result in a revision of power relations in human society as a whole. In the aforementioned long thread on Tianya, one *Hetalia* fan invoked Taoism's promotion of the feminine principle over the masculine by saying that "I don't care for macho men. Those angry young men [ultranationalists] want to be as manly as possible, but tough guys break easily."[25] Another fan remarked that *Hetalia*'s depiction of Yao as a harmless and naive *uke* is exactly the national image the Chinese government has tried to propagate abroad in past decades for the purpose of "peaceful rise," for "how could China pretend to be a stud like the United States and sow trouble everywhere?"[26]

To refute the accusation of Yao being a useless *uke*, an exasperated *Hetalia* fan elaborated her idea of *seme* and *uke*:

> What's wrong with *uke*? Does *uke* mean inferiority? Then how come there is the famous saying that "If you love him, let him be a *uke*?" . . . The attribute

of *seme/uke* is determined by personality. Yao [China] is basically not an aggressive country, and naturally he appears to be more like a *uke* compared to those aggressive Western countries. So the pairing up of Russia/China is typical and mainstream. But with Asian countries, he is more often a *seme*. Don't we have the pairings of China/Hong Kong, China/Japan? We could be both *uke* and *seme*. . . . If Yao is *seme* with those Western hunks, like the Bear Russia, I couldn't tolerate it visually.[27]

True enough, this "queer" commentary of sexual nature and national character does not call for an abandonment of the binary opposition between the aggressive and the passive. But it does attempt to eliminate the negative connotations linked to passivity, loosen the boundary between the two opposite terms, and make the switching of positions possible, so that China "could be both *uke* and *seme*" without any sense of shame. Moreover, it has read the difference between *seme* and *uke*, the West and Asia, squarely as a difference of physique (size of country) and personality (culture), so that the two parties could still construct an egalitarian relationship with and in spite of their differences. However, not all fans are willing to apply the BL philosophy to the real world. *Hetalia* fan works both pull away from and gear toward the BL framework of understanding geopolitics.

Born to be Dragon: Backward to the Empire

In January 2009, a dozen top-notch domestic manga artists copublished a *Hetalia tongrenzhi* entitled *Born to be Dragon* (hereinafter *Dragon*).[28] This professionally made ninety-two-page collection of single illustrations and comic strips soon became the most coveted *Hetalia* fanzine in China.[29] It even generates its own line of fan works, as many music videos and cosplays are based on *Dragon*, instead of *Hetalia*. *Dragon*'s canonical status in the *Hetalia* fandom is largely due to the fact that it has found a way to resolve Yao's *seme/uke* conflict and reproduced an idealized national image that fans could passionately identify with. Through a cultural logic of "both/and," rather than "either/or," and the sheer variety of artists and drawing styles, *Dragon* has worked out a complex image of Yao that is both feminine and masculine, lovely and stately, gentle and powerful. Hence, the cover of *Dragon* is graced by a vigilant *bishōnen* (beautiful boy), flying in the sky, with a panda in his bag, an unfolded blank scroll in his left hand and a writing brush in his right hand. The implied message is that China is civilized, peace-loving, but inviolable. The figure of Yao in *Dragon* is not only more militant than the easygoing, panda-hugging Yao in *Hetalia* but also less duplicitous and ruthless than Youngster C.

Yao's androgynous image is undeniably influenced by what Sun Jung has variously dubbed "East Asian soft masculinity" and "*kawaii* masculinity," referring to the kind of feminized and gentle masculinity embodied by J-Pop and K-Pop idol boy bands that have been in vogue in Asia since the 1990s.[30] Yet, unlike the Korean and Japanese bands who utilize soft masculinity as a selling point for transnational cultural consumption, the creators of *Dragon* jump on the bandwagon for a highly nationalistic agenda and formulate a set of sartorial and gender codes to represent the rise and fall of China in history precisely through the discursive fluidity inscribed in Yao's soft masculinity.

In *Hetalia*, Yao is spotted either in a green military uniform worn by Chinese soldiers in the 1930s and 1940s or in a simple jacket and pants. The latter clothing, combined with the ponytail, often recalls the "sick man of East Asia," a derogatory image of China under the Manchu regime (1644–1911) when all men were required to wear a queue and China was forced into a series of unequal treaties with foreign powers in the late nineteenth and early twentieth centuries. To disassociate from this unpleasant historical memory, some of the color pages at the beginning of *Dragon* feature Yao as an aristocratic *bishōnen* in the elegant silk robe that was worn for millennia before the establishment of the Manchu regime.[31] With more emphasis on Yao's loose and flowing locks, the image also makes the ponytail look less conspicuous. In addition, Yao is surrounded with familiar motifs of traditional high culture like flowers, wine, musical instruments, and hand scrolls. The dramatic change of clothing and setting brings back the memory of the golden ages of Chinese civilization, such as the Tang dynasty (618–907), when China enjoyed unparalleled riches, prestige, and power.

This ancient *bishōnen* figure, however, is soon replaced by a young man in modern clothing in an effort to represent China's economic and political strength in recent years. One single illustration foregrounds Yao in a pair of suspender slacks, shirt, and tie. In the background are a bunch of guys grabbing and groveling over a scattered pile of 100 yuan notes on the ground. Being the winner of this currency war that topples the dominance of the US dollar, Yao turns his back to the pathetic scene and calmly lights up a cigarette. Here China's financial power is explicitly associated with stereotypical masculine traits like cigarettes and suspender pants. In another short satire about the Mainland-Taiwan relationship, China is presented as an elder brother who tries to persuade his willful younger sister (Taiwan) to come back home. Again, Yao is wearing an unmistakable men's jacket and his shoulders are flat and broad. Although goaded by Russia to use "domestic violence" to settle the "family dispute," Yao gives up on the idea only at the last moment. The small print at the end of the comic strip reads, "Taiwan, if you don't want to see the horrible domestic violence that has happened in our neighbor's home, come back home soon." The contrast between an elder, stronger brother and a younger, weaker sister seems to assure readers that, no matter how *uke* Yao appears to be in *Hetalia*, he has the capacity to take over Taiwan by force and complete the national reunification project.[32]

Yet, when necessary, *Dragon* is also willing to portray a more feminine Yao to evoke affective identification. The longest comic strip of the fanzine, titled "The Prolonged Sleep-over," exploits the conventional metaphor of mother/land to narrate Hong Kong's separation from and final reunification with Mainland after 155 years of British occupation. Hong Kong is depicted as an unfortunate but brave "child," while Yao is figured as a suffering and caring "mother" with long, thin eyebrows, prominent round eyes and eyelashes, as well as slender fingers. Obviously, the memory of foreign invasion that happened a long time ago is still perceived to be an effective way to "forge national cohesion."[33] But this fixation on China's "Century of Humiliation" (1840–1945) in modern history might also take its toll and chart a regressive path to China's imperial past.

The ending color piece of *Dragon* presents an emotional and grandiose dialogue between a blood-smeared Yao and a *qilin*, a mythical creature of benevolence and good omen. The legendary beast assures the wounded Yao that with the "Mandate of Heaven" (*tianming*) he will live as long as the world lasts, and, born to be a dragon, he will not be defeated by any temporary setbacks. When Yao asks the *qilin*, "What's your wish?" the animal answers, "May you rule all under the heaven [*junlin tianxia*] in my lifetime." The corresponding picture shows a man with a royal crown sitting in an emperor's chair, face to face with an imposing *qilin*. This is probably the ultimate *seme* moment of Yao, as the word "under" in the phrase "all under the heaven"—a Confucian term for the "world"—indicates that Yao is figuratively on top of all other nations. According to the ancient Sinocentric geopolitical scheme, China is located at the center of the world, "both culturally and politically," and rules it with the "Mandate of Heaven." It was not until the nineteenth century that this idea of "all under the heaven" was replaced by the Western "geocultural space called the *World*" in which China is demoted from the center to the margin.[34] In the early twenty-first century when Western (American) hegemony shows a clear sign of decline and China reemerges "as a major power after one hundred and fifty years of being a weak player on the world stage,"[35] it might not be surprising that Chinese youth are eager to take pride in China's comeback and even couch their hopes for national rejuvenation in an archaic imperial discourse. After all, as Chinese historian Ge Zhaoguang has pointed out, China has not thoroughly transformed from an empire into a modern nation-state. The two identities have continued to intertwine so that "there exists a limited notion of the 'nation-state' in an unlimited consciousness of the 'empire' and the unlimited imagination of the 'empire' has been preserved in the limited recognition of the 'nation-state.'"[36]

It is significant that *Dragon* is a fanzine of "normal orientation" (*zhengchang xiang*) with hardly any hints of BL pairings. Yao is painted in an affective relationship only with Hong Kong and Taiwan, and other countries are treated mostly as enemies, rivals, or laughingstocks. Although there are three illustrations featuring Yao taking care of a younger Japan, their main purpose is probably not to pay respect to Sino-Japanese friendship but to highlight Japan's ungrateful betrayal. The old hegemonic paradigm of West versus the rest is subtly shifted to China versus the rest. Of course, not all fans embrace this thoroughly expansionist, domineering, and lonely vision of China's future; neither do they enjoy the sardonic, sadistic attacks of China's former aggressors. In an online group review of *Dragon*, one anonymous fan-reviewer wrote frankly:

I don't care much about *Dragon* because it's way too OOC [out of character].... I've talked to some buyers of *Dragon* and they all share my feelings.... I have no flattering words for Fengxi [the script writer of *Dragon*, who is actually female]. I really want to say that his "three views"[37] are way too correct. Now that we all say "the whole world is a family," why is he still so unhappy with Honda [Japan's human name in *Hetalia*]? If you despise him [Honda] so much, then don't watch *Hetalia*, don't publish a fanzine in its name! Isn't *Hetalia* the product of Honda? Asia has always been one family. *Tongrenzhi* should be used for entrusting beautiful dreams, not for venting anger.[38]

Another fan concurred, replying that strictly speaking *Dragon* is more like a fanzine of Youngster C than that of *Hetalia*.[39] So what does a "real" *Hetalia* fanzine look like? What are the "beautiful dreams" *Hetalia* fans refer to? How can fans overcome parochial nationalism to imagine a nonimperial future for China? With those questions in mind, I will turn to another highly acclaimed *Hetalia* fanzine.

Pravda Remix: Toward a Cosmopolitan Utopia

Probably only the *Pravda* ("truth" in Russian) series could match *Dragon* in terms of fame and premium value in Chinese *Hetalia* fandom. The two titles complement each other nicely as the *Pravda* series is a collection of fan fiction, whereas *Dragon* is a collection of fan art. Besides, a couple of fan artists have participated in the production of both fanzines. When *Pravda* first came out in February 2009, it created a sales spectacle on Taobao, the Chinese version of eBay. Four hundred copies of the first edition were sold out within two minutes, and two more editions had to be issued to satisfy fan demand. Encouraged by this market success, *Pravda*'s production team published a two-volume sequel, *Pravda Remix* (hereafter *Remix*), nine months later. At a total of 400 pages, *Remix* might well be the thickest *Hetalia tongrenzhi* ever published in China.

Both *Pravda* and *Remix* are categorized as BL *tongrenzhi*, featuring the pairing of Russia/China and Lithuania/Poland. The stories in *Pravda* focus on the historical period from the end of World War II to the fall of Communist regimes in Eastern Europe and the disintegration of the USSR, whereas those in *Remix* shift more freely between the past and the future. As one key contributor, Rita, comments in the "Free Talk" section of *Remix*: "If *Pravda* is about the past, then *Remix* is about the future. We have experienced too much helplessness and pain in the past so that we have all the more reasons to look forward to a better world."[40] Indeed, unlike the indignant and resentful undertone in *Dragon*, *Remix* brims with a warmth of goodwill for China's neighbors and yearns for peace and prosperity, rather than hegemony. The shipping principle of BL further helps *Remix* turn away from *Dragon*'s self-centered nationalism stemming from the "law of the jungle" and move toward an optimistic cosmopolitanism based on mutual trust and understanding among countries.

So far, Russia/China is the most popular pairing in Chinese *Hetalia* fandom, primarily because China has had an intricate love-hate relationship with the Soviet Union historically, and nothing is more fascinating to *Hetalia* fans than fiddling with historical facts. Himaruya's portrayal of Yao's suspicion and fear of Ivan Braginski (Russia's human name in *Hetalia*) tells only one side of the story. The other side is that many Chinese people, especially those who are over fifty years old, harbor a profound "Soviet complex." China used to regard the Soviet Union as the "big brother" to emulate, and Soviet songs, novels, and movies were the only foreign (Western) cultural products available in China. Most of the 1950s marks not only the peak of Sino-Soviet alliance but the golden age of the Chinese Communist regime when the whole nation was united by belief and hope. To fill the gaps and lapses in the original *Hetalia*, fans have dug up many intriguing *neta*[41] for shipping. For instance, the Sino-Soviet Treaty of Friendship, Alliance and Mutual Assistance was signed on February 14, 1950, Valentine's Day. The 2008 Russo-Georgian War broke out on the opening day of the Beijing Olympics. Three out of nine aircraft carriers of the Soviet Union or Russia were purchased by China. One uncompleted ship was refurbished into China's first aircraft carrier. Such seemingly random incidents nevertheless testify to the deep political and military ties between China and Soviet Union / Russia.

By fleshing out the complicated emotional attachment between Yao and Ivan, *Remix* embarks on a reflection of the failure of communism; the founding, breakup, and reorganization of nation-states; and the bonding and boundary between different peoples. The longest work in *Remix*, "The End of Beginning,"[42] presents a multilayered travel account set on the eve of the breakup of Soviet Union in 1991. Through dialogue and flashback, the story skillfully weaves together Yao's revisit to the Soviet Union after decades of hostility between the two countries, Ivan's return visit to Ukraine, Belarus, and the three Baltic nations before they proclaimed independence, and Yao and Ivan's travel together to Siberia and the Sino-Russian border areas. There are two high points in those slightly melancholic trips involved in remembering the dismembering of a country and the disappearance of an era. One is at the scenic Lake Baikal, where Yao and Ivan meet a group of Russian students of painting. Ivan tells Yao that he has always had an inkling that "maybe in the future we will no longer have to fight any war, even a Cold War won't be possible. Till that time . . . we would still be painting, dancing, and reciting poetry."[43] As China and Soviet Union are the two countries that suffered the heaviest casualties in World War II, no one understands Ivan's desire for peace better than Yao. The latter promises Ivan that all the good and bad, ups and downs will be remembered by "the mountains and lakes," and those memories deposited in the soil are the only true memories because no one can alter them. The moment of reconciliation between Yao and Ivan constitutes the second high point of the story. It happens at a small restaurant of the border town where all the menus are bilingual and "people of different skin colors and languages sit at the same table in noise and excitement."[44]

Both Yao and Ivan toast to the young Chinese-Russian couple who are holding a wedding there. The three-decade Sino-Russian "split" at the state level is made up symbolically by an interracial "marriage" at the individual level. After the toast, Yao confesses to Ivan, "I hated you . . . but also deeply loved you, unconditionally believed in you, and went to great length to repel you."[45] Never before had a country given him so much pain and bewilderment. Yet that era is "gone forever."

Although steeped in post-Socialist nostalgia, *Remix* is nonetheless able to rise above ideology to reflect on the fate of humanity, reminding us that communism is after all a version of cosmopolitanism. The opening story, "Cast the Route," narrates an encounter between Yao and a rank-and-file Red Army soldier, Xiao Qi, in the world-famous Long March (1934–1935), an 8,000-mile military retreat from southern to northern China.[46] Yao, the image of China, is depicted as both a mysterious immortal and an average man of flesh and bones. Having nowhere to go and no food to eat, Yao joins Xiao Qi in the march and accompanies him through the most dangerous part of the journey. Along the way, Yao gives Xiao Qi survival hints at critical moments, and Xiao Qi introduces to Yao communist ideas from Russia. After they traverse the Tibetan holy mountains, Yao disappears. But Xiao Qi completes the Long March and lives on to attend the founding ceremony of People's Republic of China. He believes that Yao is still alive and could live through any kind of hardship. Although the story shows sincere admiration for the high idealism of the older generation of revolutionaries and the intimate connection between the Chinese Communist Party and the laboring masses in the past, it is not an official revolutionary tale that eulogizes the Long March as a heroic victory of the righteous Communists over the reactionary Kuomintang troops. Instead, the story ingeniously reframes the Long March as an exile, a pilgrimage, and a basic human condition, regardless of national boundaries or ideological tendencies. Near the end of the story, Yao ponders the numerous diasporas he has gone through in history, especially when a dynasty was terminated by war or foreign invasion, and uses his own experience to empathize with migrations that have happened in Europe and America. He concludes that the human race is condemned to a permanent oscillation between settlement and migration.

Yet one might wonder why China/Japan is not a favorite pairing for fans, for, theoretically speaking, the complex feelings of admiration, envy, and animosity embedded in modern Sino-Japanese relations also provide rich material for fans to work on. To answer this question, we need to take into consideration Russia's remarkable decline in world standing and China's continuous economic boom in the twenty-first century. It is always easier for those in a superior position to forgive their former enemies, but China has not yet clearly surpassed the long-stagnant Japan, except at the level of the GDP. As Leo Ching has observed, "anti-Japanism in China is less about Japan than China's own self-image mediated through its asymmetrical power relations with Japan through its modern history."[47] Due to the lingering power imbalance between China and Japan, not many fans could get over the historical trauma of Japanese imperialism to imagine a harmonious Sino-Japanese relationship, except by viewing Japan as a subordinate younger brother in the "Asian family." *Hetalia* introduces Asian countries as brothers and sisters of the same family. Early members of the Asian family consists of two sisters, Taiwan and Vietnam, and six brothers, China, Hong Kong, Macau, Japan (human name, Kiku Honda), South Korea (human name, Yong Soo Im), and Thailand.[48] This notion of an Asian family is also echoed by Rita's short story "Blues on the Run."[49] Yet unlike some Asian family–themed fanfics that tend to be nostalgic about China's past dominance in the region, the story portrays a China that is interested more in regional economic cooperation and development than competition for regional dominance.

Set in Boao, Hainan Province, with the Boao Forum for Asia[50] as its background, "Blues on the Run" centers on Yao's unexpected encounter with Russia during the forum. At the beginning of the story, Yao takes Kiku, Yong Soo, Vietnam, Hong Kong, and Taiwan to the seaside to relax after a tiresome morning's meeting to solve the world economic crisis. At the beach, he runs into the lonely Ivan, who was just tricked out of the European tourist group by the United States. The deserted Ivan implores Yao to help him get back. After some hesitation, Yao decides to put him onboard the Asian boat, even though he knows that Ivan is not particularly welcome there. On the boat, Yao explains the local customs of pleading for luck and prosperity, as Boao is located at the mouth of three rivers, famous for its fabulous feng shui. Soon all the people on the boat reach out their left hands to grasp the auspicious wind on the river. Encouraged by Yao, even the sullen Ivan participates in the ritual and is immediately lightened by the warm wind and sunshine. Those countries "gather at this endless spring afternoon, together holding out their hands to catch those incorporeal but very beautiful things, as if national borders and frontiers no longer existed and they had been most sincere friends since their birth."[51] The story ends with the gentle fall of Ivan's left hand into Yao's right hand, hinting closer ties between the two countries.

As in her other works, Rita portrays Yao as an ordinary man, this time around, a shrewd and down-to-earth businessman who aggressively grabs every opportunity to make money and cares more about business than territorial boundaries or sovereignty. But Yao is not blinded by his greed for profit to the point of being coldhearted and unreflective. Sensing that Ivan is hurt by the abandonment of Europe and the United States, Yao reassures him that they two are in the same league in terms of popularity, a possible allusion to the regular China bashing in Western media and China's lack of allies in the course of its peaceful rise. When watching his Asian family playing on the beach, Yao thinks to himself, "Although family members and neighbors are all jerks and fools, they at least cause a lot less worry than those who-knows-what-they-are-thinking-about troublesome guys in Europe." Cultural affinity is a relative concept. Despite all the historical baggage and internal competition in Asia, most Chinese people would probably admit in the end that they feel geographically and psychologically closer to their regional neighbors than European countries.

Conclusion: Map and Mapping

I would like to conclude this chapter with a brief description of a fan-made map that accompanies Remix. It is an illustrative map of the Eurasian landmass, the chief geographical setting of the fanfic collection. Story titles, country figures, city names, representative landscapes, architecture, railways, plants, and animals are all marked out on the map, resulting in a colorful bilingual[52] and transcultural mélange of words, things, and humans. The design and the feel of the map recall those early world maps made by European cartographers and informed by either Christian ideology or colonial ambition. Maps are not faithful reflections of the objective world but projections of fantasy and desire. What the map of *Pravda Remix*, literally, "a remix of truth," has invested in is a fantasy of the BL world of grand union: a world full of connections and emotions but devoid of territorial demarcations. This fantasy has become particularly alive with the accelerating process of globalization and China's further integration into the world economic and political system.

However, the polarized trans/national visions evoked in *Dragon* and *Remix* seem to have confirmed Koichi Iwabuchi's argument that the "boundary-violating impulse" of transnational cultural flows is "nevertheless never free from nationalizing forces." As Iwabuchi quotes from Roger Rouse, "The transnational has not so much displaced the national as resituated it and thus reworked its meanings."[53] If *Dragon* is engaged in redrawing the image of China and boundaries of the self by experimenting with a more flexible gender formation, *Remix* is bent on border crossing and intercultural dialogue to reveal innate human mobility and communicativeness. These two approaches to cultural mapping might coexist in conflict and complement for a long time to come.

Acknowledgments

This research was supported by a grant for Japan-related research projects from the Sumitomo Foundation (Reg. No.: 128017). Earlier versions of the chapter were presented at "Global Polemics of BL (Boys' Love): Production, Circulation, and Censorship" held at Oita University on January 23, 2011, and "New Media and Cultural Transformation: Film, TV, Game, and Digital Communication" held at Shanghai University on December 8, 2012. I would like to thank the conference participants, especially Toshio Miyake and Earl Jackson, for their encouragement and suggestions. I am also indebted to Hongwei Bao for his stimulating feedback in the writing process.

Notes

1. Sandra Annett, "Animating Transcultural Communities: Animation Fandom in North America and East Asia from 1906–2010" (PhD diss., University of Manitoba, 2011), 271–310; Henry Jenkins, "The Cultural Context of Chinese Fan Culture: An Interview with Xiqing Zheng (Part One)" (blog), February 1, 2013, accessed May 9, 2015, http://henryjenkins.org/2013/02/the-cultural-context-of-chinese-fan-culture-an-interview-with-xiqing-zheng-part-one.html#sthash.li4BaGOo.dpuf; Toshio Miyake, "Doing Occidentalism in Contemporary Japan: Nation Anthropomorphism and Sexualized Parody in *Axis Powers Hetalia*," *Transformative Works and Cultures* 12 (2013), doi:10.3983/twc.2013.0436.
2. See, for example, Kazuko Suzuki, "Pornography or Therapy? Japanese Girls Creating the *Yaoi* Phenomenon," in *Millennium Girls: Today's Girls around the World*, ed. Sherrie A. Inness (Lanham, MD: Rowman & Littlefield, 1998), 243–67; Kazumi Nagaike, "Perverse Sexualities, Perverse Desires: Representations of Female Fantasies and *Yaoi* Manga as Pornography Directed at Women," *U.S.-Japan Women's Journal* 25 (2003): 76–103; Akiko Mizoguchi, "Male-Male Romance by and for Women in Japan: A History and the Subgenres of *Yaoi* Fictions," *U.S.-Japan Women's Journal* 25 (2003): 49–75; Dru Pagliassotti, "Better Than Romance? Japanese BL Manga and the Subgenre of Male/Male Romantic Fiction," in *Boys' Love Manga: Essays on the Sexual Ambiguity and Cross-Cultural Fandom of the Genre*, ed. Antonia Levi, Mark McHarry, and Dru Pagliassotti (Jefferson, NC: McFarland, 2010), 59–83.
3. In the Chinese context, the term *tongrennü* is often used interchangeably with the word *funü*. But the former is more closely related to the creation of fanzines/*dōjinshi* (*tongrenzhi*) and the consumption of Japanese ACG products.
4. The song is titled "Tongrennü de xinling zhi ge: Nanshou wo ye renzhe" [The soul song of fan girls: I'll bear with it even though it's trying]. It is composed by Luo Baiji and written and sung by Limao R. The complete lyrics can be found at http://blog.sina.com.cn/s/blog_497094ac010008p1.html, accessed December 25, 2014.
5. Benedict Anderson, *Imagined Communities: Reflections on the Origin and Spread of Nationalism* (London: Verso, 1983), 15.
6. See, for example, Antonia Levi, Mark McHarry, and Dru Pagliassotti, eds., *Boys' Love Manga: Essays on the Sexual Ambiguity and Cross-Cultural Fandom* (Jefferson, NC: McFarland, 2010); Mark McLelland et al., eds., *Boys Love Manga and Beyond: History, Culture, and Community in Japan* (Jackson: University Press of Mississippi, 2015).
7. Originally an amateur web comic, *Hetalia* was later published as *tankōbon*, that is, stand-alone books, and adapted into anime, games, and drama CDs.
8. Kuruma, "APH wanglu liyi tuiguang" [The promotion of APH netiquette], last modified June 9, 2009, accessed December 25, 2014, http://kuruma.holy.jp/aphm/APH_manner.htm.
9. Annett, "Animating Transcultural Communities," 291.
10. Miyake, "Doing Occidentalism."
11. *Himaruya* is written as "日丸屋," literally meaning "the house of Japanese national flag." This apparently fabricated last name seems to remind readers that the world of *Hetalia* is seen through the lens of a Japanese national. I am grateful to Earl Jackson for pointing out to me the fictional nature of this last name.

12. Himaruya, "このブログの写真は自由に使えます" [The pictures in this blog can be used freely], last modified May 11, 2008 (22:30), accessed December 25, 2014, http://himaruya.blog61.fc2.com/blog-category-5.html.
13. Participants of *"Hetalia* Only" events in Japan are also overwhelmingly female, see Miyake, "Doing Occidentalism."
14. Wukejiuyao Yanjing Kong, "Guojia niren la shizai shi tai meng le" [Country anthropomorphism, so *moe*], February 1, 2009, accessed December 25, 2014, http://www.tianya.cn/publicforum/content/funinfo/1/1368526.shtml.
15. Annett, "Animating Transcultural Communities," 298.
16. In *Hetalia*, China is given the human name of Wang Yao 王耀. The first Chinese character literally means "king," while the second character means "shining brightly."
17. In 2012, a military-political web comic titled "Nanian natu naxie shi" [That year, that rabbit, those events] gained wide popularity on the Internet with its endearing childlike drawing style, humorous cyberslang, and ultranationalist sentiments. It is probably the first political manga series in contemporary China. Interestingly, the author Niguang Feixing has admitted that his work is inspired by *Hetalia*.
18. uranusfang, November 12, 2009 (13:09:32), accessed December 27, 2014, http://bbs.tianya.cn/post-funinfo-1368526-12.shtml.
19. Mark W. MacWilliams, introduction to *Japanese Visual Culture: Explorations in the World of Manga and Anime*, ed. Mark W. MacWilliams (Armonk: M. E. Sharpe, 2008), 5.
20. This term refers to those *uke* characters that are very kind, tolerant, and have hardly any trace of masculinity.
21. Kazumi Nagaike, "Elegant Caucasians, Amorous Arabs, and Invisible Others: Signs and Images of Foreigners in Japanese BL Manga," *Intersections: Gender and Sexuality in Asia and the Pacific* 20 (2009), accessed December 25, 2014, http://intersections.anu.edu.au/issue20/nagaike.htm; Miyake, "Doing Occidentalism."
22. For more on Xianqing, see Yang and Xu's chapter in this volume.
23. The web links of those ten threads can be found at http://bbs.jjwxc.net/showmsg.php?board=3&id=331049, accessed December 27, 2014. All the links can still be opened, but most of the entries have been deleted.
24. Luobei Liya de Nixi, February 3, 2009 (15:33:21), accessed December 27, 2014, http://bbs.tianya.cn/post-funinfo-1368526-5.shtml.
25. aligaduo, February 3, 2009 (15:14:47), accessed December 27, 2014, http://bbs.tianya.cn/post-funinfo-1368526-5.shtml.
26. Gengjia Chihan Tuan, February 3, 2009 (13:33:47), accessed December 27, 2014, http://bbs.tianya.cn/post-funinfo-1368526-4.shtml.
27. merry-fish, February 3 2009 (15:03:22), accessed December 27, 2014, http://bbs.tianya.cn/post-funinfo-1368526-5.shtml.
28. Fengxi Shenlei et al. *Weilong* [Born to be dragon], 2009.
29. Jenkins, "Cultural Context."
30. Sun Jung, "The Shared Imagination of *Bishōnen*, Pan–East Asian Soft Masculinity: Reading DBSK, Youtube.com and Transcultural New Media Consumption," *Intersections: Gender and Sexuality in Asia and the Pacific* 20 (2009), accessed December 27, 2014, http://intersections.anu.edu.au/issue20/jung.htm; Sun Jung, *Korean Masculinity and Transcultural Consumption: Yonsama, Rain, Oldboy, K-Pop Idols* (Hong Kong: Hong Kong University Press, 2011), 165.

31. Some of the most well-known illustrations in *Dragon* still feature Yao in the clothing style of the Qing dynasty (1644–1911), which has caused displeasure among fans of Han Chinese Clothing (*hanfu*). Those fans had repeatedly left messages on Himaruya's blog, requesting that he draw the character of Yao in Han Chinese Clothing. In the fourth volume of *Hetalia* published in 2011, Himaruya added an image of Yao in *hanfu* and briefly explained its characteristics.

32. Taiwan is one of the few female characters in *Hetalia*. In the original series, she seems to prefer Japan to China, as one illustration drawn by Himaruya shows Taiwan angrily pointing her finger at China in defense of Japan. Japan/Taiwan is also the favorite pairing of Taiwanese *Hetalia* fans, to the dismay of some Chinese fans. Other Chinese fans, however, are "cool" about the Taiwan issue and jokingly describe China's unilateral obsession with reunification as a kind of "younger sister complex" (*meikong*). The strong emotional bond between an elder brother and a younger sister is a common theme in Japanese ACG works.

33. Kirk A. Denton, "Horror and Atrocity: Memory of Japanese Imperialism in Chinese Museums," in *Re-envisioning the Chinese Revolution: The Politics and Poetics of Collective Memories in Reform China*, ed. Ching Kwan Lee and Guobin Yang (Stanford: Stanford University Press, 2007), 250.

34. Kai-wing Chow, "Narrating Nation, Race, and National Culture: Imagining the Hanzu Identity in Modern China," in *Constructing Nationhood in Modern East Asia*, ed. Kai-wing Chow, Kevin M. Doak, and Poshek Fu (Ann Arbor: University of Michigan Press, 2001), 50.

35. Susan L. Shirk, *China: Fragile Superpower* (New York: Oxford University Press, 2008), 4.

36. Ge Zhaoguang, *Zhaizi zhongguo: chongjian youguan "zhongguo" de lishi lunshu* [Dwelling in the middle of the country: Reestablishing historical narratives of "China"] (Beijing: Zhonghua shuju, 2011), 28–29.

37. "Three views" (*sanguan*) is an acronym of three Chinese phrases: "view of world" (*shijie guan*), "view of life" (*rensheng guan*), and "view of values" (*jiazhi guan*). After the Falun Gong movement was banned in late 1990s, the Chinese government launched a campaign to indoctrinate correct Marxist views of life, world, and values in citizens. This phrase is often mentioned in *Hetalia* fandom to remind fans not to confuse historical facts with historical parody.

38. Jiang Xiaobai et al., "[Zhong] [heitaliya] [Yao zhongxin] weilong," [[Chinese] [*Hetalia*] [Yao-centered] Born to be dragon], March 31, 2010, accessed December 27, 2014, http://yellowy.blogbus.com/logs/61409690.html.

39. Z, October 16, 2010 (14:28:13), accessed December 27, 2014, http://yellowy.blogbus.com/logs/61409690.html.

40. Rita, "Free Talk," in *Pravda Remix*, 2009, 372. The cover of the fanzine bears both the English title *Pravda Remix* and the Chinese title 萬紅至理 • 回音, whereas *Dragon* only has the Chinese title 為龍.

41. *Neta* is Japanese jargon that originated in the Edo period, meaning "ingredient" or "information." It can be used to refer to the material for comedian performance on the stage, information for journalists, or the topping materials used in a sushi restaurant. The word has been widely used in Chinese ACG fandom to refer to interesting idea, plot, or laughing point that can be further worked on.

42. Rita, "The End of the Beginning," in *Pravda Remix*, 2009, 32–91. According to Rita, all the titles of her works mentioned in this chapter are borrowed from song titles of foreign bands. "The End of Beginning" is from an Irish band, God Is an Astronaut.

"Cast the Route" is from a Russian postrock band mooncake. "Blues on the Run" is from a Japanese rock band Aqua Timez. None of the bands are well known in China. Rita's familiarity with foreign subcultures reveals the exceptional cultural capital she has accumulated.

43. Ibid., 66.
44. Ibid., 75.
45. Ibid., 77.
46. Rita, "Cast the Route," in *Pravda Remix*, 2009, 5–21.
47. Leo Ching, "'Japanese Devils': The Conditions and Limits of Anti-Japanism in China," *Cultural Studies* 26.5 (2012): 712.
48. In 2011, India was added to the cast of *Hetalia*. There are also mentions of Tibet, Mongolia, and North Korea in the manga, but with no formal debut of the characters.
49. Rita, "Blues on the Run," in *Pravda Remix*, 2009, 160–72.
50. Unlike the state-led Shanghai Cooperation Organization, the Boao Forum for Asia is the foremost nonprofit nongovernment international organization housed in China to promote regional economic integration. Boao Forum for Asia, "Beijing jieshao" [Background introduction], accessed January 22, 2016, http://www.boaoforum.org/gylt/index.jhtml.
51. Rita, "Blues on the Run," 172.
52. Eight out of the eleven fanfics in *Remix* use English for their titles.
53. Koichi Iwabuchi, *Recentering Globalization: Popular Culture and Japanese Transnationalism* (Durham: Duke University Press, 2002), 17.

4

Queering the Post–*L Word* Shane in the "Garden of Eden"

Chinese Fans' Gossip about Katherine Moennig

Jing Jamie Zhao

Introduction

Overseas media and cultural products have been imported into mainland China through both legal and underground means since the beginning of the economic reformist era in the late 1970s. These foreign images and representations accordingly have been perpetuating "the popular imagination of a new lifestyle and its accompanying structure of feeling."[1] It has been well documented that transnational fan practices also help to circulate and promote unreleased or censored media commodities across the world,[2] sometimes even through "legally [or morally] questionable means."[3] Indeed, since the beginning of the twenty-first century, thanks to "the development of consumerism and electronic communication technology"[4] during the age of cultural globalization, the Chinese-speaking audience has obtained easy access to Western media, particularly American TV shows, which are translated and redistributed via peer-to-peer (P2P) networks by Chinese fan translation groups.[5] For the audience physically located in mainland China, fan-translated and fan-distributed Western media have helped to break the constraints of mainstream Chinese media and public culture that have been discursively or directly serving as the "mouthpiece"[6] of the dominant Chinese political ideology "within a developing hedonist consumer economy."[7]

The subsequent emergence of an astoundingly large-scale, cross-cultural queer fandom of the American lesbian TV show *The L Word* (Showtime, 2004–2009; *TLW* hereafter) in Chinese cyberspace should not be a total surprise. The Garden of Eden Subtitling Group (Yidianyuan Zimuzu; GE hereafter) is one of the most sizable and renowned Chinese fan translation groups and has its own distribution website and fan discussion forums.[8] Requiring a simple e-mail registration to download fan-translated videos and fan-made subtitles, post topics, and respond to threads, the GE site offers its visitors a friendly, basically open-access space to view fan discussions. Specializing in translating queer-themed Western media, GE was one of the first grassroots translation groups distributing *TLW* online with Chinese subtitles. Its subforum for fans' discussions devoted to *TLW*, originally built in early 2005 when the pirated DVDs and the digital copies of the first season of *TLW* were widely circulated in mainland China, is still active after the tenth anniversary of the premiere of *TLW*. On the site, this subforum remains one of the most popular discussion boards among those dedicated to other popular American shows, such as *Prison Break* (Fox, 2005–2009) and *The Big Bang Theory* (CBS, 2007–).[9] At first, the fan forum was created only for distributing subtitles of *TLW* and circulating its trailers and stage photos. Subsequently, along with the mounting popularity of both *TLW* and other lesbian-themed Western media among GE fans, the topics posted by the fans in the forum have broadened substantially. Gradually, the forum has been transformed into a site that not only features queer fannish practices dedicated to both the fictional characters and real-world celebrities of *TLW* but also serves as one of the most extensive Chinese queer fandoms of both female celebrities and female media characters. In early 2006, the forum was divided into three interrelated discussion boards: *South of Nowhere*, L-Themed Movies, and the *TLW* download zone.[10] As of November 2014, it had more than 6,800 threads listed and had obtained approximately 923,000 entries in total. The majority of its thread topics allow fans to voice their queer fantasies. Due to the initial Western focus of this fandom, the objects being queerly imagined by the fans in the forum are still primarily Western females.

Some media scholars have already considered the democratic potential and desiring voices of fannish subtitling and consumption of Western TV in China.[11] Meanwhile, a diversity of Chinese queer fan cultures, such as the Chinese queer fandom of Hollywood superheroes,[12] Chinese-based fandoms of Japanese Boys' Love (BL hereafter),[13] Chinese fan communities devoted to queering female celebrities in mainland China,[14] and Chinese fan sites for Hong Kong lesbian celebrities,[15] have been examined through the lenses of gender and sexuality. To enrich this existing discourse, this chapter explores online Chinese fans' queer fantasies about Western female celebrities, which are constantly conditioned by and actively speak to both local Chinese queer specificities and today's global queer trends.

A corpus of literature has already looked at the unique ways fans interpret and recreate texts in cross-cultural queer fandoms.[16] In particular, in her study of an American online fandom of the Canadian TV show *Due South*, Rhiannon Bury considers how American female fans "produc[e] a quaint, white, gay-positive Canada" by discussing intertextual information about the show.[17] Also, Fran Martin's research probes how an imagined "homoerotic 'Japan'" helps popularize Japanese BL in Taiwan and, meanwhile, creates "a reflexive zone of articulation" for Taiwanese fans to contest "local regimes of gender and sexual regulation."[18] Dwelling on Gill Valentine's concept of "imagined geography," which refers to "how we imagine space and its boundaries, how we imagine whose space it is, and how we construct 'self' and 'other,'"[19] she goes one step further to unveil a "double foreign-ness"[20] created in Taiwanese BL fandom.

As she speculates, on the one hand, the BL narratives have been imaginatively contextualized by some Taiwanese consumers within "the actual geographic spaces" of an unrealistically homoeroticized and exoticized Japan; and, on the other hand, the fantasy-focused fictional world of the BL stories narrated within this geoculturally foreign, queered Japan produce a safe, imaginative arena for Taiwanese fans' affect and negotiations.[21] This chapter follows Bury's and Martin's findings to explore a similarly paradoxical picture in online Chinese fans' "lesbian-positive" Western imaginaries. My analysis shows that, during the fans' encounter with global queer media, politics, and realities, this "double foreign-ness" feature simultaneously enables their self-reflection about local Chinese nonfictional gender and sexual issues and divulges their acculturation within offline Chinese repressive regimes of gender and sexuality.

To achieve this goal, this chapter presents a critical discourse analysis of GE fans' queer gossip surrounding the American actress Katherine Moennig, who played Shane McCutcheon, a handsome lesbian womanizer on *TLW*. The fan gossip practices involved in this research are drawn from one thread in the above-mentioned *TLW* forum dedicated to queering the real-world Moennig.[22] The "post" in the title of this chapter refers to the fans' queer reading of Moennig after the end of her legendary lesbian performance in the original five-year run of *TLW*. This type of queer reading practice is also known as real-person slash and focuses on creating queer fantasies surrounding celebrities' nonfictional lives. Originally started on April 7, 2009, the fans' queer gossip in the thread was extremely active from April 2009 to early 2011. Because Moennig has not been very active as an actress and sustained a low level of exposure after her role in *TLW*, the fan discussion in the thread eventually died down in early 2013. As of November 2014, the thread had more than 352,700 hits and over 9,200 entries. This long-term, once-intense queer gossip process illustrates well how some Chinese people, empowered by digital media, enthusiastically gather transgressive gender- and sexuality-related information from sources around the globe and voice their global homoerotic fantasies in a cyberqueer space.

Questioning the "anti-realism" of real-person slash culture and queer fandom and stardom,[23] the "cultural odorlessness,"[24] the "non-nationality"[25] of media products in transnational consumption, and the escapism in audience fantasies[26] identified in other writings on both Western and Asian fan cultures, my examination exposes how the Chinese fans' queer gossip devoted to Moennig menaces, mutates, and simultaneously is susceptible to the normative ideals, hegemonic ideologies, queer lived experiences, and real-world politics in both local and global contexts. More importantly, this research unveils the paradoxical aspects of Chinese cross-cultural queer fantasies in which fans struggle with and reformulate the seemingly fluid performances of Western female gender, sexuality, and homoerotic relationships through a transnational lens. In so doing, I demonstrate that fans' tactical and sometimes self-contradictory, Occidentalist homoeroticization of the West is significantly dissimilar to audience practices of "worlding,"[27] "domesticating cosmopolitanism,"[28] "pop cosmopolitanism,"[29] and "gross generalizations of the culture of the other"[30] during Asian transnational cultural consumption. Rather, recalibrating the significance of Chinese queer agency and subjectivity in this gossip practice, I suggest viewing it as an emblem of a cultural hybridity of the Chinese queers' performative deployment of normative ideals about the West and lesbianism to articulate repressed desiring voices, their self-reflexive interpretations of a global queer world, and their own reverberations with the local heteropatriarchal memory and contemporaneity.

Chinese Queering of the Post–*L Word* Shane Online

The finale of the sensational lesbian TV show *TLW* was aired in March of 2009. The fans' queer gossip under the post-*TLW* thread primarily focuses on Moennig's real-life gender, sexuality, and subsequent personal relationships. Although Moennig's character in *TLW*, Shane McCutcheon, is an unbelievably cool and extremely attractive, dreamy butch who consistently acts like a heartless sexual predator, Moennig herself has been very reluctant to directly disclose her own emotional life in public. In fact, she has never given a straightforward answer to any questions about her sexual preference. Yet, analogous to the cases of the previously closeted, American gay celebrities Jodie Foster and Anderson Cooper, Moennig's refusal to reveal her own sexual orientation enacts a postgay, American "glass closet"[31] discourse in which her nonheterosexuality has already become an open secret to the public because there is more than adequate information to imply it. Meanwhile, her demand for privacy as a public figure can be retained in this discourse without intentionally hiding any related information from those she would like to inform.

Indeed, widely known for her dandy butch role in *TLW*, Moennig has been frequently cast in gender-deviant or gender-ambiguous roles with lesbian (mostly butch) connotations in multiple TV shows, movies, and even music videos and commercials throughout her acting career to date. She has also been actively involved in a variety of high-profile LGBTQ causes and events. In 2013, she was employed as a brand model in the tomboy-style launch collection by Wildfang ("tomboy" in German), a US-based fashion and lifestyle company specifically for masculine-lesbian-looking apparel.[32] Moreover, in her personal life, she dates lesbians and often comfortably hangs out with her girlfriends in public places. It has been rumored that, as of October 2014, after ending a long-term, intimate relationship with the openly out, American female singer Holly Miranda, Moennig started a romantic relationship with the American actress Evan Rachel Wood.[33] Since then it seems that neither Wood nor Moennig has tried to hide their relationship from the public. They have been often spotted flirting with each other on public social networking sites and hugging each other in public in West Hollywood. When questioned by the media, the two have not attempted to deny their intimacy.

The ambiguity associated with Moennig's sexuality, together with the high-level attention about her personal life, intrigues and further encourages GE fans' queer curiosity about her. While some fans expressed their ardent anticipation of Moennig's public coming-out,[34] one fan openly admitted in her post that "it is better [for the fans if Moennig does] not make [her lesbian relationships] public. At least, it leaves us the space for homoerotic imaginations."[35] Most of the fan gossip under this thread aimed to homoerotically explore Moennig's real-world sexual orientation and gender performances. To confirm their speculation, many fans also followed Moennig and her close female friends on Twitter, lurked on diverse fan forums created by Moennig's Western fans, and translated her English news into Chinese and circulated it on the thread. Some fans who actively participated in gossip about Moennig revealed that they resided in foreign countries such as Australia, the United States, or Germany. Some posts and threads have also shown that many fans from Hong Kong or Taiwan have been lurking on the site for years, but most of these have not been very active in online posting or fan discussion.[36] During queer gossip, a few fans admitted that they often met and exchanged information with many non-Chinese fans of Moennig from the United States, Britain, Canada, Mexico, Brazil, and Malaysia on Twitter.[37] Accordingly, the information obtained and disseminated by fans under the thread was gathered from the online cross-cultural and transnational communication of a global fan community of Moennig.

GE allows its registered fans to create various types of surveys. Only registered users have access to the surveys and participate in voting. One registered user can vote only once. After voting, the fans are able to see the survey results. Of course, it is possible that some fans might create multiple online pseudonyms to vote more than once for the same survey. Nevertheless, the general demographics for the fan participants in this fandom can still be observed from the survey results. Take, for example, a survey conducted in 2006 on the sexual orientations of the fans in this queer fandom. It obtained 2,575 votes in total. The results show that 45.04 per cent of the participants are self-identified lesbian fans, 30.32 per cent are self-identified bisexual female fans, 2.32 per cent are self-identified gay male fans, 1.51 per cent are self-identified bisexual male fans, 15.14 per cent are self-identified straight female fans, and 5.68 per cent are self-identified straight male fans.[38] Another survey conducted in 2008 on *TLW* fans' educational background shows that 55.31 per cent of the total 2,052 participants are females with a college degree, 23 per cent are females with master's or doctoral degrees, and 5.26 per cent are males with a college degree or higher.[39] In addition, one survey on the fans' age distribution proves that 82.9 per cent of 1,480 fans who voted are between nineteen and thirty and above 50 per cent are between nineteen and twenty-five.[40]

A few studies have claimed that the fans involved in online queer activities are predominately young females with a "high salary, high level of education, and high social status"[41] and that slash writing and queer gossip are women's practices.[42] Some researchers also contend that male/male queer fandoms are primarily comprised of straight women who discursively express their unfulfilled, real-life heterosexual desires through their queer activities.[43] Although the outcomes of GE surveys support the point that the majority of the fans constituting queer fandom are young, highly educated females, the statistics also indicate the existence of both some males and a large number of nonheterosexual females as avid queer fans in this fandom. These data, surely, can be a starting point for further research exploring why and from what angles or perspectives fans of diverse gender and sexual identities actively participate in online queer fandoms of gender-ambiguous, potentially lesbian female media characters and celebrities. Although this research direction is beyond the focus of this chapter, the demographic formation of this queer fandom reflected in the results that is relevant to the concept of "the female homoerotic imaginary"[44] remains worth further contemplation here.

Martin deploys this phrase in her analysis of Chinese media representations of a nostalgic lesbianism, supporting Eve Kosofsky Sedgwick's theory of a universalizing view of same-sex desires "in which all gender identities fall under scrutiny rather than simply the unorthodox ones."[45] Referring to media representations of a youthful lesbian past as being "female homoerotic" rather than "lesbian," she astutely notes that the same-sex desire depicted in today's Chinese popular culture might "universally" appeal to or reside in both heterosexual and nonheterosexual females.[46] This "universal" desire and the subsequent mourning for the "vanishing" masculine tomboy whose existence is briefly tolerated in female adolescence and almost impossible within the dominant heterocentric prescriptions of Chinese female adulthood signify not a stable process of rigid lesbian identity formation but instead a commonly shared female homoerotic imaginary. Nevertheless, this discussion of the Chinese viewership dedicated to female homoerotic narratives primarily confines itself to consideration of the female audience. The aforementioned surveys revealing the sex distribution of GE fandom suggest that this "universal" female homoerotic attraction can occur within queer fan communities with a much more complicated gender and sexual composition, which ultimately implies the potential existence of interlocking cross-gender and cross-sex identifications, viewing positions, and desires within this queer imaginative space. This phenomenon might be partially invited by *TLW*'s portrayal of a wide range of nonnormative gender and sexual issues and images that deconstructs the traditional conflation of gender, sex, sexuality, and desire, including transvestitism, transsexuality, bisexuality, male gayness, queer heterosexuality, lesbian-identified males, heterosexual drag queens, lesbian drag kings, gender benders, and genderqueers. More intriguingly, GE fans' possible cross-gender and cross-sex queer interests are often conditioned by the culturally specific definitions of masculinity and femininity in this cross-cultural environment. This condition will be explored in depth later in this chapter.

Moreover, although the queer gossip in the fandom mostly focuses on celebrities rather than on fans' own real-life issues, many surveys involve topics about fans' gender identities, sexual orientations, sexual fantasies, and sexual desires, which also afford a platform for communicating about real-world topics within this fan community. For instance, two surveys ask fans to vote for the female *TLW* characters they would most like to seduce and the ones they would most like to be seduced by / have sex with.[47] Another survey asks fans to choose their favorite lesbian couple in *TLW* to have a threesome with.[48] Some surveys do not concentrate on queer imaginations but, instead, touch upon nonfictional, real-world, personal questions, such as asking about the gender(s) of the person(s) whom fans have made love with, fans' sexual orientations and preferred breast size, attitudes toward transsexual people, and opinions of love and sex as two separate experiences.[49] Following these surveys, there are always heated discussions among the fans. The intense fan discussions surrounding the real-world gender- and sexuality-related questions raised in the surveys directly challenge the scholarly understanding of fannish queer reading or cyberqueer communication as merely quixotic, escapist practices. The fans' queer gossip focusing on Moennig discussed in the next section offers an extended example of the reality-relevant nature of this fandom.

Fantasies and Realities in Online, Cross-Cultural, Queer Gossip

Some queer fandoms tend to keep their queer fantasies, queer gossip in particular, about the nonfictional, nonheterosexual potential of celebrities low profile.[50] In a few extreme cases, some fans even attempt to silence or self-silence their real-person queer gossip because these sexuality-related conversations about real-world celebrities in public spaces are often considered to be taboo and to infringe on other people's privacy.[51] Fans' self-silencing, therefore, can be understood as either a fannish way of protecting their idols or as evidence of some fans' negative attitudes or even discrimination against nonheterosexuality in the offline, real world.[52]

Nonetheless, the queer gossip discourse surrounding Moennig shows a quite different picture. Transgression of the boundaries between fantasy and reality repeatedly occurs in the fans' queer gossip. Sometimes, this transgression is even central to their queer reading of Moennig. Most of the fans actively participating in the gossip try to confirm or even spotlight her underlying lesbian identity in reality. As one fan once said while gossiping, "I believe she is gay from beginning to end, as no straight girl would be able to play the role of Shane [as successfully] as she did."[53] Some newcomers to the forum asked more experienced queer fans whether Moennig is a lesbian offstage.[54] One fan replied in this way: "If she [Moennig] is not [a lesbian], then nobody can be [a lesbian]."[55] Another fan also concurred that "she [Moennig] is already so masculine in this way, wouldn't it be a great waste if she is straight."[56] In early 2010, to prove Moennig's real-life lesbian identity, some fans used Google Earth to search for Moennig's home address in Los Angeles and obtained pictures of the street view of her house.[57] Later, one of the fans posted these pictures under the thread and matched them with some personal art photos taken by an American female fashion designer, Laura Freedman. In her post, she noted that these art photos are actually taken at Moennig's home in Los Angeles.[58] This finding was used by the fan to convince others of Moennig's offstage lesbian identity by unveiling the ambiguous yet intimate relationship between Moennig and Freedman. In July 2010, this fan found that Moennig unfollowed Freedman on Twitter.[59] Through tracking the conversations between Moennig and Holly Miranda on Twitter and circulating the pictures of the two in the thread, this fan dug out this new underground intimate relationship between the two.[60]

These creative queer practices and bold queer imaginations showcase the fans' intense desire to homoeroticize the real-world Moennig. Interestingly, this type of reality-focused, queer fantasy is not limited to fans' gossip about Moennig in this fandom. Rather, it is quite common in fans' queering of Western female celebrities more broadly. Take, for example, the fans' queer reading of some Western supermodels as revealed on the site. Some fans claimed that the Danish, potentially lesbian, female model Freja Beha Erichsen, who is also a very popular subject for fans' queer reading in GE fandom, would not break up with her rumored-to-be American girlfriend in the near future because Western countries, particularly Denmark, are very open about homosexuality. Further, according to these claims, if they do eventually break up, it would be because they personally believe that they are not suitable for each other.[61] Similarly, when queerly imagining Australian models, a few fans used their own queer lived experiences in Australia to argue that almost all people in Australia are lesbians (*quanmin les*) and these gorgeous female models can sleep with every female in an entire neighborhood.[62]

Seemingly, this general tendency of GE fandom to queerly valorize certain developed, democratic Western countries as pressure-free, homo-friendly places and Western females as sexually permissive, attractive lesbians explains why these fans do not feel uncomfortable with or do not stymie queer imaginations about real-world Western celebrities. These online homoerotic imaginaries about Western females narrated in a utopian Western queer world actually amplify the multidimensional "differences" of the objects of desire in this fandom—being foreign/non-Chinese/othered/fantastic/virtual. In turn, the "differences" from themselves help the fans loosen the bonds of offline, local, Chinese, real-world strictures against cultural, gender, sexual, and moral outcasts. Yet, a more meticulous look at Chinese cultural, social, historical, and political particularities that have been shaping this fantasy of a Western queer paradise in Chinese cyberqueer spaces might better divulge how the multifaceted "foreignness" of the intertwining of the West and queerness is tactically utilized in the fans' "disidentificatory performances"[63] in this fandom.

Certainly, the queer fantasies situated in both culturally distinct and geographically distant contexts mark a homonormative, Occidentalist queer culture among the Chinese fans. The queered West and homonormalized Western females in the fans' female homoerotic imaginaries serve as perfect narrative locales and fictive prototypes for the relocation and reification of queer voices and desires that are hardly viable in offline, real-world, mainstream Chinese society. Similar postcolonial queer fetishization of the Western gay world, as identified in many global gay studies, is believed to have been shaped by "the hegemonic Euroamerican notion of modernity"[64] and "the colonial discourse of . . . western 'civilization'"[65] that equate gayness "with whiteness"[66] or create "an idealized, romanticized view of America" for queer life abroad.[67] However, as some globalization and queer theorists have critiqued, this trend of global queer utopianism should not and cannot be simplified to the controversial view proposed by Dennis Altman that "globalization has led to an accelerated Americanization [or Westernization] and homogenization of (gay) culture."[68]

Instead, the imagined differences and even established antagonism between the West and Chineseness, although closely linked to rigid, hegemonic dichotomies of gender and sexuality, do not simply repeat "the modalities of difference . . . not only around the colonized/colonizer divide, but also a gay/straight one."[69] As Peter A. Jackson opines, "[Re]search on Asia's queer cultures reveals the local meanings of global tendencies."[70] Underlining the subjective self-positioning of postcolonial Asian queers, a body of academic work has also challenged the universalizing and overemphasizing of the influences of Western (especially American) knowledge and cultures on modern Asian queerness.[71] It instead accentuates the distinctiveness of the sex and gender cultures in diverse Asian locations that are neither similar to their Western counterparts nor to their own normative local traditions.

Also, contradictions and complexities in local audiences' global imaginations have been observed.[72] In particular, while admitting that diverse meanings can be created in different cultural contexts, John Fiske insists that local cultural characteristics can restrain the global imaginations of information consumers in certain areas.[73] Resonating with this view, a few existing studies on contemporary Chinese queerness claim that the enforcement of the opening-up policy since 1979 on the Mainland; the erasing of queer-related local history, traditions, records, and media images in modern Chinese culture; the influx of foreign information along with the blooming of media piracy and the Occidentalist political positioning of the West all together helped form the Occidentalist conceptual linkage of nonnormative genders and sexualities with the West among Chinese people.[74]

This stereotypical Chinese imagining and othering of the West as "queered" is believed to have caused various problems in the development of contemporary

Chinese queer cultures and politics. Some research shows that the formation of a new, desirable Chinese gayness has been married to a process of embodying cosmopolitanism, Westernization, and modernization, which in turn has produced a series of queer identity norms in the post-Mao era.[75] This phenomenon has further created cultural and social hierarchies within queer communities and cultural environments "along the matrices of age, attitude, location, gender, education, and class."[76] For instance, local Chinese queer media, such as Hong Kong gay films, often internalize and further "'mirror' the identities and issues of an imaginary globalized white culture . . . [and] prioritize Euro-American venues over local or regional ones in terms of distribution, rendering the formation and growth of local and regional queer cultures even more difficult."[77] However, this approach toward grasping this intrinsically problematic globalizing/Westernizing of queer possibilities in Chinese public and private cultures underestimates the Chinese audience's subjectivity and agency in the entire process. It considers the Chinese audience for queer media to be passive and subject to widespread, unrealistic representations of a queer-utopian, civilized West versus a heteronormative, backward China. In contrast, how these global queer images inspire and embolden the Chinese audience to actively interrogate and remodify the current unsatisfactory queer realities should also be given sufficient consideration.

Furthermore, the issues surrounding global queering in Asia are complicated by Occidentalist discourses in modern China. Occidentalism is believed to serve as "a postcolonialist strategy of discourse"[78] that "allo[ws] the Orient to participate actively and with indigenous creativity in the process of self-appropriation."[79] Emphasizing the postcolonial power and agency rooted in the renegade potential of Occidentalism, some postcolonial and East Asian scholars have already highlighted the unique intricacies and transformations of Chinese Occidentalist discourses. For instance, a detailed deconstructive reading of the national and political renovating of Chinese Occidentalism accomplished by Xiaomei Chen has successfully delineated the convoluted postcolonial power struggles within it. As Chen notes, two types of Occidentalism—official Occidentalism and antiofficial Occidentalism—have been formed in this process.[80] While Chinese official Occidentalism is a dominant discourse in which "the Western Other is construed by a Chinese imagination, not for the purpose of dominating it, but in order to discipline, and ultimately to dominate, the Chinese self at home";[81] antiofficial Occidentalism is a counterdiscourse of the "dissenting intellectuals"[82] of the 1980s. As Chen elaborates:

> The creation of an anti-official Occidentalism . . . was preconditioned by the parameters of Maoist political discourse, which categorized anything opposed to its political dominance as "Western" or "Westernized." . . . [T]he adoption of an Occidentalist discourse was a strategic move by dissenting intellectuals. Accused of being "Western" both by virtue of their cultural status and their political sympathies, they had little choice but to assert that

the Western Other was in fact superior to the Chinese Self. By thus accepting the inevitable official critique raised against them, whether or not it was "factually" always the case, they strengthened their anti-official status.[83]

In this sense, for certain Chinese cultural, social, and political "rebels," the seemingly "uncritical" deployment of the stereotypical, binary construction of the Western superior and the Chinese inferior transform them into "the disidentifying subject."[84] As Jose Esteban Muñoz explains, a disidentifying subject "neither opts to assimilate . . . [dominant] ideology nor strictly opposes it; rather . . . [the disidentifying subject] tactically and simultaneously works on, with, and against"[85] the top-down ideological indoctrination and repression. In this vein, the stereotyped context of a queered West employed by GE fans who are either cultural or gender/sexual nonconformists initiates a similar "antiofficial" Occidentalist, imaginative milieu within which they can surreptitiously voice "non-Chinese/Westernized" queer expressions that are annulled in the offline, mainstream Chinese realities.

I have no interest in suggesting that this fan discourse is fully politically focused or that the fans necessarily have a high degree of political awareness. Yet it should be stressed that the fans' discussion of the Western queer world as regards topics on gay politics, rather than being purely homoidealistic, is also partially self-reflexive. Sometimes, the focus of fan discussion shifts between online, fictional queer fantasies and relatively more serious discussions about queer-related political issues in offline realities. For instance, several fans (in 2009) talked about whether the legalization of gay marriage in California would actually make the United States a more homosexual-friendly country.[86] One fan replied that, according to her American friend, the flood of queer images in American mainstream media could be a Hollywood gimmick. According to this friend, many American people are still very homophobic in real life.[87] Other fans also noted that there still exist varying forms and degrees of homophobia, sexism, and racism on various occasions or in less cosmopolitan cities in Australia and Euro-America.[88] Some fans posted news about ethnically Chinese, androgynous female celebrities or self-identified lesbians who increase the exposure of nontraditional female images in mainstream media or mainland Chinese parents who publicly support gay children.[89] While a few fans expressed their hope that the entire world should be more open toward and inclusive of gender and sexual nonconformists, they also admitted that there was likely a painful and uncertain distance to travel before this expectation could be reached.[90]

Admittedly, these types of conversations among the fans occur rather randomly, thus making it hard to form any real public political debates. Also, the queer critical implications of virtual fannish practices do not guarantee a passionate, direct engagement with queer activism in offline reality. Yet, it has been argued that queer fandom can afford "queer performance spaces"[91] within which fans' cultural mediation with real-world, context-specific gender and sexual histories and politics should not be oversimplified. As Judith Butler defines:

> Performativity describes this relation of being implicated in that which one opposes, this turning of power against itself to produce alternative modalities of power, to establish a kind of political contestation that is not a "pure" opposition, a "transcendence" of contemporary relations of power, but a difficult labor of forging a future from resources inevitably impure.[92]

Viewed from this angle, the self-critical moments in the fans' queer performativity help further question the naive queer valorization of the West and meanwhile denaturalize the dominant ideological essentialization of lesbianism as an import from the West that is debarred in contemporary Chinese public cultures. In so doing, the fans' cross-cultural queer fantasies discursively reflect offline, global queer realities, negotiate dominant cultural and social constructions of gender and sexuality, and produce alternative queer spectacles and possibilities. This crucial yet ambivalent aspect of GE fandom can be further manifested by the fans' queer gossip surrounding Moennig's real-life performances of lesbian gender roles and sexuality.

Queering Moennig as the "Perfect" Butch

Gossip is found to be a "feminine discourse" that often results in "a feminization of material originally targeted at predominantly male audiences [in the patriarchal society]."[93] Some research, however, reveals a feminizing process in which female homoerotic narratives often encourage female audiences to identify with the traditionally feminine character.[94] Unlike these previous findings, this section reveals that the fans' gossip regarding the gender and sexuality of real-world celebrity Moennig serves more as "an active disidentificatory,"[95] subjective masculinizing discourse. In this process, the fans view Moennig's character Shane McCutcheon as a perfect example of androgynous butchness that is an impeccable combination of desirable masculinity and femininity.[96] This perfect butch model enables them to repicture and reevaluate real-world lesbian gender roles, sexualities, and subjectivities. In so doing, they are able to distinguish the normative yet desirable butchness created in their queer fantasies from the still existing, faint traces in contemporary everyday life of Maoist Chinese state feminism's version of female androgyny that once roughly erased (female) gender differences.[97] Meanwhile, this fan-fantasized version of perfect butchness also debunks the naturalized binarism of female femininity and male masculinity promoted in the post-Mao era.[98]

The lesbian representations in *TLW* have been widely criticized by both Western scholars and lesbian audiences for being unrealistically feminized, beautified for the mainstream male gaze.[99] Meanwhile, two actresses of *TLW*, Leisha Hailey and Moennig herself, also described the character Shane McCutcheon as an androgynous, rather than butch, lesbian during interviews.[100] Possibly due to her retention of a glass closet in public or because of her own personal preferences, Moennig in real life often exhibits a greater degree of gender variance and flexibility, rather than performing a stabilized masculine butch stereotype that "makes lesbian readable in the register of masculinity."[101]

As Judith Halberstam precisely notes, the normative butchness in mainstream Western culture "collaborates with the mainstream notion that lesbians cannot be feminine."[102] This butch normativity often serves as "the distilled and visible embodiment of lesbian desire."[103] A similar situation in Hong Kong lesbian culture in which masculine lesbians always draw local public attention to lesbianism has been detected.[104] Meanwhile, as Lucetta Yip Lo Kam has pinpointed, masculinity is "a set of gender attributes that are defined by a given culture in a specific period of time. . . . [It] can be actualized on all kinds of bodies, and each contributes to the overall understanding of the discourses of masculinity at work in a given culture."[105] The contextual specificity and social modeling of the definitions for normative and alternative masculinities have also been marked by researchers. Halberstam illustrated the discrepancy between recognizable American rural and urban female masculinities.[106] Compared to normative Western butchness, the diasporic Asian butch "situated in an Anglo-dominated lesbian scene is simply not . . . masculine enough."[107] Likewise, while androgyny in the Western context is defined as "some versions of gender mixing"[108] or "a combination of feminine and masculine traits,"[109] within the Chinese context, its standards become more complex and hard to calibrate.

A large body of research has recorded the unique and multifarious historical, political, and cultural processes in modern China that render lesbian gender performances relatively invisible. Especially in mainland China, "due to the influence of the Cultural Revolution, women [were] already under pressure to look androgynous. In addition, they live[d] in a social context where most people are ignorant of homosexuality, so they tend[ed] to relate to each other without specific gender role-playing."[110] In addition, there have been "a prevalent cultural dismissal of female sexuality" and a social tolerance (with homophobia in essence) and trivialization of female homosexuality in mainstream Chinese society,[111] all of which further muffled Chinese lesbian gendered expressions in general. Helen Leung astutely remarks on contemporary Chinese lesbian gender troubles and transregional complexities in this way: "While the butch or T or TB in Hong Kong and Taiwan most visibly marks lesbian presence because of their *difference* from the heterosexual gender of straight femininity, she would be relatively invisible in the PRC because she resembles the masculine gender of the revolutionary image of women."[112] Here, Leung refers to the female masculinity embodied in the "socialist androgyny"[113] that was promoted in the Maoist gender project, encouraging women to wear "plain-colored loose-fitting clothes," to act rebelliously and aggressively as "proletarian fighters," yet to remain "subservient to the male leaders"[114] in the workplace and stay as "sacrificing wives [and] selfless mothers in the family."[115] Consequently, it has been argued that the erasure of female gender and sexual differences in public spaces and cultures and the political naturalization of female androgyny and masculinity[116] in the Maoist era work together to force mainland Chinese women in the reform era (after 1979) to appeal for not only an awakening of feminine gender identity[117] but also "radical distinctions between femininity and masculinity."[118] Furthermore, Lisa Rofel reminds us of the generational and cohort subtleties and differences of women's gendered subject positioning that have been enabled and circumscribed by the constantly shifting objectives of state power in modern Chinese female gender narratives and politics.[119] In this vein, these past political manipulations and social engagements of female genders become the indispensable "constitutive inner limit" of the post-Mao subjects' gendered imaginaries.[120] In turn, the fans' crafting and distinguishing of contemporary lesbian gender-role imaginaries not only depend upon but also negate both previous generations' compliant performances of socialist androgyny characterized by a patriarchal hierarchy and "the post-Maoist version of natural"[121] hyperfemininity. This distinctive, paradoxical way to normalize lesbian masculinity can be seen as "a process of social distinction that . . . balances masculinity and femininity into a kind of ideal androgyny, in order to establish desirable and appropriate subjectivity."[122]

Besides, based upon the conceptualization of hybrid culture in a variety of postcolonial theories of gender, sexuality, and race,[123] hybridity itself is both "the effect of colonial power"[124] and the consequence of postcolonial and globalization processes. Accordingly, disrupted or ambiguous markers of gender, sexuality, and race can be described as "sit[es] of hybridization . . . at which competing discourses of embodiment and agency intersect [and] where global/local power relations play out."[125] Certain discourses of minoritarian subjects, thus, can enact a performative embodiment of cultural hybridity. As Muñoz says, queer hybridity, in particular, inspires "a moment of reflexivity . . . [that] is not a fixed positionality but a survival strategy that is essential for queers and postcolonial subjects who are subject to the violence that institutional structures reproduce."[126] Also, Lingchei Letty Chen expounds that "androgyny serves as a metaphor for hybridity."[127] Consequently, current androgynous televisual images of Chinese female celebrities exemplifying the "aesthetically transnational and culturally hybrid rather than purely Chinese" are said to dismantle "the cultural binaries of 'Chinese versus the foreign Other' [and] gender dichotomies . . . [, which indirectly] revea[l] constant border-crossing cultural flows and integrations in the East Asian region."[128] These entangled transnational and global discourses of information flow, cultural shaping, subject making, feminine gender, and queerness are epitomized and further convoluted within online cross-cultural queer fannish practices. The unique, hybrid characteristic of Chinese fans' homoerotic fantasies surrounding Western white female celebrities' lesbian gender and sexuality serves as both the fans' involuntary acts and painstaking survival tactics within the current mainstream, heteropatriarchal environment that possibly result from "forced assimilation, internalized self-rejection, political co-optation, social conformism, cultural mimicry, and creative transcendence."[129] It is eventually emblematic of a blending of unconscious acculturation within and subjective appropriation of global mainstream queer-related images and knowledge within Chinese cyberqueer communities.

Noticeably, unlike the aforementioned, prevailing Western view of *TLW* as a visually feminized lesbian extravaganza, most of the GE fans, due to cultural differences regarding standards of androgynous and feminine genders, see Moennig's gender and sexual performance in the show as "perfectly androgynous" (*jipin de cixiongtongti*). They persistently celebrate and highlight her performed lesbian masculinity as a superior in between existence of normative femaleness/femininity and maleness/masculinity, which is much more rebellious and visible than traditional, state-defined Chinese female androgyny. As one fan elaborated, "I think Shane is much more beautiful than many women and much more handsome than many men. No one else can be like this. There have been many other similar types of lesbians [after *TLW*]. But nobody can yet compare with her."[130]

The expressions and words used in the fans' queer gossip about Moennig sometimes are also gendered in a normative way. Some fans frequently referred to Moennig as "Master" or being "manly" (*ye/shaoye/yemen'er*). These Chinese words are usually used to refer to young, handsome, genteel, and macho males as defined by the normative, male-supremacist Chinese society. Similarly, expressions for describing charming young men or qualities for dividing "the desirable T role from the undesirable one,"[131] such as "handsome" (*shuai*) or "incredibly cool" (*taiku*), were also often used to praise Moennig's outward appearance.[132] Through employing these words to describe Moennig, the fans frame Moennig, like her character Shane, as a gender-defying female who can not only perform certain Chinese masculine characteristics but also sustain desirable, exquisite styles, inner qualities, and attractiveness during transgressive gender and sexual performances.

In this sense, it is the subtle balance of masculine and feminine elements in Moennig's butch androgyny that is most appealing to most fans. In contrast, while commenting on Moennig's art photos or on convention appearances in which she was wearing girly skirts and feminine jewelry, many fans expressed discomfort with her traditionally feminine dressing style.[133] For instance, one fan mentioned that Moennig had worn a ball gown attending the Annual GLAAD Media Awards[134] and *TLW*'s first-season premiere ceremony.[135] Another fan replied that Moennig looks great in feminine dresses because she is after all a woman.[136] Yet, some fans complained that this style is not Moennig herself but her passing identity in mainstream public spaces and implied that Moennig was forced to dress like that.[137] Many other fans said that, although Moennig is a pretty woman, girly dresses do not suit her butch persona but only make her look very "awkward" (*bieniu*) or "shocking" (*leiren*).[138] By analyzing Moennig's pose in her pictures, one fan claimed that Moennig must feel very uncomfortable wearing the dress.[139] Another fan suggested that Moennig should go back to her original Shane style, which represents her true, masculine, butch self.[140]

In addition to this negating of Moennig's feminine persona and appearance, many fans also compared Moennig with other butch lesbians from the West and Thailand. These fans sarcastically remarked that they are unable to appreciate other foreign lesbians who are hypermasculine, "pure," or transsexual butches (*chunT* or *bianxingT*) and can pass as males because these butches "look exactly the same as males."[141]

As seen from this apparently exclusionary and discriminatory gossip discourse, some fans rejected Moennig's real-life effeminate side, attempted to "butch her up," and labeled her real-world feminine persona at certain public locations as a disguise to pass as straight (or normal) in mainstream society. They resisted accepting and fantasizing about "male-imitating" or "copying-maleness" (*xiangnanren yiyang*) lesbians whose hypermasculinity possibly flattens the visual differences between lesbianism and heterosexuality and thus makes lesbianism unreadable again within a heterocentric society. This resistance can also be read as a subjective attempt to contest "the common belief, based on gender inversion, that lesbianism is based on wanting to be man."[142] The fans' rejection of normative, "passing-as-male" butchness distinguishes Moennig's female masculinity as an unrivaled embodiment of lesbian androgyny from the state-stipulated feminine and masculine ideals. In this process, Moennig, more precisely her performed androgyny in *TLW*, which visualizes lesbianism yet does not completely reproduce normative male masculinity or socialist androgyny, becomes an appropriate reference point for fans to negotiate with and work against the norms and ideals rooted in the intersection of female masculinity, female androgyny, and female homosexuality within both dominant Chinese and Western cultural settings.

More interestingly, when gossiping about Moennig's rumored girlfriends, the fan debate always focused on one central theme: whether her girlfriend was young, pretty, beautiful, or hot enough in a traditionally feminine sense for her.[143] Many fans showed great frustration when they discovered that some of her ex-girlfriends do not have normative femme/feminine looks.[144] Several fans even mocked her ex-girlfriends' outward appearance by saying that Moennig has a "rather unusual" (*xiangdang de buzou xunchanglu*) taste in terms of picking female partners.[145] In 2009, one fan posted that she observed foreign fans in some English-speaking fan sites of Moennig queerly coupling Moennig and Lindsay Lohan's ex-girlfriend Samantha Ronson, who has an outstanding, normative butch appearance.[146] Most of the fans who replied to this post questioned or even strongly rejected this imagined, masculine lesbian couple. Some refused to queer these two simply because the coupling of Moennig and Ronson would be tomboys' love (*TTL/TTlian*). The picturing of two butches in a lesbian relationship made some fans feel "totally weird" (*duoqiguai*);[147] for some, it was hard to imagine who should be sexually dominant because of their similar lesbian gender identities.[148] One fan instead supported the queer coupling of Moennig and Lohan, which seems to be more imaginable to the fans because of Lohan's normative femme/feminine look.[149]

To some extent, the ways in which fans queerly masculinized Moennig's outward look and personae and normatively gendered Moennig's lesbian relationships reveal a prevalent heteronormative thinking of lesbianism as the cultural imitation of heterosexual relationships with a rigid gender binarism of masculine butchness and feminine femmeness. Yet, the radical denying of butches' femininity and hypermasculinity and reinforcing of stereotypical butch-femme gender dynamics should not be seen as a complete, "slavish copying of heterosexual roles" as sometimes criticized by Western lesbian feminism.[150] Instead, as Richard Dyer finds, "thinking about images of gayness needs to go beyond simply dismissing stereotypes as wrong or distorted."[151] Halberstam scrupulously concurs that lesbian masculinity, stereotypes of lesbianism, and normative butch-femme gender roles do not "always and only work on behalf of a conservative representational agenda."[152]

Moreover, the unique context of China, which has muted the existence, visibility, and readability of adult, female gender and sexual deviance, possibly encourages fans' passionate searching for, embracing of, and holding on to a redefined adult, normative butchness and stereotyped butch-femme gender dynamics in a non-Chinese, homoerotic scenario. It is also this uniqueness of contemporary Chinese female gender and homoeroticism that inevitably complicates the ways in which fans' self-conflicting reworking of certain genders, identities, sexualities, and ideals surrounding Western lesbianism should be interpreted. Hence, contextualized within the larger Chinese cultural and historical context, this gossiping process can be understood as the quintessence of fans' desperate thirst for a charming adult butch role model and their subversive reiteration of heteropatriarchal ideals in butch-femme relationships in reality, although a non-Chinese, "Occidentalist" reality. It illustrates the fans' active contestation of the dominant cultural scripts in both nonfictional Chinese and Western worlds that define tomboyism, female masculinity, and lesbianism as a passing phase or a female premature stage.[153] Also, the fans' normative gendering of Moennig's lesbian relationships further reveals their eagerness for radical gender differences, even within imagined lesbianism, that have formerly been expunged and illegitimized by the state's gender politics.

For the fans, a perfect normative butch should be neither too feminine as a traditionally defined female nor too masculine as a heterosexual macho man. The butch-femme gendered lesbian relationship also cannot be visually reduced to be a pure emulation of the heteronormative sex/gender system yet should manifest an essential binary difference between lesbian femininity and masculinity. Defeminizing lesbians' butch identities, coupling butches with traditionally feminine women, and rejecting some butches' hypermasculinity, understood from this angle, can be construed as a fundamentally insubordinate means to unsettle mainstream Chinese society's minimization, erasure, ignorance, and denial of the realities of butch lesbians, adult lesbianism, and female homoeroticism in general. The referencing of normative Chinese gender and sexual ideals and traumas in the cross-cultural homoerotic imaginaries about Western females indirectly ridicules these heterocentric regulations and the dominant ideological China/West divide themselves as constructed fantasies that can be easily traversed and disavowed. This hybrid appropriation of Western lesbian celebrities by fans to voice Chinese-specific female homoerotic troubles, frustrations, and desires again represents a mixing of their delicate pessimistic dismay at current lesbian presence, recognizability, and viability within repressive Chinese realities with a utopian homofetishization of the West and a performative resistance of the hegemonic violence against gender, sexual, and cultural outcasts in contemporary China.

Conclusion

GE fans' queer gossip discourse surrounding Moennig captured in this chapter uncovers a hybrid queer cultural phenomenon that contravenes the cultural, social, political, and geographical boundaries guarding gender and sexuality. It embodies a queer cultural collision and a queer meaning contestation between the local, the cross-cultural, the transnational, and the global. On the one hand, this GE fandom, as a cyberqueer space, offers Chinese fans a relatively free and open-minded site on which to obtain access to, circulate, and discuss global queer knowledge, information, and issues and through which to voice their own gender- and sexuality-related desires. On the other hand, its fannish queer articulations operate as intricate meaning-making detours that appropriate and rescript the interconnected cultural, social, political, and historical courses in both local and global contexts in order to carve out an imaginative cultural space for queer survival. Their voices discursively intervene and are shaped by both mainstream and nonmainstream Chinese specificities within a global queer cultural environment. The self-reflexive and sometimes contradictory aspects of the fans' queer gossiping discourse validate minoritarian, survival strategies that "negotiate a phobic majoritarian public sphere."[154]

In line with the theoretical framework of queer hybridization, which "underscores the way in which *both* Western and non-Western cultures of gender and sexuality have been, and continue to be, mutually transformed through their encounters with transnationally mobile forms of sexual knowledge,"[155] I have explicated that some GE fans' global homoerotic imaginings are neither fixed reenactments of Chinese female gender and sexual histories and ideals nor complete reifications of unconstrained imaginations of the West. Instead, both the subjects' critical contestation of the dominant heteropatriarchal culture and the mixed shapings of mainstream local cultures and global information should be considered. Accordingly, this research departs from the existing theories that emphasize transnational homogenizing and geographically transcending characteristics of global queer cultures[156] and suggests studying Chinese cyberqueer cultures and spaces through the theoretical lenses of queer performativity, hybridity, and disidentification. I hope that the picture laid out here can ultimately call more scholarly attention to the self-conflicting tropes and strategic potential of today's transnational queer popular cultures.

Acknowledgments

I owe my deepest gratitude to my MA thesis advisor, Professor Elana Levine, at the University of Wisconsin–Milwaukee, from whom I have learned how to be a media scholar and have faith in my own work. Without her unflagging trust, extensive support, and great encouragement during the most frustrating time of my life, the completion of this research would not have been possible. I am also indebted to my awesome coeditors, Professor Maud Lavin and Dr. Ling Yang, for their immensely helpful feedback during the writing and revising processes of this chapter. Meanwhile, I would like to thank Professor Wai Ching Angela Wong and Professor Fran Martin for encouraging my research and kindly reading and commenting on earlier drafts of this chapter.

Notes

1. Hui Faye Xiao, "Androgynous Beauty, Virtual Sisterhood: Stardom, Fandom, and Chinese Talent Shows under Globalization," in *Super Girls, Gangstas, Freeters, and Xenomaniacs: Gender and Modernity in Global Youth Cultures*, ed. Susan Dewey and Karen J. Brison (Syracuse, NY: Syracuse University Press, 2012), 121.
2. See Henry Jenkins, *Convergence Culture: Where Old and New Media Collide* (New York: New York University Press, 2008); Henry Jenkins, Sam Ford, and Joshua Green, *Spreadable Media: Creating Value and Meaning in a Networked Culture* (New York: New York University Press, 2013).
3. Michael Z. Newman, "Free TV: File-Sharing and the Value of Television," *Television & New Media* 13.6 (2012): 469–71.
4. Koichi Iwabuchi, "Uses of Japanese Popular Culture: Trans/nationalism and Postcolonial Desire for 'Asia,'" *Emergences* 11.2 (2001): 206.
5. "Meiju meiying gaoshou dayin yinyuwang zimuzu hunzhan yijiu" [Guru of American media hiding online. The tangled fight between fansubbing groups], last modified November 8, 2009, accessed November 1, 2013, http://yule.sohu.com/20091108/n268043090.shtml.
6. Yuezhi Zhao, *Media, Market, and Democracy in China: Between the Party Line and the Bottom Line* (Urbana, Illinois: University of Illinois Press, 1998).
7. Magnus Wilson, "Didactic Escapism: New Viewing Practices among China's Digital Generation," in *Asian Popular Culture in Transition*, ed. Lorna Fitzsimmons and John A. Lent (New York: Routledge, 2013), 77.
8. The GE fan site, Yidianyuan Guowai Lianxuju Jiaoliuzhan [The Garden of Eden communication site for foreign series] is available at http://bbs.sfile2012.com/index.php.

9. The *TLW* forum is available at http://bbs.sfile2012.com/forumdisplay.php?fid=52. The earliest fan post in the forum can be traced back to the airing of the first episode of the second season in 2005.
10. *South of Nowhere* (*SON* hereafter) is an American teen lesbian TV drama produced by *The N* and broadcast from 2005 to 2008. This subboard is specifically dedicated to fans' discussion of this show. Yet, not only *TLW* and *SON* but also other various lesbian-relevant entertainment information from abroad have become a rich source of fans' queer activities on this forum.
11. See Wilson, "Didactic Escapism," 77–96; Weiyu Zhang and Chengting Mao, "Fan Activism Sustained and Challenged: Participatory Culture in Chinese Online Translation Communities," *Chinese Journal of Communication* 6.1 (2013): 45–61.
12. John Wei, "Queer Encounters between Iron Man and Chinese Boys' Love Fandom," *Transformative Works and Cultures* 17 (2014), accessed October 8, 2014, http://dx.doi.org/10.3983/twc.2014.0561.
13. See Yannan Li, "Japanese Boy-Love Manga and the Global Fandom: A Case Study of Chinese Female Readers" (MA thesis, Indiana University-Purdue University, 2009); Fran Martin, "Girls Who Love Boys' Love: Japanese Homoerotic Manga as Transnational Taiwan Culture," *Inter-Asia Cultural Studies* 13.3 (2009): 365–83; Yanrui Xu and Ling Yang, "Forbidden Love: Incest, Generational Conflict, and the Erotics of Power in Chinese BL Fiction," *Journal of Graphic Novels and Comics* 4.1 (2013): 30–43.
14. See Xin Huang, "From 'Hyper-feminine' to Androgyny: Changing Notions of Femininity in Contemporary China," in *Asian Popular Culture in Transition*, ed. Lorna Fitzsimmons and John A. Lent (New York: Routledge, 2013), 133–55; Xiao, "Androgynous Beauty," 104-24; Ling Yang and Hongwei Bao, "Queerly Intimate: Friends, Fans and Affective Communication in a *Super Girl* Fan Fiction Community," *Cultural Studies* 26.6 (2012): 842–71.
15. Eva Cheuk Yin Li, "The Absence of Fan Activism in the Queer Fandom of Ho Denise Wan See (HOCC) in Hong Kong," in "Transformative Works and Fan Activism," ed. Henry Jenkins and Sangita Shresthova, special issue *Transformative Works and Cultures* 10 (2012), doi: 10.3938/twc.2012.0325.
16. See Camille Bacon-Smith, *Enterprising Women: Television Fandom and the Creation of Popular Myth* (Philadelphia: University of Pennsylvania Press, 1992), 280; Lawrence Eng, "Anime and Manga Fandom as Networked Culture," in *Fandom Unbound: Otaku Culture in a Connected World*, ed. Mizuko Ito, Daisuke Okabe, and Izumi Tsuji (New Haven: Yale University Press, 2012), 158–78; Henry Jenkins, "Pop Cosmopolitanism: Mapping Cultural Flows in an Age of Media Convergence," in *Fans, Bloggers, and Gamers: Exploring Participatory Culture*, ed. Henry Jenkins (New York: New York University Press, 2006), 152–72.
17. Rhiannon Bury, *Cyberspaces of Their Own: Female Fandoms Online* (New York: Peter Lang, 2005), 165.
18. Martin, "Girls," 366.
19. Gill Valentine, "Imagined Geographies: Geographical Knowledges of Self and Other in Everyday Life," in *Human Geography Today*, ed. Doreen Massey, John Allen, and Philip Sarre (Cambridge: Polity Press, 1999), 48.
20. Martin, "Girls," 377.
21. Ibid., 376–77.

22. This fan thread is available at http://bbs.sfile2012.com/viewthread.php?tid=275646 &highlight=moennig. The fans' gossip in the forum is mostly in Chinese, with some sporadic English conversations, and it is translated into English by me in this research.
23. In celebrity and real-person slash studies, some scholars find that fans legitimize their queer practices by emphasizing that celebrities are not real people but fictional media constructions open to multiple readings. Yet other studies also show that queer practices are deemed highly controversial both within and beyond queer fandoms because fans' homoerotic fantasies often infringe on celebrities' privacy or stir up certain undesirable assumptions about both celebrities and fans themselves. Meanwhile, a growing body of research on queer fandom has uncovered fans' tendency to guard the boundaries between fannish homoerotic imaginaries and the real, heteronormative world within both queer and mainstream public spaces, and their refusal to be associated with nonnormative gender and sexual subjects or real-life queer topics and issues during nonfictional communication. For more detailed discussions on these points, see Karen Hellekson and Kristina Busse, eds., *Fan Fiction and Fan Communities in the Age of the Internet* (Jefferson, NC: McFarland, 2006); Anne Jamison, ed., *Fic: Why Fanfiction Is Taking Over the World* (Dallas, TX: BenBella Books, 2013); Phyllis M. Japp, Mark Meister, and Debra K. Japp, eds., *Communication Ethics, Media, and Popular Culture* (New York: Peter Lang, 2005); Li, "Japanese Boy-Love Manga"; Constance Penley, "Feminism, Psychoanalysis, and the Study of Popular Culture," in *Cultural Studies*, ed. Lawrence Grossberg, Cary Nelson, and Paula A. Treichler (New York: Routledge, 1992), 479-500; Bronwen Thomas and Julia Round, eds., *Real Lives, Celebrity Stories: Narratives of Ordinary and Extraordinary People across Media* (New York: Bloomsbury, 2014).
24. See Koichi Iwabuchi, *Recentering Globalization: Popular Culture and Japanese Transnationalism* (Durham, NC: Duke University Press, 2002).
25. See Sun Jung, "K-Pop beyond Asia: Performing Trans-nationality, Trans-sexuality, and Trans-textuality," in *Asian Popular Culture in Transition*, ed. Lorna Fitzsimmons and John A. Lent (New York: Routledge, 2013), 108–30.
26. See Bury, *Cyberspaces of Their Own*; Mark McLelland, "The Love Between 'Beautiful Boys' in Japanese Women's Comics," *Journal of Gender Studies* 9.1 (2000): 13–25; Wilson, "Didactic Escapism," 77–96.
27. Martin, "Girls," 377–79.
28. Lisa Rofel, *Desiring China: Experiments in Neoliberalism, Sexuality, and Public Culture* (Durham, NC: Duke University Press, 2007).
29. See Jenkins, "Pop Cosmopolitanism," 152–72.
30. See Kam Tan, "Global Hollywood, Narrative Transparency, and Chinese Media Poachers: Narrating Cross-Cultural Negotiations of *Friends* in South China," *Television & New Media* 12.3 (2011): 221.
31. For a more detailed definition of "glass closet," please see its first usage in 2008 by Michael Musto in *Out Magazine*'s article "The Glass Closet." It is available at http://www.out.com/entertainment/2008/09/22/glass-closet.
32. See http://www.afterellen.com/wildfang-employs-kate-moennig-megan-rapinoe-and-hannah-blilie-to-bring-you-tomboy-fashion/02/2013/.
33. See http://www.eonline.com/news/589719/evan-rachel-wood-dating-katherine-moennig-the-l-word-and-ray-donovan-star.
34. See huanyingfuchen, fan post, April 8, 2009, 11:13 a.m., http://bbs.sfile2012.com/viewthread.php?tid=275646&extra=&highlight=moennig&page=2; wenwen1213,

fan post, April 8, 2009, 1:12 p.m., http://bbs.sfile2012.com/viewthread.php?tid=275646&extra=&highlight=moennig&page=2.
35. wy124, fan post, September 25, 2010, 1:55 p.m., http://bbs.sfile2012.com/viewthread.php?tid=275646&extra=&highlight=moennig&page=358.
36. See http://bbs.sfile2012.com/viewthread.php?tid=334895&extra=page%3D1.
37. mandy0903, fan post, June 23, 2009, 1:38 p.m., http://bbs.sfile2012.com/viewthread.php?tid=275646&extra=&highlight=moennig&page=50.
38. See http://bbs.sfile2012.com/viewthread.php?tid=62152&extra=page%3D1%26amp%3Bfilter%3Dtype%26amp%3Btypeid%3D308.
39. See http://bbs.sfile2012.com/viewthread.php?tid=225141&extra=page%3D1%26amp%3Bfilter%3Dtype%26amp%3Btypeid%3D308.
40. See http://bbs.sfile2012.com/viewthread.php?tid=24296&extra=page%3D2%26amp%3Bfilter%3Dtype%26amp%3Btypeid%3D308.
41. See Jin Feng, "'Addicted to Beauty': Consuming and Producing Web-Based Chinese *Danmei* Fiction at Jinjiang," *Modern Chinese Literature and Culture* 21.2 (2009): 3; Yang and Bao, "Queerly Intimate," 843.
42. See Henry Jenkins, *Textual Poachers: Television Fans and Participatory Culture* (New York: Routledge, 1992).
43. See Bacon-Smith, *Enterprising Women*; Jenkins, *Textual Poachers*; Penley, "Feminism," 479–500.
44. Fran Martin, *Backward Glances: Contemporary Chinese Cultures and the Female Homoerotic Imaginary* (Durham, NC: Duke University Press, 2010).
45. Judith Halberstam, *Female Masculinity* (Durham, NC: Duke University Press, 1998), 162. See also Martin, *Backward Glances*, 29–30; and Eve Kosofsky Sedgwick, *Epistemology of the Closet* (Berkeley: University of California University, 1990).
46. Martin, *Backward Glances*, 16.
47. See http://bbs.sfile2012.com/viewthread.php?tid=104514&extra=page%3D1%26amp%3Bfilter%3Dtype%26amp%3Btypeid%3D308; and http://bbs.sfile2012.com/viewthread.php?tid=100148&extra=page%3D1%26amp%3Bfilter%3Dtype%26amp%3Btypeid%3D308.
48. See http://bbs.sfile2012.com/viewthread.php?tid=325183&extra=page%3D1%26amp%3Bfilter%3Dtype%26amp%3Btypeid%3D308.
49. See *http://bbs.sfile2012.com/viewthread.php?tid=364480&extra=page%3D1%26amp%3Bfilter%3Dtype%26amp%3Btypeid%3D308; http://bbs.sfile2012.com/viewthread.php?tid=290756&extra=page%3D1%26amp%3Bfilter%3Dtype%26amp%3Btypeid%3D308; http://bbs.sfile2012.com/viewthread.php?tid=125564&extra=page%3D1%26amp%3Bfilter%3Dtype%26amp%3Btypeid%3D308;* and http://bbs.sfile2012.com/viewthread.php?tid=201859&extra=page%3D2%26amp%3Bfilter%3Dtype%26amp%3Btypeid%3D308.
50. Busse, "My Life," 207–24; Li, "Absence of Fan Activism"; Xiao, "Androgynous Beauty," 102–24.
51. Ling Yang, "'Nongwan de' luomansi: chaonü tongrenwen, nüxing yuwang yu nüxing zhuyi" ["Bent" romance: Super girl slash literature, women's desires, and feminism], *Wenhua yanjiu* [Cultural Studies] 9 (2010), accessed April 8, 2012, http://wlwx.literature.org.cn/Article.aspx?ID=46197.
52. Xiao, "Androgynous Beauty," 102–24; Ling Yang, "Nongwan de."
53. wenwen1213, fan post, June 10, 2009, 11:03 a.m., http://bbs.sfile2012.com/viewthread.php?tid=275646&extra=&highlight=moennig&page=41.

54. lifeisjutst, fan post, April 23, 2011, 8:33 p.m., http://bbs.sfile2012.com/viewthread.php?tid=275646&extra=&highlight=moennig&page=366.
55. wenwen1213, fan post, April 23, 2011, 10:56 p.m., http://bbs.sfile2012.com/viewthread.php?tid=275646&extra=&highlight=moennig&page=366.
56. heehyde, fan post, April 24, 2011, 11:03 a.m., http://bbs.sfile2012.com/viewthread.php?tid=275646&extra=&highlight=moennig&page=366.
57. mandy0903, fan post, January 25, 2010, 6:27 p.m., http://bbs.sfile2012.com/viewthread.php?tid=275646&extra=&highlight=moennig&page=326.
58. wenwen1213, fan post, January 25, 2010, 11:14 a.m., http://bbs.sfile2012.com/viewthread.php?tid=275646&extra=&highlight=moennig&page=326.
59. wenwen1213, fan post, July 13, 2010, 7:17 p.m., http://bbs.sfile2012.com/viewthread.php?tid=275646&extra=&highlight=moennig&page=352.
60. wenwen1213, fan post, July 14, 2010, 8:48 p.m., http://bbs.sfile2012.com/viewthread.php?tid=275646&extra=&highlight=moennig&page=352.
61. samdream, fan post, September 25, 2011, 12:42 p.m., http://bbs.sfile2012.com/viewthread.php?tid=346706&extra=&highlight=freja&page=14.
62. sea000mus, fan post, January 27, 2012, 1:21 a.m., http://bbs.sfile2012.com/viewthread.php?tid=346706&extra=&highlight=freja&page=52; sunshisunshi, fan post, January 28, 2012, 1:36 p.m., http://bbs.sfile2012.com/viewthread.php?tid=346706&extra=&highlight=freja&page=52.
63. Jose Esteban Muñoz, *Disidentifications: Queers of Color and the Performance of Politics* (Minneapolis: University of Minnesota Press, 1999), 25.
64. Aihwa Ong, *Flexible Citizenship: The Cultural Politics of Transnationality* (Durham, NC: Duke University Press, 1999), 31.
65. Carl Stychin, *A Nation by Rights: National Cultures, Sexual Identity Politics and the Discourse of Rights* (Philadelphia, PA: Temple University Press, 1998), 200.
66. Neville Hoad, "Between the White Man's Burden and the White Man's Disease: Tracking Lesbian and Gay Human Rights in Southern Africa," *GLQ* 5.4 (1999): 564.
67. Mark Johnson, "Global Desirings and Translocal Loves: Transgendering and Same-Sex Sexualities in the Southern Philippines," *American Ethnologist* 25.4 (1998): 696.
68. Jon Binnie, *The Globalization of Sexuality* (Thousand Oaks, CA: Sage, 2004), 6. See Altman's detailed arguments in Dennis Altman, "Global Gaze/Global Gays," *GLQ* 3.4 (1997): 417–36.
69. Muñoz, *Disidentifications*, 78.
70. Peter A. Jackson, "Global Queering and Global Queer Theory: Thai [Trans]genders and [Homo]sexualities in World History," *Autrepart* 49 (2009): 17.
71. See Tom Boellstorff, *The Gay Archipelago: Sexuality and Nation in Indonesia* (Princeton, NJ: Princeton University Press, 2005); Peter A. Jackson, *Dear Uncle Go: Male Homosexuality in Thailand* (Bangkok: Bua Luang Books, 1995); Rosalind C. Morris, "Three Sexes and Four Sexualities: Redressing the Discourses on Gender and Sexuality in Contemporary Thailand," *Positions* 2.1 (1994): 15–43; Megan Sinnott, *Toms and Dees: Transgender Identity and Female Same-Sex Relationships in Thailand* (Honolulu: University of Hawai'i Press, 2004).
72. See Arjun Appadurai, *Modernity at Large: Cultural Dimensions of Globalization* (Minneapolis: University of Minnesota Press, 1996); Mike Featherstone, *Global Culture: Nationalism, Globalization and Modernity* (London: Sage, 1990).

73. John Fiske, "Act Globally, Think Locally," in *Planet TV: A Global Television Reader*, ed. Lisa Parks and Shanti Kumar (New York: New York University Press, 2003), 277.
74. See Wah Shan Chou, *Tongzhi: Politics of Same-Sex Eroticism in Chinese Societies* (New York: Haworth Press, 2000); Bret Hinsch, *Passions of the Cut Sleeve: The Male Homosexual Tradition in China* (Berkeley: University of California Press, 1990).
75. See Lucetta Y. L. Kam, *Shanghai Lalas: Female Tongzhi Communities and Politics in Urban China* (Hong Kong: Hong Kong University Press, 2013); Rofel, *Desiring China*.
76. Song Hwee Lim, "How to Be Queer in Taiwan: Translation, Appropriation, and the Construction of a Queer Identity in Taiwan," in *AsiaPacifiQueer: Rethinking Genders and Sexualities*, ed. Fran Martin et al. (Urbana: University of Illinois Press, 2008), 245.
77. Ching Yau, "Bridges and Battles," *GLQ* 12.4 (2006): 606.
78. Ning Wang, "Orientalism versus Occidentalism?," *New Literary History* 28.1 (1997): 62–63.
79. Xiaomei Chen, *Occidentalism: A Theory of Counter-discourse in Post-Mao China* (Lanham, MD: Rowman & Littlefield, 2002), 2.
80. Ibid., 1–22.
81. Ibid., 3.
82. Ibid., 23.
83. Ibid.
84. Muñoz, *Disidentifications*.
85. Ibid., 11–12.
86. See mandy0903, fan post, June 22, 2009, 1:04 p.m., http://bbs.sfile2012.com/viewthread.php?tid=275646&extra=&highlight=katherine%2Bmoennig&page=49; wenwen1213, fan post, June 22, 2009, 1:07 p.m., http://bbs.sfile2012.com/viewthread.php?tid=275646&extra=&highlight=katherine%2Bmoennig&page=49.
87. mandy0903, fan post, June 22, 2009, 1:11 p.m., http://bbs.sfile2012.com/viewthread.php?tid=275646&extra=&highlight=katherine%2Bmoennig&page=49.
88. mandy0903, fan post, June 22, 2009, 1:26 p.m., http://bbs.sfile2012.com/viewthread.php?tid=275646&extra=&highlight=katherine%2Bmoennig&page=49; phoebedawn, fan post, June 22, 2009, 6:52 p.m., http://bbs.sfile2012.com/viewthread.php?tid=275646&extra=&highlight=katherine%2Bmoennig&page=49; wenwen1213, fan post, June 22, 2009, 1:19 p.m., http://bbs.sfile2012.com/viewthread.php?tid=275646&extra=&highlight=katherine%2Bmoennig&page=49; wenwen1213, fan post, June 22, 2009, 1:21 p.m., http://bbs.sfile2012.com/viewthread.php?tid=275646&extra=&highlight=katherine%2Bmoennig&page=49; wenwen1213, fan post, June 22, 2009, 1:37 p.m., http://bbs.sfile2012.com/viewthread.php?tid=275646&extra=&highlight=katherine%2Bmoennig&page=49.
89. heehyde, fan post, April 24, 2010, 9:07 p.m., http://bbs.sfile2012.com/viewthread.php?tid=275646&extra=&highlight=katherine%2Bmoennig&page=345; heehyde, fan post, May 14, 2010, 1:35 p.m., http://bbs.sfile2012.com/viewthread.php?tid=275646&extra=&highlight=katherine%2Bmoennig&page=348; wenwen1213, fan post, May 14, 2010, 12:20 p.m., http://bbs.sfile2012.com/viewthread.php?tid=275646&extra=&highlight=katherine%2Bmoennig&page=348; wildandwindy, fan post, April 26, 2010, 12:58 p.m., http://bbs.sfile2012.com/viewthread.php?tid=275646&extra=&highlight=katherine%2Bmoennig&page=345.
90. mandy0903, fan post, June 22, 2009, 1:46 p.m., http://bbs.sfile2012.com/viewthread.php?tid=275646&extra=&highlight=katherine%2Bmoennig&page=49; pheobedawn,

fan post, June 22, 2009, 6:52 p.m., http://bbs.sfile2012.com/viewthread.php?tid=275646&extra=&highlight=katherine%2Bmoennig&page=49.
91. Marnie Pratt, "This Is the Way We Live . . . and Love!," in *Gender, Race, and Class in Media: A Critical Reader*, ed. Gail Dines and Jean M. Humez (Thousand Oaks, CA: Sage, 2011), 343.
92. Judith Butler, *Bodies That Matter: On the Discursive Limits of "Sex"* (New York: Routledge, 1993), 241.
93. Jenkins, *Textual Poachers*, 82–84.
94. Martin, *Backward Glances*.
95. Muñoz, *Disidentifications*, 103.
96. The uniqueness of the Chinese lesbian gender paradigm, the T/P or Tomboy/*Po* system, has been stressed in a few recent queer China studies. It has been argued that, different from the Western butch/femme lesbian gender identities, the T/P paradigm is built upon unstable, gendered roles, positions, and styles that can be categorized as masculine or feminine based on a set of physical qualities and personalities. Meanwhile, some research claims that the Anglo-American terms, androgyny/androgynous, cannot be used to translate "neutral sexuality" (中性; *zhongxing*) which is celebrated in contemporary Chinese-language pop cultures and has Chinese-specific historical and social trajectories. For more detailed discussions on these points, see Elisabeth L. Engebretsen, *Queer Women in Urban China: An Ethnography* (New York: Routledge, 2014), 49–55; and Eva Cheuk-Yin Li, "Approaching Transnational Chinese Queer Stardom as Zhongxing ('Neutral Sex/Gender') Sensibility," *East Asian Journal of Popular Culture* 1.1 (2015): 75–95. However, I have found that the terms "butch" and "T" or "tomboy" are used interchangeably by GE fans. Also, GE fans often use the English word "androgyny" to refer to Chinese *zhongxing* and "both feminine and masculine" (*cixiongtongti*) during their queer gossip. I think this is partially because most fans in this cross-cultural fandom have good command of English and some of them have been immersed in Western cultures for years through consuming Western entertainment information or obtaining Western lived experiences. Thus, GE queer fan culture mirrors a distinctive, hybrid, grassroots Chinese culture that inflects the combined influences of global information flows, overseas cultural experiences, and local Chinese cultural histories and conventions. Accordingly, I use the term "butch" in this chapter to refer to the performative, masculine lesbian roles and positions in the fans' queer gossip. The words "androgyny/androgynous" are employed by me to denote the fluid, in-between gender state of masculinity and femininity.
97. Mayfair Mei-hui Yang, "From Gender Erasure to Gender Difference: State Feminism, Consumer Sexuality, and Women's Public Sphere in China," in *Spaces of Their Own: Women's Public Sphere in Transnational China*, ed. Mayfair Mei-hui Yang (Minneapolis: University of Minnesota Press, 1999), 40–42.
98. Ibid., 47–64.
99. See Kim Akass and Janet McCabe, eds., *Reading "The L Word": Outing Contemporary Television* (New York: Palgrave Macmillan, 2006).
100. Michelle Kort, "Welcome Back to L World," *Advocate*, February 1, 2005, accessed April, 1, 2010, http://www.advocate.com/news/2005/01/18/welcome-back-l-world
101. Halberstam, *Female*, 177.
102. Ibid.
103. Sally Munt, *Heroic Desire: Lesbian Identity and Cultural Space* (New York: New York University Press, 1998), 122.

104. Lucetta Y. L. Kam, "Recognition through Mis-recognition: Masculine Women in Hong Kong," in *AsiaPacifiQueer: Rethinking Genders and Sexualities*, ed. Fran Martin et al. (Urbana: University of Illinois Press, 2008), 107.
105. Ibid., 100.
106. See Halberstam, *Female*, 57–58.
107. Audrey Yue, "King Victoria: Asian Drag Kings, Postcolonial Female Masculinity, and Hybrid Sexuality in Australia," in *AsiaPacifiQueer: Rethinking Genders and Sexualities*, ed. Fran Martin et al. (Urbana: University of Illinois Press, 2008), 261–62.
108. Halberstam, *Female*, 57. Also see June Singer, *Androgyny: Toward a New Theory of Sexuality* (London: Routledge, 1976), 20; Mary Anne Warren, "Is Androgyny the Answer to Sexual Stereotyping?," in *Femininity, Masculinity and Androgyny: A Modern Philosophical Discussion*, ed. Mary Vetterling-Braggin (Totowa: Littlefield, 1982), 170.
109. Huang, "From 'Hyper-feminine,'" 134.
110. John Loo, ed., *New Reader for Chinese Tongzhi* (Hong Kong: Worldson, 1999), 256.
111. Kam, *Shanghai Lalas*, 5.
112. Helen Hok-Sze Leung, "Thoughts on Lesbian Genders in Contemporary Chinese Cultures," in *Femme/Butch: New Considerations of the Way We Want to Go*, ed. Michelle Gibson and Deborah T. Meem (New York: Harrington Park Press, 2002), 129.
113. Marilyn B. Young, "Chicken Little in China: Women after the Cultural Revolution," in *Promissory Notes: Women in the Transition to Socialism*, ed. Sonia Kruks, Rayna Rapp, and Marilyn B. Young (New York: Monthly Review Press, 1989), 236.
114. Emily Honig, "Maoist Mappings of Gender: Reassessing the Red Guards," in *Chinese Femininities / Chinese Masculinities: A Reader*, ed. Susan Brownell and Jeffrey N. Wasserstrom (Berkeley: University of California Press, 2002), 255, 265.
115. Li, "Approaching Transnational Chinese Queer Stardom," 79.
116. Yang, "From Gender Erasure," 35–67.
117. Ibid., 58.
118. Rofel, *Desiring China*, 117.
119. Lisa Rofel, *Other Modernities: Gendered Yearnings in China after Socialism* (Berkeley: University of California Press, 1999), 186–87.
120. Ibid., 190.
121. Ibid., 137.
122. Engebretsen, *Queer Women*, 55.
123. See Homi K. Bhabha, *The Location of Culture* (New York: Routledge, 1994); Lingchei Letty Chen, *Writing Chinese: Reshaping Chinese Cultural Identity* (New York: Palgrave Macmillan, 2006); Meenakshi Gigi Durham, "Constructing the 'New Ethnicities': Media, Sexuality, and Diaspora Identity in the Lives of South Asian Immigrant Girls," *Critical Studies in Media Communication* 21.2 (2004): 140–61; May Joseph and Jennifer N. Fink, eds., *Performing Hybridity* (Minneapolis: University of Minnesota Press, 1999); Ella Shohat, "Notes on the Post-colonial," *Social Text* 31/32 (1992): 99–113.
124. Bhabha, *Location*, 112.
125. Durham, "Constructing," 144.
126. Muñoz, *Disidentifications*, 84.
127. Chen, *Writing Chinese*, 88.
128. Xiao, "Androgynous Beauty," 121.
129. Shohat, "Notes," 110.

130. tonijin, fan post, November 5, 2010, 5:17 p.m., http://bbs.sfile2012.com/viewthread. php?tid=275646&extra=&highlight=katherine%2Bmoennig&page=361.
131. Engebretsen, *Queer Women*, 51–52.
132. kamnic, fan post, April 8, 2009, 9:55 a.m., http://bbs.sfile2012.com/viewthread.php ?tid=275646&extra=&highlight=katherine%2Bmoennig&page=2; ly302ly, fan post, April 7, 2009, 11:55 p.m., http://bbs.sfile2012.com/viewthread.php?tid=275646& extra=&highlight=katherine%2Bmoennig&page=1; quizhuer , fan post, April 9, 2009, 5:07 p.m., http://bbs.sfile2012.com/viewthread.php?tid=275646&extra=&highlight= katherine%2Bmoennig&page=2.
133. See http://bbs.sfile2012.com/viewthread.php?tid=275646&extra=&highlight=kather ine%2Bmoennig&page=9.
134. tyj_juju, fan post, April 18, 2009, 0:17 a.m., http://bbs.sfile2012.com/viewthread.php ?tid=275646&extra=&highlight=katherine%2Bmoennig&page=8.
135. tyj_juju, fan post, April 18, 2009, 1:08 a.m., http://bbs.sfile2012.com/viewthread.php ?tid=275646&extra=&highlight=katherine%2Bmoennig&page=9.
136. Isabella527, fan post, April 18, 2009, 1:21 a.m., http://bbs.sfile2012.com/viewthread. php?tid=275646&extra=&highlight=katherine%2Bmoennig&page=10.
137. tyj_juju, fan post, April 18, 2009, 1:16 a.m., http://bbs.sfileydy.com/viewthread.php? tid=275646&extra=&highlight=katherine%2Bmoennig&page=9.
138. See huanyingfuchen , fan post, April 18, 2009, 0:41 a.m., http://bbs.sfile2012.com/ viewthread.php?tid=275646&extra=&highlight=katherine%2Bmoennig&page=9; mengbi, fan post, April 19, 2009, 2:06 p.m., http://bbs.sfile2012.com/viewthread. php?tid=275646&extra=&highlight=katherine%2Bmoennig&page=10; phoebedawn, fan post, April 18, 2009, 0:44 a.m., http://bbs.sfile2012.com/viewthread.php? tid=275646&extra=&highlight=katherine%2Bmoennig&page=9; quizhuer, fan post, April 18, 2009, 3:36 p.m., http://bbs.sfile2012.com/viewthread.php?tid=275646& extra=&highlight=katherine%2Bmoennig&page=10; roleplay, fan post, April 18, 2009, 0:26 a.m., http://bbs.sfile2012.com/viewthread.php?tid=275646&extra= &highlight=katherine%2Bmoennig&page=8; shudorm105, fan post, April 18, 2009, 0:43 a.m., http://bbs.sfile2012.com/viewthread.php?tid=275646&extra=&highlight= katherine%2Bmoennig&page=9; wenwen1213, fan post, April 18, 2009, 7:34 a.m., http://bbs.sfile2012.com/viewthread.php?tid=275646&extra=&highlight=katherine% 2Bmoennig&page=10.
139. tyj_juju, fan post, April 18, 2009, 0:54 a.m., http://bbs.sfile2012.com/viewthread.php ?tid=275646&extra=&highlight=katherine%2Bmoennig&page=9
140. shudorm105, fan post, April 18, 2009, 1:18 a.m., http://bbs.sfile2012.com/viewthread. php?tid=275646&extra=&highlight=katherine%2Bmoennig&page=10.
141. C14X, fan post, April 28, 2010, 11:37 p.m., http://bbs.sfile2012.com/viewthread.php? tid=275646&extra=&highlight=katherine%2Bmoennig&page=346; heehyde, fan post, April 29, 2010, 9:57 p.m., http://bbs.sfile2012.com/viewthread.php?tid=275646& extra=&highlight=katherine%2Bmoennig&page=346; wenwen1213, fan post, March 19, 2010, 9:00 p.m., http://bbs.sfile2012.com/viewthread.php?tid=275646& extra=&highlight=katherine%2Bmoennig&page=339; wildandwindy, fan post, April 28, 2010, 4:09 p.m., http://bbs.sfile2012.com/viewthread.php?tid=275646& extra=&highlight=katherine%2Bmoennig&page=346; wujiaojiongjiong!, fan post, March 21, 2010, 1:53 p.m., http://bbs.sfile2012.com/viewthread.php?tid=275646& extra=&highlight=katherine%2Bmoennig&page=339; xiangmingxiangdaobengkui, fan post, April 30, 2010, 11:53 p.m., http://bbs.sfile2012.com/viewthread.php?tid= 275646&extra=&highlight=katherine%2Bmoennig&page=346.

142. Engebretsen, Queer Women, 52.
143. See http://bbs.sfile2012.com/viewthread.php?tid=275646&extra=&highlight=katherine%2Bmoennig&page=327, http://bbs.sfile2012.com/viewthread.php?tid=275646&extra=&highlight=katherine%2Bmoennig&page=336, and http://bbs.sfile2012.com/viewthread.php?tid=275646&extra=&highlight=katherine%2Bmoennig&page=368.
144. C14X, fan post, March 7, 2010, 10:44 p.m., http://bbs.sfile2012.com/viewthread.php?tid=275646&extra=&highlight=katherine%2Bmoennig&page=336; heehyde, fan post, January 29, 2010, 6:56 p.m., http://bbs.sfile2012.com/viewthread.php?tid=275646&extra=&highlight=katherine%2Bmoennig&page=327; katers, fan post, January 28, 2010, 4:59 p.m., http://bbs.sfile2012.com/viewthread.php?tid=275646&extra=&highlight=katherine%2Bmoennig&page=327; lifeisjutst, fan post, May 15, 2011, 4:44 p.m., http://bbs.sfile2012.com/viewthread.php?tid=275646&extra=&highlight=katherine%2Bmoennig&page=368; wujiaojiongjiong!, fan post, January 28, 2010, 12:54 p.m., http://bbs.sfile2012.com/viewthread.php?tid=275646&extra=&highlight=katherine%2Bmoennig&page=327.
145. heehyde, fan post, January 29, 2010, 6:56 p.m., http://bbs.sfile2012.com/viewthread.php?tid=275646&extra=&highlight=katherine%2Bmoennig&page=327.
146. mandy0903, fan post, April 9, 2009, 8:49 p.m., http://bbs.sfile2012.com/viewthread.php?tid=275646&extra=&highlight=katherine%2Bmoennig&page=2.
147. tyj_juju, fan post, April 9, 2009, 8:58 p.m., http://bbs.sfile2012.com/viewthread.php?tid=275646&extra=&highlight=katherine%2Bmoennig&page=2.
148. mandy0903, fan post, April 9, 2009, 9:02 p.m., http://bbs.sfile2012.com/viewthread.php?tid=275646&extra=&highlight=katherine%2Bmoennig&page=2.
149. phoebedawn, fan post, April 9, 2009, 9:16 p.m., http://bbs.sfile2012.com/viewthread.php?tid=275646&extra=&highlight=katherine%2Bmoennig&page=2.
150. Halberstam, *Female*, 122–26.
151. Richard Dyer, *Gays and Film* (New York: Zoetrope, 1984), 31.
152. Halberstam, *Female*, 180.
153. See ibid.; Kam, "Recognition," 99–116; Martin, *Backward Glances*.
154. Muñoz, *Disidentifications*, 4.
155. Fran Martin et al., introduction to *AsiaPacifiQueer: Rethinking Genders and Sexualities*, ed. Fran Martin et al. (Urbana: University of Illinois Press, 2008), 6.
156. See Altman, "*Global Gaze*"; Arnaldo Cruz-Malave and Martin Manalansan, introduction to *Queer Globalizations: Citizenship and the Afterlife of Colonialism*, ed. Arnaldo Cruz-Malave and Martin Manalansan (New York: New York University Press, 2002), 1–10.

5
From Online BL Fandom to the CCTV *Spring Festival Gala*

The Transforming Power of Online Carnival

Shuyan Zhou

Reexamining Online Carnival and Its Political Potential

One of the most visible surfaces of Chinese cyberculture is that of entertainment. The potential relation between playful online activities and political agency has been taken into account by many scholars in recent years. As Guobin Yang has discussed in *The Power of the Internet in China*, "The playful culture in Chinese cyberspace is a central part of the heteroglossia in contemporary Chinese culture. . . . [T]his cultural plurality releases the creative energy directed at the mocking of power and authority."[1] Later, in a paper in 2011, in reviewing previous studies on the topic, Yang emphasized that play is not necessarily apolitical and noted that "the really important and interesting questions to ask are why some issues can be so passionate or more likely to arouse passions"[2] or, that is to say, how political meaning can be explored with respect to the emotional and affective power in particular online events.

Regarding the question of politics and play in Chinese Internet culture, some researchers have utilized Mikhail Bakhtin's celebrated concept of carnival to effectively elucidate political meanings of online environments in China.[3] For example, in her article "Parody and Resistance on the Chinese Internet,"[4] Hongmei Li has argued that the popularity of Internet parody/spoof (*e'gao* in Chinese) can be understood as a way by which the Chinese netizens challenge and resist the existing cultural hegemony, particularly in light of limited freedom of speech and press. In contrast to the public persona of Chinese official media, which is often rigid, serious, and humorless, and "uses distant languages to discuss stuffy ideologies," the Chinese Internet frequently exhibits another dimension of Chinese culture that is vivid, energetic, and full of pleasure, mostly because "the Internet's decentralized nature allows temporary freedom for Chinese to express their voices."[5] The parody in Li's context refers to online information created and spread by a multitude of netizens who intend to make fun of something serious. As such, Li has applied "carnival" to explain the positive meaning of Internet parody, since carnivalesque laughter, according to Bakhtin, with its inherently subversive nature against official ideologies, can reverse authority into stupidity, blur the boundaries of different social classes, embrace a diversity of people who participate in it, and celebrate "temporary liberation from the prevailing truth and from the established order."[6] Therefore, her discussion focused on the "constant struggle" between the netizens who presented a cheerful grassroots culture and the serious official culture in China; that is, by means of parody and spoof, the netizens created a carnivalesque space of laughter where more people were bound together and engaged in public events, which, according to this argument, provided strategies to resist the authority of official media, as well as the potential for social change.

To some extent, Bakhtin's theory of carnival is useful for addressing the agency of Chinese netizens. However, when in so doing netizens' culture is positioned thoroughly against the official one, this raises the suspicion that employing the political utopianism in Bakhtinian carnival can tend to romanticize and overemphasize the effectiveness of the resistance involved in netizens' play. As Li herself mentioned in the conclusion, cyberspace in China is a more contested battlefield that "indicates the complexities and difficulties in challenging the established order," and, in her words, "it is unrealistic to oversimplify the Chinese Internet as a space for resistance."[7] Yet, when she analyzes case studies of online parodies, she seems to fail to elaborate the complicated and dynamic power relations behind each of them because the relationship between cyberculture and the official culture is conceptualized as one of binary opposition. This criticism has also been made by Yang, who reminded us that

> if the metaphor of an online carnival is stretched to imply that the entire online society is a wild, lawless carnival, it may lose its analytical purchase, because it creates a sharp dichotomy between overlapping and mutually embedded forms of sociality; after all, "normal" life has its carnivalesque moments and spaces, just as online society is by no means immune from regulation.[8]

Referring to the carnival notion as well, Weizhen Lei has provided another perspective more focused on the dynamic power relations between the Internet and the other media. By analyzing the case of "Fan Paopao," which involved a heated social debate on mass media about a middle school teacher who left his students behind as he ran from danger himself during the Wenchuan earthquake in 2008, Lei especially studied how this "media event" was influenced and changed by the participation of netizens.[9] Online carnival, in this sense, made a media event more "changeable, unpredictable and decentralized," rather than under control of certain institutions, and could be seen as a "mediator" and "security gate" between the official and grassroots discourses.[10] Lei's research implied the potential power of online carnival in transgressing borders of cyberspace, thus impacting offline media. The word "carnival" in his case was applied to explain the netizens' spontaneous collective social activities. However, the playful dimension was ignored because of the affective limitations of the case. That is, the emotions expressed by netizens in Lei's case were on the whole indignant, critical, and serious, instead of a certain kind of carnivalesque laughter.

Rethinking the political potentials of online playful activities such as parody and spoof, more detailed and contextualized questions need to be addressed according to the complexities of different cases. Specifically, what kind of pleasures related to online carnival can be transformed into political discourse, and how? How will the official media respond after its authority has been mocked by netizens? To what extent does a parody or a common online joke enable netizens' self-empowerment? Will a given parody possibly be appropriated by or conspire with the official culture and thus reinforce the established social order? In addition, how and in what ways might power relations transform if the carnival goes beyond the cyberculture sphere? These questions will be explored in this chapter.

Specifically, this chapter reexamines particular effects of netizens' carnival practices, as well as the complex interactions and contradictions among cyberculture, the official culture, and consumerism in China, by centering on a specific case of "Looking for Leehom" (*zhao Lihong*) and its related media discourses in 2012 and 2013. The case has special significance because it serves as an influential online carnival, starting from an online fandom for a large number of mainly female netizens who are fond of male homoerotic fantasies and specifying those who participated in the Leehom discussions. Further, it raises large questions about resistance, complicity, and negotiation among different cultures and media, particularly considering that online carnival was appropriated by a performance on the CCTV *Spring Festival Gala* in 2013 and then commented on by newspapers and magazines. Thus, the case should be regarded as a series of dynamic events rather than a single text, since the meaning of carnival itself is constantly flowing and changing around different discourses. In the following parts, I will first explain the origin of "Looking for Leehom," with an introduction to the online Boys' Love fandom, and then inspect how the pleasure of matchmaking two Chinese-speaking male celebrities has been transferred, censored, and re-enabled between cyberculture and offline societies. In light of the enjoyment and ironic effects in the case, Bakhtin's interpretation of carnival will still be applied, nevertheless in a more prudent way. The chapter concludes by exploring the cultural and social implications of "Looking for Leehom" and the potential power of the netizens' fantasy.

Boys' Love Fandom and the Prohibition of Male Homosexuality

Boys' Love (BL) is a Japanese term for female-oriented fictional media that largely focuses on love, sex, and romance between beautiful androgynous boys or young men. Many Chinese BL fans call themselves *funü*, which literally means "rotten women," to describe their enthusiasm for fantasizing narratives seemingly rooted in male homosexuality. In the 1990s, BL as a genre of Japanese *shōjo* manga (manga for girls) began to spread into mainland China, introduced by local manga magazines and pirated manga copies from Taiwan and Hong Kong. After 2000, BL fandom continued to emerge and increase but primarily in the realm of cyberspace, due to the strict censorship of homoerotic hardcopy publications.[11] Today, there are several main websites and forums for BL writings and discussions. For example, the largest women's literature website in China, Jinjiang Literature City (Jinjiang wenxue cheng)[12] has a particular subsite for BL fiction writing, frequented by a great number of *funü*. The subsite has developed into an elaborate organization consisting of a platform for publishing BL works, an e-bookstore, and a discussion forum.[13] On the Internet, the growing fandom has not been limited to Japanese manga and anime culture, but also interrelates with the offline media covering Chinese popular culture, including Chinese martial arts, movies, TV dramas, news, popular music, and so on. It evokes a compelling sensibility by which *funü* queerly read and fantasize nonsexual male relationships, such as brotherhood, friendship, or rivalry, in the original stories or in real life into homosexual romances.

As Uli Meyer pointed out, "The avid fan starts to see homosexual dynamics everywhere: between fellow students, pop stars, even politicians. . . . BL fans are reading the world with *yaoi* [another name for erotic Boys' Love] eyes and have become perverse readers."[14] Therefore, in online BL fandom, one appealing cyber activity for *funü* is to imagine male popular stars or male celebrities in whom they are interested as a homosexual couple, by means of sharing gossip, writing fiction, and recreating photos or videos of those stars and celebrities. The fans especially like to fantasize about two male celebrities who may have a close relation portrayed in the mainstream media or have worked together in real life as lovers. According to queer theorist Eve Kosofsky Sedgwick, in modern culture, there is a cultural boundary between nonsexual male homosocial desire and sexual male homosexual desire, which is strongly dependent upon the prohibition against homosexuality.[15] Therefore, it is worth noting that when *funü* take the male celebrities' public images into their BL fantasies, the pleasure comes not merely from *funü*'s erotic desires but also from the subversion of the nonsexual social bond between two males represented in the mainstream media. This kind of BL recreation sometimes attracts other netizens who are not fans of BL eroticism per se to join in the fantasy of male celebrities' homosexuality. This is because in certain cases it can develop such a hilarious effect of parody that some netizens who don't usually follow BL may also become interested in the playful online activities of male celebrities' BL matchmaking. For example, Han Han and Guo Jingming, both popular young writers and movie directors who are often juxtaposed and compared by the mainstream newspapers and magazines as two young successful models, have become a well-known BL couple on the Internet in the past ten years, even though they have never worked with each other. Interestingly, the mass media has represented Han and Guo as competitors in their work lives, thus constructing a nonsexual and even unfriendly homosocial relationship between them, while BL fans, including a few fans of Han and Guo, turn this into a resource for their queer fantasy. A more complex reading originates from a *funü*'s BL short fiction named *Shanghai Tragic Love Story* (*Shanghai juelian*) in 2004, which seemingly depicts a male homosexual romance between Han and Guo but is actually a mockery of Guo's bad behavior of plagiarism. Hence, many netizens who have gotten interested in this BL matchmaking are neither *funü* nor fans of Han or Guo but people who like to tease the two (see Figure 5.1). In this sense, online BL fandom sometimes inseparably intertwines with Li's interpretation of Internet parody, especially when it displays resistance against celebrities' social image construction and at the same time generates a pleasure of parody from blurring the boundary between male homosocial relationships in mainstream portrayals and male homosexuality in online fantasy.

Figure 5.1

The poster of *Shanghai Tragic Love Story*, BL matchmaking of Han Han and Guo Jingming. From http://group.mtime.com/aaa/discussion/322448/, accessed June 6, 2016.

Although such male homosexual narrativizing seems a fantasy or parody for pleasure in online BL fandom, it still plays with homosexual prohibition. In contemporary China, broad social discussions about homosexuality have begun to emerge publicly since the late 1990s, and governmentally the issue of homosexuality is in an ambivalent and complicated state. The government neither prohibits homosexuality nor protects homosexual people, but rather keeps its tactical attitude as "not encouraging, not discouraging, and not promoting."[16] Homosexuality was decriminalized in 1997 with the abolishment of the "hooligan" law, and in 2001 it was also removed from the official list of mental disorders. Along with these developments, the issue has also entered academia as well as attention to related social movements as representing a marginalized social group that demands its equal rights.[17] However, representations of homosexuality in mass media still confront many difficulties. On the one hand, homosexuality remains stigmatized as "sick," "abnormal," or "perverted" in some societal news; while in entertainment news, homosexuality is often taken as a novelty, a "selling point," or a fashionable upper-middle-class lifestyle for attention grabbing, such as homosexual rumors of celebrities.[18] On the other hand, censorship from the authority controlling television and press of the explicit description of homosexual desire still persists.[19] Even on the Internet, though relevant information may be disseminated more easily and freely than it is offline, it still faces waves of online censorship.[20] For example, since homosexuality has been frequently appropriated and recreated by netizens in ways that have developed creative variants for queer desire,[21] BL fandom has also been harshly censored because of its homoerotic content.[22] Yet one feature of China's online regulation and censorship of homosexuality is that it oscillates between being strict and being lax, and it is not always effective in practice, thus leaving a quite ambiguous space for netizens to "test." Therefore, concerning the control of homosexual desire, there are several latent boundaries dividing the ways of representing homosexuality as "safe" or as "dangerous." Those boundaries stand invisibly and unstably between offline society and cyberspace, reality and fantasy, public and private, female BL fans and real male homosexuals, and play the role of filters for different homosexual representations.

Hence when *funü* homoeroticize certain male celebrities, turning them from their nonsexual social relationships as depicted in the mainstream media to BL fantasies, they are actually disturbing the boundaries that separate male homosocial desire from male homosexual desires and, explicitly or implicitly, touching on the prohibition against homosexuality. Fantasizing about two male celebrities as a couple in love, thus, may bring about subversive pleasure in *funü* discussions, which sometimes even transcends the scope of BL fandom online and begins to influence, even interfere with, the established heterosexual norms in the mainstream culture. The following case of the famous BL matchmaking of Wang Leehom and Li Yundi demonstrates how *funü*'s online male homosexual fantasies about two male celebrities can cross the borders of Internet imagination to influence offline media.

"The No. 1 Couple of the Nation" and the Consumption of Male Celebrities

Pop singer Wang Leehom and classical pianist Li Yundi[23] collaborated on a creative piano performance called "Dance of the Golden Snake" at the *Spring Festival Gala* of CCTV-1 on January 22, 2012. The duo were playing the piano together face to face, smiling, and interacting with each other. The performance triggered waves of matchmaking by numerous *funü* who were watching TV that night. For example, only a few minutes after the performance, a post appeared on China's biggest BL forum Xianqing,[24] saying Wang and Li's performance was full of "gay passion," which prompted boundless fantasies from *funü*:

> OMG, just watched the performance of Wang and Li's cooperation, I am really excited!! Leehom gave that look to Yundi, I am too shy to see it![25]

> This is the first time for me to indulge in the BL matchmaking of real people; I never thought I would connect BL fantasy with real people until this Chinese New Year's Eve![26]

Interestingly, there was a big displacement from the public performance on CCTV-1, the most authoritative media in China, to the private fantasy of male homosexuality derived from online BL fandom, which precisely produced the pleasure of parody:

> The evening report on CCGV-1[27] said, Wang and Li had done a (homo) passionate performance,[28] and I anticipate seeing this news so much![29]

> A national couple has come out, and it has gained the official certification by CCTV![30]

A week later, the number of replies to the post amounted to 2,857, followed by a second post titled "Gay Passion Piano Series" on January 30, 2012, which generated 2,778 replies in only a few days. Other similar posts under the same title followed. Up to January 4, 2013, there had been sixty-four threads on the same topic in Xianqing Forum, which means five or six threads were updated every month with 2,000–3,000 replies within each thread, forming the so-called online "Piano Threads."[31] In the "Piano Threads," *funü* could be fans of Wang or Li while at the same time fantasizing about the relationship between the two from a BL perspective, with romance and love narratives. They fictionalized the duo as characters falling in love with each other in a series of homosexual novels, poems, videos, and Photoshopped movie posters, which in turn homoromanticized the images of the two celebrities (see Figure 5.2). Wang and Li thus became the most popular "No. 1 Couple of the Nation" on the Chinese Internet,

Figure 5.2
BL matchmaking of Wang Leehom and Li Yundi. From Xianqing Forum, http://bbs.jjwxc.net/showmsg.php?board=3&keyword=%CD%F5%C1%A6%BA%EA%20%C0%EE%D4%C6%B5%CF&id=608211, accessed June 6, 2016.

celebrated not only by *funü* but also by other netizens who simply relished the carnivalesque matchmaking atmosphere.

In addition, though indirectly, this online BL fantasy stimulated commercial interests for the celebrities. After the performance at the CCTV *Spring Festival Gala*, Wang and Li received more attention on the Internet, due to the increasing number of fans for their BL pair-up. Some of those BL fans who enjoyed the matchmaking also became fans of Wang, Li, or both, for each one's good looks and musical talents were highlighted in the BL fantastic narratives. The ticket sales for their concerts quickly rose. However the two celebrities did not respond directly to these fantasies in the beginning. Rather, they chose to expose their activities together online, such as having dinner or going to the movies, taking advantage of such BL fantasies to attract more attention from the media. For example, on November 23, 2012, a photo of Wang, Li, and Li's mother was posted on Li Yundi's official Weibo, followed by lots of BL fans' replies jokingly congratulating the "No. 1 Couple of the Nation" for being accepted by their parents.[32] Some mainstream media started reporting about those fantasies in a playful tone. For example, a news item that was titled "Li Yundi said, 'I have a good relationship with Wang indeed'" in the *Southern Metropolis Daily* on November 28, 2012,[33] emphasized their close interactions and personal relationship in an ambiguous way rather than clearly denying the online rumors. To some fans, the border between fantasy and reality became more and more blurred, since the mainstream media representations of the celebrities surreptitiously supported the netizens' homoerotic fantasies, which had started out to be, after all, a queer reading of the performance in the CCTV gala:

> I went to Li's Weibo after reading the news too. It seems they have been carrying on indeed. When Li posted the photo he only mentioned his mother but not Wang. Did that mean he takes Wang as a very intimate partner?[34]
>
> I should say it is obvious that the BL pair-up of the real people is based on fantasy, but why has everybody started to take it seriously? . . . Even I myself also get the feeling that they actually have come out of the closet, how come?[35]

Undoubtedly, not all of *funü* became fans of this national BL couple. Many BL fans expressed a negative and critical attitude toward Wang and Li when they noticed the online fantasy had been appropriated by commercial speculation and consumerism. Nonetheless, because of the pervasive nature of the Internet and the push from offline media, some other netizens who used not to be fans of BL also participated in the discussion of the male homosexual gossip about Wang and Li. In addition to Xianqing Forum, which is an online community for mostly BL fans, the topic became popular in other public forums or social media such as Tianya and Weibo and even in offline media. Thus the pleasure of BL fantasies gradually exceeded the border of BL fandom and then cyberspace, and potentially interfered with the celebrities' personal life in reality.

On January 3, 2013, Wang Leehom suddenly posted a statement on his official Weibo saying: "I am a heterosexual man, and so is Li Yundi. What the hell is the pair-up of Wang and Li!? Perhaps it's just a joke, or the entertainment news, but I hope people can distinguish the truth from nonsense!"[36] This clarification initially was intended to separate him from a fantasized male homosexuality, but it unexpectedly provoked sarcasm from a number of netizens who came up with a new round of Internet parody. Wang soon got a derisive nickname on the Internet, "No. 1 Straight Guy in the Universe" (*yuzhou diyi zhinan*). Moreover, some netizens, including BL fans and nonfans who dislike Wang, started a parodic game on Weibo and Douban (a popular website in China for culture-related activities), as well as the online forums of Xianqing and Tianya, that imitated traditional Chinese poems to comfort "pathetic" Li who was "dumped" by Wang, such as,

> it is difficult to be water for one who has seen the great seas, and difficult to be gay for one who has been the straightest in universe.[37]

The erotic pleasure of fantasizing about the "No. 1 Couple of the Nation" turned into the ironic mockery of the "No. 1 Straight Guy in the Universe." The online carnival did not cease but was transformed in tandem with the reaction of the very celebrity who was suddenly worried that his social reputation would be ruined by the online homosexual rumors. The fantasy mixed with rumors further confused the authenticity of the celebrities' sexual identities. Although fantasies may seem safe at first appearance, when such desire for male homosexuality enters into reality, or in other words, transcends the border of BL fandom and cyberspace, it could trigger articulations of homophobia at any time. Under such circumstances, the incident of "Looking for Leehom," which occurred at the following year's *Spring Festival Gala* of CCTV-1 on February 9, 2013, could be understood as a symptom derived from the conflicts between excessive carnival pleasure and the heteronormative order imposed by the official media.

The Danger of "Looking for Leehom"

The CCTV *Spring Festival Gala*, with more than thirty years of history, is China's longest-running, biggest-in-scale, and most popular television entertainment show. It seems a "national carnival" for the politicians and all the people together to celebrate the most important traditional festival in China, and it often involves several art comedic forms from Chinese folk culture such as cross talk, witty skits, cross-dressing, and even some popular jokes from cyberspace. However, the comedic episodes of this pseudocarnival must be maintained within certain limits. That is, there must be a balance kept between making something funny and promoting mainstream values. As a matter of fact, every performance in the CCTV gala is strictly controlled and censored by the State Administration of Press, Publication, Radio and Television and is a direct reflection of the dominant ideology of the state, to ensure that existing social norms never be transgressed by the humor. Yet, as one recent study has implied, in recent years, the CCTV gala has tended to incorporate subcultural entertainments, especially male homosexual jokes from BL culture, to create an ambiguous space between the mainstream and subculture.[38]

At the *Spring Festival Gala* of 2013, Taiwanese magician Liu Qian partnered with Li Yundi to perform a magic show called "Magic Piano." In one of the scenes, Li Yundi was calling Liu Qian from behind a screen and Liu responded by saying "Are you looking for Leehom?"—referring to the BL matchmaking parody. The audience exploded with applause immediately. However, at 1:45 am on February 10, a few minutes after the gala ended, CCTV issued a special statement on the gala's official Weibo account, saying "the joke about Wang and Li was not designed by the directors of the Gala, but was instead Liu Qian's personal improvisation" and that "it will be deleted from the version to be rebroadcast on the next day."[39] After CCTV shook off its liability, less than an hour later, Liu Qian also issued a statement, saying Li Yundi's team proposed the joke of "Looking for Leehom" at the rehearsal before the show went on the air. "Come on! Be honest!" Liu wrote on his Weibo. On February 16, Liu's agent repeated to the mainstream media that "Looking for Leehom" was proposed by Li. On February 20, after keeping silent for ten days, Li followed by another statement denying everything Liu said, insisting that all the dialogue in the magic show was improvised and that he "never proposed or suggested any lines." On February 21, Wang and Li unfriended each other on Weibo. In the following two months, the agents of Liu and Li continued arguing about "who came up with the idea," pointing fingers at each other, which almost escalated into a lawsuit. As a result, the "No. 1 Couple of the Nation" was finally turned into an embarrassing and unnerving topic in the mainstream media that everyone was trying to get rid of.

Needless to say, CCTV started to censor the "Looking for Leehom" saga as soon as possible because the homosexual implication in the joke had crossed a line that the official program needed to maintain. After the incident, news and reviews focusing on Wang and Li started to reemerge in the mass media, this time also involving Liu. Rather than investigating the "truth" of who on earth proposed "Looking for Leehom," some critics traced the incident back to the *funü* fantasy of male homosexuality, reflecting on the reconstruction of the border between the official culture and online BL fandom. A *Morning News* commentary on February 19, 2013, for example, considered the "Looking for Leehom" incident an unsuccessful adoption of the online BL fandom. The commenter argued:

> Generally speaking, compared to the large scale of the *Spring Festival Gala* which reaches millions of mainstream people, Boys' Love should only be counted as a marginal subculture despite its popularity on the Internet. There are still many people who know little about homosexuality, how can they understand the special background of the so-called BL matchmaking of Wang and Li? The incident that occurred at the Gala can be seen as a consumption of *funü* subculture by appropriating the topic of BL matchmaking, but it was a failed one. . . . The statement issued by CCTV at the first moment, was meant to avoid offending mainstream people. . . . In fact, for the agents of the celebrities, consuming *funü* subculture is more a question of how to handle it properly. It gets the best effect when the relationship of the two celebrities is presented as more than friends but not lovers. If the joke goes too far, the mainstream audience may get offended, except for a few netizens. After all, to conduct commercial endorsement and performance, the social image of those celebrities, which ought to be sound and positive, is very important to them in the mainstream cultural market.[40]

Here the commentary appeared to provide two reasons why the adoption of online BL fandom had failed: the misuse of a joke without taking into account mainstream people and its bad effect on the celebrities' images. However, it was actually evasive about several crucial questions: for example, why will "the mainstream people get offended"? Why is it safe and beneficial for celebrities' business interests if BL matchmaking is properly used but turns toward a dark side otherwise? In other words, how in this case are the proper and improper divided? Is that to say BL fantasy is something safe, while real-world male homosexuality is dangerous to mainstream values? What if the boundary between fantasy and reality becomes ambiguous? Some online news media likewise continued to offer the criticism that the "Looking for Leehom" episode was becoming a big media hype for the celebrities, yet at the same time they never tired of introducing the BL fandom to the public, since it was where the male homosexual fantasy of Wang and Li came from.[41] BL fandom, they intimated, has been introduced as a nonmainstream entertainment for a small crowd of women or a kind of fashion derived from foreign culture. All of the critics exhibited a certain degree of anxiety, which can be deduced not only from the evident eagerness to return the transgressiveness of the male homosexual fantasy to the realm of Internet parody, the online BL fandom and the "marginal subculture," but also from the avoidance of any reference to the censorship of homosexuality implied by CCTV. The most apparent yet unspeakable reason for the failure of "Looking for Leehom" was that the homophobic prohibition, hidden at the border between official culture and online carnival, had been aroused, which prohibited "the inappropriate joke" from entering the official media in the future, thus establishing the border again. Furthermore, the prohibition worked unconsciously in a way that everyone persisted in shirking the responsibility for taking the joke across the border, without any mention of the homosexual implication of the joke. Thus the unpleasant dispute between Liu and Li indicated there was no one, in fact, who could bear the burden of disturbing the heterosexual norm in the official culture; the question of who initiated the idea of "Looking for Leehom" would never be answered.

Several months later, in November 2013, Wang and Li separately announced that they were going to get married and posted their girlfriends' photos on Weibo. What is interesting, though, is that the BL matchmaking and online parody still did not stop when both the official media and the celebrities wanted them to. On the contrary, netizens' fantasies flourished as the two celebrities sought to deny them. The name of "No. 1 Straight Guy in the Universe" for Wang became more popular. The picture that he posted online to prove his love for his fiancée was well Photoshopped by netizens who substituted Li Yundi's portrait for the woman's (see Figure 5.3). While the homophobic prohibition was induced outside cyberspace and repressed and controlled immediately, the sensation of attacking and challenging the taboo within cyberspace, however, escalated. Another new round of Internet parody was on.

Figure 5.3
BL matchmaking of Wang Leehom and Li Yundi, as a parody.
From http://www.dzdwl.com/mvqv/egaozhaopian/31981.html, accessed June 6, 2016.

The Threshold of Online Carnival

A carnival is an event in which rules of propriety are laid aside, in an area and a time set apart from the constraints of "normality" by general consensus.[42] The notion offers many comparable points to the descriptions of collective playful activities on the Chinese Internet and their relationship with offline society. In the case of "Looking for Leehom," not only were the BL fans fascinated with the matchmaking of Wang and Li, but so were other netizens who enjoyed making fun of these celebrities and participated in the online carnival practices in an alliance involved in playing with male homosexual fantasy. However, it is hard to say the case can be taken as a single resistance from the netizens against the official culture. Rather, with regard to the complex interactions among Internet culture, the official media, and the multiplatform consumption of celebrities, the case actually opens up a possibility for us to reconceptualize the question of BL fantasy as a playful online practice and its potential transformation to gender and sexuality politics, as well as the complicated power relations within the contested discourses produced by different forms of media. Three aspects help us interpret the questions raised in the case, in terms of its connection to online carnival.

First of all, as a fantasy appropriated by the offline media and accidentally by the CCTV Gala, the pleasure of BL matchmaking was constantly transformed in different contexts. Returning to the question of what kind of pleasure here in the online BL fandom could finally become a threat to the homosexual prohibition, we should trace the progress of evolving pleasures in this case of online carnival. As mentioned before, BL fantasy concerning male celebrities, with its queer reading that disturbs the boundary between nonsexual male homosocial relations and male homosexual relations, has contained in it both erotic and subversive pleasure. According to Jacques Lacan, the structure of fantasy is crucial to how desire functions because fantasy always holds the possibility that it could turn into the real, while at the same time fantasy prevents the possibility from being real.[43] In other words, fantasy intends to keep a necessary distance from reality so that it can pretend "as if" it will come true. That is why the fans' queering of male homosexuality of Wang and Li originally seemed "safe" in the BL fandom to some extent, since the pleasure from this queer reading of Wang and Li's performance is based in a fantastic and unreal dimension without any reference to male homosexuality in reality. However, when the mass media and the celebrities appropriated and connived with this fantasy, facilitating the spread of gossip and rumors online, the suspension of the possibility of male homosexuality become destabilized. The border between fantasy and reality thus was disturbed, while the pleasure of the fantasy increased. Consequently, more and more fans of the BL matchmaking of Wang and Li seemed to truly hope and believe the two were in a "real" male homosexual relation, so that the two celebrities became anxious to clarify their straight and "normal" sexual identities.

But it was impossible to halt the fantasy at that time. The BL matchmaking had unfolded an online carnival, and the pleasure unexpectedly exceeded cyberspace. Carnival here, in line with Bakhtin's emphasis on its open and fluid nature and its collective power, plays an important role that transmits the subversion of fantasy to more people and areas, until it is banned by a more powerful prohibition. When it went further at the pseudocarnival of the *Spring Festival Gala*, the BL fantasy as a joke was quickly stopped and eliminated by official censorship for its transgression, and thus it withdrew to cyberspace. CCTV, as part of the official media in China, still held its absolute authority in controlling the excessive pleasure and hence reconfirmed the border of online carnival. To the mainstream media and the celebrities, the growing pleasure was reversed into embarrassment, fear, and anger when it reached the climax, as the parody and spoof turned into something irritating. A while after the dispute of "Looking for Leehom," the online BL fantasy gradually lost its fantastic charm, and most BL fans became exhausted with it.

From the 2012 *Spring Festival Gala* that inspired the carnival of the matchmaking of Wang and Li to the gala a year later that failed to properly acknowledge the carnival, we can see that the flow of the male homosexual fantasy and its related desires created by BL fans between CCTV galas and online BL fandom was highly asymmetrical: netizens can create fantasies and parodies as they please, but a CCTV gala cannot use such parodies for entertaining effects, as the homophobic prohibition, which rests on the border between the official culture and cyberculture, is a silent but influential power behind the curtains.[44]

Therefore, the second aspect concerns the potential power from the online BL fandom against the homophobic prohibition in the mainstream. It neither means that the fans, who are fond of male homosexual fantasy, are not more homophobic than other people, nor that they find homosexual people more acceptable in reality. Rather, particularly in the case of "Looking for Leehom," by appropriating male homosexuality into netizens' fantasy and parody, the fandom creates a new form of discourse, in which male homosexuality has been transformed into an essential subversive element for the carnival. Yet, Bakhtin noted that carnival rhetoric "was always essentially ambivalent; it closely combined praise and abuse, it glorified and humiliated."[45] The homosexual joke of Wang and Li stands for such carnivalesque ambivalence: consider the incident when male homosexual matchmaking was used to make fun of the celebrity who insisted on his heterosexuality to maintain his social reputation. On one hand, the joke involved degrading the meaning of homosexuality to something absurd and devalued; on the other hand, it also incorporated homosexuality as a powerful term to resist the established order. The dynamic process of "praise and abuse" actually regenerates the discourse of homosexuality from online fandom to mainstream culture, to confront homophobic prohibition and make it visible.

In this sense, though it seems an unsuccessful adoption of online BL fandom, the censoring of "Looking for Leehom" and the subsequent disputes, from another perspective, demonstrate the possibility of the potential power generated from *funü*'s male homosexual fantasies, which can exceed the border of the fandom to interfere with reality. As Slavoj Žižek has pointed out, a fantasy is simultaneously pacifying, disarming, shattering, disturbing, and inassimilable to our reality.[46] In other words, fantasy plays a role as a double-edged sword in relation to reality—that is, to sustain the symbolic order of reality by filling it up with desires that reality cannot undertake, while also disturbing the order of reality with those desires. Although BL fantasies obviously differ from "real" male homosexuality, not to mention the fandom's intricate interactions and conflicts with online gay culture in China,[47] the pleasure of fantasizing and recreating male homosexual romances can function to transgress heteronormative boundaries both online and offline, especially when the division of reality and fantasy has been blurred by carnival practices.

Last but not least, in this case, the pleasure of carnival was also adopted by the mass media for commercial purposes. The online parody with its relation to offline media became more complicated when it got involved with the hype of celebrities and consumerism in popular culture. This kind of phenomenon is no longer new. As a so-called marginal subculture, BL fandom often faces the process of mainstream cultural appropriation, with businesses seeking to capitalize on the subversive pleasure of BL matchmaking of celebrities, which remains valuable in selling the products of those celebrities. Thus, participation in this kind of carnival sometimes tends to fall into the trap of consumerism. However, as the commentary of *Morning News* suggested, appropriating a male homosexual fantasy about celebrities is always subject to the question of "how to handle it properly," which implies the dual sides of appropriation. This case illustrates that the media hype before 2013 not only brought more focus and commercial benefits to the celebrities but also encouraged and even assisted with transmitting male homosexual fantasy across cyberculture, directly causing the incident of "Looking for Leehom." Moreover, after the BL fantasy mixed with the homosexual rumors, the more the celebrities insisted on their heterosexuality, the less of a desired reaction they got from netizens, ending up with a self-defeating joke.

Besides, it is also inappropriate to describe the netizens, including *funü*, as passive consumers by denying their agency with regard to consuming celebrities online, since there are still many BL fans who are actively aware of the mainstream cultural appropriation and who strongly detest BL matchmaking for celebrities' commercial benefits. In this light, the changing meaning of the BL matchmaking of Wang and Li, from erotic desire for male homosexuality narratives to sarcasm about celebrities' self-defense, precisely elucidates the competing discourses between fans and celebrities; that is, by reactivating the online carnival, netizens regain the power of parody to resist the celebrities' priorities and also manipulation from consumerism.

Conclusion

The relation of playful online activities and their political meanings appears more complex when the pleasure of online fantasy has been constantly appropriated, reinforced, or suspended by different media discourses. Therefore, more attention ought to be paid to specific contexts of online events, when applying Bakhtin's concept of carnival in examining Chinese netizens' parodies and subversive fantasies, and their relation to offline media. By studying BL fans' online discussions and different media discourses around the case of "Looking for Leehom," the transformative power of online carnival can be considered as the flowing of subversive pleasure that originates from BL fandom and transgresses and disturbs the established cultural boundaries of the sexual and the nonsexual, private and public, cyberspace and offline media, and fantasy and reality. In this flow, however, the ambiguous but powerful homophobic prohibition plays a significant role to regulate desire under heterosexual norms. Therefore, the phrase "Looking for Leehom," as a "slip of the tongue," is actually the excessive pleasure that temporarily slips out of the existing order in the mainstream and leaves a "strain" on the CCTV Gala.[48]

Notes

1. Guobing Yang, *The Power of the Internet in China* (New York: Columbia University Press, 2009), 90.
2. Guobing Yang, "Technology and Its Contents: Issues in the study of the Chinese Internet," *Journal of Asian Studies* 70.4 (2011): 1046.

3. For more related research, see David Kurt Herold and Peter Marolt, eds., *Online Society in China: Creating, Celebrating and Instrumentalising the Online Carnival* (London and New York: Routledge, 2011).
4. Hongmei Li, "Parody and Resistance on the Chinese Internet," in *Online Society in China: Creating, Celebrating and Instrumentalising the Online Carnival*, ed. David Kurt Herold and Peter Marolt (London and New York: Routledge, 2011), 70.
5. Ibid., 72.
6. Mikhail Bakhtin, *Rabelais and His World*, trans. Helene Iswolksy (Bloomington: Indiana University Press, 1984), 10.
7. Li, "Parody and Resistance," 85.
8. Guobing Yang, "Lightness, Wildness, and Ambivalence: China and New Media Studies," *New Media & Society* 14.1 (2012): 177.
9. Weizhen Lei, "Cong 'yishi' dao 'paidui': hulianwang dui 'meijieshijian' de chonggou" [From "ritual" to "orgy": Reconstruction of "media events" by the Internet], in *Xinmeiti shijian yanjiu* [New Media Events Research], ed. Jack Linchuan Qiu and Joseph Man Chan (Beijing: Renmin University Press, 2011), 71–72.
10. Lei, "From 'Ritual' to 'Orgy,'" 92.
11. For early history of BL in China, see Guojing Lu, "Danmei wenhua yu tongrennü qunti yanjiu" [Studies on Boys' Love culture and the fangirl community] (MA thesis, Suzhou University, 2011), 11–13.
12. The site of *Jinjiang wenxue cheng* [Jinjiang literature city] is available at http://www.jjwxc.net.
13. For more information, see Jin Feng, *Romancing the Internet: Producing and Consuming Chinese Web Romance* (Boston: Brill, 2013), 53–83.
14. Uli Meyer, "Hidden in Straight Sight: Trans*gressing Gender and Sexuality via BL," in *Boys' Love Manga: Essays on the Sexual Ambiguity and Cross-Cultural Fandom of the Genre*, ed. Antonia Levi, Mark McHarry, and Dru Pagliassotti (Jefferson, NC: MacFarland, 2010), 234.
15. Eve Kosofsky Sedgwick, *Between Men: English Literature and Male Homosocial Desire* (New York: Columbia University Press, 1985), 21–27.
16. Dazheng Tan, *Xingwenhua yu fa* [Sexual culture and law] (Shanghai: Shanghai People's Publishing House, 1998), 17.
17. For more information, see Yinhe Li and Xiaobo Wang, *Tamen de shijie: Zhongguo nantongxinglian qunluo toushi* [Their world: China's homosexual male community] (Taiyuan: Shanxi People's Publishing House, 1993); Suiming Pan, "Tongxinglian he women" [Homosexuality and us], in *Zhongguo xing geming zonglun* [Sex revolution in China: Its origin, expressions and evolution] (Gaoxiong: Wanyou Publishing House, 2006), 201–34; Yinhe Li, *Xingquanli yu fa* [Sexual rights and law] (Beijing: Science Studies Publishing House, 2009).
18. Qian Yang, "Guonei meiti dui tongxinglian xianxiang baodao de fenxi" [An analysis on the news of homosexual phenomena in the Chinese mass media], *Xinwen aihaozhe* [Journalism Lover] 2 (2011): 54–55. Please also see, Xiaomeng Zhou, "2013 nian disanjidu meiti jiance baogao" [Media monitoring report in the third quarter of 2013], *Rainbow Awards*, accessed May 20, 2015, http://www.chinarainbowawards.cn/index.php?m=content&c=index&a=show&catid=5&id=41; Tianhua Yang, "Tongxinglian qunti de meijie xingxiang jiangou" [The construction of image of homosexual groups in the mass media], *Sex-Study*, August 1, 2012, accessed May 20, 2015, http://www.sex-study.org/news.php?isweb=2&sort=158&id=1134.

19. For example, in 2007, the State Administration of Radio, Film and Television (SARFT) in issuing a plan to improve youth's ideological and moral construction by radio, film, and television, took "homosexuality" as "unhealthy content of sexuality" and declared that it "should be deleted resolutely." In 2008, SARFT added "homosexuality" into the censor list of the revised standard of film censorship. In 2010, the standard of film censorship revised in 2008 has been abolished, yet the plan instituted in 2007 still functions.
20. "Hulianwangzhan Jinzhi chuanbo yinhui, seqing deng buliangxinxi zilüguifan" [Regulation of banning the circulation of obscene, pornographic or other malicious information on websites], *China*, June 10, 2004, accessed December 23, 2013, http://www.china.com.cn/chinese/MATERIAL/583721.htm.
21. For example, rather than a simple male-to-male romance, *funü* also create different kinds of male homosexual fantasies, such as love and sex between father and son or between brothers, SM, a man giving birth to a baby after having sex with another man, and so on.
22. Several waves of online censoring and cracking down on BL fan sites have occurred in recent years, for example, see "Funü tiantian beipanxing? Zhengzhou 32 ren you beizhua" [Zhengzhou police arrested 32 BL writers], *Comicyu*, March 22, 2011, accessed December 23, 2013, http://www.comicyu.com/Html2010/2/2011/53388.html. In addition, in 2011, a woman named Ding Yanyan was arrested for uploading seven BL porn novels, and BTV-3 broadcast that news.
23. Wang Leehom (born on May 17, 1976) is a Chinese-American singer-songwriter, record producer and actor. He is currently based in Taiwan. His musical style is known for fusing Chinese elements with hip-hop and R&B. Wang has been active since 1995 and contributed to twenty-five albums. It is worth noting that there have been persistent gay rumors about Wang online for many years, though he also has had rumored romances with women. In November 2013, Wang married his Japanese-Taiwanese girlfriend. Accessed December 23, 2013, *https://en.wikipedia.org/wiki/Wang_Leehom*; Li Yundi (born on October 7, 1982) is a Chinese classical pianist. Li is best known for being the youngest pianist to win the International Frédéric Chopin Piano Competition, in 2000, at the age of eighteen. He currently resides in Beijing. Accessed December 23, 2013, https://en.wikipedia.org/wiki/Li_Yundi.
24. All *funü*'s discussion analyzed in the chapter was quoted from the forum Xianqing at http://bbs.jjwxc.net/. The forum was formerly known as Danmei Xianqing.
25. "Wang Lihong zhuiguo le Li Yundi?!!!" [Wang Leehom has dated Li Yundi?!!!], January 22, 2012, (20:49:13), accessed December 20, 2013, http://bbs.jjwxc.net/showmsg.php?board=3&keyword=%CD%F5%C1%A6%BA%EA%20%C0%EE%D4%C6%B5%CF&id=595347.
26. Jingzhe, "Wang Lihong zhuiguo le Li Yundi?!!!" [Wang Leehom has dated Li Yundi?!!!], January 20, 2012, (20:31:18), accessed December 20, 2013, http://bbs.jjwxc.net/showmsg.php?board=3&keyword=%CD%F5%C1%A6%BA%EA%20%C0%EE%D4%C6%B5%CF&id=595347.
27. CCGV refers to CCTV. Many netizens ironically call CCTV as CCAV online since AV means Adult Video; while *funü* change it into CCGV in the fandom, GV for Gay Video, which shows their love for male homosexuality.
28. The words "homo" and "passion" in Chinese sound the same as *jiqing* (gay passion).
29. Tongyi, "Wang Lihong zhuidao le Li Yundi?!!!" [Wang Leehom is dating Li Yundi?!!!], January 23, 2012, (23:12:42), accessed December 1, 2013, http://bbs.jjwxc.net/

showmsg.php?board=3&keyword=%CD%F5%C1%A6%BA%EA%20%C0%EE%D4%C6%B5%CF&id=608211.

30. Youran, "Wang Lihong zhuidao le Li Yundi?!!!" [Wang Leehom is dating Li Yundi?!!!], January 23, 2012, (23:27:03), accessed December 1, 2013, http://bbs.jjwxc.net/showmsg.php?board=3&keyword=%CD%F5%C1%A6%BA%EA%20%C0%EE%D4%C6%B5%CF&id=608211.

31. All these posts can be searched by "Gay Passionate Piano" (*Jiqing gangqin*) from the forum Xianqing, http://bbs.jjwxc.net/board.php?board=3&type=&page=1.

32. Li Yundi's Sina Weibo, Nov 23, 2012, accessed by December 1, 2013, http://weibo.com/2103206685/z6vnyB6VQ?mod=weibotime#_rnd1386935451721.

33. "Li Yundi shuo, yu Wang Lihong guanxi queshi tinghao" [Li Yundi said, "I have a good relationship with Wang indeed"], *Southern Metropolis Daily*, November 28, 2012.

34. "Wang Lihong zhuidao le Li Yundi?!!!" [Wang Leehom is dating Li Yundi?!!!], November 29, 2012, (01:25:33), accessed December 1, 2013, http://bbs.jjwxc.net/showmsg.php?board=3&keyword=%CD%F5%C1%A6%BA%EA%20%C0%EE%D4%C6%B5%CF&id=608211.

35. "Wang Lihong zhuidao le Li Yundi?!!!" [Wang Leehom is dating Li Yundi?!!!], November 24, 2012, (02:31:52), accessed December 1, 2013, http://bbs.jjwxc.net/showmsg.php?board=3&keyword=%CD%F5%C1%A6%BA%EA%20%C0%EE%D4%C6%B5%CF&id=608211.

36. Wang Leehom's Sina Weibo, January 3, 2013, accessed December 1, 2013, http://weibo.com/1793285524/zcO6tDEsE?mod=weibotime.

37. "Cengjing canghai nanweishui, zhagong shuo ta bushi ji" [It is difficult to be water for one who has seen the great seas, and difficult to be gay for one who has been the straightest in universe], *Tianya*, accessed December 1, 2013, http://bbs.tianya.cn/post-funinfo-3873429-1.shtml. The original poem has been translated as "It is difficult to be water for one who has seen the great seas, and difficult to be clouds for one who has seen the Yangtze Gorges" by Lin Yutang; it means "To a sophisticated person there is nothing new under the sun."

38. Hailong Xu and Lewen Zhang, "Zhongqu de dansheng—jinlai yangshichunwan xiaoping dui danmei yawenhua de shoubian" [The birth of "a middle stage"—The incorporation of *tanbi* subculture into CCTV *Spring Festival Gala*], *Journal of Nanyang Normal University (Social Sciences)*, 13.10 (2014): 51–55.

39. CCTV's official Weibo, accessed December 20, 2013, http://weibo.com/2210168325/zirStCOSq?mod=weibotime.

40. Jianzhong Li, "Zhao Lihong shi xiaofei funü wenhua" [Looking for Leehom is a consumption of *funü*'s culture], *Morning News*, February 19, 2013. The author's own translation.

41. For example, "Zhao Lihong shi meiti chaozuo, wangluo majie youyingjia meishujia" [Looking for Leehom seems to be a media hype, no losers for the online quarrel], *Ifeng*, February 20, 2013, accessed December 20, 2013, http://ent.ifeng.com/tv/special/shenianchunwan/content-4/detail_2013_02/20/22315168_0.shtml; "Gouxueju zhao Lihong, jiji caisuanxiu" [The melodrama of looking for Leehom: How many seasons in total?], *Sohu*, February 22, 2013, accessed December 20, 2013, http://yule.sohu.com/20130222/n366717256.shtml.

42. Bakhtin, *Rabelais and His World*, 10.

43. Sean Homer, *Jacques Lacan* (London and New York: Routledge, 2005), 85–89.

44. This homophobic prohibition described here actually is not a stable, straightforward one. It is said CCTV sometimes exploits implicit homosexual connotations but rarely accepts explicit homoerotic narratives.
45. Bakhtin, *Rabelais and His World*, 418.
46. Slavoj Žižek, *Welcome to the Desert of the Real: Five Essays on September 11 and Related Dates* (New York: Verso, 2002), 18.
47. For example, there are some gay netizens who express a very unpleasant and negative attitude to some BL fans; they usually believe the consumption of male homosexuality by those BL fans distorts gay men's representation to the public and creates a misperception that a male homosexual must be beautiful, aesthetic, and even unreal. However, there are also some gay netizens who participate in the online BL fandom, especially the BL literature websites, and some who write or read the literature defined as BL genre as well.
48. In addition, there are still many questions left with regard to the case that this chapter is unable to cover: for example, how do nonfans respond to the BL matchmaking of Wang and Li? What are the conflicts between the separated fan groups of Wang and Li, especially after the incident of "Looking for Leehom"? What is the difference between online BL fantasy and male homosexual rumors? Is there any harm to the celebrities when their fans have imposed the BL fantasy on them? Further investigation should be done from these different angles. As regarding the events, the competition between multiple discourses on the Internet is no less intense or complicated than it is offline.

6
Dongfang Bubai, Online Fandom, and the Gender Politics of a Legendary Queer Icon in Post-Mao China

Egret Lulu Zhou

Introduction

As one of the most influential popular writers in contemporary China, martial arts novelist Jin Yong (Louis Cha) is famous for his characterizations: his major characters have become a part of cultural imaginaries and practices of Chinese communities all over the world.[1] Most of the actors and actresses who have played Jin Yong's characters in adapted films and TV dramas have either risen to stardom or had their careers rejuvenated as a result. As well, Chinese literature scholars have poured energy into Jin Yong studies, in doing so mainly adopting textual analysis of his novels as their method.[2] However, reception studies of Jin Yong's work are regrettably rare, especially the ones with qualitative empirical bases. Nowadays, when fan studies has gradually moved from its underground status to the center stage of popular culture studies, it is high time we reevaluate Jin Yong and his characters with a new academic lens in order to better understand how he has impacted and continues to impact generations of Chinese popular culture. This chapter, thus, aims to research the online fan cultures of one of Jin Yong's classic characters, Dongfang Bubai (the Invincible East, DFBB hereafter), in post-Mao China.

This character plays a supporting role in *The Smiling, Proud Wanderer* (*Xiao'ao jianghu*, 1967–1969)[3] but still is extraordinarily unique and popular. DFBB is the only queer character in Jin Yong's heterocentric martial arts worlds presented in his fifteen novels: a man castrates himself and falls in love with another man. In addition, DFBB is one of the most famous fictional characters in contemporary China, whose fans are so active that their online activities have made this character rank among the top ten in the "Literary Character" menu in Baidu Post Bar (Baidu tieba, the most popular Chinese online forum).[4] Actually, this character's prominent status could not have been achieved without some adaptation versions. Suggested by incomplete statistics, *The Smiling, Proud Wanderer* has been adapted a multitude of times into various films, TV dramas, video games, and other transmedia productions throughout these five decades, topping all

Jin's novels.[5] Among the adaptations, Hong Kong director Tsui Hark's film *Swordsman II* (*Xiao'ao jianghu zhi Dongfang Bubai*, 1991) and Chinese television producer-scriptwriter Yu Zheng's *Swordsman* (*Xiao'ao jianghu*, 2013) seem to have garnered the most attention. Tsui broke ground by using DFBB as the leading role and casting a female star, redefining the role from an ugly villain in Jin Yong's novel to an enchanting queer icon; and Yu had inherited Tsui's adaptation strategies and further changed DFBB's gender to a woman.

This chapter focuses on the fandom of Yu's new DFBB, situating it within DFBB's adaptation history. By presenting an actress in a female role, this latest DFBB story not only sustains gay readings but also invites those that focus on heterosexual and lesbian romances. I will first analyze DFBB's images in Jin Yong's, Tsui's, and Yu's stories, then identity fans' multiple reading tactics of the new DFBB through examining fan discussions and fan-made artifacts, especially fan webisodes and their related photo collages. The methodology is composed of textual analysis and "Internet ethnography."[6] Starting immediately after the airing of this drama up to this writing, I have frequently visited its fan communities on various websites. And fans' comments on this drama's Sina Weibo (microblog, the Chinese version of Twitter) official webpage, as well as the Baidu Post Bar of DFBB and the actress Joe Chen (Chen Chiao-En), who plays the new DFBB in Yu's version, are my main data collection sites in cyberspace.[7] In 2013 in focused research, I spent two months reading, classifying, and saving its every piece of (re)tweeting, as well as every comment following. And with this I've explored these questions: How do fans understand the new DFBB? What are the main reading tactics that have emerged in their communities? What are the consequences of these reading positions, and why?

Jin Yong, Male Homosexuality, and the Great Cultural Revolution

In Jin Yong's original novel, as the biggest martial arts school in that fictional world, the Sun and Moon Holy Sect (Riyueshenjiao, the sect hereafter) is notorious for its "evilness" and is publicly opposed by five so-called decent schools. The whole story is constructed around one pivot: fighting for the most valuable martial arts secret manuscript, which requires men to self-castrate. There are two copies. One is obtained by DFBB, who follows the requirement and cuts off his testicles, imprisons the hierarch of the sect—Ren Woxing—and usurps his leadership. After this, DFBB kills his concubines and falls in love with a man Yang Lianting (YLT hereafter). Thereafter, DFBB lets YLT deal with all the administrative work of the sect and stays in a secret boudoir. Another copy of this manuscript is obtained by Hua Mountain School, but Linghu Chong (LHC hereafter), who is the leading character of the whole story, refuses to pocket it, and so keeps his genitals intact. Throughout this book, LHC is loved by three women, including the daughter of Ren Woxing—Ren Yingying (RYY hereafter).

After RYY gradually wins the heart of LHC, she persuades him to collaborate with her and her father's trusted followers to form a group to help her father resume leadership. The group saves Ren Woxing from prison and then sneaks into DFBB's boudoir by holding YLT hostage. Jin Yong had used the Chinese character *yao* (demon or monster) five times to indirectly describe DFBB in the eyes of the group, emphasizing "normal" people's anxieties about DFBB. In their eyes, DFBB's pink clothes, makeup, and caring behavior toward LYT were both *qiguai* (weird) and *e'xin* (disgusting).[8] Since DFBB is invincible, RYY tries to attack YLT to distract DFBB. In rescuing YLT, DFBB is killed. After that, Ren Woxing resumes his position as the sect's hierarch. In the end, LHC and RYY are said to live happily together in seclusion.

Generally speaking, Jin Yong's descriptions of DFBB are dramatic and unrealistic; and he himself had admitted that self-castration is not a required condition for gay relations in the postscript of the newly edited version.[9] In fact, Jin Yong's intentions were in another realm: criticism of mainland China's party politics during the Great Cultural Revolution (1966–1976). Some critics claimed that DFBB could be read as a representation of Mao Zedong, Lin Biao, or other political leaders in the Chinese Communist Party at that time.[10] Actually, there is a long tradition in China for literati and historians to interpret "social anomalies such as dislocations in gender as implicative of moral disruption in the broader political cosmos."[11] Seen in this light, it is fair to say that Jin Yong had achieved political criticism at the cost of exploring DFBB's love, gender, and sexual life.

Tsui Hark, Transgender Casting, and Hong Kong's Postcolonial Experiences

Thanks to Tsui's film *Swordsman II* (1991),[12] DFBB has transformed from an "abnormal monster" into a "cross-dressing goddess."[13] Jin Yong had been strongly opposed to the casting of a female star—Brigitte Lin (Lin Ching-hsia)—in this male role, for fear that Lin was too beautiful to play a male role and portray a part in a male homosexual relationship.[14] However, Tsui had insisted on using Lin, and this film turned out to be a huge success.

At the beginning of this movie, DFBB appears as the hierarch of the sect. LHC (played by Jet Li Lianjie) bumps into him and misrecognizes him as a woman, and the two fall in love at first sight. RYY loves LHC, but he loves DFBB without knowing his true identity as the male hierarch of the "vicious" sect; DFBB has a female concubine named Cici who loves him very much, but he begins to turn his affection from Cici to LHC.[15] One night, when LHC sneaks into DFBB's room, he bumps into the "woman" he misses so much. In the name of love, DFBB has asked Cici, the "true" woman, to pretend to be him and sleep with LHC. Finally, when the group of RYY, her father, and LHC attacks DFBB, LHC discovers that the "woman" he loves is actually the notorious self-castrated man—DFBB. Ren Woxing and RYY laugh about DFBB's transgender identity, while LHC is shocked and furious. When the group defeats DFBB, LHC tries very hard to save DFBB and asks him whether he was the "woman" who had slept with him. DFBB refuses to answer this question to make LHC remember him forever, and then DFBB commits suicide.

This film is centered on DFBB and LHC's love, instead of power struggles and martial arts fighting. But this love story is by no means "staid, coherent, and heterosexual."[16] There is a split between the fictional male character DFBB and the real female star Lin. For Chow Wah Shan, this film is just a heterosexual clichéd romance packaged as a seemingly gay love story, for it had defused all the anxieties that could have been aroused in many viewers by gay love if the role had been played by a male actor.[17] Yau Ching's attitude, however, was more balanced, with the claim that the love story in this film had allowed two different kinds of spectatorial pleasure at the same time, for it could be read as gay love (between DFBB and LHC) or heterosexual romance (between Jet Li and Bridgett Lin) at different moments by different audiences.[18] Most recently, Helen Hok-Sze Leung has pointed out that we are well advised to read DFBB as a transgender woman whose subjectivities were self-fashioned gradually in the film.[19]

In addition to representing love stories, Tsui had not given up political sarcasm, for he had crystallized Jin Yong's vague metaphor into evident embodiment: not only had he made DFBB recite a famous poem written by Mao Zedong in his film, he had also dressed DFBB in bright red, which is an evident mark of Maoist China.[20] To Yau, DFBB might represent the forcible, authoritarian political power of the People's Republic of China (PRC) government particularly as feared by Hong Kong people before the coming of the 1997 handover;[21] however, Roland Chu contended that the most radical dynamic of pleasure in this film is the prospect of loving the monster: the taboo of embracing the abject.[22] Whether feared or embraced, DFBB could be seen as a symptom of the complicated sentiments toward the political pressures of 1997 in Hong Kong. If, as Leung has insightfully observed, a contemporary queer culture in Hong Kong is paradigmatic of the city's postcolonial experience,[23] then a political reading of Tsui's DFBB is not far fetched. In general, to explore love, gender, and sexuality does not necessarily lead to a dilution of political sarcasm, and Tsui has balanced these themes in a clever way.

Yu Zheng, Miss Dongfang, and the Post-Mao Chinese Television Industry

In post-Mao China, the rapid transformations from a socialist planned economy to a capitalist market economy have brought about various problems in all walks of life. In the television industry, while we have witnessed a dramatic rise in the numbers of TV dramas China produces every year,[24] there are widely circulated worries about their quality. And the *leiju* (shocking dramas) is a new term coined by Chinese netizens to express their disappointment about them. *Swordsman*

(2013) was also called a "shocking drama,"[25] largely because it was produced by Yu Zheng, who is notorious for his history of "copying and pasting," and even plagiarism.[26] Paradoxically, Yu's dramas are always commercially successful, and *Swordsman* is not an exception. After the first-round airing by the Hunan Satellite TV channel in the lunar new year of 2013, *Swordsman* was soon snapped up by various online video companies and other TV stations, becoming that year's most popular mainland Chinese–aired TV drama whose click ratio exceeded 1 billion within one month.[27] Not coincidentally, Joe Chen, the Taiwanese actress who plays DFBB, also had her stardom greatly reignited; Chen's number of fans on Sina Weibo steadily shot up from about 6 million to 30 million within several months after the airing of this TV drama.[28]

In the TV drama, DFBB is a woman whose parents deserted her in a war. In an incident when she is chased by gangs, she is saved by the former hierarch of the sect. She becomes his disciple, joins the sect, and pretends to be a man in public spaces. After many years, she climbs into the position of the hierarch by imprisoning Ren Woxing, thus becoming the most powerful martial arts fighter in that world. One day, she wants to know what true love is and pretends to be a prostitute in a brothel where she encounters LHC. She loves him at first sight, but not vice versa. At first, she is still cross-dressing in men's clothes, but her gender identity is discovered by LHC by accident. This time, LHC is loved by four women, including RYY and DFBB. DFBB takes the initiative to love LHC and sacrifices almost everything for him. LHC is touched and decides to pay her back with his love. However, on the second day of their mutual declaration of love, LHC learns DFBB's true status as the hierarch of the sect, and he wounds her with a sword, breaking up with her. RYY, who has won the heart of LHC, persuades him to collaborate with her to save her father and sneak in to DFBB's boudoir. This time, DFBB is not dead, but she gives up her hierarch's position. Trying very hard to forget LHC but failing, DFBB finally commits suicide to save RYY's life and let her be with LHC in the end.

On the surface, this is a "clean" story: there is a very little relation between DFBB and Mao Zedong, and DFBB is not queer but a "true" woman played by an actress. Compared with Jin Yong's and Tsui's versions, Yu's DFBB seems to have nothing to do with the explorations of either formal politics or gender politics. Given that male homosexuality is the most distinct feature of this legendary queer icon, DFBB's Baidu Post Bar, which is the most prominent online forum of this character, has banned any discussions of the new DFBB and declared that an "authentic" DFBB should never be a woman, but a gay man.[29] As a result, fans of Yu's DFBB have moved to other cyberforums, and fans of Jin Yong and Tsui's DFBB have stayed in this forum. Now that the new DFBB is a female character played by a female star, somewhat contradictorily, both TV industrial practitioners and online fans have not forgotten nor stopped imagining and articulating this characters' queer possibilities. In what follows, I will closely examine the various queer reading tactics that have emerged in online fan communities.

Gay Reading and the *Tongzhi* Movement in Cyberspace

Among all the three basic reading positions, the gay reading might be the most surprising on account of the new DFBB's female identity, and the fact that the new DFBB has been excluded from DFBB's Baidu Post Bar is another indication that a female DFBB might be "harmful" for fans who want to understand the love between DFBB and LHC as a gay story. Understandable maybe, but Yu's story of DFBB and LHC could also be enjoyed imaginatively by some fans as a gay love, and in any case their criticisms were not about the casting but instead involved other factors related to industrial and social structures:

> No matter what specific version, no matter how feminine DFBB is trying to be, and even if you cast an actress into this role, he is essentially a man. As a result, no matter what changes the director can make, he is never able to make two men together in the ending. Otherwise, it will be censored. (Fan_no.01)

> Because the male-male love could not be accepted by "the party" . . . what am I saying? OMG (Fan_no.02)

> This TV drama educated us that gay love would never come into fruition, persuading us to go back to those mainstream values. It is quite boring! (Fan_no.03)

These fans were disappointed by the failure of a gay love, and they tried to understand it (or its nonexistence) as a result of media representation politics in terms of gay identities that are deeply situated in the social contexts of the originating place: mainland China's media censorship systems controlled by the party-state. TV dramas, as the most popular entertainment in contemporary China, have always been strictly monitored and regulated by the State Administration of Press, Publication, Radio, Film and Television. Scholarship on Chinese TV industry studies has pointed out that the state regulations on TV dramas, in addition to being harsh, are also unclear and complicated. The lack of explicit censorship criteria tends to encourage self-censorship, and "television dramas broadcast during prime time on CCTV and provincial satellite channels are the most heavily censored and monitored because of their vast audience size."[30] Since *Swordsman* had been broadcast by the Hunan Satellite TV channel, the most popular TV channel in contemporary China, it is almost impossible for it to represent a consummated gay love between two leading players. Nonetheless, fans were not only highly aware of such censorship system preferences, they also related gay readings to Internet gay and lesbian movements:

> If I remember correctly, DFBB must be a castrated man . . . and there is a love story between the Hero LHC and DFBB in this new TV drama. . . . Is it going to exhibit "engaging in gay love" (*gaoji*) in public? If so, let me wish them happy together forever! #Supporting *Tongzhi* and Be Against the Discrimination# (Fan_no.04)

Reading DFBB as a gay man, this fan linked popular culture to activism about gender politics and *tongzhi* (gay) issues. There is a slogan attached after the fan's comments, with the mark # in both the beginning and end. The use of such double marks operates as a special function in Weibo so that words placed between them can be searched much more easily. Notably, the slogan comes from the ongoing antidiscrimination *tongzhi* movement launched by the Hong Kong lesbian star Denise Ho Wan See.[31] So, interconnectedness between popular culture and politics is evident here. Reading the new DFBB as a gay man, thus, could result in either criticisms about gay representations in mainstream TV media or articulations of public awareness of *tongzhi* movements in the contemporary Chinese cyberspace.

Perhaps more interesting, the industry also promoted gay readings to garner attention in cyberspace. For example, the online video company LeTV (*leshi* TV) that had bought the copyright of this drama had even announced its intention to invite audience members to celebrate the male-male romantic plots:

> The most respectable character in this drama is DFBB. In order to fulfill the potential of gay love in this drama, and for LHC, he had done a transsexual operation to become a woman! Friends, let's engage in gay loves![32]

As an online video company, LeTV enjoys relatively more freedom than satellite TV stations do in terms of content censorship, but such "celebration" of male homosexuality by TV industrial discourses is a double-edged sword: at first glance, it seems to contribute to the visibility of male homosexuality in media discourses; nonetheless, its logic of gay love is, of course, unrealistic, because there is no necessity for a man to become a woman to engage in a gay relationship. Not insignificantly, this is appropriation of DFBB's historical status as a queer icon by industry practitioners to create a media buzz and maximize profits. Topics of male homosexuality, such as "let's engage in gay loves," have proved to be both sensational and controversial, resulting in high click rates in the industry's online threads and posts. In any case, it appears that reading the new DFBB as a gay man is possible, both in fan communities and industry discourses.

Heterosexuality, Leftover Women, and the Backlash against Feminism in Post-Mao China

There are also other fans who read the new DFBB as a "pure" woman and her love with LHC as a heterosexual romance between a beautiful woman and a handsome man. In the process of reading DFBB as a heterosexual love seeker, discourses of feminism and patriarchy have also emerged in fan communities:

> Since LHC had mentioned that DFBB is the person who treated him most well, why did he dump her and end up together with RYY? His excuse is rather fake, since both DFBB and RYY are members of the Sect. The only thing I learnt from it is that men tend to be afraid of women who are stronger than them! It is ridiculous! (Fan_no.05)

This fan was complaining that Chinese men tend to marry weaker women, thus criticizing men's spousal-choice tastes. In post-Mao China, there is an implicit yet powerful gendered clause stipulating that women marry up and men marry down, and any vaguely respectable man would not be willing to practice hypergamy at any rate—preferring instead to preserve his reputation.[33] With this logic, as the most powerful martial arts fighter and the hierarch of the biggest school in that world, DFBB's social status as a woman is too high for marriage with a man; thus, the love between DFBB and LHC is doomed to fail. In this light, some fans have pointed out that the new DFBB could be understood as a representative example of an embarrassed, often stigmatized, and widely existent group of women in post-Mao China—*shengnü* (leftover women):

> I think DFBB is a *shengnü*, she is old and powerful, just like other *shengnü* around us now. You know, it is difficult for a *shengnü* to get married. This drama is another boring *shengnü* story in today's Chinese TV circles. (Fan_no.06)

"Leftover woman" is a derogatory term used to describe a woman with "three highs": highly educated, high professional status, and a relatively high age (in the "marriage market") in post-Mao China. These women's single status is usually deemed not independent and liberated but shameful and disgraceful. In Sandy To's study, the fifty "leftover woman" interviewed were ones who wanted to lead "conventional" marital lives and had actively tried many strategies to find suitable partners; however, few of them have been successful in love and marriage, evidencing the popularity of the "male-as-superior" pattern of marriage partner choice in post-Mao China. Being both superior and older, the new DFBB seems to be unmarriageable, like many "leftover women" in this patriarchal Chinese society.

Another leftover-women researcher, Leta Hong Fincher, has compared women's status in Maoist China with that in post-Mao China, contending that gains in women's rights related to the state feminist slogan "women hold up half the sky" proclaimed by Mao have been gradually eroded in China's postsocialist era. Actually, there are no "leftover" women; it is a label concocted by the government to achieve demographic goals linked to promoting marriage, population planning, and maintaining social stability.[34] More importantly, the media has played a pivotal role in constructing, sensationalizing, and stigmatizing the myth of the "leftover" women.[35] Concomitantly, we have witnessed a series of recent TV dramas featuring the characters of various "leftover" women in China, in which these women's only goal is to find a true love and marry, such as *Wanhun* (Late marriage, 2010), *Yiyi xiangqianchong* (Go, Yiyi go!, 2010), *Shengnü de xinhun shenghuo* (The marriage lives of a leftover woman, 2011), *Zanmen jiehunba* (We get married, 2013), *Yipu erzhu* (A servant of two masters, 2014), etc. Most of these dramas are centered on one plotline: a "leftover" woman tries very hard to get married and has to overcome all sorts of difficulties and obstacles in the processes of seeking love; none of them remain happy and comfortable as single women, though they all excel in different careers. In our case, DFBB seems to be tired of her professional status, and all she wants is a "true love," and she tries very hard to achieve this goal. She is a desperate "leftover" woman in this vision, and fan no. 06 expressed boredom about watching such stories again and again, thus criticizing the media's double stakes in both capitalizing on and dramatizing the myth of "leftover" women.

I am not celebrating Yu's drama's contributions to transposing a post-Mao social problem onto an old story created in the Maoist era; in fact, Yu has never used the discourse of "leftover" women to promote his drama. What I want to stress, however, is that this "heterosexual reading position" proposed by some fans has enriched our understanding of this legendary queer icon, which can hardly be achieved in Jin Yong's and Tsui's versions. Reading the new DFBB as a heterosexual love–seeking "leftover" woman, hence, could also be productive, for it might lead to a feminist criticism that is rather important and relevant in post-Mao China when patriarchy and gender inequality have had a resurgence in spite of the so-called economic miracle.

Lesbian Love, Incest Taboo, and Subcharacters in Fan-Made Stories

Fans not only read the new DFBB in complicated and critical ways, they also participate in retelling DFBB's stories in their own versions, enriching the images of DFBB in creative and innovative respects. Their stories are told in various fan-made artifacts, such as fan fiction, videos and MVs, photo collages, and webisodes. A thorough study of these fan stories is beyond this chapter's scope, but most of these stories share the same motif: star-centered character subdividing. While most existing fan studies use fan fictions as objects of analysis,[36] in this case, webisodes are the most mature and developed fan artifacts, which till now have not received enough academic attention. Usually, webisodes are minidramas composed of several or dozens of episodes and circulated online.[37] My focus, then, is on how this shared motif works in these fan-made webisodes.

In the TV drama, Yu designed dozens of costumes for the new DFBB to change her gender identity in different situations: sometimes she has to pretend to be a man, but sometimes she can disclose her true identity as a woman. Accordingly, fans have creatively made their own DFBB stories by dividing DFBB's characters into several subcharacters, some male dressed and some female dressed, and they are all played by the same star, Chen. In terms of plot narrative, a common depiction of these subcharacters' family relations, names, costumes, and personalities is like this one provided by fan no. 07, who called her story *The Dongfang Family* (*Dongfang nayijiazi*, 2013) (see Figure 6.1):

1. The older sister: Dongfang Bubai (in female and male red formal costume of the hierarch of the sect), powerful and domineering
2. The older brother: Dong Fangbo (in male casual costume), talented and caring

3. The younger sister: Dongfang Bai (in female casual costume), haughty and lovely
4. The youngest brother: Dong Bofang (in male casual costume with a black hat), vivacious and humorous

Figure 6.1

Fan-made photo collage: *The Dongfang Family*.

Fan no. 07's work is representative of this motif: these four subcharacters are the absolute leading roles, who fall in love with each other in a promiscuous way in different fan works, while other characters have all become supporting, if not redundant. For example, LHC, who used to be the central role in every official version, is usually mocked or trivialized in these fan stories. Many fan artifacts are based on *The Dongfang Family*'s narrative structure, including fan webisodes *Anecdotes of the New Swordsman* (*Xin xiao'ao jianghu waizhuan*, 2013), *The Four Dongfang Babies' Mini Theater* (*Dongfang sibaojia de xiaojuchang*, 2013), *The Dongfang Family's Theater* (*Dongfang yijia juchang*, 2013), *The Double Dong* (*Shuangdong*, 2013), and *Dongfang Encounters Dongfang* (*Dongfang yudao Dongfang*, 2013). Usually, the subcharacters of the new DFBB are natural brother and sisters in one family; otherwise, it is hard to explain why they look the same and are played by one actress. Not only do the family members engage in love relations, they sometimes have sex with each other. Scholarship has already indicated that some fans have a particular investment in incest storylines,[38] and there is a popular subgenre—father and son incest love—in Chinese BL stories;[39] it comes as no surprise that fans in this case have broken the incest taboo to remake their own DFBB in the realms of fantasy and storytelling.

And such incestuous love and sex relations are also lesbian because these fan artifacts are star centered. As the new DFBB is prohibited in DFBB's Baidu Post Bar, many of the new fans come to Chen's Baidu Post Bar to develop their fan cultures, and the fan-made artifacts that use this motif are generally developed, posted, and circulated on Chen's Baidu Post Bar, emphasizing the salience of Chen's stardom in fans' stories of DFBB. In the context of a star-centered fandom, the love and sex relations among the family members are not only incestuous but also lesbian, for all the characters are actually played by the same female star. In Figure 6.2, for example, we can see the possibilities of promiscuous lesbian relations among different subcharacters of DFBB who are all played by Chen.

Figure 6.2
Photo collage of the queer family.

The lesbian readings, thus, could be identified here. In these fan-made webisodes, it is much more desirable for the new DFBB to experience love among the subcharacters, or to love herself, than love the so-called Zha Chong (the scumbag LHC). (Because he does not return DFBB's love and has wounded her for an inexplicable reason, he is thought by these fans to be a scumbag.) Many fans have expressed strong disdain for LHC and sympathy toward DFBB, for instance:

> LHC does not deserve our Miss Dongfang; I'd prefer to see love between Dongfang Bubai and Dongfang Bai, instead of a heart-breaking love between LHC and DFBB. (Fan no. 08)

Rather than regretting a failed love between LHC and DFBB, the fans have remade their own versions of the new DFBB to satisfy their own desires. Almost all the stories that use this shared motif are related in happy and pleasant tones, superseding the heartbroken sentiments in Yu's official TV drama. But this shared motif is not without its limitations. Usually, when LHC wants to develop a gay relationship with DFBB's subcharacters or any other male character, he is despised, pushed away, or intimidated (see Figure 6.3).

Similar sentiments could also be found in another long webisode *Five Joes Make One Drama*, in which one of the male subcharacters of DFBB has directly expressed his hatred by saying, "Throughout my life, I have hated gays the

Figure 6.3
A capture from a fan-made webisode *Anecdotes of the New Swordsman*. DFBB's male subcharacter (left) had pushed away LHC (right), saying: "Get out of here! Ye [a self-proclaimed term for a man in powerful status] don't engage in gay relations!"

most," when he finds that LHC and other male characters are intimate. I suggest two considerations here. One is that fans who made these stories using this shared motif might support lesbian readings while resisting gay readings; the other is that lesbian readings in fantasy stories do not guarantee a prohomosexuality political expression in this case. This is not to devalue fan stories, because "queer positions, queer readings, and queer pleasures are part of a reception space that stands simultaneously beside and within that created by heterosexual and straight positions,"[40] as Alexander Doty has observed. And Western research on slash has also argued that, for some fans, a queer awareness is irrelevant or intrusive in slash stories.[41] Thus, the coexistence of the lesbian family and sentiments of homophobia in these fan-made stories that share the same motif reverberates with other scholars' claims about the entanglements of queer and heteronormative sentiments.

Coda

After studying the online fan cultures of the new DFBB mainly through fan comments and fan-made webisodes, I have identified and analyzed three queer reading positions: gay readings, heterosexual readings, and lesbian readings. Given that the new DFBB is a woman in Yu's new TV drama, these queer reading tactics are much more creative, innovative, and even radical than official stories churned out by the television industry in post-Mao China. Fans' creative readings have transformed a shocking drama into a valuable cultural resource that could be explored in multiple directions with multiple consequences.

This chapter contributes to current research in three ways: first, this reception study tries to revolutionize Jin Yong studies by adopting a newly developed fan studies' approach to enrich our understandings of Jin Yong's classic characters. For decades, scholars have written on Jin Yong mainly through the lens of textual analysis, and it is high time to rejuvenate Jin Yong studies with reception studies' theoretical rigor given the huge impact of Jin Yong's works in the Chinese communities all over the world. Furthermore, since English studies of Jin Yong are also rare, this chapter aims to bring about more recognition and awareness of Jin Yong studies' significance in international academia. Second, this chapter may extend and complicate our understanding of fan cultures by going beyond fan fiction studies to use fan-made webisodes as objects of analysis. As I argued earlier, Chen's stardom has played a pivotal role in articulating lesbian expressions in fan webisodes in ways that cannot be achieved in fan fiction. Thus, and third, for gender and queer studies, this chapter provides us with a much more complicated and entangled case to investigate the simultaneous symbiosis and conflicts of queer and nonqueer articulations in fan cultures; for example, heterosexual readings exist besides gay and lesbian readings, and within lesbian readings there are also antigay expressions.

Acknowledgments

This chapter received a start-up research grant from the Education University of Hong Kong, as research titled *Dongfang Bubai's Queer Fandom in Contemporary Chinese Cyberspaces* (RG 72/2014–2015R).

Notes

1. David Wang, "Xu" [Preface], in *Jin Yong xiaoshuo guoji xueshu yantaohui lunwenji* [Proceedings of the International Conference on Jin Yong's Novels], ed. Qiu Gui Wang (Taipei: Yuan-Liou Publishing, 1999), i.
2. Chen Pingyuan, *Wuxia xiaoshuo leixing yanjiu* [Genre studies of martial arts novels] (Beijing: People's Literature Publishing, 1992); Yan Jiayan, *Jin Yong xiaoshuo lungao* [Essays on Jin Yong's novels] (Beijing: Peking University Press, 2007); Chen Mo, *Renwu Jin Yong* [Characters of Jin Yong] (Beijing: Oriental Publishing, 2008).
3. There are roughly three versions of Jin Yong's novels: the original serial version published in newspapers from 1955 to 1972, the second book version published in 1980s, and the newly edited book version published in the 2000s. Compared to other novels of Jin Yong, *The Smiling, Proud Wanderer* has just been slightly modified, and this chapter uses the newly edited book version published by Minghe She (Hong Kong) in 2006.
4. "Wenxue renwu renqi paihangbang" [The popularity ranking of literary characters], Baidu Post Bar, accessed July 14, 2015, http://tieba.baidu.com/sign/index?kw=%E4%B8%9C%E6%96%B9%E4%B8%8D%E8%B4%A5&ie=utf-8#current_forum.
5. "Meili wudi: Xiao'ao Jianghu sishinian beigaibian N ci" [The unparalleled charm: The smiling, proud wanderer has been remade for N times within four decades], *China News*, July 10, 2013, accessed July 14, 2015, http://finance.chinanews.com/it/2013/07-10/5025779.shtml.
6. Christine Hine, *Virtual Ethnography* (London: Sage, 2000); Angela Cora Garcia et al., "Ethnographic Approaches to the Internet and Computer-Mediated Communication," *Journal of Contemporary Ethnography* 38.1 (2009): 52–84. Actually, my position in this research follows a fan studies' classic tradition—that of the "aca-fan," as proposed by Henry Jenkins. More specifically, I have long been a fan of Jin Yong, Hong Kong cinema, and Chinese TV dramas. Henry Jenkins, *Fans, Bloggers, and Gamers: Exploring Participatory Culture* (New York: New York University Press, 2006), 11–12.
7. The drama's official Weibo account was highly active during the production and first-round airing period from September 3, 2012, to April 7, 2013, producing 1,135 threads and still attracting 72,766 followers even in the middle of 2015, though the number of comments and retweets are too huge and fluid to be counted. And it had retweeted various information from other Weibo players, such as stars, directors, TV stations, electronic and traditional media, as well as fan clubs and individual fans. "The TV Drama Swordsman," *Sina Weibo*, accessed July 14, 2015, http://www.weibo.com/xajh2012. As I will point out later, DFBB's Baidu Post Bar has banned any discussion of the new DFBB, thus, the fans of the new DFBB have generally moved to other cyberspaces, especially Chen's Baidu Post Bar, to develop their fandom.
8. Jin Yong, *Xiao'ao Jianghu* [The smiling, proud wanderer] (Hong Kong: Minghe She, 2006), 1326.
9. Jin, *Xiao'ao Jianghu*, 1752.

10. Margaret Ng, *Jin Yong xiaoshuo de nanzi* [The men in Jin Yong's novels] (Taipei: Yuan-Liou Publishing, 1998), 109; Chen Fangying, "*Xiao'ao Jianghu* zhong de yishu yu renwu" [The arts and characters in *The Smiling, Proud Wanderer*], in *Jin Yong xiaoshuo guoji xueshu yantaohui lunwenji* [Proceedings of the International Conference on Jin Yong's Novels], ed. Qiu Gui Wang (Taipei: Yuan-Liou Publishing, 1999), 232.
11. Judith Zeitlin, *Historian of the Strange: Pu Songling and the Chinese Classical Tale* (Stanford, CA: Stanford University Press, 1993), 104; Howard Chiang, "Archiving Peripheral Taiwan: The Prodigy of the Human and Historical Narration," *Radical History Review* 120 (2014): 209.
12. *Swordsman II* (1991) is a sequel to *Swordsman* (1990), which was more "faithful" to Jin Yong's novels, and its plotlines resolve around LHC.
13. Chow Wah Shan, *Tongzhi lun* [On *tongzhi*] (Hong Kong: Hong Kong Homosexual Research Society, 1995), 298.
14. Akiko Tetsuy, *Yongyuan de Lin Ching Hsia* [The last star of the East: Brigitte Lin Ching Hsia and her films] (Taipei: Locus Publishing, 2008), 79.
15. There is no YLT in the movie.
16. Roland Chu, "*Swordsman II* and *The East Is Red*: The 'Hong Kong Film', Entertainment, and Gender," *Bright Lights: Film Journal*, January 1, 2001, accessed July 14, 2015, http://brightlightsfilm.com/swordsman-ii-east-red-hong-kong-film-entertainment-gender.
17. Chow, *Tongzhi lun*, 275–318.
18. Yau Ching, *Xingbie guangying: Xianggang dianying zhongde xing yu xingbie wenhua yanjiu* [Sexing shadows: Gender and sexualities in Hong Kong cinema] (Hong Kong: Hong Kong Film Critics Society, 2005), 85–91.
19. Helen Hok-Sze Leung, *Undercurrents: Queer Culture and Postcolonial Hong Kong* (Vancouver: University of British Columbia Press, 2008), 65–84.
20. Moreover, in 1993, he had produced a sequel of this film titled *Dongfang Bubai zhi fengyun zaiqi* in Chinese and *East Is Red* in English. And the latter is a very popular socialist song in China, whose lyrics link Mao Zedong to the Red Sun rising from the East.
21. Yau, *Xingbie guangying*, 90.
22. Chu, "*Swordsman II*."
23. Leung, *Undercurrents*, 5.
24. In 2012, China became the biggest TV drama–producing country in the world, with an annual output of 170,000 episodes, while the US output is 5,000 episodes. "Dianshiju nianchanliang" [The annual output of TV dramas], *Sina News*, August 27, 2013, accessed July 14, 2015, http://dailynews.sina.com/gb/ent/tv/sinacn/20130827/02294909558.html.
25. "Leiju *Xiao'ao Jianghu* weihe hong? Jiulinghou: Mei Yu Zheng sheizhi Jin Yong" [Why is the shocking drama swordsman so popular? The post-1990s: We wouldn't know Jin Yong if there were no Yu Zheng], *Xinhua Net*, February 27, 2013, accessed July 14, 2015, http://education.news.cn/2013-02/27/c_124393012.htm.
26. "Qiong Yao qisu Yu Zheng chaoxi" [Qiong Yao has sued Yu Zheng for plagiarism], *Sina Entertainment*, December 26, 2014, accessed July 14, 2015, http://ent.sina.com.cn/f/v/qyjbyz/.
27. "Dianshiju wangluo dianjilü" [The online click ratio of TV dramas], *Sina Entertainment*, April 16, 2013, accessed December 26, 2014, http://ent.sina.com.cn/v/m/2013-04-16/14283901301.shtml.

28. "Chen Chiao En's Weibo," *Sina Weibo*, accessed December 26, 2014, http://www.weibo.com/chenchiaoen.
29. "Benba bu zhichi xinban Dongfang guniang" [The Miss Dongfang in the new version will not be supported in our forum], Baidu Post Bar, February 23, 2013, accessed July 14, 2015, http://tieba.baidu.com/p/2179038616.
30. Ruoyun Bai, *Staging Corruption: Chinese Television and Politics* (Vancouver: University of British Columbia Press, 2014), 54–63.
31. Coincidently, this movement had been launched just before the first-round airing of this drama. This movement, though it is based in Hong Kong, has been supported by other mainland Chinese and Taiwanese stars (such as Zhou Xun and Ariel Lin), in ways that have circulated in Chinese cyberspaces. "He Yunshi faqi chengtongzhi fanqishi yundong" [Ho Wan See Denise launches a movement of 'supporting the homosexuals and be against the discriminations'], *Sina Ladies*, January 15, 2013, accessed December 27, 2014, http://eladies.sina.com.cn/qg/2013/0115/15441207565.shtml. See Eva Li's chapter in this book on Ho's fandom.
32. "Zheshi yige gaoji de shidai" [This is an era of engaging in gay love!], *Sina Weibo*, February 16, 2013, accessed December 27, 2014, https://freeweibo.com/weibo/3546426354853926.
33. Sandy To, *China's Leftover Women: Late Marriage among Professional Women and Its Consequences* (New York: Routledge, 2015), 38.
34. Leta Hong Fincher, *Leftover Women: The Resurgence of Gender Inequality in China* (London: Zed Books, 2014), 6.
35. Ibid., 2.
36. Fan fiction studies, from the inception of fan studies in the early 1990s, has dominated fan studies throughout recent decades. Important works include: Henry Jenkins, *Textual Poachers: Television Fans and Participatory Culture* (New York: Routledge, 1992); Christine Scodari and Jenna L. Felder, "Creating a Pocket Universe: 'Shippers,' Fan Fiction, and the *X-Files* Online," *Communication Studies* 51.3 (2000): 238–57; Karen Hellekson and Kristina Busse, eds., *Fan Fiction and Fan Communities in the Age of the Internet: New Essays* (Jefferson, NC: McFarland, 2006); Karen Hellekson and Kristina Busse, eds., *The Fan Fiction Studies Reader* (Iowa City: University of Iowa Press, 2014).
37. Technically, fans cut video clips from Yu's drama and re-edit them into a new video, adding some comic and cartoon graphics, and they make subtitles for it; for the audio part, fans look for various background music and audio effect clips from different sources, such as video games and other films and TV programs. Most of these webisodes are well made, with titles and theme songs, and some of them are even dubbed by fans themselves or by borrowing audio clips from Chen's other TV dramas.
38. Dru Pagliassotti, "GloBLisation and Hybridisation: Publishers' Strategies for Bringing Boys' Love to the United States," *Intersections: Gender and Sexuality in Asia and the Pacific* 20 (2009), accessed July 14, 2015, http://intersections.anu.edu.au/issue20/pagliassotti.htm.
39. Yanrui Xu and Ling Yang, "Forbidden Love: Incest, Generational Conflict, and the Erotics of Power in Chinese BL Fiction," *Journal of Graphic Novels and Comics* 4.1 (2013): 30–43.
40. Alexander Doty, *Making Things Perfectly Queer: Interpreting Mass Culture* (Minneapolis: University of Minnesota Press, 1993), 15.

41. Shoshanna Green, Cynthia Jenkins, and Henry Jenkins, "Normal Female Interest in Men Bonking: Selections from *The Terra Nostra Underground* and *Strange Bedfellows*," in *Theorizing Fandom: Fans, Subculture and Identity*, ed. Cheryl Harris and Alison Alexander (Cresskill, NJ: Hampton Press, 1998), 22.

II.

Hong Kong

7
Desiring Queer, Negotiating Normal

Denise Ho (HOCC) Fandom before and after the Coming-Out

Eva Cheuk Yin Li

Introduction

Denise Wan-See Ho (a.k.a. HOCC) is one of the few celebrities in the East Asian Chinese-language entertainment industry to have come out as a lesbian in public. This chapter explores the entanglement and tension in HOCC fandom in Hong Kong between the desire to be queer and the struggle with normativity before and after her coming-out. By adopting the terms "queer" and "normal" as analytical tools, I contextualize the queer fan culture of HOCC by demonstrating the interplay among fans' lived experience, sexual cultures in Hong Kong, and global information flows. Queer reading arises when the boundary between queer and normal is contested. It is fans' frustration with (hetero)normativity that enacts queer fan practices. Nonetheless, living in a heteronormative society also means that fans are constantly seeking or being compelled to normalize and police such practices.

I use "queer" in two ways. The first refers to the process of production of meaning as analogous to a "flexible space for the expression of all aspects of non-, anti-, contra-, and straight cultural production and reception."[1] It is an attitude that goes beyond binarism in gender (male/female) and in sexuality (heterosexuality/homosexuality).[2] Therefore, queer positions and queer readings are not marginal to but always parts of the erotic center of culture because queer often operates within the nonqueer and vice versa.[3] Second, I use "queer" as the provisional academic shorthand for LGBT identities.[4] The scholarship in queer Asia studies has suggested that Western post-Stonewall LGBT identities may not be directly applicable to the hybrid formation of nonheterosexual and nonnormative genders and sexualities in Asia.[5] Instead, these genders and sexualities are the results of the complex interplay between historical trajectories and global forces. In Hong Kong, both the English term "queer" and its Chinese translation *ku'er* (Hanyu pinyin) / *hukji* (Cantonese romanization) are rarely used in everyday life. When referring to or self-identifying as queer, informants of this study used terms such as *gei* (gay), *les* (lesbian), *lyun* (bent), TB (tomboy or butch lesbian), homo (homosexual), *tongzhi/tung zi*,[6] and *zi gei jan* (we).[7]

There are three meanings of "normal" in this chapter. The first is the concept of heteronormativity coined by Michael Warner.[8] Heteronormativity assumes that all social actors are heterosexual and reproductive by default. It is a set of structural and institutional arrangements that privileges certain sexual practices and relationships such as being heterosexual, married, and monogamous.[9] The second meaning of "normal" refers to a conformist type of queer politics that normalizes the differences between homosexuals and heterosexuals. There has been a shift in Anglo-American queer politics since the 1990s from confrontational politics such as coming out and mass protest to normalization stressing integration and respectability, which turns out to be an "antipolitical" politics reducing queer politics to the mere quest for equal rights.[10] Likewise, in Hong Kong, since the decriminalization of male homosexuality in 1991, the local *tongzhi* movement has always preferred normalization over confrontation. This has been further complicated by both the colonial government (1842–1997), which depoliticized local society, and the postcolonial government, which essentialized Chinese culture as social harmony.[11] The third meaning of "normal" in this chapter is the concept of homonormativity coined by Lisa Duggan as a critique of the new organizing principle in contemporary Anglo-American queer politics.[12] Duggan argued that the new emphasis on domesticity and consumption in queer politics has been accompanied and fostered by neoliberal politics, which narrowly defines democracy as the privatization of public, affective, and economic life.[13] Nonetheless, homonormativity is not parallel to nor comparable with heteronormativity since the structure of queer lives is never commensurate with the institutional and structural perpetuation of heterosexuality.[14]

Normal is an impossible ideal for everyone, especially the queer.[15] When discussing sexuality and gender in mainland China and Hong Kong, Yau Ching highlighted the relativity and specificity of normal as an ideal being negotiated and fine-tuned at different historical conjunctures and in different power structures.[16] Yau observed that instead of resisting normativity, queer subjects in China and Hong Kong attempted to access and achieve normativity because of socialization and internalized homophobia. Yau used the example of gay boys' desire to sleep with straight boys to illustrate the paradoxical moment that queers confirmed their impossibility to be normal only when they were being closest to the ideal of normal.[17] Before coming out, the ambivalence of HOCC's sexuality was an important part of her stardom that allowed fans' playful speculation, evidenced by the vibrant queer fan culture. Fans celebrated the pleasure of queer reading but at the same time enacted a kind of self-discipline about it as regards HOCC. After HOCC came out, that is, after her "queerness" was confirmed, instead of fading, the tension between queer and normal has shifted from the heteronormative negotiation of a "proper" female gender and accorded sexuality to the negotiation of a "proper" lesbian embodiment. I argue that the shift is circumscribed by the changing sexual culture and queer politics in Hong Kong regulated by the strategic alliance of postcolonial administration, Chinese family, and religion.

Data for this study are drawn from semi-structured interviews and participant observation conducted between 2009 and 2014: the first stage between February 2009 and May 2010 for my MPhil thesis and the second stage in mid-2014 as part of my PhD research. Informants interviewed in the first stage (n = 13) were recruited from the official fan club of HOCC, the HOCC International Fan Club (HOCC IFC). Informants for the second stage (n = 20) were recruited through snowball sampling, including four who had been interviewed in the first stage.[18] Interviews lasted from thirty minutes to three hours and were conducted in Cantonese or Mandarin. Transcripts were translated into English. In total, I have interviewed twenty-nine self-identified fans of HOCC: twenty-five female and four male whose ages ranged from sixteen to thirty-five. All of them are Hong Kong natives except one, who is from eastern China and had lived in Hong Kong for two years at the time of the interview. Educational background varied from secondary education to graduate school, and years of fandom ranged from four to more than ten years. All the names appearing in this chapter are pseudonyms. In terms of self-identified sexuality, there are eight lesbians, three gay men, eighteen straights, and three "ambivalent" at the time of interview.[19]

Queer reception goes beyond identity politics and one's sexual identities.[20] In particular, most subjects in Chinese societies may not be able to afford to politicize their identities.[21] Furthermore, there are inconsistencies of identity and fan practices, such as lesbian fans denying HOCC's sexuality and straight fans enjoying queer reading. For this purpose, I did not restrict myself to recruiting informants of a particular sexuality.[22] Identities are multiple and relational. Fandom is defined by not only observable practices such as consumption pattern and affective investment[23] but also the fabrication of one's public and intimate life. A fan is also a partner, sibling, offspring, colleague, friend, opinion leader, and so on of other members in the society. Hence, queer fan practices are always relational and situated in a wider nexus of social relations. My multiple positions as an aca-fan researcher, a Hong Kong native, and a cisgender queer woman when engaging with HOCC's texts and interacting with informants well demonstrates the importance of reflexivity and intersectionality of fan practices.[24] This chapter does not aim to generalize HOCC fandom but to present a picture of its queer fan culture fabricated by my informants' stories.

HOCC Stardom[25]

> During my teenage years, I thought of starting a revolution. Revolution is not only about mass protest and being heroic but also standing out and staying firm in one's faith. . . . I have been a persevering person in fans' eyes. To thank them for their support over the years, I shall hold on to what I believe in.[26]

HOCC was born in Hong Kong in 1977 and spent most of her teenage years in Montreal, Canada. She returned to Hong Kong to enter and win the championship of the fifteenth New Talent Quest in 1996 and later became the only female student of Cantopop diva Anita Mui. She established her own music label Goomusic in 2001. In September 2004, she joined the East Asia Music (Holdings) Limited, which granted her autonomy in production, for which she was always grateful. She was one of the best-selling singers in Hong Kong from 2006 to 2014.[27] She was awarded the Golden Prize of Female Singer 2006 and voted by audience members as My Favorite Female Singer 2013 in the Ultimate Song Chart Awards Presentation, among many others.[28] Her popularity has grown in transnational and transcultural Chinese societies after she issued two Mandarin albums, which earned her nominations for the Best Mandarin Female Singer at the Golden Melody Awards in 2012 and 2014.[29] In the musical drama *Awakening*, she impersonated the male lead Jia Baoyu and performed 109 shows in mainland China, Hong Kong, Macau, Taiwan, and Singapore between 2011 and 2013. After her active participation in the civil rights movements in Hong Kong, HOCC became an independent musician in 2015.[30]

HOCC can be regarded as an idiosyncratic cultural producer since she is one of the few Hong Kong singers who has repeatedly produced songs with queer overtones. Working closely with queer lyricist Wyman Wong,[31] she has produced songs such as "Rose Mary" ("Lou si maa lei") and its sequel "Goodbye Rose Mary" ("Zoi gin lou si maa lei") on lesbianism,[32] "Rolls Royce" ("Lou si loi si") on male same-sex eroticism, "Coffee in a Cola Bottle" ("Hei seoi zeon leoi dik gaa fe") on transgenderism, and "Illuminati" ("Kwong ming wui") on queer solidarity. In 2005, she produced and performed in the well-received musical stage play *Butterfly Lovers* (*Loeng zuk haa sai cyun kei*), a reinterpretation of the well-known Chinese heterosexual tragic legend *Butterfly Lovers*. Specifically, a twist was added to touch upon homoeroticism and transgenderism.[33] Although HOCC's songs cover a wide range of themes, songs that are said to have queer undertones are often award winning and constantly highlighted by the media in order to further speculate about her sexuality.

HOCC's gender representation has been considered nonnormative since the late 1990s, when most female singers embodied normative or hyper femininity, by, for instance, wearing high heels and skirts, putting on heavy makeup, and having long hair. HOCC had appeared as a long-haired rocker singing songs of soft rock genre in her debut album *first* in 2001. Over the years, HOCC's hair has gotten shorter, and it has become one of the major concerns of fans panicked or excited by gossip about her lesbianism. Apparently, HOCC did not intend to replicate the androgynous style of her predecessors such as Anita Mui and Anthony Yiu-ming Wong. However, she has remained an androgynous icon in the industry.[34] She was given the title Most Handsome in Golden Melody Awards Presentation in 2012 by the Taiwanese media and Prince Charming (*Naam san*) in 2014 by Hong Kong Golden, a popular local Internet forum famous for parody. Although these titles were largely for fun and sometimes mockery, they suggest that HOCC's gender representation has gradually been received less negatively by the public.

Figure 7.1
Yes! Cards (collectible issued by teen magazine *Yes!*) of HOCC, 2001–2004. Courtesy of Kaitlyn.

Furthermore, speculation on HOCC's sexuality and love affairs involving other female celebrities, on which the queer fan culture was largely centered, has been a frequent topic in local tabloids since the early 2000s. Before coming out, HOCC remained low profile and did not deny her alleged homosexuality. Unsurprisingly, this incited more gossip. The following interviews conducted in 2003 demonstrated her attitude toward such speculation:

> In my opinion, being a lesbian or not isn't a big deal.[35]

> If I cared about others speculating on my sexuality, I would not have sung songs like "Goodbye Rose Mary." I have anticipated people discussing . . . I don't feel offended. In fact, I find it funny. . . . It is futile to clarify since there are always excuses to scrutinize my sexuality.[36]

The most well-known piece of gossip was the alleged decade-long same-sex romance with Joey Yung, a top female singer in Hong Kong. The gossip emerged in the early 2000s, but both of them seldom admitted to being a couple in public.[37] HOCC was also alleged to have had a short-term heterosexual relationship with singer Wilfred Lau in the early 2000s. In HOCC fandom, there were two groups of fans, *goocho* and *sigoo*, who respectively supported HOCC's homosexual relationship with Joey Yung (thereafter Goo/Cho) and her heterosexual relationship with Wilfred Lau (thereafter Si/Goo). The name of these pairings was derived from the stars' given name or nickname: *Goo* (mushroom) is the nickname of

HOCC; *Cho* is the first character of Yung's first name in Cantonese; *Si* is the first character of Lau's nickname, *Si hing* (senior male fellow).[38] There were significantly more supporters of Goo/Cho than Si/Goo, because there was more "evidence" supporting the former, and HOCC and Yung individually had more successful careers than Lau in the mid-2000s. Fans who disliked Goo/Cho and insisted on HOCC's heterosexuality were labelled as anti-*goocho*. In addition, whether before or after coming out, HOCC's sexuality has been under public attack.[39] She was occasionally portrayed as an aggressive butch lesbian. For example, a report published by *Apple Daily* on December 1, 2002, called HOCC a "flirty king." Nevertheless, HOCC seldom responded to these reports since she considered sexuality a private matter.

Situating Queer Fan Culture: *Tongzhi* in Hong Kong

Although it is now generally agreed that audience reception and practices are situated in a complex web of transnational exchanges and converging global media culture, local trajectories and social structure remain prominent in shaping these activities. Therefore, I argue that the queer fan culture in HOCC fandom is embedded in the sexual and gender cultures in Hong Kong, in particular, the situation of *tongzhi* there. Meanwhile, fans have negotiated and challenged these norms and regulations by developing various tactics and drawing from transnational and global media.

The *tongzhi* movement in Hong Kong has experienced recurrent backlash since its emergence in the 1980s. After a decade of legal and social debates on the practice of homosexuality triggered by the controversial suicide of Scottish police inspector John MacLennan in 1980,[40] homosexual conduct between males over the age of twenty-one in private was decriminalized in 1991. This consequentially confined local *tongzhi* movement to the fight for private rights and normalization.[41] After the handover of sovereignty in 1997, the postcolonial government, the heteropatriarchal Chinese family, and religion have become the three key sites of dominance that have regulated and shaped sexuality.[42] The postcolonial Special Administrative Region Government established on July 1, 1997, is an illiberal quasi-democratic regime, which has hindered both the queer and nonqueer in fighting for full political rights and citizenship.[43] Second, the notion of the Chinese family in Hong Kong has been established and constructed into a powerful self-regulating site of heteronormativity since the colonial period.[44] The congested living conditions in Hong Kong as a result of the state's capitalist land use policy further closets homosexuality under familial heteronormativity.[45] Third, religion mainly in the form of evangelical activism has been influential in Hong Kong, not only because of the fact that a significant proportion of local education, medical, and social services are provided by Christian churches and organizations, but also on account of the rise of activist groups focusing on sex and morality since 1997.[46] These evangelical activist groups privilege the heterosexual, monogamous, and nuclear family as the ideal prototype for social order and public morality in order to press for their political agenda.[47] The postcolonial government, Chinese family, and religion have formed a strategic alliance that Kong and colleagues called "the trinity of governance."[48] For example, in 2005, the government appointed the Society of Truth and Light, an evangelical group well known for its homophobic stance and activism, to develop the curriculum of moral and civil education for the training of secondary school teachers and principals.[49]

Legally, there are no ordinances against discrimination based on sexual orientation. Same-sex marriage or registered partnership is not recognized. Lesbians and gays are mostly closeted, and homosexuality is rarely discussed publicly.[50] Public acceptance of homosexuality has gradually increased, but public opinion remains divided. A survey launched by the colonial government in 1995 showed a low level of public acceptance.[51] A decade later, divergent views persisted, especially on whether homosexuals were "psychologically normal" and whether homosexuality was in conflict with family and community values.[52] Furthermore, discrimination has been widely observed and experienced by sexual minorities.[53] Deprivation of formal political rights has channeled queer sensibilities in Hong Kong to cultural production and economic consumption since the 1980s.[54] *Tongzhi* spaces such as gay consumption spaces have flourished since the 1990s, and lesbian consumption spaces have also emerged, albeit on a smaller scale.[55] The International Day against Homophobia Hong Kong event since 2005, Hong Kong Pride Parade since 2008 (except in 2010), and Pink Dot Hong Kong (since 2014) have attracted the media spotlight, and the number of participants has grown over the years. The number of participants in the pride parade (more than 9,000) and Pink Dot (more than 15,000) in 2015 hit the record high as reported by their respective organizers.

In terms of gender diversity, although there had been improvements since the late 1990s, recent studies have suggested that gender stereotypes in different realms of social life have prevailed and the public has remained divided on them.[56] Regarding legal protection, support for antidiscrimination legislation has doubled over the past decade, accounting for more than half of the population in 2015.[57] Nonetheless, there is increased opposition to same-sex marriage or registered partnership at the same time.[58] Concerning lesbians in particular, social visibility has been low if not neglected. Although legal criminalization has been focused solely on male homosexuality because sexual intercourse is defined by the presence of male genitalia and the act of penetration, lesbianism has been regulated in different social and intimate spaces such as those of family, church, school, and workplace.[59] Regarding media representation, both lesbians and gays have been negatively portrayed in newspaper and magazines since the 1990s.[60] Biased and heteronormative representations of queers have been observed in prime time television dramas.[61] Recently, there has been an emergent homonormative media culture focused on upper-class celebrity lesbian relationships, usually featuring a wealthy butch providing for a femme partner.[62]

Queer Fan Culture before HOCC's Coming-Out

The queer fan culture of HOCC has been predominantly centered on Goo/Cho. Prior to HOCC's coming out, the ambiguity of her sexuality provided resources for queer fan practices and fantasy. Fantasy is always a playful and significant part of fandom.[63] Fantasy and reality are not mutually exclusive since we can never understand nor experience social reality "objectively."[64] The realms of queer and normal are usually blurred since fans engage in fantasy to negotiate their own identities, desires, and preferences.[65]

> I like HOCC and Yung. If I read news about them going out together, I am happy. I don't know why but I feel happy for HOCC. She said she had loved a person for seven years. That person must be Joey Yung. (Summer, age twenty-seven, straight, interview in 2009)

Fans produced their own knowledge of Goo/Cho by homoeroticizing, collaging, and circulating materials including news, pictures, blog entries, and so on. They justified their activities by upholding the slogan "Imagination Is Free" (*waan soeng si min fai dik*), borrowing from the theme of HOCC's open-air concert "Happiness Is Free" ("Faai lok si min fai dik") in 2009. Summer actively looked for and enjoyed reading information about Goo/Cho. Her everyday routine included carefully reading every photo of HOCC on social networking sites for clues such as couple bracelets, known as "fishing-line bracelets" (*jyu si sau lin*) for their almost unnoticeable thinness.

Felicity (age twenty-four, lesbian, interview in 2008) claimed that she had a lot of "credible insider information" on Goo/Cho. Throughout the three-hour interview, she kept showing me the matching content in HOCC's and Yung's blog entries.[66] Similar to many fans, she refused the *goocho* identification since she believed that if HOCC was known as a lesbian, it would be scandalous and detrimental to her career. Therefore, she felt obliged to keep the discussion discreet.

Informants were aware of managing the boundary between normal and queer in online discussions.[67] Many informants enjoyed queer reading and playing with gossip about HOCC collectively, but they also acknowledged the prevalence of heteronormative values within the fan community and in society in general. The major fan online platform, the HOCC IFC forum,[68] became a site of heteronormativity since HOCC's sexuality and Goo/Cho were considered sensitive topics. Fans were advised not to discuss these issues in the forum because some of them worried that the discussion, usually with "evidence" collected by fans, would attract paparazzi and adversely affect her career in the Chinese-speaking world. Disputes in the forum were common, as in this typical example:

It usually starts with an ordinary thread, for example, discussing recent photos of HOCC. Someone commented "very cool" [*hou jing*] and others agreed by adding "very cool boy" [*hou jing zai*]. Some would condemn this comment and defend HOCC by insisting "very cool girl" [*hou jing neoi*]. . . . Very often those saying "a very cool girl" won at the end. (Megan, age sixteen, lesbian, interview in 2009)

Felicity had a similar experience of being criticized for starting a thread about a news report about the speculated "affairs" of HOCC and Sammi Cheng.[69] Because of the verification system of the IFC forum, some fans did not dare to risk having their account blocked by challenging these subtle regulations of discussion. As a result, some would discuss Goo/Cho elsewhere or in private, remaining silent on such matters in the forum.

Not only was the fan club forum a site of heteronormativity, but fans who expressed high-profile support of Goo/Cho in public, such as at concerts and fan events, were also marginalized. Informants would not easily disclose their attitude toward Goo/Cho at fan events. I have witnessed a small incident suggesting the precariousness of *goocho*s. It was 7:30 p.m. on October 10, 2010, the second night of HOCC's *Supergoo* concert. I was wandering outside the Yellow Gate of the Hong Kong Coliseum, a parking area encircled by barricades, where I met Kaitlyn (age twenty-four, lesbian) and her friends.

Eva: Why are you here? HOCC has burnt incense and cut roasted pig yesterday.[70]

Kaitlyn: (*Whispers*) We're waiting for Joey Yung. She can only come tonight as she has to go overseas tomorrow.

Another friend of Kaitlyn joined the conversation.

Kaitlyn's friend: Are the other people waiting here *goochos* as well?

Kaitlyn: (*Whispers*) Sh!!!!!! Don't speak it loud.

On the same evening, inside the concert hall, when HOCC was singing "Rose Mary," a song about lesbian romance, Yung was seen running along the aisle to her seat in the auditorium. Many fans along the aisle stood up to cheer and witness that moment.[71] Intriguingly, the concert hall, which Kaitlyn and other informants had assumed to be a heteronormative space because of the presence of anti-Goo/Cho fans and paparazzi, became a queer space where many joyously celebrated and welcomed Goo/Cho.

Since Goo/Cho discussion was not welcome in the official forum, some fans relocated their discussion to Internet forums Blur-F and Utopia. Blur-F was a local lesbian Internet forum set up in 1998. There was a thread about a tabloid reporting HOCC, Yung, and Yung's mother having barbecue together at Christmas in 2008, which then quickly became a Goo/Cho discussion thread and attracted HOCC fans, including straight fans who had not heard of Blur-F before.[72] Between December 2008 and January 2010, there were 570 pages of discussion with 11,386 posts.

> I am very happy as I can discuss Goo/Cho freely. I remember somebody warned us about HOCC IFC's reaction in the thread. Then someone else posted the link in HOCC's blog and HOCC's reply seemed to be positive. I was extremely happy! I even wonder if HOCC has a Blur-F account (*chuckles*)! (Felicity, interview in 2009)

Partially inspired by the long discussion thread in Blur-F, Kaitlyn established Utopia (pseudonym) in 2009, which was dedicated to Goo/Cho discussion online. It flourished after HOCC's "accidental" coming out in mid-2009.[73] *Goochos* gathered there to share information and circulate fan fiction and Goo/Cho videos. It served as an alternative space for Goo/Cho discussion and articulation until mid-2012 when Goo/Cho was "officially over."

Fan art, fan video, and femslash were the major forms of queer fan cultural production. Fans collaged photos of HOCC and Yung to highlight the duplication of their clothes and accessory items. Some of them also produced and circulated cartoon illustrations about the interaction between a mushroom, which was the literal meaning of HOCC's nickname Goo, and a rabbit resembling the Dutch cartoon character Miffy, which was Yung's favorite cartoon character. These illustrations often appeared in fan videos as well. All the informants interviewed in the first stage of data collection had either heard of or watched Goo/Cho videos. Fans juxtaposed and edited songs, audio interviews, video clips, and pictures of HOCC and Yung from news reports, Facebook, Weibo,[74] and blogs to articulate the Goo/Cho romance.[75] These fan videos were uploaded to YouTube and reuploaded to mainland Chinese video sharing sites such as Tudou and Youku.[76] They usually showcased photo hunts of HOCC and Yung's duplicated outfits, accessories, and personal belongings. While Kaitlyn equated these videos with those played in wedding banquets, Summer, who self-identified as straight, found them touching even after repeated watching. Some of my informants admitted that they watched Goo/Cho fan videos much more frequently than HOCC's concert DVDs.

Comparatively, femslash was less known to fans. Femslash, also known as female slash, femmeslash, or girlslash, is derived from the term "slash," which refers to fans' writing of romantic or erotic relationships between two male characters; with femslash it is two female characters.[77] There has been limited scholarship on femslash, compared to that on slash.[78] While slash has been argued to be subversive for liberating straight women's erotic desires,[79] it is unclear whether established arguments on slash can be equally applied to the subculturally and erotically distinctive practice of femslash.[80] In HOCC fandom, femslash was largely circulated in a restricted area in Utopia. By the end of May 2009, there were fifty titles contributed by twenty-two registered members. All of them were based on the public personae of HOCC and Yung. Most of the stories used nicknames for HOCC and Yung.[81] New fictional characters were sometimes added. Recontextualization was common, such as stories of life after death, court romance in imperial China, and college romance. Plots mainly focused on the emotional interactions and homosocial bonding between the female characters. The lead female characters (symbolizing HOCC and Yung) were usually well behaved and monogamous. Although it has been observed that femslash fandom in Anglo-American contexts has a strong overlap with the desire for nonfictional lesbian representation,[82] research in non-Western femslash fandom has suggested that nonfictional lesbian topics and the voices of queer-identified fans are often neglected.[83] Goo/Cho femslash deliberately kept explicit lesbian erotic scenes invisible. The only explicit homoerotic scene was the two female protagonists, presumably the characters of HOCC and Yung, caressing each other, and the chapter ended there. This attracted many replies requesting sex scenes in the next chapter. However, the subsequent chapter began with a morning-after scene.

Recognizing readers' strong requests for same-sex erotic scenes, Kaitlyn insisted on keeping the forum "clean," despite the fact that femslash was accessible to a small group of registered forum users only. She was not very worried that the female same-sex erotic content would run afoul of the Control of Obscene and Indecent Articles Ordinance in Hong Kong but was deeply anxious that those materials could attract media attention and consequently harm HOCC's career. This demonstrated the strange relations of queer and normal in the realm of sex; on the one hand, sex is supposed to be "normal" as a human instinct, but, on the other hand, it is never treated "normally" if it disrupts psychic and cultural meanings.[84] Studies on gender and sexuality in Hong Kong also suggested that it was not even "normal" (usual) for women to talk about "normal" sex, that is, straight sex, in both public and private.[85] Furthermore, as 40 percent of educational service in Hong Kong has been provided by Christian organizations, sex-positive education has been banned from or rarely existed in the curricula in these schools.[86]

In keeping with the aforementioned example of a typical fan dispute on HOCC's gender and sexuality, the paradoxical relation between normal and queer is also salient when fans negotiated HOCC's embodiment. *Zhongxing*, which literally means "neutral gender and/or sex," is a generic term in East Asian Chinese societies used to refer to a person (usually female) who does not do gender normatively.[87] HOCC has been repeatedly associated with *zhongxing* in tabloids and fan discussion. As an ambiguous, generic, and depoliticized term, *zhongxing* has proved to be a convenient excuse when fans faced the questioning of others.

> My sister used to worry about my sexuality because I was very sporty and I mixed with tomboys at school. Whenever I watched HOCC on television, she teased me by saying "HOCC is gay." Then I would fire back, "no, she's just *zhongxing*!" It's hilarious when I look back. I was so silly (*chuckles*). (Hannah, age twenty-seven, straight, interview in 2014)

When facing scrutiny within her family, a heteronormative site, Hannah manipulated the ambivalence of *zhongxing* to normalize HOCC's gender representation and divert the questioning of her sexuality. On the other hand, Kaitlyn cared less about the implication of *zhongxing*.

> I am fine as long as she does not look either B or G. (Kaitlyn, interview in 2009)

It is intriguing that Kaitlyn neglected the sex categories of female and male and directly took the localized lesbian genders B and G as points of reference. B or TB stands for tomboy, a localized term approximating butch lesbian in Hong Kong but not entirely reducible to "butch."[88] G or TBG stands for tomboy's girl, a localized term approximating femme lesbian. Presumably, TB dates TBG, but these labels are relational, and there are no agreements on what a TB is.[89] Instead of recognizing and celebrating HOCC's "queer"' embodiment of in-betweenness (being between masculine and feminine and between male and female), Kaitlyn's negotiation of HOCC's embodiment suggested the normalizing tendency toward fixity and the elimination of ambivalence.

Many informants interviewed in both stages of data collection had mixed feelings about *zhongxing*, but they generally welcomed it. Some of them considered *zhongxing* as the least offensive way to hint that one is a TB. Hence, *zhongxing* could be regarded as a normalizing term to "neutralize" (as its Chinese characters literally mean) the social existence and public visibility of women with nonnormative gender and sexuality, usually in the form of being masculine. However, informants' welcoming attitude of using *zhongxing* to describe HOCC legitimized her queer if not ambivalent gender embodiments and sexuality. Without carrying the disapproving implication borne by labels such as tomboy, *naam jan po* (mannish woman), and so on, *zhongxing* made the contestation and negotiation of ambivalence possible and yielded the potentiality to challenge the heteronormative regulation of female bodies.

While there were fans happily engaging in queer fan culture, others struggled. Sheena, who saw herself as "100 percent straight," strongly rejected Goo/Cho, despite having studied in a girls' school for seven years. Lesbian relationships were normatively constructed in girls' schools but also repressed by heteronormative school regimes.[90] During the interview, Sheena hinted that she was used to seeing lesbians around but she disliked lesbian relationships because she considered herself a "traditional" woman who wanted to get married to a member of the opposite sex and then procreate. Therefore, she manipulated the ambiguity that HOCC left for her sexuality:

> I feel very frustrated after reading all the gossip. . . . I force myself to read it because I have to know everything about her. I keep telling myself that those were mere speculations. (Sheena, age eighteen, straight, interview in 2009)

Inconsistencies of fan identities and fan practices were not uncommon. Erin was a tomboyish girl who had a short and trendy hairstyle. Her views on HOCC's sexuality surprised me:

> I am a woman who loves other women. I know how troublesome it can be. I wish HOCC could date a guy. Wilfred Lau treats her well. HOCC has to face so many challenges and criticisms at work. She really needs a guy who can protect her. Deep inside my heart, men and women are different. Men are for women to rely on. HOCC supports me mentally. So I wish that she is supported by another person. Joey Yung does not have this "function" (*chuckles*). I can imagine how HOCC, after a tiring day of work, has to take care of Yung and write letters to comfort her in case they had a fight the night before. (Erin, age eighteen, lesbian, interview in 2009)

In a context where more than three-quarters of the population had observed discrimination against *tongzhi* and frequently witnessed the negative portrayal of lesbians and gays in the media,[91] Erin acknowledged the privilege of being heterosexual and wished HOCC to be free from the "troubles" of being a lesbian. Her position not only demonstrated the internalization of heteronormativity and the stigmatization of the queer but also highlighted queers' love-hate relationship with normal.

Turning Points in 2012: "Breakup" and Coming-Out

Elsewhere I have discussed the unlikelihood of fan queer activism in HOCC fandom due to an internal schism over Goo/Cho and external social repression.[92] The internal schism changed drastically in 2012 when two incidents took place. The first was the "end" of Goo/Cho, the decade-long legendary gossip as described by informants. On the afternoon of an ordinary day in June 2012, I received dozens of text messages from (former) informants, friends, and colleagues about this "breaking news." HOCC's alleged ex-boyfriend Wilfred Lau, publicly admitted his relationship with Yung. A few days before this announcement, HOCC posted in Weibo that she felt like she had been "stabbed." Ironically, this was widely perceived to be the "official" end as well as a long overdue recognition of the purported relationship between HOCC and Yung.

> I was heartbroken. After the outbreak of the news, everyone including *goochos* or *sigoo* wept together. Many people in Hong Kong knew their relationship and some may have accepted them as a couple already. Even members of the Hong Kong Golden (where members were mostly homophobic) and BabyKingdom (a conservative local parenting forum) were sympathetic toward HOCC. (Olivia, age twenty-seven, lesbian, interview in 2014)

The second incident was HOCC's coming-out in the Hong Kong Pride Parade on November 10, 2012.

> In the face of discrimination, silence is no longer an option. . . . If I can speak out and say something that might—even in the smallest inkling—push us further down the path toward equal rights, I feel that all of my own reservations and concerns are insignificant.

> I haven't found the right occasion for long. On this occasion of love, peace, and tolerance, I have my friends, colleagues, and family with me. I feel that I have the obligation to stand out and fight for more love, peace, and tolerance. I'd like to say this proudly—I am *tongzhi*!
> I believe that the world can be a better place.[93]

HOCC's coming-out can be read as the direct response to the discontent with the "trinity of governance" in Hong Kong. In subsequent interviews, HOCC admitted that her decision to come out was made only after the Legislative Council rejected the launch of a public consultation regarding the legislation of an ordinance against discrimination based on sexual orientation on November 7, 2012. Although more than 60 percent of the population supported the legislation to protect individuals of different sexualities from discrimination,[94] the legislation had been delayed because half of the legislators in the quasi-democratic system were not elected by universal suffrage and thus not accountable to the public. With the strong influence of evangelical activist groups that supported narrowly defined "traditional Chinese family values," official public consultation about the anti-discrimination ordinance was dropped. After coming out, HOCC cofounded the *tongzhi* group Big Love Alliance with other celebrities, activists, and politicians.[95] She became more vocal and involved in the *tongzhi* movement as well as other social movements, which was welcomed and appreciated by most of my informants.[96]

After coming out, HOCC was said to have a new female partner, but fans were less keen to follow this relationship. Some informants admitted that they enjoyed the pleasure of juxtaposing materials and speculating in secret. Therefore, they lost interest when materials about HOCC and her alleged new partner were all readily available on social networking sites such as Facebook and Instagram. While there were a few fan blogs remembering Goo/Cho, most informants had lost the motivation to follow HOCC's new relationship. Kaitlyn's forum, Utopia, which had been dedicated to Goo/Cho discussion, was restructured for solely discussing HOCC. Nonetheless, the tension between queer and normal did not fade, since heteronormativity remained prevalent both within her fandom and in Hong Kong.

There were fans who (still) struggled with HOCC's lesbianism. Sheena, whom I had interviewed in 2009, was one of them. She continued to develop tactics to normalize HOCC's sexuality:

> I've been O-mouthed [Cantonese slang meaning "gobsmacked"] for the whole day! Whatever. I admire her courage but I don't think it's necessary to come out. If she didn't come out, there would still be room for imagination. Now, nothing is left. I used to be very happy whenever there was gossip about her and male singers. I am not discriminating against homosexuals.... But I am a very traditional person. I will accept her as bisexual because Lau used to be her boyfriend. She's not a lesbian. (Sheena, age twenty-three, straight, interview in 2014)

In spite of her denial of HOCC's lesbianism, Sheena remained a faithful supporter of HOCC's participation in social movements, even though she did not see the need to fight for *tongzhi* rights. Sheena's attitude reflected a heteronormative sex hierarchy, where bisexuality ("half-normal") is less discriminated against than homosexuality ("abnormal"). By emphasizing her nondiscriminatory attitude toward bisexuality, Sheena tried to normalize her hidden homophobic sentiments. Therefore, she was not only normalizing her hierarchy of queers but also her beliefs and values. Nonetheless, this hierarchy varied among different fans. For example, Kaitlyn, who used to be a lesbian, and Joyce, whose self-identified sexuality was "ambivalent," heavily denounced Yung's bisexuality as "unfaithful." Their view resembles the dualistic (hetero/homosexuality) sex hierarchy that stigmatizes bisexuality and undermines the agency of the individual sexual subject. It also demonstrates the marginalization of bisexuality within sexual minorities.[97]

Discussion about the homonormative code of "proper" lesbian embodiment also arose after HOCC's coming out. Hazel expressed her discontent with HOCC's coming-out outfit:

> It would be better if she was less boyish on that day. She was very manly. Her hairstyle was boyish and she dressed herself in a white top, black suit jacket, and sunglasses. Maybe she wants to present herself as a tough woman.... I'd prefer her coming out in a more feminine outfit. That would be more convincing. (Hazel, age twenty-nine, lesbian, interview in 2014)

Figure 7.2
HOCC in the Hong Kong Pride Parade on November 10, 2012. Courtesy of *Apple Daily Hong Kong*.

Many informants noticed that there has been an increased frequency of HOCC dressing in feminine and sexy outfits. For example, she wore a Louis Vuitton deep-V dress at the Golden Melody Awards Presentation in 2014 and showed her half-naked upper body on the cover of *Marie Claire* (Taiwan issue, July 2014). Joyce had mixed feelings about this:

> I think she did that deliberately. She wants to show us that a lesbian can be girly too. . . . But I am confused. It seems to me that she overdoes femininity (*giggles*). She can just be what she used to be. She looks great in a T-shirt and jeans. Anyhow, it's good to show people that a lesbian is not necessarily a TB, but it's too much for me! (Joyce, age twenty-three, straight, interview in 2014)

Although many informants acknowledged that HOCC did not identify herself as a TB, some found HOCC in a feminine outfit unfamiliar. Joyce's negotiation and evaluation of HOCC's post-coming-out embodiment illustrated the style of TB in Hong Kong culture in which TBs are often addressed and communicated with as men and are frequently treated with hostility.[98] Mainstream heterosexual culture often pictures and represents lesbians through a heteronormative lens. For example, there is a strong stereotype that a lesbian relationship must consist of a TB and a TBG. Many informants appreciated HOCC's intention to break through such a heteronormative stereotyping of lesbianism by emphasizing in-betweenness in her gender performativity after coming out. As HOCC once mentioned, "I am here to reverse the narrow definition of gender."[99]

Megan was inspired by HOCC's coming-out. She used this to negotiate the "ideal" lesbian relationship and experiment with her gender performativity. She was one of the informants reinterviewed in 2014. Since our first interview in late 2009, she had transformed from a masculine TB to a feminine-looking lesbian who had short hair and wore makeup.

> It is definitely related to my current partner. But HOCC did make me think more deeply. Being lesbian doesn't require one to be TB. I can be simultaneously gentle, caring, and protective. I think I am now a *Pure* instead of TB.[100] If HOCC can let go of her masculine outward appearance, why can't I do the same? (Megan, age twenty-one, lesbian, interview in 2014)

She used to see *zhongxing* negatively. Her view of that has changed as well:

> *Zhongxing* is nice. Hongkongers are too backward to understand lesbianism. Why can't we appreciate the diversity in lesbianism like that in *The L Word*?[101] Hongkongers see *zhongxing* women like HOCC as TB but in the West, people may not think so. They will probably appreciate *zhongxing*.

She then shared with me her recent "*The L Word* experiment": going to a luxurious hotel for fine dining in a very sexy and feminine outfit with her femme partner and how that confused waiters and other customers. She found this experience interesting and felt relieved about her gender performativity. On one hand, her criticism of the gender and sexual "backwardness" in Hong Kong was not uncommon, which easily fell into the widely shared Anglo-American-centric view of gender and sexual modernity. On the other hand, despite the fact that *The L Word* has been criticized for being highly selective in its representation of lesbians and even reinforcing heteronormativity,[102] Megan tactically employed American pop culture to challenge local norms and explore alternative gender performativity.

Lastly, fans' negotiation of HOCC's post-coming-out embodiment demonstrated the operation of homonormativity in negotiating the notion of a "proper" and respectable lesbian. This highlights the shift within the tension of queer and normal. Many informants felt uncomfortable when HOCC was associated with outward masculinity. Joyce, in particular, despised the new TB fans of HOCC who were immature and rude:

> There is a lot of MK-looking TB trying to act like a man.[103] When HOCC was rising to fame in 2006, some TB said, "HOCC, stop pretending to be a TB!" Come on, HOCC never said she's a TB. . . . Now, those TB suddenly proclaim that they adore HOCC. They are so shallow. They adore HOCC because she came out and think that she is cool. I hate those MK [TB]. (Joyce, age twenty-three, straight, interview in 2014)

Samantha, who had a "typical TB-look"—wearing a pair of bold black glasses and spiky short hair—was also uneasy with HOCC being associated with TB:

> I once saw a photo of HOCC together with the helpers of the Big Love Alliance. Many of them were . . . boyish girls. I think this makes the older generation see HOCC even more negatively. I don't know if it's good or bad, but it seems to stir up the whole issue [lesbianism and the presence of TB]. The older generation, like my mom, dislikes outspoken people and gay people. HOCC is both! I'd rather hide my fandom now. (Samantha, age twenty-three, lesbian, interview in 2014)

Samantha's uneasiness could be unpacked by deploying the three layers of meanings of "normal." Her discomfort with the public visibility of masculine women and assumption of all masculine girls being lesbian implied the internalization of heteronormative values. The anxiety over the *tongzhi* movement being "misrepresented" by masculine lesbians and thus losing public support illustrated the normalizing view of queer politics, which resembled the closeting of butch lesbians in the queer movement in the United States.[104] In Hong Kong, besides being wealthy, healthy, good looking, and filial as discussed in the literature on Chinese homonormativity,[105] the homonormative code of a "proper" lesbian also included the avoidance of overt masculinity in hairstyle, outfit, and comportment. In this way, normalization of queer politics and homonormativity unintentionally works hand in hand with heteronormativity in policing fans' negotiation of HOCC's queer embodiment.

Conclusion

By demonstrating the queer fan culture in HOCC fandom before and after her coming-out, this chapter presents the entangling relations of queer and normal. Under the strategic alliance of the postcolonial government, heteropatriarchal Chinese family, and religion, which has powerfully shaped sexual cultures and reinforced heteronormative values in Hong Kong, HOCC fans have struggled when negotiating HOCC's gender and sexuality and their own. Before HOCC came out, queer reading was celebrated but precariously negotiated. Although many informants enjoyed queer reading and playing with the ambivalence in HOCC's sexuality, they were self-disciplined in both online and offline discussions out of fear of jeopardizing HOCC's career. The "official" end of Goo/Cho and HOCC's coming-out in 2012 were significant in reshaping the queer fan culture. HOCC's coming-out could be regarded as related to discontent with heteronormative dominance and oppression of *tongzhi* in Hong Kong. Instead of following HOCC's alleged new same-sex relationship, fans shifted their attention to negotiating her lesbian embodiment. The anxiety over the "proper" embodiment of a lesbian and "correct" representation of the *tongzhi* movement vividly demonstrated the intricate relations between heteronormativity and normalization in queer politics, as well as the new emerging homonormative codes in queer fan culture. The quest for normal has therefore fostered the homonormative understanding of queer. Nonetheless, the contingency and constant contestation of queer and normal also allowed the possibility of transgression and transformation, as, for example, in the use of the ambivalent notion of *zhongxing* that has "neutralized" the social visibility of queer and made possible the challenge of normal.

Lastly, what is normal and what is queer? Can one be normally queer or queerly normal? These are not mere wordplays but possible positions as a result of their intricate relationality and constant contestation operating at multiple levels. Situated within macrostructural and micropolitical forces, HOCC fans in Hong Kong desire to be queer by transgressing normal and paradoxically desire to be normal by tactically negotiating the limits of queer.

Acknowledgments

This chapter is based on my MPhil thesis completed in 2011 and my PhD research, which is partially supported by the Chiang Ching-kuo Foundation for International Scholarly Exchange and King's College London Hong Kong Scholarship. I would like to thank *Apple Daily Hong Kong* and Kaitlyn for permitting me to use their photos, the HOCC International Fan Club for its assistance in recruiting informants in 2009, and my informants for their trust and sharing. I would like to express my profound gratitude to Dr. Ng Chun-Hung and Dr. Travis Kong in the Department of Sociology at the University of Hong Kong and Professor Chris Berry and Dr. Victor Fan in the Department of Film Studies at King's College London. My gratitude also goes to the editors of this book and anonymous reviewers for their insightful comments on earlier drafts.

Notes

1. Alexander Doty, *Making Things Perfectly Queer: Interpreting Mass Culture* (Minneapolis: University of Minnesota Press, 1993), 3.
2. Ibid., 3–4.
3. Ibid.
4. Ara Wilson, "Queering Asia," *Intersections: Gender, History and Culture in the Asian Context* 14 (2006), accessed September 20, 2013, http://intersections.anu.edu.au/issue14/wilson.html.
5. For example, Peter A. Jackson, "An Explosion of Thai Identities: Global Queering and Re-imagining Queer Theory," *Culture, Health & Sexuality* 2.4 (2000): 405–24; Peter A. Jackson, "Capitalism and Global Queering: National Markets, Parallels among Sexual Cultures, and Multiple Queer Modernities," *GLQ: A Journal of Lesbian and Gay Studies* 15.3 (2009): 357–95; Fran Martin et al., eds., *AsiaPacifiQueer: Rethinking Genders and Sexualities* (Urbana: University of Illinois Press, 2008).
6. *Tongzhi* (Hanyu pinyin) / *tung zi* (Cantonese romanization), which literally means "comrade," is the generic term referring to lesbian and gay in Chinese contexts. See, for example, Travis S. K. Kong, *Chinese Male Homosexualities: Memba,* Tongzhi *and* Golden Boy (Oxon: Routledge, 2011), 14.
7. Although Hanyu pinyin is the most widely used Chinese romanization system, it is based on Mandarin pronunciation, which does not represent the local linguistic customs of Cantonese spoken by most Han Chinese in Hong Kong. In this chapter, I transliterate Chinese terms used in Hong Kong in Cantonese romanization according to the Jyutping system developed by Linguistic Society of Hong Kong, with tone indicators omitted. Personal names will follow individuals' preferences.
8. Michael Warner, "Introduction: Fear of a Queer Planet," *Social Text* 29 (1991): 3–17.
9. Michael Warner, *The Trouble with Normal: Sex, Politics, and the Ethics of Queer Life* (Cambridge, MA: Harvard University Press, 1999); Gayle Rubin, "Thinking Sex: Notes for a Radical Theory of the Politics of Sexuality," in *The Lesbian and Gay Studies Reader*, ed. Henry Abelove, Michèle Aina Barale, and David M. Halperin (London: Routledge, 1993), 100–33.
10. Steven Seidman, "From Identity to Queer Politics: Shifts in Normative Heterosexuality and the Meaning of Citizenship," *Citizenship Studies* 5.3 (2001): 321; Warner, *Trouble*, 24–25, 60. In the United States, national gay politics has been reduced to two issues, marriage and military service. See also Andrew Sullivan, *Virtually Normal* (New York: Vintage Books, 1995).
11. Kong, *Chinese Male Homosexualities*, ch. 2; Day Wong, "(Post-)identity Politics and Anti-normalization: (Homo)sexual Rights Movement," in *Remaking Citizenship in Hong Kong*, ed. Agnes S. Ku and Ngai Pun (Oxon: RoutledgeCurzon, 2004), 195–214.
12. Lisa Duggan, "The New Homonormativity: The Sexual Politics of Neoliberalism," in *Materializing Democracy: Toward a Revitalized Cultural Politics*, ed. Russ Castronovo and Dana D. Nelson (Durham, NC: Duke University Press, 2002), 175–94.
13. Ibid., 179–80.
14. Ibid., 191n9.

15. Warner, *Trouble*, 54–55.
16. Yau Ching, "Dreaming of Normal While Sleeping with Impossible: Introduction," in *As Normal as Possible: Negotiating Sexuality and Gender in Mainland China and Hong Kong*, ed. Yau Ching (Hong Kong: Hong Kong University Press, 2010), 3–4.
17. Ibid., 3.
18. The HOCC IFC was founded in 2002. About two-thirds of all the informants were once its members. Some did not renew the annual membership or have never joined because of the stigma of being a fan or for practical reasons such as having alternative access to concert tickets.
19. All lesbian and gay informants except one were closeted in workplace. Three had come out to their families at the time of interview.
20. Doty, *Making Things*, 15.
21. Yau, "Dreaming of Normal," 2.
22. Although some of the informants adored HOCC for reasons other than her queerness, once they self-identified as fans of HOCC, whose gender and sexuality is always under public scrutiny, the negotiation with HOCC's gender and sexuality became inevitable.
23. Cornel Sandvoss, *Fans: The Mirror of Consumption* (Cambridge: Polity Press, 2005), 8; Lawrence Grossberg, "Is There a Fan in the House? The Affective Sensibility of Fandom," in *The Adoring Audience: Fan Culture and Popular Media*, ed. Lisa A. Lewis (London: Routledge, 1992), 50–65.
24. Cisgender refers to individuals whose body and personal identity match with the gender assigned at birth. This term aims to replace "nontransgender" so as to decentralize gender narratives that base on biological facts. Kristen Schilt and Laurel Westbrook, "Doing Gender, Doing Heteronormativity: 'Gender Normals,' Transgender People, and the Social Maintenance of Heterosexuality," *Gender & Society* 23.4 (August 1, 2009): 461.
25. For textual analysis of HOCC's stardom, see Wai-man Vivian Au, "The Queer Female Stardom: Emerging from Transnational Chinese Singing Contests" (MPhil thesis, University of Hong Kong, 2012), ch. 1; Nicholas Wong, "Dialogue Two: From Rose Mary to Rolls Royce; Denise Ho X Wyman Wong Queerness in Denise Ho's Music," in *Fe/male Bodies*, ed. Daryl Cheung et al. (Hong Kong: Kubrick, 2005), 62–68; Rainsta Lai, "Dialogue Two: Rose/Mary/Rose-Mary: The Blurring of Gender Boundaries," in *Fe/male Bodies*, ed. Daryl Cheung et al. (Hong Kong: Kubrick, 2005), 56–61.
26. *Music Dream: Ho Denise Wan See*, produced by RTHK, first broadcast June 13, 2010, by TVB. Directed and written by Winnie Ho.
27. "Hong Kong Top Sales Music Award Presented [2001–2014]," International Federation of the Phonographic Industry (Hong Kong Group) Limited, accessed May 1, 2015, http://www.ifpihk.org/hong-kong-top-sales-music-award-presented-01-14/hong-kong-top-sales-music-award-presented/2014.
28. The Ultimate Song Chart of the Commercial Radio Hong Kong is one of the major local music charts.
29. The Golden Melody Awards is an annual Taiwanese music award for popular and traditional music, which is widely considered one of the most important awards in Mandopop.

30. "Ho Wan See: Ngo dik duk laap syun jin, jyu 2015 nin" [HOCC: My declaration of independence 2015], *Apple Daily*, March 23, 2015, accessed April 19, 2015, http://hk.apple.nextmedia.com/enews/realtime/20150323/53560989.
31. Names of the following songs are translated into English by me.
32. The former song is about the romance between Rose and Mary, and the latter is about their breakup.
33. This new story was set in modern times. Rolls (played by male singer Endy Chow) and Royce (played by HOCC) were a pair of heterosexual lovers. Royce had been killed in an accident and was born into a biological male Joe (played by male actor Joey Leung) in the life after death. Rolls, Joe, and other characters struggled with gender and sexuality as the story developed.
34. Kong, *Chinese Male Homosexualities*, 65.
35. "Ho bat ci ngo—Ho Wan See" [Why not be like me—Denise Ho], *Sing kei luk zau hon* [Saturday Magazine], March 29, 2003, 20.
36. "Tung sing lyun Ho Wan See" [Homosexual Denise Ho], *Faai zau hon* [Weekly express], April 30, 2003, accessed March 5, 2015, http://www.xpweekly.com/share/xpweekly/0245/ent/20030430ent0072/content.htm.
37. HOCC had "accidentally" come out in a game show in 2009 but she subsequently denied it. See Eva Cheuk-Yin Li, "Exploring the Productiveness of Fans: A Study of Ho Denise Wan See (HOCC) Fandom" (MPhil thesis, University of Hong Kong, 2011), 197–208. Yung acknowledged her intimate relationship with HOCC in an interview published by *Oriental Daily* on October 24, 2011, which stirred up discussion among lesbians in the Chinese-speaking world. See Denise Tse-Shang Tang, "An Unruly Death: Queer Media in Hong Kong," *GLQ: A Journal of Lesbian and Gay Studies* 18.4 (2012): 602–3. However, Yung denied it in another report published by *Oriental Daily* on October 25, 2011.
38. Both *Goo* and *Cho* are not formal but convenient Cantonese transliterations widely used by fans.
39. After coming out, HOCC was once asked by a journalist whether she would consider undergoing sex reassignment surgery, after the Court of Final Appeal had ruled transsexuals having the right to marry in May 2013, which illustrated public misunderstanding of sexual minorities. In late 2014, HOCC's sexuality was attacked by pro-government supporters for her prodemocratic stance on universal suffrage during the Umbrella Revolution or Occupy Central in Hong Kong.
40. For a brief summary of the case, see Kong, *Chinese Male Homosexualities*, 49.
41. Kong, *Chinese Male Homosexualities*, 50–51.
42. Travis S. K. Kong, Sky Hoi Leung Lau, and Eva Cheuk Yin Li, "The Fourth Wave? A Critical Reflection on the *Tongzhi* Movement in Hong Kong," in *Routledge Handbook of Sexuality Studies in East Asia*, ed. Mark McLelland and Vera Mackie (London: Routledge, 2015), 189–90.
43. Ibid., 189.
44. Aihwa Ong, "On the Edge of Empires: Flexible Citizenship among Chinese in Diaspora," *positions* 1.3 (1993): 753–62.
45. Travis S. K. Kong, "A Fading *Tongzhi* Heterotopia: Hong Kong Older Gay Men's Use of Spaces," *Sexualities* 15.8 (2012): 899–901.
46. Kong, Lau, and Li, "Fourth Wave?" 190.

47. Wai Ching Angela Wong, "The Politics of Sexual Morality and Evangelical Activism in Hong Kong," *Inter-Asia Cultural Studies* 14.3 (2013): 340–60.
48. Kong, Lau, and Li, "Fourth Wave?" 190.
49. Denise Tse-Shang Tang, *Conditional Spaces: Hong Kong Lesbian Desires and Everyday Life* (Hong Kong University Press, 2011), 74–75.
50. Ting-Yiu Robert Chung et al., *Hong Kong LGBT Climate Study 2011–12*, Survey Report (Hong Kong: Public Opinion Programme, University of Hong Kong, May 14, 2012), accessed March 5, 2015, http://hkupop.hku.hk/english/report/LGBT2011_12/content/resources/report.pdf.
51. MVA Hong Kong Limited, *Survey on Public Attitudes towards Homosexuals, Report Prepared for the Home Affairs Bureau, Hong Kong Special Administrative Region Government*, March 2005, 1, accessed March 5, 2015, http://www.legco.gov.hk/yr05-06/english/panels/ha/papers/ha0310cb2-public-homosexuals-e.pdf.
52. Ibid., 8.
53. Ting-yiu Robert Chung, Ka-lai Karie Pang, and Wing-Yi Winnie Lee, *Survey on Hong Kong Public's Attitudes towards Rights of People of Different Sexual Orientations* (Hong Kong: Public Opinion Programme, University of Hong Kong, November 7, 2012), accessed March 5, 2015, *http://hkupop.hku.hk/english/report/LGBT_CydHo/content/resources/report.pdf*; Yiu-tung Suen et al., *Study on Legislation against Discrimination on the Grounds of Sexual Orientation, Gender Identity and Intersex Status* (Hong Kong: Equal Opportunities Commission, 2016), accessed June 1, 2016, *http://www.eoc.org.hk/eoc/upload/ResearchReport/20161251750293418312.pdf*.
54. Kong, *Chinese Male Homosexualities*, ch. 2.
55. Ibid.; Tang, *Conditional Spaces*, ch. 2.
56. For studies between late 1990s and early 2000s, see Lucetta Yip Lo Kam, "Recognition through Mis-recognition: Masculine Women in Hong Kong," in *AsiaPacifiQueer: Rethinking Genders and Sexualities*, ed. Fran Martin et al. (Urbana: University of Illinois Press, 2008), 99–116; Anthony Fung and Eric Ma, "Formal vs. Informal Use of Television and Sex-Role Stereotyping in Hong Kong," *Sex Roles* 42.1/2 (2000): 57–81. For gender stereotypes in the late 2000s, see Equal Opportunities Committee, Hong Kong Special Administrative Region Government, *Study on Public Perception of Portrayal of Female Gender in the Hong Kong Media—Executive Summary* (Hong Kong: Social Sciences Research Centre, University of Hong Kong, commissioned by the Equal Opportunities Commission, 2009), accessed March 1, 2015, http://www.eoc.org.hk/eoc/upload/20096111239594027760.pdf; Women's Commission, Hong Kong Special Administrative Region Government, *Findings of Survey on Community Perception on Gender Issues* (Hong Kong: Women's Commission, 2009), accessed March 1, 2015, http://www.women.gov.hk/download/research/Community-perception-survey-findings.pdf.
57. Suen et al., *Study on Legislation against Discrimination*.
58. Ting-Yiu Robert Chung et al., *Survey on Hong Kong Public's Attitudes towards Rights of People of Different Sexual Orientations* (Hong Kong: Public Opinion Programme, University of Hong Kong, October 23, 2013), accessed March 1, 2015, http://hkupop.hku.hk/english/report/LGBT_CydHo2013/content/resources/report.pdf; Chung, Pang, and Lee, *Survey on Hong Kong Public's Attitudes*, November 7, 2012.
59. Tang, *Conditional Spaces*; Carmen Ka Man Tong, "Being a Young Tomboy in Hong Kong: The Life and Identity Construction of Lesbian Schoolgirls," in *AsiaPacifiQueer:*

Rethinking Genders and Sexualities, ed. Fran Martin et al. (Urbana: University of Illinois Press, 2008), 117–30.

60. Wah Shan Chow, *Tung zi leon* [On *tongzhi*], second edition (Hong Kong: Hong Kong Queer Press, 1997), ch. 8.
61. Nütong Xueshe, a local *tongzhi* organization, studied the representation of *tongzhi* in dramas produced by TVB, the major station providing free television service between 1976 and 2012, and found that more than 70 percent involved homophobic content such as portraying *tongzhi* as criminals or deviants. Nütong Xueshe, "Zeoi 'hung tung' kek zaap syun geoi" [Voting for the most homophobic television drama], n.d., accessed December 2, 2016, https://sites.google.com/site/gayvotetvb/home; "TVB jau tiu hung tung fong cing sik" [TVB has a homophobic formula], *Apple Daily*, December 3, 2012, accessed March 1, 2015, http://hk.apple.nextmedia.com/news/art/20121203/18088948.
62. Tang, "Unruly Death," 608–10.
63. Matt Hills, *Fan Cultures* (Oxon: Routledge, 2002), ch. 4; Ien Ang, *Living Room Wars: Rethinking Media Audiences for a Postmodern World* (New York: Routledge, 1996), 92; C. Lee Harrington and Denise D. Bielby, *Soap Fans: Pursuing Pleasure and Making Meaning in Everyday Life* (Philadelphia: Temple University Press, 1995); C. Lee Harrington and Denise D. Bielby, "Flow, Home, and Media Pleasures," *The Journal of Popular Culture* 38.5 (2005): 846.
64. John Fiske, *Reading the Popular* (Boston: Unwin Hyman, 1989), 124.
65. Michael DeAngelis, *Gay Fandom and Crossover Stardom: James Dean, Mel Gibson, and Keanu Reeves* (Durham, NC: Duke University Press, 2001), 5.
66. HOCC and Yung used to have their individual public blogs in Yahoo! Hong Kong. Yahoo! shut down all its blog service in 2013.
67. Goo/Cho was also discussed by mainland Chinese fans and lesbian in online platforms, even after the "official" end of Goo/Cho in 2012. According to some informants, discussion in mainland Chinese forums could be much more explicit. Nonetheless, most Hong Kong fans did not engage in discussion in the mainland Chinese Internet.
68. The HOCC IFC forum is available here: http://www.hocc.cc/forum/index.php. It was established in 2005 to replace the former official discussion bulletin *HOCC School*. One has to register an account to participate in discussion. Forum users who have joined the HOCC IFC could access an exclusive discussion board on exclusive resources such as videos, photos, and tickets for events. Discussion in the forum has been inactive since the setting up of HOCC Facebook Fan Page in 2008, where HOCC frequently interacted with fans.
69. Sammi Cheng is a top-selling Cantopop female singer and actress in Hong Kong.
70. This ritual is performed before concerts or movie filming to pray for safety and success.
71. Audience response was included in the concert DVD of *SuperGoo*. See Li, "Exploring the Productiveness of Fans," 209–10.
72. "Aa si zip zoi zou ji mou neoi taan cyun siu" [HOCC took Joey Yung and mother to barbeque], *Blur-F*, December 25, 2008, accessed February 1, 2010, http://www.Blur-F.net/forum/viewthread.php?tid=41695&extra=page%3D1&page=1. The thread was locked by the forum administrator in January 2010 and Blur-F was shut down in 2012. A copy has been downloaded. The thread was archived at *Internet Archive*, July 2,

2010, accessed November 30, 2016, https://web.archive.org/web/20100702181808/http://www.blurf.net/forum/viewthread.php?tid=41695&extra=page%3D1&page=1.

73. To keep the forum discreet, Kaitlyn has tightened the registration procedure. The forum has been restructured several times since 2009.

74. Weibo, literally meaning microblog, is a popular social networking site in mainland China. Since both Facebook and Twitter are blocked in mainland China, celebrities in Hong Kong and Taiwan registered Weibo accounts to interact with mainland Chinese fans. HOCC's Weibo account was removed in October 2014 because of her support of the Umbrella Revolution in Hong Kong.

75. For example, fans widely believed that HOCC's song "The Red Roof" ("Hung uk deng") and Yung's song "The Yellow Gate" ("Wong sik daai mun") referred to the house of Miffy, the Dutch cartoon character that Yung adored. Both songs were written and arranged by Carl Wong, with lyrics by Wyman Wong.

76. Some of the Goo/Cho fan videos on YouTube were removed by users after the "official" breakup of Goo/Cho in mid-2012. There were a few left in late 2014 by searching with keyword *goocho* (in Chinese or English).

77. Julie Levin Russo, "Textual Orientation: Queer Female Fandom Online," in *The Routledge Companion to Media and Gender*, ed. Cynthia Carter, Linda Steiner, and Lisa McLaughlin (London: Routledge, 2014), 452.

78. Ibid., 453.

79. Henry Jenkins, *Textual Poachers: Television Fans and Participatory Culture* (New York: Routledge, 1992), 191–92.

80. Russo, "Textual Orientation," 453.

81. For example, the character of HOCC would be named *C* or *See* while that of Joey Yung would be named *Cho*, *Yee*, or other Chinese names with the same Cantonese pronunciation. Sometimes, the two protagonists were given new names, but authors would indicate them by other personal attributes such as zodiac signs: Taurus for the HOCC character and Gemini for the Yung character.

82. Russo, "Textual Orientation," 457.

83. Jing Jamie Zhao, "Fandom as a Middle Ground: Fictive Queer Fantasies and Real-World Lesbianism in *FSCN*," in "Access/Trespass," special conference issue, *Media Fields Journal* 10 (2014), accessed February 10, 2016, http://mediafieldsjournal.squarespace.com/fandom-as-a-middle-ground/.

84. Warner, *Trouble*, 54–58.

85. Sik Ying Ho and Ka Tat Tsang, "The Things Girls Shouldn't See: Relocating the Penis in Sex Education in Hong Kong," in *Gendering Hong Kong*, ed. Anita Kit-wa Chan and Wai Ling Wong (Hong Kong: Oxford University Press, 2004), 690–708.

86. Wong, "Politics of Sexual Morality," 343–44; Tang, *Conditional Spaces*, 74–75.

87. This term is widely used in mainland China, Hong Kong, and Taiwan. *Zhongxing* (Hanyu pinyin), *zung sing* (Cantonese romanization) and *jhong sing* (Tongyong pinyin for Mandarin in Taiwan) all share the same written characters. See Eva Cheuk-Yin Li, "Approaching Transnational Chinese Queer Stardom as Zhongxing ('Neutral Sex/Gender') Sensibility," *East Asian Journal of Popular Culture* 1.1 (2015): 75–95.

88. Helen Hok-Sze Leung, "Loving in the Stillness of Earthquakes: Ho Yuk—Let's Love Hong Kong," in *Ho Yuk—Let's Love Hong Kong: Script and Critical Essays*, ed. Ching Yau (Hong Kong: Youth Literary Press, 2002), 61.

89. Lucetta Yip Lo Kam, "This Gender Called TB" TB 這性別, *E-journal on Hong Kong Cultural and Social Studies* 2 (2002), accessed September 25, 2008, http://www.hku.hk/hkcsp/ccex/ehkcss01/frame.html?mid=1&smid=1&ssmid=7 (site now defunct).
90. Tang, *Conditional Spaces*, 75–81.
91. Chung et al., *Survey on Hong Kong Public's Attitudes*, October 23, 2013, 6.
92. Cheuk Yin Li, "The Absence of Fan Activism in the Queer Fandom of Ho Denise Wan See (HOCC) in Hong Kong," in "Transformative Works and Fan Activism," edited by Henry Jenkins and Sangita Shresthova, special issue, *Transformative Works and Cultures* 10 (2012), doi:10.3983/twc.2012.0325.
93. The first paragraph is translated into English by Arthur Tam and the rest is translated by me. Arthur Tam, "HOCC: Gay . . . and Happy!," *Time Out Hong Kong*, December 19, 2012, 12.
94. Chung et al., *Survey on Hong Kong Public's Attitudes*, October 23, 2013, 7.
95. The promotion of "big love" can be seen as an attempt to normalize queer politics for public empathy, which risks downplaying institutional and structural inequality sustained by heteronormativity.
96. For example, she spoke on the issue of transsexual marriage in the Legislative Council Bills Committee meeting in April 2014. She has participated in the Umbrella Revolution for universal suffrage in Hong Kong and cofounded Hong Kong Shield to monitor authorities' abuse of violence during the movement in late 2014.
97. Bisexuals have been stigmatized as "promiscuous" and further marginalized within lesbian and gay communities for being unreliable and easily attracted by the privilege of heterosexual relationships. For a literature review of research on attitudes towards bisexuality, see Tania Israel and Jonathan J. Mohr, "Attitudes toward Bisexual Women and Men," *Journal of Bisexuality* 4.1/2 (2004): 120–23. For bi-negativity within the lesbian community, see Kirsten McLean, "Inside, Outside, Nowhere: Bisexual Men and Women in the Gay and Lesbian Community," *Journal of Bisexuality* 8.1/2 (2008): 67–68. In Hong Kong, there has been little attention paid to bisexuals compared with that to lesbians and gays. A small-scale survey conducted in 1999 and 2000 suggested that the general public tended to tolerate the existence of bisexuality based on the human rights discourse. Nonetheless, the survey also reported widespread misunderstanding and stigmatization of bisexuals as "morally weak" and "promiscuous". Anson Hoi Shan Mak, *Soeng sing cing juk* [Bisexual desires], ed. Mary Ann Pui Wai King (Hong Kong: Hong Kong Women Christian Council, 2000), 67–69.
98. Leung, "Loving," 61.
99. HOCC Facebook Fan Page, last modified May 27, 2014, accessed February 10, 2016, https://zh-tw.facebook.com/HOCCHOCC/posts/10154199771680230.
100. "Pure" is a lesbian gender in Hong Kong referring to those who refuse the categories TB or TBG, or whose appearance cannot be recognized as TB or TBG. Its equivalence are H in mainland China and *bu fen* in Taiwan.
101. *The L Word* is an American television drama that ran from 2004 to 2009 about a group of lesbians, bisexuals, and transgenders living in Los Angeles.
102. Samuel A. Chambers, "Heteronormativity and the L Word: From a Politics of Representation to a Politics of Norms," in *Reading "The L Word": Outing Contemporary Television*, ed. Kim Akass, Janet McCabe, and Sarah Warn (London: I. B. Tauris, 2006), 81–98.

103. MK is the abbreviation of Mongkok, a district on the Kowloon Peninsula in Hong Kong known for attracting young people and hosting trendy fashion shops. It is also a derogatory slang referring to hipsters trying to be trendy but in fact failing, as well as people with poor fashion taste.
104. Shane Phelan, "Public Discourse and the Closeting of Butch Lesbians," in *Butch/Femme: Inside Lesbian Gender*, ed. Sally R. Munt (London: Cassell, 1998), 191–99.
105. Kong, *Chinese Male Homosexualities*, ch. 7; Tang, "Unruly Death"; Lucetta Yip Lo Kam, *Shanghai Lalas: Female Tongzhi Communities and Politics in Urban China* (Hong Kong: Hong Kong University Press, 2012).

8
Hong Kong–Based Fans of Mainland Idol Li Yuchun

Elective Belonging, Gender Ambiguity, and Rooted Cosmopolitanism

Maud Lavin

> Yes, I have been to Li Yuchun's concerts [on the Mainland]. The signs and banners at her concerts are different from normal concert culture. Different groups in age, geography, education, and occupation all have special banners that hang around the concert halls. They are very warm, yet funny. . . . When the concert is over and everyone leaves, all the Corns pick up trash around them and leave everything in order. This is very rare. I think there is not much difference between Hong Kong people and mainland people. Even though mainland China has some "locusts" [derogatory term used by some Hong Kongers to refer to mainland people], there are many people who are well educated and have great manners. We can't just talk about people from mainland China as a whole. There are some cultural differences between Hong Kong and the Mainland, but I feel like some Hong Kong people make this too much of a big deal. (Hong Kong–based student, born on the Mainland in Chongqing)[1]

From the handover of Hong Kong to the People's Republic of China (PRC) in 1997 to the present, urgent governmental questions of democracy and power have been and continue to be contested between Hong Kong and mainland China, most visibly in the Umbrella Revolution of 2014 when more than 100,000 protesting Hong Kongers occupied the city's streets.[2] During this posthandover period and preceding it, though, there has also been a related but quieter discourse about issues of bigotry toward Mainlanders in Hong Kong. This discourse is, as well, an urgent one in the everyday lives of Hong Kong residents—particularly the more than 30 percent of Hong Kong residents who were born on the Mainland.[3] It is this substantial minority of Hong Kong residents born on the Mainland that interests me here. In this chapter, I explore one thread of the complex weave of how they might employ mass cultural fandom, among other factors, in negotiating such bigotry and, complementarily, feelings of belonging. The thread or case study I focus on is such usage in feelings of complex belonging among Hong Kong–based, Mainland-born fans and followers of mainland idol Li Yuchun. I include both those who self-define as fans, that is, enthusiastic *devotées*, and a selection of those studying in Hong Kong whom I describe as followers (by followers I mean those who keep up with a star with interest but are not necessarily fans; in this chapter this category includes the academics interviewed). Both groups contribute to the reception culture and affective climate that forms around a celebrity in a given locale.[4]

In this exploration, I do not look to fandoms to completely solve multifaceted bigotry but instead explore how potentially transformative elements are raised within a specific case.[5] In discussing Hong Kong–based Mainlander fandom and viewers of a mainland idol, I am considering the use of mass cultural consumption to negotiate border crossing and elective belonging in ways that are primarily separate from identification with local or national governments. I am focusing on fans and followers of Li Yuchun, whom I would mainly describe, following Mica Nava,[6] as rooted cosmopolitans. In addition to their balancing loyalty to Hong Kong with the Mainland and international knowingness, their readings of Li Yuchun fit here too, either through their music tastes, their educational capital, or their willingness to read one aspect of mainland culture against the grain of the government's highly mythologized claim of univocality. As one Mainlander living in Hong Kong who describes herself as a "fresh graduate" asserts and implicitly self-identifies, "I think Li Yuchun's fans are quite cosmopolitan."[7] Many also identify with a feminine-inflected gender and sexual ambiguity that involves, at this time in the evolution of Li's persona, connection to a fashionable gender neutrality, a relatively noncontroversial (and therefore fairly easy to activate) contribution to rewriting a script of what it means to be a Chinese woman.

Singing star Li Yuchun is a rich focus for fan and viewer discussions because for many her (primarily) *zhongxing* or gender-neutral style and behaviors represent a flexibly androgynous figure who appealingly suggests a range of options for femininities and sexualities.[8] Specifically, her most well-known public persona is *zhongxing* with additional connotations of a tomboy style, although she appears in other visual styles as well. Fans with quite different intersectional identities can and do employ her representations to perform a striking variety of gender and sexuality readings. Some read her as queer, some as straight, many as her own kind of woman. In addition and connected to these gender and sexuality issues as well as migrancy ones of elective belonging,[9] she has particular resonance for some Mainlander fans and interested followers living in Hong Kong.

When I say "resonance," I use it as an umbrella affective term denoting meaningfulness; this need not be felt as an active member of a fandom, although there is a sturdy, persistent, unofficial group of fans (mainland- and Hong Kong–born) based in Hong Kong, who travel to the Mainland to see Li Yuchun's yearly "Why Me" concerts and other appearances of hers, who avidly follow her on Sina Weibo (the Chinese version of Twitter) and Baidu Post Bar (Baidu tieba) (and for some Hong Kongers Facebook), who connect online and with Mainland-based fans, and who have remained loyal to her for years. Li Yuchun is important to her Hong Kong–based fans, and they love her. I also include in this chapter followers for whom Li Yuchun has meaning as those who keep themselves informed about her because of her status as both a mainstream mainland idol and a famous tomboy.

Li Yuchun's exceptional popularity began when she won the 2005 *Super Girl* (*Chaoji nüsheng*), a reality TV show produced by Hunan Satellite TV. *Super Girl* was a contest show featuring competing amateur singers and attracting millions of viewers. For the 2005 finale when Li won, there were more than 400 million viewers, a number that amounts to more than the populations of the United States and Canada combined.[10] The show ran from 2004 to 2006, was halted by the government for three years, and then returned from 2009 to 2011—when it was again stopped, this time apparently permanently. In 2006, Liu Zhongde, a former Chinese culture minister and a member then of the National Committee of the Chinese People's Political Consultative Conference, served as a spokesperson against *Super Girl*, decrying its lowbrow quality and the subservience to the market it represented (via profits made by Hunan Satellite TV and telecom operators who made considerable money from the text messages of support, i.e., voting), and declaring that its youth audience was being "poisoned" and that contestants appeared wearing "vulgar fashion."[11] Notably Li Yuchun and other winners of later years, whom it is surmised were following her style, often appeared as androgynous tomboys, authentic new New Women from the provinces, sincere and fresh in their talent. In the press about Li's win, it is often mentioned that her androgyny signaled different kinds of independence. For some viewers (for some adamantly not) she also represented minoritarian sexuality.[12]

For the short-lived but impactful *Super Girl* TV show, whose viewers "voted" or expressed preferences for singers via SMS (short message service), the surprise is not how many viewers the show garnered. Instead the surprise—given the current state of the PRC music industry—is that any of the winners have become megastars in China and have turned profits for their production companies on the level of superstardom understood to function in, say, Korea and the United States.

Nationally, as scholar Ling Yang has analyzed, in an uneasy and sometimes fractious collusion between fans and her record companies, Taihe Rye Music Company (2005–2011) and EE-Media (2011–present, as of this writing in 2014), sales of Li Yuchun's DVDs and CDs have skyrocketed. These sales have been promoted by producer/consumer (prosumer) Corn fans, who initiate in-store promotions, Li-branded charity work, online post bars, and even Li media-promotion kits. The fans themselves have taken on or significantly contributed to what is in the West thought of as the jobs of the publicists and music production companies. This has continued even as Li Yuchun's fame has risen to spectacular heights and may be the chief pragmatic factor behind her rise.[13]

Li Yuchun, as arguably mainland China's best-known tomboy since 2005, is, in a way that has to do with celebrity gossip but also transcends it, the consumable "property" of so many interested in gender and sexuality fluidities in China, including those in Hong Kong. Li Yuchun has long had her antifans too, who call her "Brother Chun" (*chunge*) and deride her androgynous appearance. And, as has been well documented, she not only has fans who bond through their enthusiasm for her but also has loyal fans who dislike each other intensely, often disagreeing along lines of what they think Li Yuchun's (unspoken) sexuality might be.[14] (She has at least one fan, probably more, who has used her to come out to her mother.[15]) Her commercial success has garnered her many imitators, and some argue her sellable apparent queerness has even been requested of other reality TV competitors by TV stations.[16] Some find her too faux-innocent or even slightly quaint in this, her eleventh year of fame. In 2011, though, she was designated as the top-earning young Chinese entertainment star, including those in the movie and music worlds. In the 2010s, she is often seen modeling on fashion runways and endorsing such product lines as L'Oréal. Since 2009, she has appeared in three historical-drama movies in supporting roles as a warrior woman, including Fang Hong in *Bodyguards and Assassins* (*Shiyue weicheng*, Teddy Chan, 2009, Hong Kong), which earned her a Hong Kong Film Award nomination for Best Supporting Actress. So, while some may still associate her with *Super Girl*, she has in fact become mainstream and financially formidable while also retaining her somewhat nonconformist persona in public. She never discusses her sexuality, nor does she, even in her thirties, a time by which most mainland women are married,[17] appear with a boyfriend or a male date. That is unusual.

Almost all Li Yuchun's fans and most interested viewers are women. Lucetta Kam has written about how Li Yuchun and other tomboy-style singers are used and debated by those in China who self-define as lesbian.[18] Li is also the subject of gossip, analysis, interest, and opinion among those who are not fans but are still involved viewers.[19] I interviewed some academic followers in Hong Kong as well as fans, and the academic viewers had engaged analyses about Li Yuchun's sexuality, including opinions that had changed over the years. They were also well aware that in Hong Kong, of course, a tomboy appearance is not new, as can be easily seen in recent decades of Hong Kong mass music culture. Further in Hong Kong Li Yuchun is not at all "the most famous tomboy"; instead, HOCC (Denise Wan-See Ho), who came out as lesbian in 2012, probably is. HOCC is known for her activism in favor of Hong Kong democracy and gay rights as well as her music. But, in a place like Hong Kong, where, as one interviewee put it, many "look down on Mainlanders" and Mainland-originated pop music,[20] Li Yuchun is still taken seriously as the subject of articulate and opinionated gender and sexuality gossip and for a number of those academics in cultural studies and gender studies in Hong Kong as a person to follow in terms of her public persona—a star whose persona one keeps informed about.

Li Yuchun is easily perceived as cosmopolitan because she does international tours and endorsements for international fashion brands, and in this context she functions as, to paraphrase an academic viewer, a fresh face for China.[21] She may be lesbian, she is definitely private about her sexuality, and her public comments are resolutely those of someone devoted to her music and to keeping her privacy. Her primary persona is that of a woman who desires to be different, *zhongxing* or gender neutral, involved in her work, and private. None of these are shocking, but at the same time none of these are norms, except in some areas of the transnational Asian music world, usually for men. So Li Yuchun's persona as of 2016 sits squarely in the mainstream in terms of her massive popularity, but is still outside heteromarital Chinese norms for women, in ways that can be read as cosmopolitan and even fashionable, but not merely fashionable. She could be counted as a kind of cosmopolitan girl next door by Mainlander followers living in Hong Kong. For instance, a Mainlander fan of the 1990s or late 1980s cohort, who has moved to Hong Kong to study or work and also who partakes in person in Hong Kong popular culture (for a long time, along with Taiwanese music, popular on the Mainland), may be someone who is looking for a new but still thoroughly Chinese script in terms of gender or sexuality or who simply feels comfortable enjoying a border-crossing star who is also from the Mainland. Knowing about Li Yuchun, gossiping about her, staying lightly informed about her could be, along with other strands of mainland and Hong Kong everyday cultures, useful to employ in the process of elective belonging to Hong Kong, an elective belonging that can be felt passionately and deeply, but one that has to be negotiated over time, particularly in light of prejudices.

This sense of belonging also relates, of course, to feelings of friendship—having friends, being able to make friends, having relationships that could potentially be imagined as turning into friendships. And in this area, the functions of fandom are key. As Hong Kong music teacher Mengjun Lin, born in Fujian, says, connecting herself to both Mainland-based and Hong Kong–based fans:

> I am in touch with some Hong Kong Corns as well as some Corns from the Mainland who study or work in Hong Kong like myself. If I compare myself to mainland Corns, I don't see any significant differences. Hong Kong Corns will speak more Mandarin when they chat with us, and we will also learn Cantonese from them. We all become friends because of Chunchun, it's some kind of fate.[22]

For a related project in 2014 and 2015, I interviewed twenty-three mainland fans of Li Yuchun based in Beijing and other large cities and active online in the fandom.[23] Although, as Ling Yang and Hongwei Bao have analyzed, affective bonds online and offline for Mainland-based fans of Li are powerful,[24] in my interviews of Hong Kong–based and Mainland-based fans, an imaginary about friendship was more often articulated by the Hong Kong–based fans, whereas the Mainland-based ones, although asked generally similar questions, tended to talk directly about Li Yuchun and their perceptions of her and less about other fans. A larger study might determine how comparatively large a role longing for friendship might play among fans who have moved away from their home base to an environment well known to be unfriendly to them; here I can raise it as a valuable question and can hypothesize that this aspect of the fannish imaginary would be key for such a population. Interestingly, even the few Hong Kong–born among the Hong Kong–based fans of Li tended to bring up friendship, particularly cross-border friendship, which makes sense to me, as joining this fandom as a Hong Konger would likely mean interacting—and wanting to interact—with mainland fans (and also traveling to the Mainland). For example, Beatrice, a Hong Kong–born fan working as a teacher in Hong Kong relates:

> I only have close communication with two or three Corns from the Mainland. We . . . met each other during a "Why Me" concert. I consider them my friends. One time at a Shanghai "Why Me" concert, one of my Corn friends gave me a birthday cake that was identical to the one that Chunchun had at her 2013 birthday. This person also picked me up and sent me back to the hotel. We didn't really know each other before that.[25]

In the main, my exploration has to do with how this mainland, tomboy-appearing idol can function in quite mainstream culture in terms of Mainlanders settled in Hong Kong who are her fans or simply knowledgeable viewers. Unlike some in fan studies, I am not looking to locate cultish devotion in fans nor transgression in a star. I am thinking about how people can use elements of mainstream culture to help write their own always evolving identity scripts, and in this case ones that are rooted in an elected place that can carry deep desires of belonging. Hong Kong is Chinese and it also is international, cosmopolitan, supposedly—or at least in its subcultures if not commonly—open to gender and sexuality minorities; has more freedom of expression as a Special Administrative Region than elsewhere in China; and has relatively little pollution. It also has great inequality in class and assets, and it is an expensive place to live. The decision to stay in Hong Kong is not an easy one to negotiate.

Over a six-month period, March through August 2014, I followed fan sites with the assistance of researchers Xiaorui Zhu-Nowell and Star Sijia Liu, and I did fifteen interviews, composed of seven fan and eight academic followers, not a huge sampling but an informative one, since Li Yuchun is the subject of fine-tuned analysis for most of the respondents. Although I interviewed mainly Mainlanders living in Hong Kong, I also included a few respondents who are Hong Kong–born enthusiasts and commenters to consider their attitudes as well in this fandom picture. I focus mainly, though, on selected Mainlander residents in Hong Kong and how their sense of Li Yuchun's ambiguous sexuality, (by now) noncontroversial success, mild but stubborn nonconformism, and her cosmopolitanism might be of use to them.

Li's public persona could even be described as "queer light." Here I use "queer light" in a *non*dismissive way as a light, publicly acceptable to mainstream culture, appearance of queerness as a nonstraight identity that may mean lesbian or other minoritarian sexuality *or* might signify more generally a nontraditional, nonnormative woman. In other words, I take the connotative blurring of a lesbian-seeming appearance and a nonnormative woman seriously.[26] Even a semblance of gender bending could also fit within this definition of queer light.

Here, too, following John Nguyet Erni, the Cantonese term *bin tai* is useful to consider, meaning literally a changing state of affairs but used in Hong Kong culture as "a common lexicon referring to all real or imagined perversions designated as a deviation from or subversion of reproductive, heterosexual, family-centered norms of the body, gender, and sexuality."[27] In the hope of democratically changing norms through, among other elements, the potential uses of new stereotypes, in this case of Li Yuchun's popularized T-style, the imaginary I participate in is to jog such terms as *bin tai* and "tomboy" away from insults and toward a positive expansion of functional differences in daily life.

Prejudices against Mainlanders

I should clarify here what I mean by prejudices against Mainlanders. There is an important difference between, on the one hand, Hong Kong residents being concerned about the flood of mainland tourists taxing resources in the city[28] and, on the other, the bigotry expressed toward Mainlanders, residents or not, on the subway, in the street, in workplaces, and for some mainland women in and around marriages.[29] As legal scholar Carol Jones points out, these prejudices have long colonial and postcolonial roots:

> In a reversal of fortunes [in the 2000s], the [Mainlander] newcomers were often better-off than the locals, sometimes conspicuously so. Hong Kongers have long seen themselves as superior to their "Ah Chan" Mainland "country cousins," but the Asian Financial Crisis and the SARS outbreak impacted negatively on Hong Kong just as China's prosperity grew.[30]

As cultural analyst David Volodzko bluntly summarizes, "Hong Kong is not without a palpable air of superiority, partly the effect of wealth and partly the facility its people enjoy with English."[31]

As one journalistic venue reports, "Unfortunately, frustration with the Chinese government has, at times, translated to vitriol toward Mainland Chinese visitors in Hong Kong. Those who come as tourists from Mainland China are called locusts."[32] This familiar comment, however, ignores the impact of discrimination on residents born on the Mainland, as does in fact much of the Hong Kong journalistic coverage of tourism issues.

In Hong Kong, it is all too easy to find publicly articulated evidence of these prejudices expressed in language used in a range of locales to articulate racism and bigotry. To take one example, the Hong Kong–based website "Spot the Mainlander" describes mainland Chinese as dirty, uncouth, crude, and animalistic.[33] Further, in words and images reminiscent of cultural historian Klaus Theweleit's analysis of certain German masculinities' lineage of hate, the website focuses on Mainlanders' release of bodily fluids, such as urinating.[34] An outside observer might theorize that some of these prejudices are projections of fear and hatred related to policy issues, but this is of course not a justification of bigotries against individuals.

Still, even at a fraught contemporary time of negotiation between the Hong Kong populace and the central Beijing government, these prejudices link to the heritage of the Cold War, with the British-run capitalist-financial center of Hong Kong being culturally as well as economically pitted against the supposedly backward and un-Western-civilized, not to mention "communist" Mainland. In contemporary East Asia, the legacies of such tensions, as well as others newly created by mineral and navigational right conflicts and other economic competition, remain open questions. Significantly there are blurrings between government actions and attitudes toward mainland Chinese people, ones that cannot be easily untangled. But historical untangling is not the main focus here; harm to individuals due to bigotry is—as are possibilities of cultural negotiation. In a recent Hong Kong Institute of Education study of 1,083 migrants (not residents yet) in the city from the Mainland, "nearly 57 percent perceived daily discrimination."[35]

A longer study could trace a number of mass culture sites where Hong Konger–Mainlander discussions intersect in vivid and evolving ways—Cantopop songs or, say, popular *wuxia* (martial arts) films come quickly to mind, and in fact *wuxia* movie production when involving coproduction between Hong Kong and mainland entities nicely parallels such fan interactions and potential interactions. Yet in this chapter I focus mainly on Hong Kong–based, Mainland-born fans and interested followers of mainland idol Li Yuchun, using the intertwining of three key factors—Li's somewhat contested but hugely popular status as a fresh face of mainland China, her cosmopolitan gender-bending persona, and the fact that her online following is dominated by women—together to trace within this fraught context issues of daily life and fan interest in gender and sexuality and how these might open avenues for cross-border seeing and being seen in potentially new ways.

Mainland-Born Hong Kong Fans

The affective layerings of the border crossings, in fandoms and sometimes geographically, enacted by these Hong Kong fans and followers of Li's can also be explored as they reverberate with intimate attitudes toward her *zhongxing* qualities. How do Li Yuchun's *zhongxing* looks matter to Hong Kong fans and in turn to their attitudes toward her as a mainland star? Could her special status as homegrown, tomboyish winner of the 2005 *Super Girl*, montaged with her subsequent international-star style encourage an empathic cosmopolitanism in her Hong Kong fans? Do they encourage Mainlanders living in Hong Kong to envision it as a cosmopolitan space that includes them?

Is Li Yuchun's gender and sexual ambiguity part of her appeal to Hong Kong–based fans or instead, as some have argued, subsumed into a kind of mythological innocent femininity?[36] Specifically I want to know whether these fans and followers read Li Yuchun (as Chengzhou He has written about the Chinese cross-dressing male star Li Yugang) as "a symbol of liminality for progress and liberalization in the present Chinese society" or whether their following of Li Yuchun is tied to other reasons.[37] With these attitudinal questions, an ethnographic approach is called for, and I use e-mail interviews and textual analysis of fan comments to explore them in the context of cross-border tensions. Of the fifteen people interviewed, seven self-identified as avid fans.

Five out of these seven interviewed Hong Kong fans were born on the Mainland (a university student from Chongqing, a music teacher originally from Fujian, a retail worker born in Zhejiang, and two, a new university graduate and a twelfth grader, referring to their birthplace as more generically the Mainland), with two others, a teacher and an administrative buyer, born in Hong Kong. Most preferred to be referred to as anonymous or with a pseudonym in this chapter.

To a person the fan interviewees expressed admiration for Li Yuchun because of her independence, her uniqueness, her "specialty and honesty," and her being "really true to herself." They were also united in seeing Li Yuchun as someone who followed her own dreams, particularly in making her own music and not becoming a puppet of the entertainment industry. For instance, Hong Kong–born fan Little Fish states, "I am grateful that she shares with us her inner world music. From the lyrics one writes, you can tell a lot of that person's character and thoughts. Truly heartfelt words and emotions don't lie. I can conclude that my favorite quality of Li is her sincerity."[38]

It is possible to see this common perception of Li Yuchun's sincerity and uniqueness as being of use to Mainland-born female fans who have resettled to live in Hong Kong, a place perceived as, and for some desired as, a more individualistic culture. A twelfth grader, who moved with her family to Hong Kong from the Mainland when she was in sixth grade, praises Li Yuchun: "She always follows her own dream" (*jianchi ziji de lixiang*).[39]

As fan and music teacher, Mainland-born Mengjun Lin articulates:

> She's very unique. When I first arrived in Hong Kong the biggest difference I experienced was how diverse Hong Kong is. The people here prefer uniqueness and don't want to be the same as everyone else. I think this might be the reason that Li Yuchun is very popular in Hong Kong and overseas, her uniqueness. In my eyes, she's totally different from Korean and/or Japanese stars that I know of. She's not a "star product" from the mass plant. Her charm comes from her natural personality. If you want me to use a term to describe her, I would use "unique" [*weiyi*, only one].[40]

Mengjun Lin, born in Ningde, Fujian, and having completed her undergraduate degree at Xiamen University, had come to Hong Kong for graduate study and stayed to work and live. For her, it seems that the Li Yuchun fandom had even become a kind of model for the cross-language and cross-cultural friendship she has sought in Hong Kong. She continues:

> My first "Why Me" concert was Shenzhen's "Why Me." It was super fun and exciting. That year, I came to Hong Kong for my graduate study. It was a

fresh start for my own life. The same year, at the Shenzhen concert, I became friends with the Corn that sat next to me. Because of her, I became friends with many other Hong Kong Corns and friends. It was also fate of sorts. I feel like all the people I met in Hong Kong or Mainland are very kind, especially Hong Kong. When I first came to Hong Kong, I could barely speak Cantonese. I had to communicate through Mandarin and hand gestures. People understand that, and they tried their best to communicate with me in Mandarin. They even apologized for their poor Mandarin. I feel very warm in the strange city. Even though there is news that reports conflicts between the two, I think it is all problems stemming from communication issues and cultural differences. Therefore, we need to keep an even stronger commitment to fostering communication between each other.[41]

And, unsurprisingly, there is some idealization of fan bonding in keeping with this desire and also, I would guess, with the affective intensity of fandom itself. As a Zhejiang-born female fan working in retail in Hong Kong expresses it, "I think no matter if they are from Hong Kong or the Mainland, a fan's love for Li Yuchun is the same. We all love her from the bottom of our hearts."[42]

Not everyone, though, experienced the reality of these desired friendships in idealized terms. The Zhejiang-born interviewee starts out optimistically, "I think Hong Kong Corns and mainland Corns are not that different." But she continues, "Maybe Hong Kong fans are colder and more distant? Why do I say colder and more distant? . . . Even though you may have met each other at different events before, they still won't come up and talk to you."[43]

Yet, even idealized fannish attitudes have concrete results for some. As active fan, Hong Kong–born Little Fish reports:

> I was born in Hong Kong and am now studying in a university in Beijing. My major is theater literature. When I applied to universities, all the schools I applied to were in Beijing. I wanted to study in Beijing so I would be able to have more chances to see Li Yuchun. During summer vacations, I always go back to Hong Kong for some short-term jobs, mostly administrative.[44]

One example of pragmatic bonding is cross-border fan cooperation in surmounting ticket-purchasing challenges. As Hong Kong–born Little Fish outlines:

> The concert in 2009, I organized younger [Hong Kong] Corns to go to Guangzhou together to see that concert. It was very memorable. We also got some help from the Corns in Shenzhen on the way. I don't really care where people come from; Corns from other places helped us a lot as well. Because it is hard to buy Li's concert tickets in Hong Kong (especially difficult for younger students who do not have online banking), we can't buy them online. So many Shenzhen Corns were helping us to purchase the tickets.[45]

Fans disagreed on the issue of Li's *zhongxing* or gender-neutral style. Of course, in Sinitic cultures, connotations adhering to *zhongxing* vary according to time and place. In contemporary Hong Kong, the *zhongxing* style can be interpreted as connoting a lesbian-identified tomboyness or instead as merely a style with a tinge of commodified queerness to signify an independence from gender norms, or an intersection of the two. For purposes of these cross-border considerations, I am identifying Li Yuchun's *zhongxing* or gender-neutral style as queer light, with some tomboy connotations of queerness subsumed within Li Yuchun's cosmopolitan persona. In the collection of signs that are a part of Li Yuchun's image, a grassroots Chineseness also melds with this cosmopolitan, transnational style. She is a transnational, androgynous star "with Chinese characteristics." The set of gender and sexuality signs that are a part of Li Yuchun's persona figure differently for different fans and followers, as can be illustrated by responses here to my questions, using different keywords including *zhongxing* and "tomboy," regarding the star's gender appearance.

One Mainland-born fan responded definitively, "Yes, she is a tomboy. Yes, I agree with that and that's her greatest contribution, I think."[46] Others embraced Li Yuchun's style as even more ambiguous than gender neutral might imply:

> *Zhongxing* style is one of her symbols. She's not doing it for any purpose. She just likes a less flashy style. She would wear skirts during her concerts and fashion shoots. Maybe her dressing style is close to *zhongxing*, but deep down she is very beautiful [*meili*] and charming [*wumei*]. She's very different from other *zhongxing* singers. Even though her dressing style is close to *zhongxing*, her dance moves are very sexy and enchanting. I wouldn't use the term "tomboy" to describe her either. I would use "handsome, beautiful, and stylish" to describe her.[47]

Hong Konger Beatrice dances back and forth between identifying or not with Li Yuchun's montage of masculine and feminine characteristics: "I normally use 'handsome, cute, stylish, unique, and pretty' to describe her to my friends (both Corns and non-Corns). I'll also sometimes use the term 'very manly' [*hao 'man'*] to describe her tougher fashion style."[48]

Finally, the theme of a Chinese pride in Li Yuchun as a natural "new New Woman" beauty who embodies the goal of self-making[49] came up repeatedly in the fan comments, sometimes in keeping with Li's *zhongxing* style, sometimes differentiating her style as more unique: "Maybe to an outsider's eyes Li Yuchun styles herself in a *zhongxing* look, but her *zhongxing* look contains lots of Chinese traditional beauty. It's an implicit beauty under a cool surface."[50] This quote can be interpreted as both citing yet distancing Li's appeal from her *zhongxing* look as (primarily) cosmopolitan and reclaiming her handsome and beautiful cool as Chinese.

Hong Kong Aca-Gossip

The people I know best who live in Hong Kong tend to be affiliated with universities as graduate students or faculty, and I interviewed some of these friends and acquaintances about Li Yuchun—although, as it happened, they did not describe themselves as fans.[51] As I researched this chapter, I became aware that to focus exclusively on people in Hong Kong who self-define as fans of Li Yuchun's would be to tell only part of the story, and that also important was the opinion, gossip, analysis, enjoyment, and attention that those generally interested in Li Yuchun were generating. In fact, in my comings and goings to Hong Kong for work and family reasons from 2010 to 2014, I talked with a number of Hong Kong–based people (mainly women) about Li Yuchun, and it was extremely rare to find one who, whether or not she described herself as a fan, was anything but well informed and quite opinionated about Li Yuchun, her public persona, her music, and her sexuality. Although all the academic interviewees seem to be thriving professionally in Hong Kong, it did not make the Mainland-born ones immune to the realization that, as one scholar summed up bluntly, "HKers generally look down on mainland people."[52] Thus, for academic followers born on the Mainland, gossip about Li also reinforced a selective and elected sense of belonging—here to one of many cosmopolitan and gender- and sexually ambiguous parts of mainland culture as well as to academic, and, for many, popular culture in Hong Kong. (As with many fandoms, follower gossip and participation as well as fan participation together create discursive space around a celebrity or other cultural object.)

Further, interest in Li Yuchun has generated stimulating scholarship among a number of academics involved in gender, sexuality, and Asian cultural studies. The discourse around Li in academic circles via publications alongside gossip is in total a rich and evolving text for discussion of contemporary Chinese and Sinophone femininities.[53] Here I use the word "gossip" in signifying types of communication that are coded for semipublic and semiprivate homosocial circulation and inflected as feminine.[54] In fan studies, as mentioned, there is an active discourse on the aca-fan, the academic who is also a fan and may be writing from that fannish obsession and enthusiasm while also using analytical tools and bibliography. However, the word "fan" in this discourse can close off some of the resonance in the affective reception and reinterpretation of a mass culture text or celebrity persona. The interested followers also generate buzz, contribute to meaning making, and communicate affectively using the mass-culture object. It is in this way that the gossip I analyze here among interested academics is also a methodological emphasis. I assert that followers—in my usage, those interested but not self-defined as fans—matter in cultural studies when emphasizing and exploring issues in reception: here, cross-border usage of mass culture to contribute to elective belonging, and also how issues of genders and sexualities play in.[55]

I enjoy talking about Li Yuchun and am a part of this homosociality; for me, too, this fan and follower gossip and analysis has been part of building friendships. I am also a follower of Li Yuchun, albeit one born in the United States. For this chapter, I partly formalized such discussions via e-mail interviews with eight Hong Kong–based academics (six identified as women of a variety of different sexual orientations and two as gay men), some of which followed up more informal discussions. Questions I asked included, among others (1) A classic, gossipy question about *zhongxing* stars: In thinking about imaginaries related to Li Yuchun, what do you believe Li Yuchun's sexual orientation is? On what do you base your supposition? And (2) Do you consider yourself a fan of Li Yuchun's or merely interested? As I usually do in interviews, I also asked the interviewees how they wanted to be referred to, and all but one did not want to use their real name. I take this mainly as a sign that in gossiping about, among other things, sexuality we were stepping away from academic codes; specifically, although there is a copious academic archive of publications on sexuality, it rarely includes guessing what someone "is." The academic published voice, in the lingua franca English, called "academic English," also differentiates itself from both fanspeak with its heightened if also sometimes ironic affect and gossip codes, which are often inflected as feminine. Most of my academic interviewees are female emerging scholars and, too, I would suppose, subject to some pressure to appear in print in the "neutral" (read masculine-inflected authority) tone of academic English and not to splash around in print in their gossip, even thoughtful gossip, voices. Although it is common for academics to also self-define as fans in one way or another, none of these eight described themselves as a fan of Li Yuchun's. However, all but one were not only interested in the discourses around the star but quite knowledgeable and opinionated about them—and hypothetical issues about Li Yuchun's sexuality.

As mentioned "tomboy" has a wide range of cultural associations at this point in Hong Kong and on the Mainland. In Hong Kong it can be merely a sartorial and hair style connoting urbanity and contemporaneity as well as a pushing against conformist behaviors for women through envisioning the self with a feminized masculine style. For others it can connote lesbian sexuality, especially butch sexuality. There is blurring and overlap between these categories. To my read, the ambiguity is quite important as it allows some, even if mild, blurring of a heteronormative public appearance for women. Again, this is where queer light is not really light at all. Via a tomboy look, it can weigh in for heterosexual or lesbian women or others who self-define differently as signaling a gender nonconformativity and a pushing against a generalized set of norms that *can*, say, be associated with long hair in Hong Kong and on the Mainland—women as family caregivers, women as traditionally feminine, women as the "indoors person," women not working outside the home or with jobs as secondary to the husband's career. The tomboy look is not necessarily radical, though, and can signify a fashion or a slight deviation from norms—it can vary, in other words, in how individuals use it. Li Yuchun, although she has appeared in a variety of styles, came to fame as a tomboy on *Super Girl* and most often when appearing "in her own clothes" (that is clothes she seems to have selected to wear on her own time in semipublic spaces like airports) adheres consistently to a tomboy style.

Most interesting to me is that, first, almost all the interviewees had quite detailed and well-argued opinions about Li Yuchun's sexuality, and, second, almost none of these matched or duplicated each other.

Some were cynical about what they saw as Li Yuchun's performing queerness for possible market value. As one emerging scholar working in Hong Kong, anonymous, born and raised on the Mainland, heterosexual, and female, asserted:

> I guess she is originally heterosexual; however, after her rising to stardom, she might pretend to be somehow ambivalent [about her] sexuality, if not directly homosexual. She and her management know quite well that the very queerness is one of her selling points, especially in the condition that her [appearance] is not that really good among the Chinese stars. My supposition is based on the observations that she controls her images very carefully (there is no evidence to be leaked), but allowing the fans to imagine and write about her queerness freely.[56]

Others chose to identify Li Yuchun as lesbian, and this hypothesized but knowing stance is a powerful part of the role gossip plays in cross-border belonging. For instance, a doctoral student in Hong Kong, born on the Mainland, and who self-identifies as a tomboy/lesbian opines:

> I think she is lesbian in reality. Although I'm not a fan of LY, I did follow some online discussions around her sexual orientation a few years ago. I still remember that there were some erotic, or say intimate, photos of her and another female circulated online. They were half-naked in the pictures and the other female was sitting on LY's lap, I think. They were also kissing each other in one photo. Back then, there were a lot of people talking about these photos online, not only her fans or antifans. Some people said that the one in these photos was not LY. But, I think it seems very obvious to me that she's a lesbian, mainly due to my own academic identity and gender/sexuality. Her persona is very "lesbian" to me. And gender and sexual identities are always performative and fluid. So, why can't she be a lesbian? She never said she's not one. And like heterosexuality, lesbianism does not need self-defense.[57]

Yet others underlined that what matters about Li Yuchun's persona is that it is not stereotypically and traditionally Chinese-feminine. Another graduate student, born on the Mainland and pursuing her doctorate in Hong Kong, who defines herself as female and heterosexual, said, "As far as I'm concerned, most of her fans in [the] Mainland [are] female. I suppose she is performing a lesbian/just-not-straight-style for her fans. Because I think what she was before her overnight popularity [was] just some girl who [didn't] fit in the stereotypes of femininity."[58] Here I would assert that Li Yuchun's persistent singleness even more perhaps than her (culturally standard) public silence about her sexuality, a singleness that has persisted to her present age of thirty, is perhaps the most nonconformist element of her public persona.[59] In general, that singleness figures in the gossip and calculations about Li as well.

The idea of Li projecting a persona of gender and sexual ambiguity has particular appeal. As an emerging Hong Kong–based scholar, male and born on the Mainland, puts it:

> I think the images of LYC do provoke the speculation of her sexual identity as a lesbian, since she has a more masculine dressing style, lower voice and

displays personalities that deviate from the traditional feminine image. However, personally I wouldn't label her directly as lesbian, because I believe the most attractive feature about LYC is the sense of gender neutrality and sexual fluidity.

And in response to the question about how LY's being a mainland star might figure in Hong Kong, he continues:

I suppose she does enjoy international fame at least to some extent. Based on my observation LYC's gender neutral style is not rare in HK, especially in the case of young people. Therefore, I wouldn't say LYC represents something "new" or "shocking" to HKers but as a public figure she might symbolize a kind of "opening-up" of gender expression or even queer space in the Mainland to some.[60]

This kind of dual, seemingly easy (but actually related to lived experiences in both locales) readership skill, then, is a mark of cross-border elective belonging.

A feminine-inflected androgyny in a mainland idol has meaningful connotations to interested Hong Kong residents. As one doctoral student asserts, "I think LY still represents a kind of mainland Chinese grassroots pop culture and a type of young, androgynous potentially lesbian image from China. This kind of image was pretty rare in mainland China before her popularity."[61]

In an e-mail conversation, Eva Cheuk Yin Li, a contributor to this volume, who was born in Hong Kong and is now completing her doctorate at King's College in London and who has done research on Li Yuchun's reception in East Asia, emphasized the perceptual importance of Li Yuchun's sexuality as ambivalent.[62] I agree that this ambivalence is key, along with Li's cosmopolitan draw, one rooted in the Mainland but also legible across borders. It allows for a range of active gossip and complex cross-border readings related to elective belongings in followers, particularly those interested in Li's cosmopolitanism, her gender-neutral identity, or both.

Among Mainland-born, Hong Kong–dwelling fans, their self-identification as Corns can involve cosmopolitanism rooted in both the Mainland and Hong Kong. Finally, for Hong Kong–born Corns who have joined the fandom, their affinity lays the groundwork for friendships with Mainlanders even in a context of bigotry. Overall, this chapter analyzes the attitudes of Li Yuchun followers and fans among Mainland-born Hong Kong dwellers who are negotiating belonging in a fraught cultural terrain.

Notes

1. Anonymous, Hong Kong–based student, born on the Mainland in Chongqing, e-mail July 8, 2014, translated by Xiaorui Zhu-Nowell. Corns, *yumi*, are Li Yuchun fans; *yumi* is the Chinese word for "corn" and is here a homophone of the first syllable in Yuchun and the word *mi* meaning fan. Fan interviewees were located through their 2014 activity on the Baidu HKCL (Hong Kong Chris Li) Post Bar. For example, the thread http://tieba.baidu.com/p/1043659818 on the Golden Melody Awards,

accessed May 28, 2014. Follower interviewees were located through the author's friends and acquaintances, using the snowballing method to build numbers.

2. NPR, "How to Measure a Crowd, without the Political Numbers," October 5, 2014, accessed November 28, 2016, http://www.npr.org/2014/10/05/353849607/how-to-measure-a-crowd-without-the-political-numbers.

3. The Hong Kong Census and Statistics Department calculates that, as of 2011, of the Hong Kong resident population, 30.98 percent, or 2,190,973, had been born on the Mainland. http://www.census2011.gov.hk/en/build-your-census-tables.html and e-mail from Research Manager (Social) Willis Lam, December 17, 2014.

4. There is a rich discourse on aca-fans, academics in fan studies who are also fans. For instance, see Henry Jenkins, "Acafandom and Beyond: Concluding Thoughts" (blog), October 22, 2011, accessed January 11, 2016, henryjenkins.org/2011/10/acafandom_and_beyond_concludin.html; and also Mark Duffett's "Researching Fandom," in his *Understanding Fandom: An Introduction to the Study of Media Fan Culture* (New York: Bloomsbury Academic, 2013), 255–76. Yet the emphasis on the "fan" side of these discussions is still limited to dedicated, enthusiastic fans. Thus, my discussion in this chapter, while drawing from such aca-fan discussions, is closer and more indebted to scholarly considerations of gossip in reception studies such as Erin Meyers, *Dishing Dirt in the Digital Age: Celebrity Gossip Blogs and Participatory Media Culture* (New York: Peter Lang, 2013).

5. I both am positively influenced by and deviate from the scholarly tradition of fan studies scholars such as Sang-Yeon Sung and Yoshitaka Mori who have queried issues of bigotry and its potential transformation via elements of fan discourses. However, in this chapter I focus more on those who are in the discriminated-against group and are negotiating feelings of belonging rather than those expressing bigotry. Sang-Yeon Sung, "Constructing a New Image: Hallyu in Taiwan," *European Journal of East Asian Studies* 9.1 (2010): 25–45; Yoshitaka Mori, "*Winter Sonata* and Cultural Practices of Active Fans in Japan: Considering Middle-Age Women as Cultural Agents," in *East Asian Popular Culture: Analysing the Korean Wave*, ed. Chua Beng Huat and Koichi Iwabuchi (Hong Kong: Hong Kong University Press, 2008), 127–42.

6. Mica Nava, *Visceral Cosmopolitanism: Gender, Culture and the Normalisation of Difference* (Oxford: Berg, 2007). What I call "rooted cosmopolitanism" Nava refers to as a subjectivity that involves a "normalizing of difference," a cosmopolitan outlook that "not only is visceral and vernacular but also domestic," evident and practiced in everyday life (12–13).

7. Anonymous, Mainland-born "fresh graduate," e-mail in English July 21, 2014.

8. See Eva Cheuk-Yin Li's discussion of *zhongxing* in "Approaching Transnational Chinese Queer Stardom as *Zhongxing* (Neutral Sex/Gender) Sensibility," *East Asian Journal of Popular Culture* 1:1 (2015), 75–95.

9. Brian Longhurst, Gaynor Bagnall, and Mike Savage, "Place, Belonging, and the Diffused Audience," in *Fandom: Identities and Community in a Mediated World*, ed. Jonathan Gray, Cornel Sandvoss, and C. Lee Harrington (New York: New York University Press, 2007), 125–38.

10. Audrey Yue and Haiqing Yu, "China's Super Girl: Mobile Youth Cultures and New Sexualities," in *Youth Media in the Asia Pacific Region*, ed. Usha M. Rodrigues and Belinda Smaill (Newcastle, UK: Cambridge Scholars Publishing, 2008), 118.

11. "'Super Girls' Sparks Controversy over 'Vulgarity,'" *People's Daily Online*, accessed September 7, 2012, http://english.peopledaily.com.cn/200605/03/eng20060503_262793.html.

12. Ling Yang and Hongwei Bao, "Queerly Intimate: Friends, Fans and Affective Communication in a *Super Girl* Fan Fiction Community," *Cultural Studies* 26.6 (2012): 842–71.
13. Ling Yang, "All for Love: The Corn Fandom, Prosumers and the Chinese Way of Creating a Superstar," *International Journal of Cultural Studies* 12.5 (2009): 527–43.
14. Yang and Bao, "Queerly Intimate."
15. Lucetta Yip Lo Kam, *Shanghai Lalas: Female Tongzhi Communities and Politics in Urban China* (Hong Kong: Hong Kong University Press, 2012), 75.
16. Jing Jamie Zhao, "Fandom as a Middle Ground: Fictive Queer Fantasies and Real-World Lesbianism in *FSCN*," in "Access/Trespass," special conference issue, *Media Fields Journal* 10 (2014), accessed February 10, 2016, http://mediafieldsjournal.squarespace.com/fandom-as-a-middle-ground/. And on sellable queerness, see Egret Lulu Zhou's chapter in this volume.
17. In 2005 the mean age for PRC women for first marriage was 23.6; in the country's largest city, Shanghai, 24.1. Deborah S. Davis and Sara L. Friedman, *Wives, Husbands, and Lovers: Marriage and Sexuality in Hong Kong, Taiwan, and Urban China*, ed. Deborah S. Davis and Sara L. Friedman (Stanford, CA: Stanford University Press, 2014), 7, table 1.1, Mean age at first marriage, 1970–2005.
18. Lucetta Yip Lo Kam, "Desiring T, Desiring Self: 'T-Style' Pop Singers and Lesbian Culture in China," *Journal of Lesbian Studies* 18.3 (2014): 252–65.
19. Matt Hills, "Media Academics as Media Audiences," in *Fandom: Identities and Communities in a Mediated World*, ed. Jonathan Gray, Cornel Sandvoss, and C. Lee Harrington (New York: New York University Press, 2007), 33–47.
20. Anonymous, cultural studies scholar in Hong Kong, born Mainland, e-mail August 26, 2014. Note: throughout this chapter, if no translator is cited for an interview quote, the interviewee responded in English.
21. Ms. Ng [pseud.], doctoral student in Hong Kong, born in Hong Kong, heterosexual, e-mail September 8, 2014.
22. Mengjun Lin, e-mail interview July 21, 2014, translated by Xiaorui Zhu-Nowell.
23. These interviewees were found through their online activity in Baidu Post Bar such as http://tieba.baidu.com/f?kw=%CA%A5%C4%C9%B0%D9%B4%A8&fr=ala0&tpl=5. Star Sijia Liu is the research assistant for this project.
24. Yang and Bao, "Queerly Intimate."
25. Beatrice [pseud.], Hong Kong teacher, born in Hong Kong, e-mail July 21, 2014, translated by Xiaorui Zhu-Nowell.
26. Here I find Jose Esteban Muñoz's concept of disidentification useful as signaling that a range of women looking to deviate from various femininity norms might choose to disidentify to a degree with a lesbian-seeming look or persona. José Esteban Muñoz, *Disidentifications: Queers of Colors and the Performance of Politics* (Minneapolis: University of Minnesota Press, 1999).
27. John Nguyet Erni, "Marriage Rights for Transgender People in Hong Kong," in *Wives, Husbands, and Lovers: Marriage and Sexuality in Hong Kong, Taiwan, and Urban China*, ed. Deborah S. Davis and Sara L. Friedman (Stanford: Stanford University Press, 2014), 196.
28. In 2015, mainland Chinese comprised the largest tourist visitor percentage for Hong Kong, at 77 percent of the total. Mainland Chinese tourists numbered 45.8 million arrivals. www.tourism.gov.hk/english/statistics/statistics_perform.html, accessed November 30, 2016.

29. Linda To, "Hong Kong Should Help Vulnerable Mainland Immigrants, Not Denigrate Them," *South China Morning Post*, August 28, 2014, http://www.scmp.com/print/comment/insight-opinion/article/1581222/hong-kong-should-help-vulnerable-mainland-immigrants-not.
30. Carol Jones, "Lost in China? Mainlandisation and Resistance in Post-1997 Hong Kong," *Taiwan in Comparative Perspectives* 5 (2014): 22–23.
31. David Volodzko, "Self-Perceptions Strain Hong Kong-Mainland Relations," *Diplomat*, September 14, 2014, accessed November 29, 2016, http://thediplomat.com/2014/09/self-perceptions-strain-hong-kong-mainland-relations/.
32. Brendon Hong, "Hackers Attack Hong Kong Pro-Democracy Websites," *Daily Beast*, June 19, 2014, accessed June 19, 2014. http://www.thedailybeast.com/articles/2014/06/18/hackers-attack-hong-kong-pro-democracy-websites.html.
33. "Spot the Mainlander," *Dictionary of Politically Incorrect Hong Kong Cantonese: Politically Incorrect Views from Hong Kong*, accessed June 19, 2014, badcanto.wordpress.com/spot-the-mainlander/.
34. Klaus Theweleit, *Male Fantasies*, Vol. 1, *Women, Floods, Bodies, History*, trans. Chris Turner et al. (Minneapolis: University of Minnesota Press, 1987).
35. Peter Kammerer, "Open Hong Kong Must Not Tolerate Discrimination against Migrants," *South China Morning Post*, June 8, 2015, accessed June 8, 2015, www.scmp.com/print/comment/insight-opinion/article/1818329/open-hong-kong-must-not-tolerate-discrimination-against.
36. For the subsumed argument, see Xin Huang, "From 'Hyper-feminine' to Androgyny: Changing Notions of Femininity in Contemporary China," in *Asian Popular Culture in Transition*, ed. Lorna FitzSimmons and John A. Lent (New York: Routledge, 2013), 133–55.
37. Chengzhou He, "Trespassing, Crisis and Renewal: Li Yugang and Cross-Dressing Performance," *Differences: A Journal of Feminist Cultural Studies* 24.2 (2013): 167.
38. Little Fish [pseud.], active fan since 2008, born in Hong Kong, e-mail July 14, 2014, translated by Xiaorui Zhu-Nowell.
39. Anonymous, born on the Mainland, in twelfth grade in Hong Kong at time of interview, e-mail September 7, 2014, translated by Star Sijia Liu.
40. Mengjun Lin, Hong Kong–based music teacher, Mainland-born in Ningde, Fujian, undergraduate studies Xiamen, graduate studies Hong Kong, e-mail July 21, 2014, translated by Xiaorui Zhu-Nowell.
41. Ibid.
42. Anonymous, works in Hong Kong in retail, Mainland-born in Zhejiang, e-mail July 5, 2014, translated by Xiaorui Zhu-Nowell.
43. Anonymous, born, Zhejiang, e-mail interview July 5, 2014, translated by Xiaorui Zhu-Nowell.
44. Little Fish, e-mail July 14, 2014.
45. Ibid.
46. Anonymous, Hong Kong–based recent graduate, Mainland-born, e-mail July 21, 2014.
47. Anonymous, e-mail July 11, 2014, translated by Xiaorui Zhu-Nowell.
48. Beatrice, Hong Kong–born and Hong Kong–based teacher, e-mail July 21, 2014, translated by Xiaorui Zhu-Nowell.

49. Fran Martin, "The Gender of Mobility," *Intersections: Gender and Sexuality in Asia and the Pacific* 35 (2014), accessed January 5, 2016, http://intersections.anu.edu.au/issue35/martin.htm.
50. Anonymous, born in Zhejiang, e-mail July 5, 2014, translated by Xiaorui Zhu-Nowell.
51. Hills, "Media Academics as Media Audiences," 33–47.
52. Anonymous, born Mainland, e-mail interview August 17, 2014.
53. For scholars who have published on Li Yuchun, see especially Kam, "Desiring T, Desiring Self," 252–65; Li, "Approaching Transnational Chinese Queer Stardom," 75–95; Huike Wen, "'Diversifying' Masculinity: Super Girls, Happy Boys, Cross-Dressers, and Real Men on Chinese Media," *ASIA Network Exchange: A Journal for Asian Studies in the Liberal Arts* 21.1 (2013): 1–11; http://asianetworkexchange.org/index.php/ane/article/view/75/152; Hui Faye Xiao, "Androgynous Beauty, Virtual Sisterhood," in *Super Girls, Gangstas, Freeters, and Xenomaniacs: Gender and Modernity in Global Youth Cultures*, ed. Susan Dewey and Karen Brison (Syracuse, NY: Syracuse University Press, 2012), 104–24; Huang, "From 'Hyper-Feminine'," 133–55; Yang, "All for Love," 527–43; Yang and Bao, "Queerly Intimate," 842–71; Yue and Yu, "China's Super Girl,"117–34; Jing Jamie Zhao, "Articulating the 'L' Word Online: A Study of Chinese Slash Fandom of *Super Girl*" (MA thesis, University of Wisconsin–Milwaukee, 2012).
54. Irit Rogoff, "Gossip as Testimony," (1996) in *The Feminism and Visual Culture Reader*, ed. Amelia Jones (New York: Routledge, 2003), 268–76.
55. Erin Meyers in *Dishing Dirt*, page 30, usefully reminds us about celebrity gossip, "the well-knowingness of the celebrity works to reduce the intervening social distance between strangers by acting as a social conduit, bringing individuals together around shared knowledge and the creation of shared social values." And Helen Hok-Sze Leung analyzes the importance of queer celebrity gossip in self-making in her *Undercurrents: Queer Culture and Postcolonial Hong Kong* (Vancouver: University of British Columbia Press, 2008), 90–92.
56. Anonymous, Mainland-born, e-mail interview August 17, 2014.
57. Anonymous, doctoral student, Mainland-born, e-mail interview August 11, 2014.
58. Anonymous, doctoral student, Mainland-born, e-mail interview August 21, 2014.
59. See, for instance, Deborah S. Davis, "On the Limits of Personal Autonomy: PRC Law and the Institution of Marriage," 41–61, and Yong Cai and Wang Feng, "(Re)emergence of Late Marriage in Shanghai: From Collective Synchronization to Individual Choice," 97–117, in *Wives, Husbands, and Lovers: Marriage and Sexuality in Hong Kong, Taiwan, and Urban China*, ed. Deborah S. Davis and Sara L. Friedman (Stanford: Stanford University Press, 2014).
60. Anonymous, doctoral student, Mainland-born, e-mail interview August 21, 2014.
61. Anonymous, doctoral student, Mainland-born, e-mail interview August 11, 2014.
62. E-mail with Eva Cheuk Yin Li, September 10, 2014.

III.

Taiwan

9
Exploring the Significance of "Japaneseness"

A Case Study of Fujoshi's *BL Fantasies in Taiwan*

Weijung Chang

Situating Taiwanese *Fujoshi* Culture in the Japanophilia Context

Fujoshi, defined as girls who read male homoerotic texts such as BL (Boys' Love) or *yaoi*, originated in the fan culture of Japanese *shōjo manga*.[1] The core activities of *fujoshi* culture are to create fantasies about male homoerotic relationships or to reinterpret existing male homosocial relationships as *gong/shou*[2] couplings in fictional narratives or both. As a part of the globalization of Japanese popular culture, *fujoshi* culture also has emerged and become visible in Taiwan since the late 1990s, but, in fact, the introduction of Japanese male-male homoerotic manga can be traced back to an earlier period. (Fran Martin's chapter in this volume discusses this history in depth by giving a thorough overview of the development of the manga industry in Taiwan.)

The rapidly changing social context since the late 1980s brought indirect results for Taiwanese consumption of the vast range of Japanese manga. The processes of liberalization and democratization sped up after the lifting of martial law in 1987, including the abolition of manga censorship in 1988. Moreover, because of the Copyrights Act passed in 1992, many manga publishers started to contract with Japanese publishers to publish Japanese manga legally. As a result, nowadays, Japanese manga, including BL, occupies the majority of Taiwan's local manga market. There are lots of BL manga in bookstores or rental bookstores, and *yaoi* fan fiction is also popular. Not only are readers of BL texts increasing in numbers, but both amateur and professional artists participate actively in original or secondary creations.[3] Together these texts and related fan practices construct *fujoshi* culture in Taiwan.

However, the construction and localization of *fujoshi* culture in Taiwan is not simply the inevitable result of cultural dissemination. It has been widely recognized that Taiwan has the most noticeable "pro-Japanese" attitude among former Japanese colonial regions in Asia. One of the most representative examples is the "Japanophilia phenomenon," that is, a "feverish passion" for Japanese popular culture and Japanese cultural products that began to take shape between the late 1990s to the early 2000s.[4] People who enthusiastically consume products imbued with "Japaneseness" or get involved with Japanese popular culture are referred to as Japanophiles. Because of the diversification of consumption and acceptance of Japaneseness, I suggest expanding the range of Japanophilia and redefining it to include *fujoshi* culture. Although *fujoshi* culture has not been previously accounted for as relating to the Japanophilia phenomenon, its practices embrace the concept of Japanophilia in that participants tend to place Japaneseness at the center of their everyday lives.[5]

The main purpose of this chapter is to examine the localization of *fujoshi* culture in Taiwan by situating it within the context of Japanophilia. I intend to answer the following questions: How has *fujoshi* culture been localized in the Japanophilia context? What is the symbolic significance of Japaneseness in Taiwanese *fujoshi* practice? To answer these two questions, I will elaborate on the Japanophilia context in relation to Taiwanese *fujoshi* culture. Furthermore, I reveal the role Japaneseness plays in Taiwanese *fujoshi* culture by exploring how Taiwanese *fujoshi* practice constructs BL fantasy. Ultimately, by clarifying how local sociocultural context shapes the construction of today's hybridized popular cultures and lived experiences, I hope this research can bring a new perspective to help analyze cross–East Asian *fujoshi* cultures.

To be more specific, in this research, I examine BL fantasies of Taiwanese *fujoshi* by interviewing twelve Taiwanese *fujoshi*.[6] To analyze how Japaneseness functions as a Japanophilic cultural element in their BL fantasies, I pay careful attention to the interviewees' practices in constructing BL fantasies and in relating themselves to Japaneseness. The following table shows the profile of the twelve interviewees.

Overview of the Japanophilia Context

In my earlier work, I focused on media attention to the Japanophilia phenomenon and pointed out a trajectory of how social recognition of Japanophilia has changed since this term had been created.[7] Because Japanophilia arose as a consequence of the Cable Television Broadcast Act in 1993, which lifted the ban on Japanese TV dramas, it was colloquially and generically recognized as referring to the passion for Japanese TV drama or related media products. However, accompanied by mass media coverage, the employment of this term in the more recent Taiwanese context by the general public has started to deviate and broaden from that initial usage. That is, the appropriation and localization of Japanese elements—such as the use of common Japanese cooking ingredients to create Taiwanese dishes, TV dramas based on Japanese manga with every protagonist maintaining a Japanese name, or the use of elements of Japanese fashion in the local fashion industry—has appeared in a large proportion of Taiwanese news reports published since 2000. In addition, the acceptance of Japanese

Table 9.1
Profile of Taiwanese *fujoshi*

	Age	Occupation	Linguistic ability in Japanese	Experience of visiting Japan	Period of being a *fujoshi*	Category of interests
A	30s	Office worker in Taiwan	Fluent in conversational Japanese	Travel, one-year working holiday	About 10 years since the second year of university	Voice actors, *Kamen Rider* TV show, Otome games, Sengoku-period warriors
B	20s	Japanese language school student in Japan	Fluent in conversational Japanese	Residing in Japan	About 14 years since junior high school	Manga, animation, games, Sengoku-period warriors
C	20s	Graduate student in Taiwan	Basic level	Travel	About 10 years since the third year of junior high school	Manga, animation, the Johnny's idol groups, the Niconico Dōga singers
D	20s	Undergraduate student in Japan	Fluent in conversational Japanese	Four-year overseas education in Japan University	Over 10 years since elementary school	Manga, animation, voice actors, idols, vocaloids, Sengoku-period warriors
E	20s	Office worker in Taiwan	Fluent in conversational Japanese	One-year foreign exchange	About 10 years since elementary school	Voice actors, manga, novels
F	20s	Office worker in Taiwan	Not a speaker	None	Contingently touched in elementary school; became interested since the second year in high school	Novels

Table 9.1
(continued)

	Age	Occupation	Linguistic ability in Japanese	Experience of visiting Japan	Period of being a *fujoshi*	Category of interests
G	20s	Undergraduate student in Taiwan	Not a speaker	None	About 10 years since the sixth grade	Novels, manga
H	20s	Undergraduate student in Taiwan	Fluent in conversational Japanese	Travel	About 10 years since junior high school	Novels, manga
I	30s	Graduate student in America	Fluent in conversational Japanese	Travel, short-term visit for research	About 10 years since high school	Manga, Japanese television drama, Japanese movies, the Johnny's idol group
J	30s	Office worker in Taiwan	Basic level	Travel	About 10 years since high school	Visual bands
K	20s	Office worker in Taiwan	Fluent in conversational Japanese	Travel, business trip	About 10 years since junior high school	Manga, animation
L	20s	Office worker in Taiwan	Fluent in conversational Japanese	Travel	Over 10 years since junior high school	Manga, animation, the Niconico Dōga singers

otaku culture (which includes manga, animation, *tongrenzhi*,[8] cosplay,[9] and other related products or practices) and its associated practices in the local context has also been connected to the Japanophilia context. Although the number of news articles related to Japanophilia started to decline after 2002,[10] still, the enthusiasm for learning Japanese and the appropriation of Japanese vocabulary into a Chinese context became social phenomena deserving of attention in the mass media.

Such transformation of how the Taiwanese mass media perceived "Japanophilia" shows that the localization of "Japaneseness," which refers to all elements or symbols representing the image or association of Japan or evoking the imaginary of Japan, became socially recognized as an important part of Japanophilia.[11] Accordingly, I consider "Japaneseness" as a key element to focus on when analyzing the Japanophilia context.

Existing studies on Japanophilia in Taiwanese academia correspond with the transformation in the public understanding of Japanophilia. In the early 2000s, most of the research concentrated on the consumption and acceptance of mainstream Japanese entertainment media, especially the interest in Japanese TV dramas. Later, more scholars started to show interest in the acceptance and construction of *otaku* culture in the local context. For instance, Tzuyao Lee's focus on the creativity of practices in the *tongrenzhi* and cosplay communities,[12] Shihyun Chang's chronological study on the development of the *tongrenzhi* fairs in Taiwan,[13] and Chih-lan Tsai's situating of Taiwanese BL novels in the Taiwanese women's writing tradition[14] all manifest the localization of Japanese *otaku* culture and BL culture, and expand the diversity of the acceptance and localization of Japaneseness in the Japanophilia context.

Japaneseness is also an important element to focus on when analyzing Japanophiles, who are difficult to define as a community that has concrete boundaries or a clear sense of solidarity.[15] Existing studies about Japanophiles not only indicate that they share at some level their common desire for Japaneseness but also their motivation for keeping in touch or associating themselves with Japaneseness. For instance, in Lee's study mentioned above, he interviewed several *danbangke* (merchants who travel around trading on their own or parallel import retailers) who owned small stores selling Japanese products obtained by private importing. He argued that these *danbangke* are Japanophiles who associate themselves with Japaneseness through their form of business, and, at the same time, they also try to connect with other Japanophile consumers.[16] Yufen Ko[17] and Iyun Lee's[18] studies explored the issue of how Japanophile fans of Japanese TV drama linked themselves with Japaneseness by watching TV dramas or even by discussing them with other fans on the Internet. Moreover, Yizhen Chen investigated how female fans of Johnny's idol groups use the Internet and computer technologies to watch real-time Japanese TV programs and thus construct feelings of getting close to Japaneseness on a temporal axis.[19] Although each study demonstrates different types of Japanophiles and different kinds of imagined cultural identities related to Japan, these studies share a common focus in revealing the enthusiastic motivation of constantly associating oneself with Japaneseness. Following this ongoing dialogue, I suggest defining Japanophiles not by the objects they devote themselves to but by the strong desire or motivation to associate themselves with Japaneseness.

Japaneseness is the element that not only constructs the base of Japanophilia but also shapes Japanophiles' core desires. At a time when the rich and multifaceted Japanese popular culture has taken root and flourished in Taiwan through Japanophiles' consumption, performances, and daily practices, the role of Japaneseness in those practices remains one of the most intriguing issues to explore. Accordingly, my analysis of Taiwanese *fujoshi* culture contextualizes the acceptance and localization of BL against this Japanophilia background and focuses on how Japaneseness functions as a significant element in Taiwanese *fujoshi* practices.

The Japanophile Taiwanese *Fujoshi*

In this section, I first explore details of how Taiwanese *fujoshi* construct BL fantasies in their daily practices. In this essay I define "BL fantasies" as the processes and pleasures accompanying fantasizing about male homoerotic relationships in the context of *fujoshi* practices. According to my interviews, most of the Taiwanese *fujoshi* encountered BL texts in their adolescence, and most of these texts were Chinese translations of Japanese manga. For instance, interviewee H said:

> When I was in junior high school, I went to cram school. After cram school, I usually went to a rental library with my friend. I loved reading *shōjo manga*, but one day, my friend recommended *The Ice-Cold Demon's Tale* [*Koori no mamono no monogatari / Bing zhi mo wuyu*] to me and said, "It's kind of interesting." Later, she recommended to me *Desperate Love* (*Zetsuai 1989 / Jue'ai 1989*), and I totally fell in love with BL.

In general among the interviewees, those who were enchanted by the male homoerotism in these Japanese texts started their adolescent lives as *fujoshi*. They not only consumed BL manga or novels but also enjoyed the processes of constructing BL fantasies about male-male close relationships. This finding supports the conclusion drawn by Patrick W. Galbraith[20] and Pinzhi Liu[21] that BL fantasy and such pleasures strengthen each other, thus framing a very important part of *fujoshi* common practice.

My interviews demonstrate that the Japanophilia context is deeply and broadly rooted in Taiwanese *fujoshi* practices, in roughly two ways. The first is the general preference for Japaneseness in their daily lives. For instance, some interviewees, like interviewees I and J, not only read Japanese BL works but also show a consistent preference for Japanese pop artists. They pay great attention to details of the close relationship between specific members of idol groups or rock bands and construct BL fantasies about them. In addition, despite the wide range of Japan-originated cultural products such as manga, animation, music, TV dramas, or variety shows that are translated into Mandarin, some *fujoshi* prefer to consume in the original language regardless of whether they understand Japanese or not.

A tendency to regard the Japanese language itself as a unique enchantment of Japaneseness was also found in my interviews. For instance, even though they did not understand any Japanese, interviewees A and E both had the experience of being addicted to certain voice actors of Japanese BL drama CDs in their adolescence. They stated that most of the drama CDs they listened to were based on BL manga, so they could understand the stories by reading Chinese editions of those manga or scanlations[22] on the Internet. However, their statements imply that it was not the stories but the texture, the performance of male voice actors, or even their Japanese intonations that attracted them most. Interviewee E devoted herself to voice actors and went to their concerts and talk shows to experience the enchantment of their voices. Interviewee A said that she used to listen to BL drama CDs before bedtime, because she could relax and become happy from hearing voice actors' voices, allowing her to fall deeply asleep. In other words, seemingly separate from the homoerotic elements in BL drama CDs, by purely concentrating on voice actors' voice performances in Japanese, they created a form of *moe*[23] which may include romantic imagination, enchantment, happiness, and pleasure. The examples provided here indicate that whether a *fujoshi* understands Japanese or not, Japanese as a foreign language can possibly be considered as an element which facilitates or inspires fantasy.

Contrastingly, the case of interviewee B reflects a way to fantasize about Japanese language based on its historical and linguistic structure. Interviewee B who is addicted to the coupling of the Sengoku-period warriors Date Masamune and his retainer Katakura Kojūrō mentioned that she was fascinated with Katakura's use of Japanese honorifics and the phrases used by samurai in the Sengoku period (1467–1573/1603)[24] such as *ikemasenu* or *degozaru*.[25] She said that it is because such Japanese terms and phrasing present both the signature of the historical period and the strict hierarchical relation between the characters. In the context in which one understands Japanese, Japanese grammar and honorifics are regarded as symbols facilitating fantasizing about a BL couplings' relationship, and their social/historical context as well.

Other cases such as interviewees who prefer Japanese-version animations to the Chinese-dubbed ones, or listen to or sing Japanese animation songs also show the preference for "Japaneseness." The feeling of *moe* is also closely related to Japaneseness. For instance, many *fujoshi* said that they gain a feeling of *moe* from characters' attributes such as black hair, glasses, *tsundere*,[26] or uniforms, which are frequently depicted in Japanese manga. Generally speaking, *fujoshi*'s cultural capital tends to include details about characters and couplings in Japanese texts, skills to distinguish Japanese voice actors, or information about new releases in Japan. Exchanging such information and knowledge plays a fundamental role in *fujoshi*'s personal communications and relationships. For instance, interviewees A and B are friends in private and both are fans of the game/animation/theater series called Sengoku BASARA. They not only talked about voice actors and theater actors of the Sengoku BASARA series but also exchanged responses to BL manga and animation, and even went to a karaoke bar together several times. Interviewees H, J, and K also shared the experience of traveling to Japan with their *fujoshi* friends and buying hundreds of BL manga at bookstores. All these examples reveal the strong preference for Japaneseness in Taiwanese *fujoshi* practice.

The second way is the employment of Japaneseness in their fan practices. For instance, some *fujoshi* use Japanese-style pen names or Japanese vocabulary when communicating with other *fujoshi*. The most obvious example is that they frequently use the Japanese term *moe* instead of its Mandarin translation *meng* to express their excitement and pleasure about BL couplings. Fan fiction involving Japanese singers or manga characters written in Mandarin (and sometimes also containing several Japanese words/vocabulary/sentences) or involving fantasies about Taiwanese politicians[27] are good examples of the localization of BL. Teri Silvio's study on Pili puppetry fan fiction even demonstrates how some female fans who also identify themselves as *fujoshi* combine Taiwanese traditional culture with aesthetics and illustrating skills effected by Japanese manga to create BL *tongrenzhi* of Pili puppetry.[28] The case of interviewee B shows more detail about how localization of BL is embedded in a *fujoshi*'s practice. B talked about her enthusiasm for Sengoku BASARA featuring Sengoku-period warriors. She not only paid great attention to the master-servant relationship between the characters Date Masamune and Katakura Kojūrō but also traced their historical records in order to create manga and novels about them. She used Mandarin mainly in her novel creations, but since she is now a foreign worker in Japan with strong Japanese language skills, she used plenty of Japanese sentences and vocabulary (sometimes even Japanese dialects) in her short manga even though most of her readers are Taiwanese.

The fact that *fujoshi* are constantly surrounded by Japaneseness implies that *fujoshi* practices are embedded in the Japanophilia context and that *fujoshi* share the desire for Japaneseness with other types of Japanophiles. This commonality is seen in interviewee A's and C's self-identifications in a complicated way. C identified herself as a Japanophile, because "Japaneseness[29] is like something at the center of my life. . . . Things I like or am interested in are all surrounded with it." To the contrary, A rejected the label of Japanophile for she has "no interest in Japanese TV drama" and "does not blindly value all Japanese products." Yet, she admitted that "when choosing something, say, simply a chair, and say there are some materials which are made-in-Taiwan and others are made-in-Japan, I probably would first give a glance at or just choose the Japanese one." Although such interviewees as A do not necessarily identify themselves as Japanophiles, their close relationship with Japaneseness is undeniable.

This result implies the complicated overlap between *fujoshi* culture and the Japanophilia context, as well as between *fujoshi* and Japanophiles. On the one hand, *fujoshi* and Japanophiles share the commonality that Japaneseness occupies a large part of their life. Yet *fujoshi* do not necessarily identify themselves clearly as Japanophiles. Some of them, like interviewee A mentioned above, even show resistance to the negative image often applied to Japanophiles. On the other hand, although in most studies the fact of *fujoshi* consuming Japanese BL manga seems to be self-evident, what this strong preference for Japaneseness means in Taiwanese *fujoshi* culture has rarely been discussed.

The above analysis has shown the importance of the structural passion and shared desire for Japaneseness under the Japanophilia context. Based on the strong attitude of preference and desire for Japaneseness evidenced in my interviews, I turn now to an elaboration on how Japaneseness matters with regard to Taiwanese *fujoshi*'s BL fantasies. Moreover, with the premise that BL fantasies and the accompanying pleasures of *moe* are at the core of *fujoshi* culture, I suggest that a consideration of those pleasures would be key to clarify how Japaneseness functions in Taiwanese *fujoshi*'s fantasies. In the next section, I will further explore the context of the transformation of the social meanings of Japaneseness and its relation with Taiwanese *fujoshi*'s BL fantasies.

The Role Japaneseness Plays in BL Fantasies

Martin has paid careful attention to the role of Japaneseness in Taiwanese *fujoshi* culture.[30] First, she persuasively critiqued Koichi Iwabuchi's argument that the worldwide impact of Japanese cultural products is due to their "cultural odorlessness."[31] Instead, she provided strong evidence proving that the desirable Japaneseness acts as an important element for facilitating or inspiring fantasy particularly in the BL context. On the one hand, she indicated how Taiwanese readers use BL to create an imaginative geography of "Japan" that is characterized by homoeroticism. On the other hand, she also showed how the readers establish a social subworld where *fujoshi* are linked together. Her argument on imaginary geography and Japaneseness inspires me to delve further concerning these issues in light of the complex Taiwan-Japan relationship.

The first point I employ to look more carefully into Japaneseness is that, given the lingering influence of Japanese colonial history—such as the continuing existence of Japanese architecture, artifacts, institutions, and living habits in Taiwanese society—Japaneseness has become part of material lives of *fujoshi*, and its foreignness has been reduced. Second, we need to understand the formation and transformation of pro-Japan attitudes in Taiwan and the social significance of Japaneseness. The pro-Japanese sentiment has been explained both as an effect of the Kōminka Movement, the Imperialization Movement, 1937–1945, during the Japanese colonial period, and as a result of the contrast Taiwanese people observed between Japanese colonialism and the autocratic Nationalist government during the martial law period. Many studies have focused on the nostalgia for colonial powers in postcolonial countries, especially when political oppression from the new government betrays people's expectations for a liberated nation.[32]

The process of how the pro-Japanese sentiment had gradually taken shape under the radical changes in the Taiwanese historical and political environment further relates to the symbolization of Japaneseness. During the colonial period, Taiwanese people constructed their view of Japan, a hybrid based on actual experiences with Japanese residents in Taiwan and imaginary concepts of Japan proper.[33] Such a view of Japan was later transformed into a collective romanticized memory of colonial experience during the postwar martial law eras. During those eras of political conflicts, Japaneseness was idealized as the symbol of modernity with positive meanings, contrasting with the corrupt Nationalist government.[34] Since then Japaneseness has continued to be constructed as the symbol of modernity in the Japanophilia context but in a different way. It has been argued that Japanophile audiences were enchanted by Japanese TV dramas because these dramas provide concrete and accessible images and models of modernity in East Asia.[35] In the case of Taiwan, because of its complicated historical process in relation to Japan, Japaneseness is both a homely, mundane element deeply rooted in Taiwanese people's daily lives as well as an essentially foreign attribute subject to constant reimagination and reinvention. This double feature of Japaneseness, highly specific to Taiwanese society, is precisely what makes it so desirable to Taiwanese Japanophiles. This local configuration of Japaneseness is crucial to our understanding of its significance in relation to BL fantasy.

Since I have showed that Japaneseness occupies part of Taiwanese *fujoshi*'s daily lives, fantasies facilitated by Japaneseness could indeed be experienced with a particular intimacy in *fujoshi*'s private lives. It has been discussed in many Japanese *fujoshi* studies that the BL coupling could represent some women's ideal type of romantic love or the ultimate pure love, for *gong* and *shou*, who have homogeneous bodies but heterogeneous personalities, share a relatively equal and intensely closely paired relationship.[36] My interviews also show a similar attitude. For instance, interviewee I situated the coupling of Johnny's idol group's members as evoking "something like a unicorn or myth." Interviewee L said that she always wishes for the couple's happiness when reading BL manga. Interviewee L even talked about how she projected her ideal partner in a romantic relationship on one BL manga character.[37] Although their ideal type for romantic love might differ among interviewees, these examples show a common pattern of projecting an ideal type of romantic relationship onto BL couplings.

Anthony Giddens has provided a lucid analysis of the transformation of intimacy in modern society.[38] He points out that if romantic love represents a kind of everlasting and "one-and-only" intimate relationship, confluent love then is a type of pure, idealist relationship that is characterized by high modernity, egalitarianism, reciprocity, and democracy. Drawing on Giddens's distinction between romantic love and confluent love, we can see that the BL genre has combined elements of both types. In recent years, BL coupling has gradually evolved from an indulging aesthetics of the *shōnen-ai* (Boys' Love) era, in which two characters are intimately bounded and one character cannot live without the other, into an aesthetics that focuses on egalitarianism, reciprocity, and complementariness. While it is true that most *fujoshi* have their favorite "one-and-only" BL pairings, which often embody their ideals of pure intimacy, BL works as a whole represent an imaginary collective of diverse, fluid, pure intimacies. Unlike Giddens, who believes that men prefer short-term sexual relationships and, contrastingly, who chooses lesbianism as an example of confluent love, *fujoshi* project their ideals of confluent love onto distinctively male bodies. In so doing, they create a utopia of love in which the male characters strive hard for personal happiness. In these utopian love fantasies, the male couples form a faithful and egalitarian relationship whether they come to a happy ending or bad ending. We may even argue that the confluent love often portrayed in BL is purer and more idealistic than that described by Giddens. In short, BL articulates Taiwanese *fujoshi*'s craving for a highly modernized and idealized model of intimate relationship. This process of idealization could be regarded as corresponding to a key characteristic of Japanophila, that is, a belief in Japaneseness as symbolizing the ideal of modernity.

Another important question that needs to be further explored is how the relationship between Taiwanese *fujoshi* and Japaneseness might change, given the context of increased cross-cultural or cross-regional mobility. Japan seems to be within reach to Taiwanese *fujoshi*, and thus the cultural "distance" seems to be gradually disappearing. Does this change strengthen the familiarity and weaken the foreignness of Japaneseness or even prevent Taiwanese people from desiring or fantasizing about Japaneseness? Iyun Lee argued that when Japanophiles (in her case, the term referred to the fans of Japanese TV drama) have had the chance to gradually become closer with "authentic" Japanese culture, such as experiencing a long-term stay in Japan, they tend to become disillusioned in their expectations for or imaginations about Japan/Japaneseness.[39] However, the results shown in my research seem to be far more complicated.

Most of my interviewees experienced short-term or long-term stays in Japan, and they share paradoxical feelings of getting geographically or culturally close to Japan. On the one hand, making a pilgrimage to the "authentic" home of Japaneseness brought them pleasure and satisfaction. On the other hand, even though they were in Japan surrounded with "authentic" Japaneseness, that situation contrarily reminded them of the differences and foreignness between them and Japaneseness. Yet, interestingly, these paradoxical feelings strengthened their desire for Japaneseness rather than weakened it. For instance, both interviewees A and C shared a feeling of anxiety during their stay in Japan because it ironically made them realize that although they kept constructing familiarity with Japaneseness by consuming Japanese cultural materials, it could not perfectly bridge the distance between them and the country's culture. Yet that anxiety never stops them from traveling to Japan, not to mention from continually consuming Japanese products and culture in their daily lives. Since first attending a concert of her favorite Japanese singer in Tokyo in 2013, interviewee C has traveled frequently to Japan for sightseeing and concerts. Interviewee A even started a collection of *yukata*[40] and other kimono styles. She not only enthusiastically researches this traditional Japanese clothing culture but also tries to coordinate it with her contemporary experience by taking pictures in Japanesque landscapes of herself wearing kimonos. When she recently traveled to Japan in 2015, she even went cherry-blossom viewing and shopping wearing a kimono to practice a kimono lifestyle, because she was unable to go out in kimono outfits freely in Taiwan. Japan seems to provide her with a physical environment to indulge in her passion for kimono and act out her ideal Japanese lifestyle. All these acts of interviewees C and A are attempts to routinize Japaneseness in real life, through which we can gain a glimpse of how the desire for Japaneseness, BL fantasy, and pleasure are intertwined and embedded in the everyday practices of Taiwanese *fujoshi*. These examples thus imply the special feature of Taiwanese *fujoshi*, that is, a shared lifestyle of constructing BL fantasies facilitated by Japaneseness, enjoying the enchantment of Japaneseness, and at the same time continually desiring Japaneseness.

Conclusion

This chapter first gave an overview of the development of the Japanophilia phenomenon to indicate that Japaneseness is the core element necessary to comprehend both the Japanophilia context and the sharing of desire among Japanophiles. I thus analyzed Taiwanese *fujoshi* culture within the Japanophilia context focusing on the element of Japaneseness. I argued that the role Japaneseness plays in Taiwanese *fujoshi*'s BL fantasies, which facilitates their desire for confluent intimacy, is heavily related to the historical, political, and social context in which both the familiarity and foreignness of Japaneseness have been gradually shaped. This explains the importance of the Japanophilia context to Taiwanese *fujoshi*'s BL fantasies and the significant meanings of Japaneseness to the contemporary Taiwanese social context.

The analysis based on my interviews shows how gender, sexuality, and national and cultural practices intersect with each other, resulting in the creation of fantasies and pleasures, in the sense that the construction of Taiwanese *fujoshi* BL fantasies contains a range of women's attitudes toward male homoerotism and their desire for Japaneseness. It presents a specific perspective, that of Taiwan, to explore how *fujoshi* cultures are practiced and localized under different social contexts. What is more, it also suggests a situating of Taiwan as an exemplary mediator within the East Asian cultural sphere by indicating how the complicated historical, political, and cultural relations with Japan have contributed to shape a kind of hybrid cultural practice.

Notes

1. This chapter was developed from a presentation at the Cultural Typhoon Conference held on June 28, 2014, titled "Analyzing Sexuality in Japanophilia Culture in Taiwan: A Case Study of Taiwanese Japanophile *Fujoshi's* Fantasy" (presented in Japanese). I have modified my analysis based on the comments received at the presentation and my further investigation. For more details about *Fujoshi*, see Kazumi Nagaike and Tomoko Aoyama, "What Is Japanese 'BL Studies'? A Historical and Analytical Overview," in *Boys Love Manga and Beyond: History, Culture, and Community in Japan*, ed. Mark McLelland et al. (Jackson: University Press of Mississippi, 2015), 119–40.
2. *Gong* refers to the top or dominant character; while *shou* refers to the bottom or passive character in a BL coupling.
3. BL fans in Taiwan translate the Japanese term *fujoshi* into the Mandarin term *funü* (腐女, rotten women), although some prefer to use *fujoshi*. Because the term *fujoshi* is widely used in academic fields and because *funü* could be easily confused with the word *funü* (婦女, adult women), I use the term *fujoshi* instead of *funü* throughout this chapter.
4. See, for example, Ming-Tsung Lee, "Qinri de qinggan jiegou yu hari de zhuti: Yige kuashidai rentong zhengzhi de kaocha" [The "pro-Japan" emotional structure and the "Japanophile" subjects: A study on diachronous identity politics], paper presented at the annual meeting for the Taiwanese Sociological Association, Xinchu, Tsinghua University, December 4–5, 2004; Keita Matsushita, "Diffusion of Japanese Media Culture and Forming 'Japanese Image' in Taiwan," *Mejiro Journal of Humanities* 4 (2008): 121–34; Weijung Chang, "Analyzing the Relationship with 'Japaneseness' from the Life Story of a Taiwanese Japanophile Girl," *Journal of Japan Oral History Association* 10 (2014): 77–98. Lee focuses on the pro-Japanese attitude and claims that it should be regarded as an important structural context of the general acceptance of Japanese culture in Taiwan. I agree with his argument and aim to explore how this pro-Japanese structure has influenced diverse dimensions in the contemporary Taiwanese cultural and social context.
5. Fran Martin, "Girls Who Love Boys' Love: Japanese Homoerotic Manga as Transnational Taiwan Culture," *Inter-Asia Cultural Studies* 13.3 (2012): 365–83; Chang, "Analyzing the Relationship with 'Japaneseness,'" 77–98.
6. I did most of the interviews in 2011 except for A and C. During 2013 and 2014, I interviewed C, a new interviewee and conducted additional interviews with A. Because they both helped me with other research on life stories of Japanophiles, I interviewed each of them five times. Prior to the interviews I was acquainted with interviewees B, C, and I, while the other interviewees were users of the BL-related bulletin boards who responded to the interview requests I posted. I conducted interviews in person, usually in public spaces like cafés or restaurants, and used the IC recorder to record the interviews. The average length of one interview was around two hours. Profiles of these interviewees (seen in Table 1) are records taken at the time of the interview.
7. For more details, see Chang, "Analyzing the Relationship with 'Japaneseness,'" 77–98; Weijung Chang, "Gendered/Sexualized Transformation of Japanophilia: The Symbolization and the Localization of 'Japaneseness' in Taiwan," paper presented at

the annual meeting for the North America Taiwan Studies Association, Boston, MA, Harvard University, June 12–13, 2015.
8. *Tongrenzhi*, or *dōjinshi* in Japanese refers to amateur publications such as manga, novels, and fan fictions.
9. "Cosplay" is a portmanteau of the words "costume play," which refers to the activity in which participants wear costumes to represent a specific character (mostly in manga, animation, games, or movies).
10. In terms of the news coverage of that year, I consider the controversy over the publication of Yoshinori Kobayashi's manga in which the author asserted that Taiwanese women volunteered to be comfort women for Japanese soldiers during World War II, as well as the accompanying criticisms against Japanophilia to be directly and causally related to this decline of media attention. For more details, see Chang, "Analyzing the Relationship with 'Japaneseness,'" 77–98.
11. See Chang, "Analyzing the Relationship with 'Japaneseness,'" 77–98; Chang, "Gendered/Sexualized Transformation of Japanophilia."
12. Tzuyao Lee, "Dongman yuzhaizu de huanxiang shijie: Yi Taiwan de tongren chuangyan huodong wei yanjiu duixiang" [A fantasy theme criticism of *dōjinshi* and cosplay in Taiwan] (MA thesis, Fu Jen Catholic University, 2004).
13. Shihyun Chang, "Ciwenhua jingji zhi zhanxian: Lun Taiwan tongrenzhi de zaidi bianqian" [The power of subcultural economics: A discussion about the local transformation of *Dōjinshi* in Taiwan] (MA thesis, National Taiwan Normal University, 2006).
14. Chih-lan Tsai, "Nüxing huanxiang guodu zhong de chuncui aiqing—lun Taiwan BL xiaoshuo" [The pure love in the kingdom of women's fantasy—on BL novels in Taiwan] (MA thesis, National Taiwan Normal University, 2011).
15. Lee, "'Pro-Japan' Emotional Structure," 12.
16. Ibid.
17. Yufen Ko, "Nihon no aidoru dorama to taiwan niokeru yokubō no katachi" [The Japanese idol drama and the shape of desire in Taiwan], in *Global Prism*, ed. Koichi Iwabuchi (Tokyo: Heibonsha, 2003), 151–82.
18. Iyun Lee, "The Japanese Image Made by the Japanese Dramas in Taiwan," *Journal of Mass Communication Studies* 69 (2006): 108–25.
19. Yizhen Chen, *A Research on Johnny's Fans in Taiwan* (Tokyo: Seikyusha, 2014).
20. Patrick W. Galbraith, "Fantasy Play and Transgressive Intimacy among 'Rotten Girls' in Contemporary Japan," *Signs* 37.1 (2011): 211–32.
21. Pinzhi Liu, "Funü de huanxiang yu wang/wangxiang" [A study on *fujoshi*'s queer reading experience] (MA thesis, National Kaohsiung Normal University, 2014).
22. Scanlation is the process of scanning, translating, and editing foreign manga into another language without authorization.
23. *Moe* refers here to the excitement that *fujoshi* feel about erotic relationships between males. See Galbraith, "Fantasy Play and Transgressive Intimacy."
24. The ending of the Sengoku Period is debated by many scholars but it is argued that either the end of Muromachi period (1573) or the end of Azuchi-momoyama period (1603) is counted as the end of Sengoku period.
25. *Ikemasenu* is the courteous expression of "must not." *Degozaru* is the honorific expression of "is." These kinds of terms were used until the Meiji era (1868–1912).

26. *Tsundere* is a Japanese character terminology that describes a person who is initially cold toward another person but in some situations suddenly shows his or her warm or shy side.
27. For instance, the competition between Chen Shuibian and Ma Yingjiu, who were the presidential candidates of Democratic Progressive Party and Kuomingtang, respectively, or more recently the trusting relationship between President Ma Yinjiu and former secretary-general of the National Security Council Jin Bucong excite some Taiwanese *fujoshi*'s curiosity. Narratives of BL fantasy about these politicians can be easily found on the Internet.
28. Teri Silvio, "BL/Q: The Aesthetics of Pili Puppetry Fan Fiction," in *Popular Culture in Taiwan: Charismatic Modernity*, ed. Marc L. Moskowitz (London: Routledge, 2013), 149–66.
29. In her words, "日本/Japan," but I consider "Japaneseness" to be a more accurate word to express her intended meaning.
30. See Martin, "Girls Who Love Boys' Love."
31. Koichi Iwabuchi, *Transnational Japan* (Tokyo: Iwanami Shoten, 2001), 27–33; Koichi Iwabuchi, *Recentering Globalization: Popular Culture and Japanese Transnationalism* (Durham, NC: Duke University Press, 2002), 24–32. In the Japanese version in 2001, he originally used the Japanese phrase *bunkatekimushūsei* (文化的無臭性) and explained in notes that this phrase, although it was used by some Japanese scholars, seems unfamiliar in English.
32. See, for example, Iyun Lee, "The Conflict between the Reality and Illusion—the Implication of the Re-emergence of the Japanese Image on Postwar Taiwan, 1945–1949," *Journal of Information Studies, Interfaculty Initiative in Information Studies the University of Tokyo* 69 (2005): 137–60; Jintang Tsai, "The Views of Japan by Taiwanese People Who Had Lived during the Japanese and Kuomintang Colonization Periods," trans. Takuju Mizukuchi, in *Sengo taiwan niokeru nihon: Shokuminchi keiken no renzoku, henbō, riyō* ["Japan" in the post-war Taiwan: The continuity, transformation and appropriation of the colonized experiences], ed. Masako Igarashi and Yuko Mio (Tokyo: Fukyosya, 2006), 19–60; Peifeng Chen, "Enka no zaichika: Jūsōtekina shokuminchibunka kara no jijosaisei no michi" [The localization of Enka: The road from the multicolonial culture to self-helping rebirth], in *Higashi ajia sinjidai no nihon to Taiwan* [Japan and Taiwan in the new age of East Asia], ed. Jun Nishikawa and Hsinhuang Hsiao (Tokyo: Akashi book, 2010), 239–300.
33. See, for example, Shunichi Horie, "Futatsu no 'Nihon': Hakkaminkei wo chūshin tosuru Taiwanjin no 'Nihon ishiki'" [Two "Japans": The Taiwanese Hakka people's "consciousness of Japan"], in *Sengo Taiwan niokeru nihon: Shokuminchi keiken no renzoku, henbō, riyō* ["Japan" in the postwar Taiwan: The continuity, transformation and appropriation of the colonized experiences], ed. Masako Igarashi and Yuko Mio (Tokyo: Fukyosya, 2006), 121–54; Peixian Xu, *Taiyang qixia de mofa xuexiao: Rizhi Taiwan xinshi jiaoyu de dansheng* [The magic school under the sun flag: New style of education in Taiwan during the colonial period] (Taipei: Dongcun, 2012).
34. See, for example, Zhihui Huang, "Posutokoroniaru Taiwan ni okeru jūsōkōzō: Nihon to chūka" [The multilayered structure in postcolonial Taiwan: Japan and China], in *Higashi ajia shinjidai no nihon to Taiwan* [Japan and Taiwan in the new era of East Asia], ed. Jun Nishikawa and Hsinhuang Hsiao (Tokyo: Akashi Shoten, 2010), 159–93; Xu, *Magic School under the Sun Flag*.
35. See Iwabuchi, *Transnational Japan*; Ko, "Japanese Idol Drama and the Shape of Desire in Taiwan."

36. See, for example, Chizuko Ueno, *Hatsujyō sōchi* [The apparatus of eroticism] (Tokyo: Chikuma Shobō, 2002); Kazumi Nagaike, "Perverse Sexualities, Perversive Desires: Representation of Female Fantasies and *Yaoi* Manga as Pornography Directed at Women," *U.S-Japan Women's Journal* 25 (2003): 76–103; Junko Kaneda, "Yaoi ron, asu no tameni sono 2" [The theory of *yaoi*: For the future 2] *Yuriika*, December 2007, 48–54.
37. It does not mean that she considered directly the character as her ideal partner. It is more accurate to comprehend through her narrative that this character provided a concrete image of her ideal partner.
38. Anthony Giddens, *The Transformation of Intimacy: Sexuality, Love, and Eroticism in Modern Societies* (Stanford: Stanford University Press, 1992).
39. Lee, "Japanese Image," 108–25.
40. *Yukata* is a casual form of kimono, worn by both men and women, usually in the summer.

10
Girls Who Love Boys' Love

BL as Goods to Think with in Taiwan (with a Revised and Updated Coda)

Fran Martin

Amid the plethora of intraregionally mobile texts, forms, and practices that constitute the lifeworlds of teenagers and young adults in Taiwan today, the phenomenon of BL (Boys' Love) manga stands out as a particularly rich site for cultural analysis. Vast numbers of young women in Taiwan are engaged in reading, making, trading, discussing, and reenacting these originally Japanese narratives of love, sex, and romance between boys and young men, creating an extremely dense and ideologically complex form of participatory pop culture. In this chapter, which arises from interviews I conducted with female BL fans in Taipei in 2005, I seek to avoid assumptions about how the manga will tend to be interpreted based on their generic structures and aim instead to center the readers' own accounts of their reading pleasures and interpretative practices.[1] Ultimately, though, I am less interested in synthesizing the *content* of these readerly "microtheories" into a "macrotheory" capable of taking account of all of them than in exploring the social significance of the *processes* interlinking the field of discourses and practices around BL in Taiwan. My interest does not lie in evaluating how progressive or subversive are the specific ideas about gender and sexuality articulated by these readers. Rather, I want to argue for the important social function of the BL scene itself as an arena—a "discursive battlefield," in Akiko Mizoguchi's inspired phrase—where complex debates about gender and sexuality can be played out, in all their internal contradiction, through the construction and trading of the fans' own reflexive theorizations.[2] The BL scene in Taiwan is no feminist utopia or zone of unilateral sexual-political progressiveness, but what is important, I argue, is that it *exists*, as a participatory space created with immense imaginative energy and generative of great pleasure and intellectual as well as affective engagement for its largely female participants. Or perhaps one should say, of Taiwan's BL culture as discussed here, it *existed*—for the material presented in these pages needs to be historicized quite specifically as a view of the scene as it was in early 2005. In July that year, the Government Information Office brought into force a new law governing the classification of printed materials in Taiwan that legally restricts BL material to readers eighteen years of age and over. I return to consider the implications of this in the conclusion, but it is worth noting at the outset that the enforcement of the new ratings system just after this study was concluded brings into even clearer focus the social utility of the complex, organic scene that the ratings measure so crudely attempts to regulate.

Following a sketch of the modern transnational history of Japanese manga in Taiwan, the chapter introduces the specificities of BL as a genre in Taiwan, including its various subgenres and modes of production as well as the activities of the BL fan subculture (*tongrenzhi*). The chapter then presents some of the results of my interview-based study. I spoke with a total of thirty women between the ages of nineteen and thirty-four, including some who produced their own BL texts and were otherwise active in the *tongrenzhi* subculture, plus one male professional manga editor. Participants were interviewed both singly and in friendship groups, with each semistructured interview lasting between one and two hours. My questions focused on two aspects of the women's interactions with BL narratives, which this chapter addresses in turn. First, I consider questions of gender, sexuality, and generation. Second, I consider BL's relation to imagined geographies, specifically, its enabling of imaginative engagements with "Japan" and "Japaneseness." In addition to the general point, above, about the *social utility* of the BL world, the other part of my central argument concerns *how it works*. What is especially interesting, I argue, is how the gender/sexuality aspect and the geographic aspect intersect, so that the imaginative geography of a homoerotic "Japan" that is notably distinct from readers' own everyday lifeworlds in Taiwan facilitates the formation of a reflexive zone of articulation where the fans work through a range of responses to *local* regimes of gender and sexual regulation. In other words, as the imagined elsewhere of "BL Japan" is drawn into inevitable comparison with the experiential here-and-now of the lives of its young women readers in Taiwan, the BL scene becomes a space that enables the readers to articulate their own feeling and thinking to themselves.

A Transnational History of Manga in Taiwan

In Japan, it was during the 1950s that *shōjo manga* (girls' comics) eclipsed other forms of cultural expression, such as popular magazine fiction, to become the dominant element in modern *shōjo bunka* (girls' culture).[3] The *shōjo manga* genre diversified greatly in the 1970s, when women authors began to outnumber male ones, and it is was during this decade that *shōnen-ai* (BL) manga began to appear, inaugurated by the Showa 24 Generation (1949 Generation) of women manga artists, including Moto Hagio, Yumiko Oshima, Keiko Takemiya, and Reiko Yamagishi. Yukari Fujimoto, manga editor and prominent commentator on *shōjo manga*, frames the Japanese *shōnen-ai* subgenre as an outgrowth of the "transvestite girls" subgenre, in which girl characters cross-dress to accomplish daring deeds, beginning with Osamu Tezuka's *Princess Knight* (1953–1956).[4]

In these "transvestite" manga, she proposes, girls symbolically "became" boys both to pursue otherwise off-limits social status and power and to distance themselves from the troublesome, sometimes fearful, associations of female sexuality. In Fujimoto's analysis, shōnen-ai comics were a logical outgrowth of this earlier "transvestite" tendency, with the young "female" characters now even more thoroughly in disguise: decked out in male bodies as well as masculine attire. In Fujimoto's analysis, the new development also grew out of these artists' collective impatience with conventional heterosexual romance narratives. Classic works from this initial period of shōnen-ai production include Moto Hagio's *November Gymnasium* (1971) and Keiko Takemiya's *Song of Wind and Trees* (1976).[5] Shōnen-ai manga, also known as bishōnen, yaoi, or bōizu rabu, remains a major genre in Japan up to the present day, incorporating a plethora of different styles and subgenres, with its largest readership found among heterosexual-identified girls and women.[6] Without doubt, the yaoi fan community in Japan functions as a kind of critical, girl-dominated subworld; in Mizoguchi's words, even "an unprecedented, effective political arena for women with the potential for [feminist and queer] activism."[7]

Following the immediate postwar period of intense political censorship of culture in Taiwan, local comic art blossomed between the mid-1950s and the mid-1960s, largely in the form of children's comics in periodicals and dedicated volumes, yet not without elements of social satire.[8] In 1966, however, the Administrative Yuan brought into force the Guidelines on Printed Serial Publications Measure.[9] This political censorship law drastically limited the permissible content of locally written comics; as a result, informally copied editions of Japanese manga began to proliferate in the local market.[10] In 1976, a Taiwanese publisher created a test case by submitting a pirated Japanese manga to the censorship body; when it was formally approved for publication, local publishers saw that the censors did not intend to apply the harsh standards of the measure to Japanese imports.[11] The year 1976 thus marks the beginning of the "piracy period" (*daoban shidai*), when Taiwanese publishers began publishing a massive volume of pirated photocopies of Japanese manga. The censors did not significantly interfere with their content, aside from requesting slight modifications to explicit sexual scenes and, in an attempt to limit the cultural influence of the former colonizer over the population, mandating that all Japanese names and place-names had to be converted to Chinese equivalents.[12] Many major Taiwanese manga publishers were set up during the piracy period and established their foothold in the market by selling the cheaply copied Japanese works.[13] Pirated Japanese manga dominated the market until the early 1990s, when formal copyright contracts were finally drawn up between the Japanese publishers and the Taiwanese translators and distributors. Japanese manga continues to dominate the Taiwanese manga market today, albeit now in copyright-cleared editions, alongside much smaller niche markets in manga from Hong Kong, South Korea, and Taiwan itself.

It is difficult to piece together an accurate picture of exactly which manga series circulated during the piracy period. Photocopying, translation, and minor editing were carried out by the various Taiwanese publishing houses in an informal, ad hoc fashion, and no reliable records remain of precisely what content reached Taiwanese readers.[14] But given the prominence of *shōnen-ai* as a subgenre of girls' manga in Japan since the 1970s, and the lack of official restriction on the content of Japanese manga pirated in Taiwan, it seems probable that the major *shōnen-ai* works of that period and after will have made their way to Taiwanese readers. Certainly, the young readers interviewed for this study were very familiar with iconic *shōnen-ai* works of the 1980s, such as Marimo Ragawa's *New York, New York* (NYNY/*Niuyue, Niuyue*, 1988) and Minami Ozaki's *Desperate Love* (*Zetsuai*/*Jue'ai*, 1989), and some of the slightly older respondents recalled having read 1970s works like *Song of Wind and Trees* in childhood.

The 1990s witnessed a surge in the popularity of BL, and today in Taiwan BL forms a major niche market within the broader category of girls' manga (*shaonü manhua*), with hundreds if not thousands of titles currently available. Today Taiwan's BL culture encompasses a range of texts, practices, and sites far exceeding its original instance in the Japanese comics. The consolidation of a local fan world, known as *tongrenzhi* following the Japanese *dōjinshi*, is particularly notable. Several interviewees pointed out that commercial BL's popularity boom in Taiwan over the past decade can in fact be traced back to the rise of the local *tongrenzhi* subculture during the early 1990s: the commercial publishing industry followed the lead of fan production.[15]

In Taiwan, BL manga comes into existence either through commercial publication, most often by Taiwanese publishing houses translating Japanese originals under license, or informally, created by the *tongrenzhi* fans. *Tongrenzhi* in Taiwan is a flourishing fan subculture perhaps broadly comparable to, albeit also distinct from, slash subcultures in the United States and elsewhere.[16] It is based around writing, drawing, making, and consuming the fans' own homoerotic mangas, stories, and related products, and gathering together at conventions to buy, sell, wear, and share this wealth of fan-produced material.[17] The *tongrenzhi* culture intersects with the broader cosplay youth culture, in which fans dress up en masse in elaborate homemade costumes representing favorite characters from popular media culture. BL narratives may be written by *tongrenzhi* participants either as original stories or as creative extensions of existing works, making explicit homoerotic subtexts to originally "straight" works (such as TV dramas or boys' mangas), as in slash fan production.[18] *Tongrenzhi* works may take the form of comics or popular novels, which in Taiwan are closely allied forms of BL cultural production and are often written and read by the same groups of people. *Tongrenzhi* works may be distributed either in hardcopy or electronically via the Internet, and, as a result of the popularization of *tongrenzhi* cyberworlds, readers in Taiwan can now consume *tongrenzhi* works by women from across Japan, China, Hong Kong, as well as Taiwan itself. This dense and intricate network, connecting tens of thousands of readers with varying degrees of investment in fan activities—from simply reading the manga to contributing to Internet discussions to regular participation in conventions to authoring original BL works—constitutes the material, social aspect of the BL "world" that is this chapter's central subject.

BL Taxonomies as Subcultural Capital

The range of works covered by the term BL in Taiwan is extremely broad and internally differentiated by a number of factors. These include generic distinctions in both narrative (fantasy versus social-realist) and presentation of sexual content (romantic versus pornographic conventions), mode of production (commercial versus fan-produced), textual form (novel versus manga versus illustrated novel versus anime), tone (from the comic or satirical to the deadly earnest), and so on. There exists a significant body of critical works on BL texts and fandoms in Japan, many of which emphasize the sexually and socially empowering function for women fans of writing and reading these stories of love and sex between men.[19] Since the majority of BL texts that circulate in Taiwan originate in Japan, this material provides a useful context for understanding the phenomenon of BL in Taiwan. But the results of the present study also indicate that BL and its taxonomies may in some cases be slightly differently understood by Taiwanese as compared with Japanese readers. In this section, I present a summary account of the cumulative popular taxonomy of the field that was communicated to me in interviews.

Pure-love BL: In this subgenre, an emphasis on "pure love" (*chun'ai* or *chunqing*) between young men is often accompanied by an association with the Japanese homoerotic aesthetic of 耽美 (*tanbi/danmei*), which was understood by the Taiwanese readers to imply a somewhat refined appreciation of young men's aesthetic beauty without necessary recourse to explicitly sexual imagery. This type of BL focuses on highly idealized romances between beautiful boys or young men. The erotic element may be clearly indicated, with scenes of kissing and sex, or, often, it may remain highly ambiguous (*aimei*) and sub-textual. Frequently there is an emphasis on the "normality" of the characters: they declare explicitly that they are "not homosexual" but simply in love with a unique individual who "happens to be" male.[20] Generally, plots omit reference to the real-life social censure of same-sex sexual relations; what is presented instead is a fantasy world free from homophobia where same-sex love is universally accepted. Pure-love BL tended to be seen as a "young" genre, aimed primarily at adolescent female readers, in distinction from the more sexually explicit "ladies' comics" (*shunü manhua*) targeted at slightly older women.

To contextualize the above points, it is crucial to note that "girl-directed" (*nüxingxiang*) BL manga was considered by the vast majority of interviewees to be clearly and obviously distinct from gay (*tongzhi*) narratives. Mandy, a twenty-seven-year-old administrative assistant and herself an author of popular romance novels (both heterosexual romances and BL works), voiced this idea from the perspective of a BL producer:

> It's my hope that people could approach BL material with a more relaxed attitude, and not necessarily see it as having anything to do with gays. It's true that it's written about them, but we [authors] really don't want to talk about things that we don't—to tell the truth, we don't know much about gayness, and we don't know much about boys, either. We just want to make girls see that things like this do exist, and that they shouldn't be prejudiced, because in fact *all* love is beautiful, both gay and nongay, it's all beautiful.

Similar distinctions between the feminine fantasy world of BL and the masculine real-life world of gay male culture were made repeatedly by interviewees.

As its title suggests, the thematic and ideological center of the pure-love subgenre, even when sex scenes are included, is romantic love. One interviewee observed succinctly, "BL mangas always take love as their central axis—not like regular porn mangas, which just focus on sex."[21] Pure-love BL narratives presume and nurture a belief in love as an irresistible force in human life; as in heterosexual romance, love is the central motivating power propelling the protagonists and the action. Indeed, parallels are frequently drawn, both by manga critics and by its consumers, between this subgenre and conventional heterosexual romance stories (known as *yanqing xiaoshuo*, or more colloquially, "BG" stories—"boy-girl" romance). Several of the interviewees for this project were fans of BG romance narratives as well as BL manga, and some framed pure-love BL as simply the conventional feminine genre of boy-girl romance transposed onto two protagonists of the same sex—a reading strengthened by the commonness of polarized sexual roles and hyperfeminized bottom/insertee characters (*shou*) within the genre. Hong, a twenty-seven-year-old accountant, put it this way:

> I read something interesting about this once. It said that nowadays when girls read BL, sometimes they project aspects of their own real life onto the bottom/insertee character. When you look at it like that, there's actually no difference between [BL] and conventional romance stories.

Simao, a twenty-seven-year-old T (tomboy; i.e., butch lesbian) research student, had less patience with what she perceived as naïve straight women appropriating queer imagery for their own romantic and sexual fantasies:

> I think those BL girls are so idiotic. . . . When they see two cute boys making love they go, oh wow, that's so cool, and they think that's what being gay means. . . . Those girls really piss me off. . . . I think to them, BL is basically a version of [straight girls'] romance. . . . I suspect that deep down inside, those girls who claim to be so excited about seeing [two men] making love are actually harboring a fantasy about a knight in shining armor coming to rescue them.

Critical commentators on BL in both Japan and Taiwan, too, have been quick to point out the generic and ideological parallels between pure-love BL and conventional popular romance.[22] Especially in light of the strong gendered distinction between tops and bottoms and the insistent feminization of the bottom/insertee role, it may even be questionable the extent to which such narratives should be interpreted as strictly concerning relations between "two men."[23] Jui-ping Chung makes an apposite comparison between BL plots of the pure-love variety and the works of Taiwanese "romance queen," popular novelist Qiong Yao. In both, she notes, narratives center on the ability of the lovers' pure romantic passion to sweep aside petty worldly concerns—whether these be parental opposition, in the case of many of Qiong Yao's works, or conventional gender and sexual roles, in the case of BL.[24] Despite initial appearances, then, given the readers' understanding of its central thematic focus as being firmly on the ideological value and overwhelming power of romantic love, the pure-love subgenre of homoerotic manga probably has more in common with the conventional "women's genre" of popular romance than it does with gay male cultural production.[25]

H-ban (H-version) BL: The H (sometimes pronounced Japanese-style as *ecchi*) in the designation of this subgenre references both the first letter of the English transliteration of the Japanese term *hentai* (*biantai*), meaning perverted or sexually explicit, and the initial of the English term "hard"; *ban* means "edition." *H-ban* differs from the pure-love subgenre mainly in its degree of sexual explicitness and in the ratio of romantic versus pornographic conventions it deploys. Here, elements of pornography—a graphic focus on sexual organs, extended and detailed sex scenes interrupting the narrative flow, the unabashedness of its function for sexual arousal, and so on—begin to impinge on the central romance narratives, placing this subgenre arguably somewhere between the romantic pure-love subgenre and the pornographic *nan-nan* genre (see below).[26] The thematic and ideological focus of the *H-ban* BL subgenre oscillates between romantic love and sex.

In addition to these two major subgenres of "girl-directed" BL, there exist also another two: *nan-nan* manga—male-on-male pornography in manga form—and *tongzhi*, or gay, manga. *Nan-nan* manga is generally commercially produced and dominated by explicit sex scenes with little plot development. Its thematic and ideological focus is squarely on sexual pleasure. The Taiwanese BL readers understood it to be read by both gay men and adult straight women. Like *H-ban* BL, *nan-nan* can be described as *H*; it is also referred to as *A-man* (X-rated manga) or simply as *seqing manhua* or *qingyu manhua*: pornographic or erotic manga. Meanwhile, those comics designated by Taiwanese readers as *tongzhi manhua* self-consciously present gay lives with a modicum of social realism, complete with representations of parental homophobia, the difficulty of the coming-out process, a hostile surrounding society, and gay men's struggles to find a place within it. The readership for *tongzhi* manga is popularly understood to comprise a mix of gay men, straight young women, and lesbians. The thematic and ideological core of this genre is identity: coming to terms with one's sexuality, learning to express it, revealing it to the world, and creating a life around it, similarly to the globalizing literary genre of the popular coming-out story.

Interestingly, despite the widespread understanding that they are directed at men, a significant number of participants in this study did confess to being readers of these latter two categories. In particular, women (both straight-identifying and queer) who actively preferred and sought out social-realist *tongzhi* manga in preference to the fantasy-romance narratives of "girl-directed" BL constituted a very notable subgroup.[27] Together with the at-times somewhat fuzzy definitional boundaries of BL itself in Taiwan—in particular, the fact that it is not infrequently thought to include these latter two categories as well as the girl-directed subgenres above—this problematizes certain common assumptions about BL as a genre; especially the idea that it is *primarily* concerned with straight women reading homoerotic romance fantasies. The above taxonomy suggests that this oft-discussed scenario may in fact be just one among several, which also include both straight and queer women reading social-realist *tongzhi* narratives, Ts and feminine heterosexuals reading *nan-nan* porn, and so on.[28]

On one hand, the material presented above is useful for what it reveals about the empirical makeup of the field—the genres, subgenres, styles, and forms of BL as a series of textual products. But also, even more interestingly, this material can be seen as a product of the Taiwan fans' own cultural labor. In this sense the above taxonomy, as a shared body of knowledge, functions as subcultural capital: an intellectual object with value in its own right, the collective product and property of the fans who, in turn, are linked together as a community partly through their shared labor of classifying the material and drawing hierarchical distinctions within it.[29] In explaining these classifications to me, these BL readers were *performing* their own fandom through the manipulation and mastery of this complex information (the same is true, of course, of all of the discussions analyzed below). We now turn to the issue of the cultural labor that the BL texts perform for their Taiwanese fans in relation to local discourses on gender and sexuality.

Gender, Sexuality, and Generation

At the time of this study, the BL fandom in Taiwan was generationally confined to readers under the age of about forty. In this section, I argue that the genre's novel treatment of the topics of both gender and same-sex sexuality meshes with emergent discourses that are critical of still-dominant patriarchal and heteronormative ideologies.[30] My suggestion is that the popularity of these narratives of gender and sexual nonconformity among young women in Taiwan links to a series of broader shifts in the available discourses on love, sex, gender, and sexual identity, and may be related to in-process modifications to mainstream ideologies in these areas, which are arguably beginning—albeit unevenly—to incorporate elements of feminist and antihomophobic critique. But this is not the same as proposing that the BL and its fandom is unilaterally antihomophobic; as Akatsuka notes, a key characteristic of many girl-directed BL narratives is the copresence of homoeroticism within heteronormativity, typically in the form of one or more protagonists' heated denials of actually being gay.[31] Rather than claiming that Taiwan's BL scene is straightforwardly antihomophobic, my point is rather that the scene provides a discursive arena for ongoing arguments around the meaning and politics of nonstraight sexualities, and these arguments draw from and extend available discourses on sexuality currently being hashed out within the wider culture.

First, then, to the question of same-sex sexuality. As the above fan taxonomy makes clear in its differentiation of the *tongzhi* subgenre from BL more broadly, the relation between the categories BL and gayness is by no means straightforward. However, given their narrative thematization of sexual and romantic relations between men, BL texts certainly do *raise the topic* of male homosexuality, albeit often in a symbolic or allegorical rather than a literal or realist way. Many of the women interviewed reported that they felt the need to hide their BL fandom from their parents, since that generation has a less liberal attitude to same-sex sexual relations than that held by the women themselves.

> Zirong (a twenty-five-year-old project manager in a small design/manufacturing business): I leave them [BL comics] lying around at home, and once my mum came in and saw one of them, and I could tell that she really wanted to ask why I would read such a thing. But she never asked me—I always wonder how come she didn't.
>
> Brenda (a twenty-five-year-old electronic engineer): My mum and dad have seen the comics in my room, too. My dad ran off and asked my elder sister: Is your sister a homosexual? He didn't dare ask me directly. After a while he got used to it, and nowadays it's only when we're having company that he'll say, "How about you tidy up those piles of comics?"

Some women also linked readership of BL comics and novels with their generation's more or less liberal attitudes toward male homosexuality, either citing BL as a catalyst for the liberalization of their thinking or, vice versa, citing generational change as the reason they are relatively receptive to homosexual-themed materials in the first place. As Ata, a twenty-four-year-old web bookstore employee put it, her own generation tended to think, "If you don't want to love girls but love boys instead, or if a girl doesn't love boys but loves other girls, that's your own business—and what's wrong with that?" whereas "adults—people of around forty to fifty years of age—grew up during the martial law period, and they think that you have to conform to a certain set of rules in order to be a good citizen." Very broadly speaking, then, the BL phenomenon plausibly relates to a wider generational shift in available discourses on sexuality, a shift that can be attributed in part to the arrival of the transnationally mobile vectors of gay and lesbian politics, activism, theory, art, film, and literature in Taiwan since the early 1990s.[32] The liberal discourses that some of the interviewees voiced on gay acceptance, gay normality, gay rights, and the triviality of gender as a deciding factor in romantic love carry strong echoes of gay-friendly rhetoric since the 1990s in the broader culture. This is a generation that has come of age with these rhetorics (if not generally their effective implementation) looming large in the public arena.

Yet although many interviewees made use of this emergent discourse linking the homosexual topic to the positively valued ideologies of personal autonomy and sexual liberation, nonetheless as a whole the group was internally conflicted about the value and meaning of gayness in relation to BL. Consider Mandy's discussion, quoted above, in which she sought actively to delink BL love stories from the topic of gayness via a universalizing rhetoric on the beauty of *all* love, in comparison with Simao's expression (also quoted above) of her impatience with precisely this "idiotic," willful straightening of queer content for hetero fantasy. Reports of arguments along these lines in online forums arose frequently during interviews. Such conflicts provided the ideological context, often, for those readers who actively preferred social-realist *tongzhi* narratives to fantasy-romance BL, citing the greater fidelity of the former to "real-life" gay experience as an attractive feature.[33] Thus, while none of the women interviewed expressed active hostility to the idea of homosexuality, discussions uncovered an array of different theories of the value and meaning of same-sex sexuality in BL texts, underscoring the function of the BL scene as a forum for the collective working out of ambivalence on the topic.

Among this group of interviewees, in addition to discussions of same-sex sexuality, the idea that interaction with BL texts enabled young women actively to engage with questions of *gender* was among the most frequently expressed. Specifically, clusters of reflexive "folk-theories" emerged on BL fandom as a form of protofeminist cultural critique, on the one hand, and as a means for readers symbolically to negotiate their own gendered identities, on the other.[34] For example, on the question of why straight girls should prefer stories about love between two boys over stories about love between a boy and a girl, several interviewees offered critiques of the representation of girl characters in mainstream girls' manga. Emma, a nineteen-year-old first-year university student said:

> In boys' manga, they make the girl characters completely dumb and ditzy; in girls' manga, they make them all innocent. But most girls don't like those sorts of girl characters. They think: hey, this girl is obviously totally dumb, why would she be with him? . . . If the cute guy ended up with a girl character that everyone could relate to, that'd be OK; they'd accept it. But if he went with a [dippy] girl, then you tend to think he'd be better off with a boy.

While this theory frames BL as a resistant response by "most girls" to the questionable gender politics of popular cross-sex romance, Zirong and her friend Brenda offered a different interpretation. They suggested that the objectification of men's bodies in H-version BL could be seen as "payback" by women for women's objectification within patriarchal culture as a whole. The discussion (personalized, this time, but still self-consciously reflexive and theoretical) went like this:

> Z: I think the reason I read BL is because I don't really like boys. . . . To make use of some gender theory for a moment: I think that BL has to do with the objectification of men, and that's what I like about it. . . . When girls read BL they make a certain emotional investment in it. Sometimes, a component of that investment involves objectification. Myself, that's the component that I enjoy.
>
> B: It's true—all the stuff she reads is really extreme. Sometimes I think when she's reading it she's just like a guy watching a porn flick.

It is also worth noting an extremely common countertheory about BL and gender politics. Finduilas, a nineteen-year-old student and fan of *tongrenzhi* fiction focusing on the BL potential of the *Lord of the Rings* narratives, gave succinct expression to this popularly cited theory:

> Before I understood BL, I asked my friends why they so liked to read this stuff. Their response was to say that when you're reading a text and you really like one of the male characters in it—like him so much that you don't want him to get together with any other girl—then you'd rather he got together with a boy.

This alternative theory of the relationship between BL and "real-life" gender relations inverts the theories voiced by Emma and Zirong, above: sexual jealousy and competitiveness, rather than a critique of the sexism of mainstream romance and pornography, is posited as the reason why young women prefer manga that couples boys with other boys. But as with the discussion above on homosexuality, the point here is not to adjudicate whether the BL phenomenon is ultimately progressive or regressive for a feminist cultural politics. For again, it is crucial to note that Finduilas was not straightforwardly revealing a personal response to the texts; rather, she was constructing a theory about why other girls (her friends, girls in general) enjoy them. This entails developing a reflexive theory of "what girls are like": at this moment in our conversation, girls were constructed as jealous of other girls getting together with a boy (character) they like. This theory-making aspect indicates, counterintuitively perhaps, that these fictional texts about love between boys become a means for women readers to think about the character of their own relations *with other women*: Is this relation to be understood as one of protofeminist solidarity? Or a sexual competitiveness that facilitates a voyeuristic desire to see two young men together? Finding the "right" answers to these questions is less important than recognizing the opportunity that BL affords young women to share the process of collectively thinking them through in a women-dominated cultural space.

Other responses suggested that BL may be useful to young women readers for the ways in which it facilitates more direct negotiation with the readers' own gendered and sexual identities. Illustrating the immense complexity of potential reader identifications with the already complex representations of gender in this genre of manga, Shaomo, a twenty-one-year-old university student, related the following:

> I remember one manga by Satosumi Takaguchi, I think it was called *The Rainbow-Colored Mask*. . . . It was about a youth who'd been abused by his family, and had a stint in hospital. . . . Just then they were practicing "cosmetic therapy," and they taught him how to apply nail polish and whatever. After the boy recovered, he'd often make himself up. He got a job in a nightclub, and became a hostess, the most beautiful one there. He was a boy, but yet he was the most beautiful woman—that's right! The reason I like that manga is that the youth is normally a boy, but then he dresses up real *sexy*.[35] And when he makes himself up, he makes up every single surface of his body, and transforms himself into the image that he really wants to be, and he does it all so meticulously and with such concentration. Although for me, it's only a matter of deciding whether this time I'll dress up as a sexy girl for cosplay—I wouldn't dress up like that in my ordinary life, because [cosplay] is a kind of ritual; a ritual that allows me to perform in a certain way, and allows me, through that process, to experience a new consciousness of a different sort of life. I think it's the same for that boy [in the manga].

Shaomo identifies with a fictional representation of a feminized Japanese boy not by virtue of any shared "original" gender but rather through her pleasurable recognition of the agential self-transformation that the character's cross-dressing represents. The distinction between Shaomo's and the character's socially ascribed genders is strongly downplayed in her account. She feels a bond with him/her not actually *despite* but more accurately *without any necessary reference to* her own "underlying" sex and gender. While she highlights the contradiction of the character as a "boy" being simultaneously "the most beautiful woman," it is as though her own socially ascribed status as a "girl" momentarily disappears from view in her identification with the self-transforming boy-woman character. It is worth noting that the kind of "sexy" femininity described here is in reality likely to be a highly anxious one for young middle-class women like Shaomo, with elements of popular youth culture and media encouraging them to enact it while the dominant parental culture of "respectable" middle-class femininity strongly stigmatizes it (perhaps it is for this reason that Shaomo noted that she "wouldn't dress up like that in [her] ordinary life").[36] For both the cosplaying Shaomo and the sex-working character, this form of sexualized femininity is made into a theatrical mask to be taken up and set down at will. According to her theory, their pleasure inheres precisely in the intentionality of and high degree of ritualized *control* exercised over their performance of a pleasurable yet somewhat taboo femininity (and, of course, the telling of the story itself constitutes yet another self-making performance, for Shaomo, as she constructed herself as "fan" for me, the researcher). The manga lends Shaomo the imaginative resources to rethink, reconfigure, and take control of her own relation to this ambivalent image of adult heterosexual femininity, while floating momentarily free from her own socially ascribed identity as a "girl."

The responses analyzed in this section have shown how interaction with BL texts enables these readers collectively to think, talk, and write about socially dominant and emergent ideologies on gender and sexuality. They do so sometimes in critical ways and at other times not, collectively working through and working on the ideological contradictions inherent in the array of incommensurable discourses currently available for interpreting both feminine gender and same-sex sexuality. Some readers formulate constructions of male homosexuality in line with emergent discourses of liberal sexual pluralism; others express attachment to the idea of a universalized romantic love that makes gay identity irrelevant; some voice a protofeminist critique of the sexism of mainstream romance and pornography genres; indirectly, some think through the question of women's intragender relations; others experiment with socially taboo forms of gendered and sexual self-making. The readers' collective exploration of such an array of ideas about gender and sexuality has led me to propose, elsewhere, that the BL culture in Taiwan could be considered as a form of counterpublic, along the lines theorized by Michael Warner.[37] Here, I would like to somewhat temper that observation. While the ideals of gender and sexual diversity broadly valued within the BL subculture might be said to run counter to currently dominant formations, nonetheless, as I have tried to show, significant elements within the BL scene in fact reproduce ambivalences around both homosexuality and feminine gender from the broader culture. While in some ways the BL scene acts like a counterpublic in Warner's sense, what is of greatest interest for me is less its *specific ideological stance* (radical versus conservative) than its *broad social function* as a discursive space created by and for young women themselves to actively work through these questions.

Transnational Imaginaries

If BL enables its female fans to engage imaginatively with what is ostensibly a sex-gender "other" in its representations of same-sex loving boys, then it also prompts such an engagement with a cultural-national other: Japan. In this section, I approach the interviewees' discussions about culture and place in the BL texts with the aim of framing their experience of the texts' "Japaneseness" as a form of *imagined geography*. This concept has been defined by cultural geographer Gill Valentine as referring to "how we imagine space and its boundaries, how we imagine whose space it is, and how we construct 'self' and 'other.' . . . [Cultural geographies] are produced and reproduced in everyday life as a result of individual as well as collective actions."[38] Relatedly, Arjun Appadurai has observed that under conditions of accelerating globalization, the imagination—particularly the imagination of forms of geographic space such as regions composed of interrelating nations and localities—takes on a newly prominent social role.[39] How, then, does the idea of "Japan" figure for these Taiwanese women through their everyday life practices of manga reading?

One of the most influential theories in recent years about why Japanese cultural products should have met with such success in overseas markets is the theory of these products' "cultural odorlessness" (*mukokuseki*).[40] In Koichi Iwabuchi's account, which Neal K. Akatsuka has recently cited as an explanation for Japanese BL's popularity in the United States, Japanese cultural industries have actively striven to rid their products, including manga and anime, of the cultural "odor" of Japaneseness to facilitate the localization and hence acceptance of these "culturally neutral commodities" by consumers outside Japan.[41] Candang Zhuxi, a male editor at a manga publishing house interviewed as part of this project, voiced a colloquial version of the theory when I asked him his opinion on how Taiwanese readers were able to identify with ostensibly Japanese manga characters:

> We can leave aside the question of whether one is Taiwanese or Japanese, leave aside the question of nationality. [Readers] just say that they like this manga. . . . They have no concept of nationality, the only relation is between the individual and the story. This is the method that has enabled Japanese manga to become so successful, that is, they enable the reader to become the protagonist, so that there is no difference in nationality. . . . [Instead,] it's a very pure relation between the book and the reader.

However, contradicting this theory, the only time that any of the Taiwanese manga readers interviewed for this study stated that they were *un*aware of the texts' Japaneseness was in memories of the period between 1976 and the late 1980s, when the Kuomintang government mandated the Sinicization of all Japanese personal and place names. Today, however, the readers interviewed were relatively conscious of the comics' Japaneseness. They cited, first, *cultural content*, including the details of Japanese daily life (sailor-suit school uniforms, tatami rooms, Japanese foodways, religious ceremonies, the role of social clubs in schools, bowing, the codified ritual of love confession), perceived Japanese cultural prejudices (the Japanese team invariably winning at sports tournaments, the representation of both Western and Chinese cultures in an exoticized manner), and perceived Japanese philosophies and attitudes (a melancholy, Zen-like existential resignation; collectivism; self-sacrifice; rigid social hierarchy; company loyalty). Second, readers cited culturally marked *formal and graphic conventions* such as the fine lines, high print quality, and characteristic drawing style of Japanese manga; the Japanese-inflected "translatese" of the dialogue (seen in the absence of the second-person pronoun and in hierarchical modes of address); and the overdetermined symbolism of certain repeated images (cherry blossom, flying birds, chrysanthemums). Third, and most interestingly, some interviewees made direct links between their practice of manga reading and their personal experiences of tourism in Japan. Malfoy, a nineteen-year-old university student, related:

> I went to Japan with four of my friends from high school. We planned to go to the Tokyo Tower and the Tokyo City Hall. Why? Because that's where the bishop was, in CLAMP's manga, X. I've been taken over by [manga] to the extent that as I stood there looking at the Tokyo Tower, the first thought I had was "This is where that story took place!" When I went to Odaiba to see the Rainbow Bridge, the first thing I thought of was my two favorite characters: that's the perspective through which I saw Japan, . . . part of my way of looking now takes manga as a starting point.

Petit, a twenty-nine-year-old administrator in a computer games company, had a comparable memory of her trip to Tokyo:

> I did get that feeling, that cherry-blossom feeling. Because the place I went to was Kabuki-chō, where a lot of manga are set. Actually I ended up there by accident, after getting lost—I was looking for a manga store, and I couldn't find it (laughs), and I ended up there. And I got this feeling of *"This* place appears in those manga backdrops"—I was *so* moved! (guffaws)

Far from suggesting that Japanese manga have been effectively indigenized as a localized, "culturally odorless" form for these Taiwanese readers, these responses reveal a process whereby manga narratives are imaginatively mapped onto the actual geographic spaces of Tokyo.[42] In these cases, part of the pleasure of the texts seems to inhere not in cultural odorlessness but on the contrary in a desirable, exotic "fragrance" of recognizable Japaneseness.

Fantasy Worlds

While the fictional worlds represented in manga narratives are clearly marked, in the responses discussed above, with a flavor of Japaneseness that relates in some sense to real-world Japan, other responses drew a clearer line between the fantasy world of BL manga and Japan as a real place. Although marked by a perceptible aura of general Japaneseness, the manga narratives seemed to these readers to take place in a kind of parallel universe—"manga world." Giselle, for example, distinguished between real-world Tokyo and "manga-Tokyo" and between real Japanese people and "manga-people" as characters. Xiao Tou, a twenty-five-year-old T university student, elaborated a comparable theory:

> Regardless of whether the location is made clear—and even if it *is* made clear—what attracts our attention, what makes us dwell imaginatively [on the manga] is not the location. . . . It's the plot, and the feelings that it reflects or projects to us. So [manga] *have* no space or time. I think that one takes oneself, one's own emotions, and projects them there, and then [is able to] feel them, that's how it works.

Xiao Tou proposed a theory of Japanese manga as a combined mediator/reflector/projector for the Taiwan reader's own affective experience: the texts both reflect and project feelings onto the reader, and at the same time the reader projects her own feelings onto the text and then, after mediation through its plot, is able to "re-feel" them herself. In one way, Xiao Tou's response seems to mirror the *mukokuseki* thesis discussed above. But it is important to note that at other times during the same interview Xiao Tou pointed out many features of Japanese manga that made her consciously aware of their Japanese "fragrance." How and why can a cultural product that is manifestly marked by its "foreign" flavor lend itself so effectively to the kind of intimate affective mediation that Xiao Tou and others theorized? The answer may lie in a particular modality of engagement between reader and text, characteristic of fantasy genres, which is among the engagement modalities enabled by some forms of BL.

Mandy, introduced above, offered the following interpretation of the appeal of BL. Her comments relate to the seeming anomaly of so many straight-identifying women reading male same-sex romance narratives, but the logic she outlined is also interesting to consider in relation to Taiwanese readers' negotiations with the palpable Japaneseness of the form:

> M: Sometimes people read things looking for a kind of analogy/consonance/substitution (*jituo*). But if you read about something that you understand very well in real life, it's hard to find an analogy in it.
>
> F: So BL is good for finding analogies?
>
> M: I mean because they're boys, and I have no way of really understanding what boys are, so I think: well perhaps this is what they're like, and I'm able to project my own thoughts onto them [as characters]. But when everyone [i.e., all the characters] are girls, you can't have any fantasies about them, so it's harder. I mean to me it just feels wrong, not to the extent of being distasteful, but when I want to read something I wouldn't choose [a text about girls].

With the concept of analogy, Mandy proposed here that it is precisely BL manga's thematic distance from the real-life world of young women that enables it to become such an effective screen for the projection of readerly affect and fantasy. I suggest that a similar logic may be at work vis-à-vis the texts' notable fragrance of Japaneseness. Scholars including Fujimoto, Nakamura and Matsuo, and Akatsuka have made related arguments about how fantasy worlds and liminal genders in certain fictional representations, distanced as they are from the daily lived experience of their female audiences, allow for novel and productive forms of gendered identification that both "transcend" and implicitly critique the constraints of normative femininity.[43] We might conclude, then, that it is precisely the differentness of BL's fictional worlds from the Taiwanese readers' own lifeworlds—at the level of both gender and national-cultural identification—that makes them such fertile ground for imaginative and affective appropriation. If a direct thematic focus on "Taiwanese young women" would be prohibitive because of its overfamiliarity and unavoidable associations with the irksome

Girls Who Love Boys' Love

limitations associated with that subject position in readers' own social experience, the texts' focus on "Japanese boys" enables a pleasurable exploration of an expansive imaginative, affective, and erotic space—"BL world"—that, precisely because of its double foreignness, is relatively unencumbered by such inhibitive associations. Thus, the world of "boys in Japan" that BL presents turns out to be central, in the fantasy mode of engagement, in the ongoing processes of reflecting on and negotiating with readers' own real-world social positioning as women in Taiwan.[44]

This chapter has engaged two related thematics: on one hand, the zone of contestation around gender and sexuality activated in Taiwanese women's BL engagements; on the other hand, the imaginative geography of "Japan" that the BL texts construct for these readers. Elsewhere, I have proposed the idea of "worlding" as a name for the kinds of imaginative and material practices that BL fans engage in, encompassing both their subjective engagement with the homoerotic "manga-world" in the BL texts themselves and their social engagement with the subcultural world of the local *tongrenzhi* fandom.[45] I now return here to that idea of worlding as a means of linking BL's imaginative geographies with its function as facilitator of a young women's discursive arena. As I intend it, worlding refers, on the one hand, to the ways in which Taiwanese readers use the BL texts to imagine a geocultural world and reflect on their relation to it—that is, to create an imaginative geography of a "Japan" that is characterized by sex-gender ambiguity/fluidity/nonconformity, where beautiful boys enact romance narratives and enjoy passionate sex with each other. On the other hand, worlding describes the ways in which BL facilitates young Taiwanese women linking up with each other into a social subworld at a local level, as a community of readers, fans, and creators of BL narratives.

Coda: Reflections Ten Years On

The interviews that revealed these aspects of Taiwan's BL world took place during early 2005 against a backdrop of widespread and energized public debate over the looming implementation of a new ratings system, announced by the body then known as the Government Information Office (whose function was taken over in 2012 by the new Ministry of Culture) in the final months of 2004. The Measure Governing the Ratings Systems of Publications and Pre-recorded Video would see the vast majority of BL manga volumes subject to restriction to readers over eighteen years of age by means of shrink-wrapped plastic covers, "Over 18s only" stickers, and relocation to restricted sections of bookshops.[46] The aim of the measure was to carve out a category that is closed to minors but accessible to over-18s: an "indecent" category in between "general" and "obscene" (the latter prohibited under criminal law). This new category, as currently defined, includes "those things that through language, text, dialogue, sound, graphics, or photographs excessively depict sexual behavior, indecent plots, or naked human sex organs."⁴⁷ Despite an energetic struggle against the implementation of the measure by a broad-based anticensorship lobby, the law was ultimately passed, with print items affected as of July 1, 2005 (slight revisions to the law were made in 2012). At first glance, the measure may appear innocuous enough: not an instance of outright banning of materials but rather only their restriction to an adult readership. But, as scathing critics among my interviewees were quick to point out, because the definition of indecency is so vague, and because the measure leaves the onus on publishers and retailers themselves to classify and appropriately mark publications, they will tend to self-police and are unlikely to risk stocking materials that *could be interpreted* as "indecent," hence inviting a hefty fine (up to around US$15,000), suspension of publication rights up to a year, or both. Moreover, a major portion of the BL world involves young women under the age of eighteen. Despite the fact that, in practice, it has turned out ten years on that very few manga book and rental stores rigorously check patrons' age, technically, under the measure, these adolescent women are classified along with children and denied *legal* access to the texts that form the imaginative basis for the BL world that this chapter has described.

In the decade since the fieldwork presented in this chapter was carried out, Taiwan's BL scene has been affected significantly—like so many aspects of popular and youth culture—by the ever-increasing accessibility of broadband-enabled Internet technologies in everyday life. In 2015, a majority of BL fans access and circulate their BL materials online. Hence, the material impact of the measure governing the classification of printed publications has waned since its promulgation a decade ago, with Internet content regulated more laxly than printed materials due both to looser regulatory frameworks for online content and the difficulty of ascertaining its country of origin. At the end of 2014, two Taiwanese publishing houses, Tong Li and Sharp Point, even established Taiwan's first legal BL e-zines, featuring both Taiwanese and Japanese series, which continue to run at the time of writing in 2015.⁴⁸ Internet communication is, however, obviously not completely exempt from regulation and the moral panics that often underlie the regulation of media content for youth, in particular. Between 2004 and 2012, a regulation mandating age-based restrictions on accessing Internet content was in effect in Taiwan; like the measure on the classification of printed publications and video, this regulation was framed with reference to Taiwan's Protection of Children and Youths Welfare and Rights Act (promulgated in 2003).⁴⁹ While the regulation on Internet content was ultimately abolished by the National Communications Commission, it was replaced in 2012 by the establishment of a watchdog body, the Institute of Watch Internet Network (*sic*) or iWIN, which is charged with "protecting" youth from "harmful" Internet content: a vague category that arguably encompasses many BL materials (although as far as I am aware at the time of writing, no cases have successfully been brought against BL sites).⁵⁰

Feminist scholar and social activist Josephine Chuen-juei Ho pointed out that developments such as these are not merely idiosyncratic quirks of Taiwan's domestic legal system. Rather, they may be seen as intrinsically linked to transnational developments, as Taiwan's successive governments strive to bring its international image into line with benchmarks set by intergovernmental organizations such as, most relevantly here, the UN Convention on the Rights of the Child.[51] Ho demonstrated how local conservative nongovernmental organizations are able to work in concert with the government's continuing anxieties over Taiwan's lack of nation-state status and concomitant desire to be seen to bring the island's laws into line with international benchmarks in order to push forward a series of new legal measures regulating local cultural production, among them those regulating materials legally accessible to "youth" in both printed and electronic forms. But, paradoxically, by rendering illegal access to the textual tools with which adolescent girls and young women have creatively constructed their *own* forms of critical social space, the effect of such measures is to culturally impoverish those very "children" who are framed as the target of the state's protection.

The effects of the trends in cultural-sexual regulation that Ho described are certainly not limited to Taiwan. In recent years, for example, a long-running debate raged in Australia regarding the former Labor government's plans to institute a nationwide ISP-level Internet filter to protect children from the effects of harmful material, including "child abuse materials"—a category into which many if not most BL texts would fall, according to the category's extremely broad and fuzzy definition.[52] While that plan was in the end quietly abandoned, the dangerously vague definition of "child abuse materials" in Australian law remains.[53] Meanwhile, in Japan, Mark McLelland detailed recent developments in child protection laws that similarly impact BL communities with their crude and fuzzy definitions of what constitute "harmful" materials, and bespeak what McLelland, following Habermas, sees as a wider transnational trend toward "the juridification of the imagination."[54] The concern I would like to raise in closing this chapter, which has explored in detail the complex, vibrant, and creative world of Taiwan's BL fandom, is that the application of such legal content-regulation measures may be detrimental to the ways in which youth cultures actually work—organically, chaotically, productively. Such measures may function like a broad-spectrum antibiotic that kills off useful as well as harmful forms of life. Drawing its energies from one kind of informal transnational imaginary, Taiwan's BL culture and comparable worlds elsewhere are now clearly at risk from transnational desires of another, more official kind.

Notes

1. In referring to my interviewees as "women," I refer to their ascribed gendered position within the broader social context rather than to any presumed gendered

position adopted while reading BL texts; as we will see, gendered identification in reading is often marked precisely by its *dissonance* with socially ascribed gender.

2. Akiko Mizoguchi, "Theorizing Comics/Manga as a Productive Forum: *Yaoi* and Beyond," in *Comics Worlds and the Worlds of Comics: Towards Scholarship on a Global Scale*, ed. Jaqueline Berndt (Kyoto: International Manga Research Centre, Kyoto Seika University, 2011), 146, accessed April 21, 2016, http://imrc.jp/lecture/2009/12/comics-in-the-world.html.

3. Fusami Ogi, "Gender Insubordination in Japanese Comic (Manga) for Girls," in *Illustrating Asia: Comics, Humour Magazines, and Picture Books*, ed. John A. Lent (Honolulu: University of Hawai'i Press, 2001), 172; Hiromi Tsichuya Dollase, "Mad Girls in the Attic: Louisa May Alcott, Yoshiya Nobuko and the Development of Shōjo Culture" (PhD diss., Purdue University, 2003), 220. Both Ogi and Dollase frame *shōjo manga* as a logical extension of the literary *shōjo* aesthetic and style created by Yoshiya Nobuko in her often homoerotic popular girls' fiction, complete with its large-eyed, fine-limbed character illustrations.

4. Yukari Fujimoto, "Shōjo manga ni okeru 'Shōnen-ai' no imi" [The significance of "Shōnen-ai" in shōjo manga], in *Nyū feminizumu rebyū* [New Feminism Review] 2 (May 1991, unpublished translation by Taeko Yamada, accessed March 23, 2015, http://www.matt-thorn.com/shoujo_manga/fujimoto.php.

5. James Welker, "Drawing Out Lesbians: Blurred Representations of Lesbian Desire in *Shōjo* Manga," in *Lesbian Voices, Canada and the World*, ed. Subhash Chandra (New Delhi: Allied Publishing, 2006), 156–84, "Beautiful, Borrowed, and Bent: Boys' Love as Girls' Love in *Shōjo* Manga," *Signs: A Journal of Women and Culture in Society* 31.3 (2006): 841–70, and "Lilies of the Margin: Beautiful Boys and Lesbian Identities," in *AsiaPacifiQueer: Rethinking Gender and Sexuality in the Asia-Pacific*, ed. Fran Martin et al. (Urbana and Chicago: University of Illinois Press, 2008), 46–66; Mark McLelland, "The Love Between 'Beautiful Boys' in Japanese Women's Comics," *Journal of Gender Studies* 9.1 (2000): 13–25.

6. The term *yaoi* derives alternately from initials of the Japanese phrase "no climax, no point, no meaning" or from the phrase "Stop, my arse hurts!"; both possibilities underscore the pornographic convention, in this subgenre, of narrative development overwhelmed by graphic depictions of sex acts. Fujimoto, "Significance of *Shōnen-ai* in Shōjo Manga."

7. Mizoguchi, "Theorizing Comics/Manga," 164.

8. Jui-ping Chung, "Tongxinglian manhua duzhe zhi texing yu shiyong dongji zhi guanlianxing yanjiu" [A study of the relationship between the characteristics and users' motivation of readers of homosexual manga] (MA thesis, Chinese Culture University, 1999), 19–22; Shu-chu Wei, "Shaping a Cultural Identity: The Picture Book and Cartoons in Taiwan, 1945–1980," in *Illustrating Asia: Comics, Humour Magazines, and Picture Books*, ed. John A. Lent (Honolulu: University of Hawai'i Press, 2001), 64–84.

9. Chung, "Study of the Relationship," 20.

10. Wei, "Shaping a Cultural Identity," 68–69; see also John A. Lent, "Local Comic Books and the Curse of Manga in Hong Kong, South Korea and Taiwan," *Asian Journal of Communication* 9.1 (1999): 108–28; and John A. Lent, "Comics in East Asian Countries: A Contemporary Survey," *Journal of Popular Culture* 29.1 (1995): 185–98; and Wai-ming Ng, "A Comparative Study of Japanese Comics in Southeast Asia and East Asia," *International Journal of Comic Art* (Spring 2000): 45–56; and Wai-ming Ng, *The Impact*

of *Japanese Comics and Animation in Asia*, last modified 2002, accessed September 10, 2003, http://www.jef.or.jp/en/jti/200207_006.html.
11. Chung, "Study of the Relationship," 20.
12. This stipulation remained in place until the mid-1980s. Candang Zhuxi (Taiwanese manga editor) in discussion with the author, March–April 2005.
13. For example, Taiwan's Tong Li Comics, which went on to become the island's largest publisher of Japanese manga, was established in 1977; it has since published over 1,000 Japanese series. Yi Shi Man, today trading as Da Ran, was set up during the same period. Lent, "Local Comic Books," 122–26. See also the account of Tong Li's history at Tong Li Comics a, accessed May 5, 2010, http://www.tongli.com.tw/index.aspx.
14. Candang Zhuxi, interview.
15. This mirrors a parallel development in Japan: the key example here is the CLAMP collective, which is a group of women manga artists now producing *shōnen-ai* works commercially, but which began as a *dōjinshi* circle in the late 1980s. CLAMP's works were among the favorites of many of the Taiwanese interviewees.
16. Slash culture is the subject of an extensive field of critical commentary that, similarly to commentary on the BL phenomenon, tends to underscore the productive and empowering aspects of the fandom for the young women who are its principal participants. Some key texts include Constance Penley, "Feminism, Psychoanalysis, and the Study of Popular Culture," in *Cultural Studies*, ed. Lawrence Grossberg, Cary Nelson, and Paula Triechler (Routledge: New York, 1992), 479–500; Constance Penley, "Brownian Motion: Women, Tactics and Technology," in *Technoculture*, ed. Constance Penley and Andrew Ross (Minneapolis: University of Minnesota Press, 1991), 135–62; and Constance Penley, *NASA/Trek: Popular Science and Sex in America* (London: Verso, 1997); Joanna Russ, "Pornography by Women, for Women, with Love," in *Magic Mommas, Trembling Sisters, Puritans and Perverts* (New York: Crossing Press, 1985), 79–99; Will Brooker, "Slash and Other Stories," in *Using the Force: Creativity, Community and "Star Wars" Fans* (London: Continuum, 2003), 129–72; Shoshanna Green, Cynthia Jenkins, and Harry Jenkins, "Normal Female Interest in Men Bonking: Selections from *The Terra Nostra Underground* and *Strange Bedfellows*," in *Theorizing Fandom: Fans, Subculture and Identity*, ed. Cheryl Harris and Alison Alexander (Cresskill, NJ: Hampton Press, 1998), 9–38; Mirna Cicioni, "Male Pair-Bonds and Female Desire in Fan Slash Writing," in *Theorizing Fandom: Fans, Subculture and Identity*, ed. Cheryl Harris and Alison Alexander (Cresskill NJ: Hampton Press, 1998), 153–77; and Camille Bacon-Smith, "Homoerotic Romance," in *Enterprising Women: Television Fandom and the Creation of Popular Myth* (Philadelphia: University of Pennsylvania Press, 1992), 228–54.
17. On *tongrenzhi* and cosplay in Taiwan, see, for example, Teri Silvio, "Informationalized Affect: The Body in Taiwanese Digital Video Puppetry and Cosplay," in *Embodied Modernities: Corporeality, Representation, and Chinese Cultures*, ed. Fran Martin and Larissa Heinrich (Honolulu: University of Hawai'i Press, 2006), 195–217; and Lin Yi-min, "Why Are They 'Obsessed'? An Exploration of the *Tong-Ren-Zhi* Phenomenon among Teenagers in Taiwan," *Inter-Asia Cultural Studies* 2.3 (2001): 447–53.
18. The pleasurable imaginative activity of "slashing" or pairing up existing male characters is known among Taiwanese fans as *peidui*: matching couples.
19. See for example Fujimoto, "Significance of 'Shōnen-ai' in Shōjo Manga"; Sharon Kinsella, "Amateur Manga Subculture," in *Adult Manga: Culture and Power in*

Contemporary Japanese Society (Richmond: Curzon Press, 2000), 10–238; Sharalyn Orbaugh, ed., "Manga," special issue, *US-Japan Women's Journal* 25 (2003): 3–7; Mark McLelland, "The World of *Yaoi*: The Internet, Censorship and the Global 'Boys' Love' Fandom," *The Australian Feminist Law Journal* 23 (2005): 61–77; Mark McLelland and Seunghyun Yoo, "The International Yaoi Boys' Love Fandom and the Regulation of Virtual Child Pornography: The Implications of Current Legislation," *Sexuality, Research and Social Policy* 4.1 (2007): 93–104; and McLelland, "The Love between 'Beautiful Boys'"; Wim Lunsing, "*Yaoi Ronsō*: Discussing Depictions of Male Homosexuality in Japanese Girls' Comics, Gay Comics and Gay Pornography," *Intersections: Gender, History and Culture in the Asian Context* 12 (January 2006), accessed December 1, 2016, http://intersections.anu.edu.au/issue12/lunsing.html; Frederik L. Schodt, "Regulation versus Fantasy" in *Manga! Manga! The World of Japanese Comics*, ed. Frederik L. Schodt (Tokyo: Kodansha International, 1983), 120–37; Veruska Sabucco, "Guided Fan Fiction: Western 'Readings' of Japanese Homosexual-Themed Texts," in *Mobile Cultures: New Media in Queer Asia*, ed. Chris Berry, Fran Martin, and Audrey Yue (Durham, NC: Duke University Press, 2003), 70–86; Tomoko Aoyama, "Transgendering Shōjo Shōsetsu: Girls' Inter-text/Sex-uality," in *Genders, Transgenders and Sexualities in Japan*, ed. Mark McLelland and Romit Dasgupta (London and New York: Routledge, 2005), 49–64; Matthew Thorn, "Girls and Women Getting Out of Hand: The Pleasure and Politics of Japan's Amateur Comics Community," in *Fanning the Flames: Fans and Consumer Culture in Contemporary Japan*, ed. William W. Kelly (Albany, NY: State University of New York Press, 2004), 169–88; Mizoguchi, "Theorizing Comics/Manga"; and, on BL in the USA and some other non-Japanese reception contexts, the essays in Antonia Levi, Mark McHarry, and Dru Pagliassotti, eds., *Boys' Love Manga: Essays on the Sexual Ambiguity and Cross-Cultural Fandom of the Genre* (Jefferson, NC: McFarland, 2010).

20. One interviewee plausibly suggested that this quasigeneric convention may arise from a similar ideology in Minami Ozaki's seminal work of 1989, *Desperate Love* (*Jue'ai*) (Hong, in discussion with the author, March–April 2005).
21. Nights, in discussion with the author, March–April 2005.
22. See Fujimoto, "Significance of 'Shōnen-ai in Shōjo Manga'".
23. Mizoguchi, "Male-Male Romance by and for Women in Japan: A History and the Subgenres of *Yaoi* Fictions," *U.S.-Japan Women's Journal* 25 (2003): 56.
24. Chung, "Study of the Relationship," 36. On the popular romance in Taiwan and other queer appropriations of Qiong Yao-style romance, see Chapter 3 in Fran Martin, *Backward Glances: Contemporary Chinese Culture and the Female Homoerotic Imaginary* (Durham, NC: Duke University Press, 2010).
25. See also Dru Pagliassotti, "Better Than Romance? Japanese BL Manga and the Subgenre of Male/Male Romance Fiction," in *Boys' Love Manga: Essays on the Sexual Ambiguity and Cross-Cultural Fandom of the Genre*, ed. Antonia Levi, Mark McHarry, and Dru Pagliassotti (Jefferson, NC: McFarland, 2010), 59–83.
26. Distinction between the pure-love and the *H-ban* subgenres of BL is also common in the critical literature. Chung, "Study of the Relationship," 6; Ping-chun Liu, "Jiegou liuxing wenhua de quanli guiji: Shixi Taiwan manhua wenhua" [Deconstructing the power trajectory of popular culture: An analysis of manga culture in Taiwan] (PhD diss., National Cheng-chi University, 2003), 177.
27. Cf. Mizoguchi, "Theorizing Comics/Manga," 159.
28. On the queer potential of gendered and sexual identification for fans as well as creators of BL, see Uli Meyer, "Hidden in Straight Sight: Trans*gressing Gender

and Sexuality via BL," in *Boys' Love Manga: Essays on the Sexual Ambiguity and Cross-Cultural Fandom of the Genre*, eds. Antonia Levi, Mark McHarry, and Dru Pagliassotti (Jefferson, NC: McFarland and Company, 2010), 232–56.
29. On subcultural capital, see Sarah Thornton, *Club Cultures: Music, Media and Subcultural Capital* (Oxford: Polity Press, 1995).
30. I intend "emergent" and "dominant" in Raymond Williams' sense of these terms. See Raymond Williams, "Dominant, Residual and Emergent," in *Marxism and Literature*, ed. Raymond Williams (Oxford: Oxford University Press, 1978), 121–27.
31. Cf. Neal K. Akatsuka, "Uttering the Absurd, Revaluing the Abject: Femininity and the Disavowal of Homosexuality in Transnational Boys' Love Manga," in *Boys' Love Manga: Essays on the Sexual Ambiguity and Cross-Cultural Fandom of the Genre*, ed. Antonia Levi, Mark McHarry, and Dru Pagliassotti (Jefferson, NC: McFarland and Company, 2010), 159–76.
32. For further detail on the indigenization of global gay and lesbian culture in Taiwan during the 1990s, see Fran Martin, *Situating Sexualities: Queer Representation in Taiwanese Fiction, Film and Public Culture* (Hong Kong: Hong Kong University Press, 2003).
33. A similar desire of "gay realness" among the American *yaoi* fans is discussed in Alexis Hall, "Gay or *Gei*? Reading 'Realness' in Japanese *Yaoi* Manga," in *Boys' Love Manga: Essays on the Sexual Ambiguity and Cross-Cultural Fandom of the Genre*, ed. Antonia Levi, Mark McHarry, and Dru Pagliassotti (Jefferson, NC: McFarland and Company, 2010), 211–20.
34. I discuss the idea of BL fandom as a mode of "folk-theorizing" in detail in Fran Martin, "Comics as Everyday Theory: The Counterpublic World of Taiwanese Women Fans of Japanese Homoerotic Manga," in *Cultural Theory and Everyday Practice*, ed. Katrina Schlunke and Nicole Anderson (Oxford: Oxford University Press, 2008), 164–76.
35. Shaomo said the word "sexy" in English.
36. For key articles critiquing the cultural hegemony of forms of "respectable femininity" in Taiwan, see Naifei Ding, "Parasites and Prostitutes in the House of State Feminism," *Inter-Asia Cultural Studies* 1.2 (2000): 305–18; Hans Tao-ming Huang, "State Power, Prostitution and Sexual Order in Taiwan: Towards a Genealogical Critique of 'Virtuous Custom,'" *Inter-Asia Cultural Studies* 5.2 (2004): 237–62; and Josephine Chuen-juei Ho, "From Spice Girls to *Enjo Kosai*: Formations of Teenage Girls' Sexualities in Taiwan," *Inter-Asia Cultural Studies* 4.2 (2003): 325–36; and Josephine Chuen-juei Ho, "Self-Empowerment and 'Professionalization': Conversations with Taiwanese Sex Workers," *Inter-Asia Cultural Studies* 2.2 (2000): 283–99.
37. See Martin, "Comics as Everyday Theory"; and Michael Warner, *Publics and Counterpublics* (New York: Zone Books, 2002), 56. This observation is inspired by McLelland and Yoo, "International *Yaoi* Boys' Love Fandom." On women's public spheres in transnational China, see Mayfair Yang, ed., *Spaces of Their Own: Women's Public Sphere in Transnational China* (Minneapolis and London: University of Minnesota Press, 1999).
38. Gill Valentine, "Imagined Geographies: Geographical Knowledges of Self and Other in Everyday Life," in *Human Geography Today*, ed. Doreen Massey, John Allen, and Philip Sarre (Cambridge: Polity Press, 1999), 48.
39. Arjun Appadurai, "Grassroots Globalization and the Research Imagination," *Public Culture* 12.1 (2000): 1–19.
40. For a critical discussion, see Koichi Iwabuchi, *Recentering Globalization: Popular Culture and Japanese Transnationalism* (Durham, NC: Duke University Press, 2002).

41. See Koichi Iwabuchi, "Return to Asia? Japan in the Asian Audiovisual Market," in *Consuming Ethnicity and Nationalism: Asian Experiences*, ed. Kosaku Yoshino (London: Curzon Press, 1999), 177–99; Koichi Iwabuchi, "Purposeless Globalisation or Idealess Japanisation? Japanese Cultural Industries in Asia," *Culture and Policy* 7.1 (1996): 33–42; and Iwabuchi, *Recentering Globalization*, 27–28; and Akatsuka, "Uttering the Absurd," 160.

42. It is worth noting, too, that contra the *mukokuseki* thesis, respondents frequently paralleled—rather than contrasted—the "Japanese" flavor of Japanese cultural products (manga, TV dramas) with the "American" flavor of American ones (comics, TV series, Hollywood films). The latter they tended to associate with a bold, coarse aesthetic sense and cultural values including hero worship, individualism, sexual libertinism, and infantilism.

43. Fujimoto speculates that the unpopularity of GL with girls, as compared to BL, may be connected with the relative familiarity of the subject matter, hence its unamenability to pleasurable fantasy. Yukari Fujimoto, *Watashi no ibasho wa doko ni aru no—shōjo manga ga utsusu kokoro no katachi*, translated by Taeko Yamada as *Where Is my Place? Reflections of the Heart in Shōjo Manga* (Tokyo: Gakuyo Shobo, 1998), 177–206. This was borne out somewhat by my discussions with the Taiwanese interviewees. Cf. Nakamura and Matsuo on why female Takarazuka fans have trouble forming close identification with female-feminine stars/roles on stage, as distinct from their identificatory bond with the female masculinity of Takarazuka performers; Karen Nakamura and Matsuo Hisako, "Female Masculinity and Fantasy Spaces: Transcending Genders in the Takarazuka Theatre and Japanese Popular Culture," in *Men and Masculinities in Contemporary Japan: Dislocating the Salaryman Doxa*, ed. James E. Roberson and Nobue Suzuki (New York: Routledge Curzon, 2003), 59–76; Akatsuka applies a similar logic to male femininity in BL comics, "Uttering the Absurd," 169.

44. However, making this observation is not the same as concluding that BL *always only* functions as a fantasy genre. Rather, fantasy constitutes *one* modality of engagement available to some readers of some texts. It exists alongside the other modes noted above, which include somewhat more realist engagements vis-à-vis social issues of homosexuality and homophobia, and vis-à-vis Japan as a more specific imagined geography.

45. Martin, "Comics as Everyday Theory."

46. Taiwan Ministry of Culture, "Chuban pinji luying jiemudai fenji guanli banfa" [Measure for the management of ratings systems for publications and video programs], 2012, accessed February 18, 2015, http://www.moc.gov.tw/law.do?method=find&id=363.

47. Ibid., Clause 5, part 4.

48. See Sharp Point Comics website, accessed February 24, 2015, http://www.spp.com.tw/comic.htm; and "Events," Tong Li Comics b, accessed February 24, 2015, http://www.tongli.com.tw/webpages/events/2014/TCA2015/ebook1.htm.

49. The Republic of China, Laws & Regulations Database, "Regulations for the rating of Internet Content (Abolished)," accessed February 18, 2015, http://law.moj.gov.tw/LawClass/LawContent.aspx?PCODE=P0050021.

50. For example, complaints may be lodged online by members of the public against websites with "pornographic or obscene" content, defined as including "obscenity, nudity, [or] provocative, erotic pictures." *iWin*, accessed February 18, 2015, http://www.win.org.tw/iwin/; see also Li-jen Liu, "Fei neirong fenji ershao shangwang gai fanghu jigou" [Content ratings abolished; children and youth to be protected online

by an organization, instead], *Liberty Times Net*, May 17, 2012, accessed February 18, 2015, http://news.ltn.com.tw/news/life/paper/584380.

51. Josephine Chuen-juei Ho, "Queer Existence under Global Governance: A Taiwan Exemplar," *positions: east asia cultures critique* 18.2 (2010): 537–54.

52. For a thorough critique of the Internet filter plan, see Mark McLelland, "Australia's Proposed Internet Filtering System: Its Implications for Animation, Comics and Gaming (ACG) and Slash Fan Communities," *Media International Australia* 134 (February 2010): 7–19.

53. Mark McLelland, "Australia's 'Child-Abuse Material' Legislation, Internet Regulation and the Juridification of the Imagination," *International Journal of Cultural Studies* 15.5 (2012): 467–83.

54. Mark McLelland, "Sex, Censorship and Media Regulation in Japan: A Historical Overview," in *Routledge Handbook of Sexuality Studies in East Asia*, ed. Mark McLelland and Vera Mackie (Oxford: Routledge, 2014): 402–13.

Works Cited

Akass, Kim, and Janet McCabe, eds. *Reading "The L Word": Outing Contemporary Television*. New York: Palgrave Macmillan, 2006.

Akatsuka, Neal K. "Uttering the Absurd, Revaluing the Abject: Femininity and the Disavowal of Homosexuality in Transnational Boys' Love Manga." In *Boys' Love Manga: Essays on the Sexual Ambiguity and Cross-Cultural Fandom of the Genre*, edited by Antonia Levi, Mark McHarry, and Dru Pagliassotti, 159–76. Jefferson, NC: McFarland and Company, 2010.

Allison, Anne. "Portable Monsters and Commodity Cuteness: Pokémon as Japan's New Global Power." *Postcolonial Studies* 6 (2003): 381–95.

Altman, Dennis. "Global Gaze/Global Gays." *GLQ* 3.4 (1997): 417–36.

Anderson, Benedict. *Imagined Communities: Reflections on the Origin and Spread of Nationalism*. London: Verso, 1983.

Ang, Ien. *Living Room Wars: Rethinking Media Audiences for a Postmodern World*. New York: Routledge, 1996.

Annett, Sandra. "Animating Transcultural Communities: Animation Fandom in North America and East Asia from 1906–2010." PhD diss., University of Manitoba, 2011.

Aoyagi, Hiroshi. *Islands of Eight Million Smiles: Idol Performance and Symbolic Production in Contemporary Japan*. Cambridge, MA: Harvard University Press, 2005.

Aoyama, Tomoko. "Transgendering Shōjo Shōsetsu: Girls' Inter-text/Sex-uality." In *Genders, Transgenders and Sexualities in Japan*, edited by Mark McLelland and Romit Dasgupta, 49–64. London and New York: Routledge, 2005.

Appadurai, Arjun. "Grassroots Globalization and the Research Imagination." *Public Culture* 12.1 (2000): 1–19.

———. *Modernity at Large: Cultural Dimensions of Globalization*. Minneapolis: University of Minnesota Press, 1996.

Arnold, Carrie. "Cuteness Inspires Aggression." *Scientific American Mind* 24 (July/August 2013). Accessed October 5, 2014. http://www.nature.com/scientificamericanmind/journal/v24/n3/pdf/scientificamericanmind0713-18b.pdf.

Arnold, Matthew. *Culture and Anarchy*. Edited with an introduction by J. Dover Wilson. Cambridge: Cambridge University Press, 1960.

Ashcraft, Brian. "What Is Japan's Fetish This Week—Male Daughters." Last modified May 26, 2011. Accessed September 8, 2014. http://kotaku.com/5804979/what-is-japans-fetish-this-week-male-daughters.

Au, Wai-man Vivian. "The Queer Female Stardom: Emerging from Transnational Chinese Singing Contests." MPhil thesis, University of Hong Kong, 2012.

Bacon-Smith, Camille. *Enterprising Women: Television Fandom and the Creation of Popular Myth*. Philadelphia: University of Pennsylvania Press, 1992.

———. "Homoerotic Romance." In *Enterprising Women: Television Fandom and the Creation of Popular Myth*, 228–54. Philadelphia: University of Pennsylvania Press, 1992.

Bai, Ruoyun. *Staging Corruption: Chinese Television and Politics*. Vancouver: University of British Columbia Press, 2014.

Bakhtin, Mikhail. *Rabelais and His World*. Translated by Helene Iswolksy. Bloomington: Indiana University Press, 1984.

Balkind, Nicola. *Fan Phenomena: "The Hunger Games."* Chicago: University of Chicago Press, 2014.

Bao, Hongwei. "'Queer Comrades': Transnational Popular Culture, Queer Sociality, and Socialist Legacy." *English Language Notes* 49.1 (2011): 131–37.

BBC. "Gay Love Theory as Fans Relish Sherlock in China," January 2, 2014. Accessed July 24, 2015. http://www.bbc.com/news/blogs-china-blog-25550426.

Berry, Chris. "The Chinese Side of the Mountain." *Film Quarterly* 60.3 (2007): 32–37.

———. "*East Palace, West Palace*: Staging Gay Life in China." *Jump Cut: A Review of Contemporary Media* 42 (1998): 84–89.

———. "The Sacred, the Profane, and the Domestic in Cui Zi'en's Cinema." *positions: East Asia Cultures Critique* 12.1 (2004): 195–201.

———. "*Wedding Banquet*: A Family (Melodrama) Affair." In *Chinese Films in Focus: 25 New Takes*, edited by Chris Berry, 183–90. London: British Film Institute, 2003.

Berry, Chris, Nicola Liscutin, and Jonathan D. Mackintosh, eds. *Cultural Studies and Cultural Industries in Northeast Asia: What a Difference a Region Makes*. Hong Kong: Hong Kong University Press, 2009.

Bhabha, Homi K. *The Location of Culture*. New York: Routledge, 1994.

Binnie, Jon. *The Globalization of Sexuality*. Thousand Oaks, CA: Sage, 2004.

Boellstorff, Tom. *The Gay Archipelago: Sexuality and Nation in Indonesia*. Princeton: Princeton University Press, 2005.

Brooker, Will. "Slash and Other Stories." In *Using the Force: Creativity, Community and "Star Wars" Fans*, 129–72. London: Continuum, 2003.

———. *Using the Force: Creativity, Community and "Star Wars" Fans*. London: Continuum, 2003.

Bury, Rhiannon. *Cyberspaces of Their Own: Female Fandoms Online*. New York: Peter Lang, 2005.

Butler, Judith. *Bodies That Matter: On the Discursive Limits of "Sex."* New York: Routledge, 1993.

———. *Gender Trouble: Feminism and the Subversion of Identity*. New York: Routledge, 1990.

———. *Gender Trouble: Feminism and the Subversion of Identity; with an Introduction by the Author*. Second edition. New York and London: Routledge, 2006.

Cai, Yong, and Wang Feng. "(Re)emergence of Late Marriage in Shanghai: From Collective Synchronization to Individual Choice." In *Wives, Husbands, and Lovers: Marriage and Sexuality in Hong Kong, Taiwan, and Urban China*, edited by Deborah S. Davis and Sara L. Friedman, 97–117. Stanford: Stanford University Press, 2014.

Chambers, Samuel A. "Heteronormativity and *The L Word*: From a Politics of Representation to a Politics of Norms." In *Reading "The L Word": Outing Contemporary*

Works Cited

Television, edited by Kim Akass, Janet McCabe, and Sarah Warn, 81–98. London: I. B. Tauris, 2006.

Chang, Shihyun. "Ciwenhua jingji zhi zhanxian: Lun Taiwan tongrenzhi de zaidi bianqian" [The power of subcultural economics: Discussion about the local transformation of *Dōjinshi* in Taiwan]. MA thesis, National Taiwan Normal University. 2006.

Chang, Weijung. "Analyzing the Construction of Sexuality from 'BL Fantasy': A Case Study of Taiwanese *Fujoshi*'s Fantasy Practice in 'Butler Cafés.'" *Journal of Women and Gender Studies* 32 (2013): 97–133.

———. "Analyzing the Relationship with 'Japaneseness' from the Life Story of a Taiwanese Japanophile Girl." *Journal of Japan Oral History Association* 10 (2014): 77–98.

———. "Gendered/Sexualized Transformation of Japanophilia: The Symbolization and the Localization of 'Japaneseness' in Taiwan." Paper presented at the annual meeting for the North America Taiwan Studies Association, Boston, MA, Harvard University, June 12–13, 2015.

———. "The Sexuality of 'BL Fantasy' in Taiwan: A Case Study of Taiwanese *Fujoshi*'s Fantasy Practice." *Journal of the Graduate School of Humanities and Sciences* 15 (2012): 291–99.

Chang, Yin-Huei. "Qiangwei chanrao shizijia: BL yuetingren wenhua yanjiu" [Crucifix entwined with roses: A cultural study of BL audience]. MA thesis, National Taiwan University, 2007.

Chao, Shih-chen. "Grotesque Eroticism in the *Danmei* Genre: The Case of Lucifer's Club in Chinese Cyberspace." *Porn Studies* 1.3 (2016): 65–76.

Chen, Fangying. "*Xiao'ao jianghu* zhong de yishu yu renwu" [The arts and characters in *The Smiling, Proud Wanderer*]. In *Jin Yong xiaoshuo guoji xueshu yantaohui lunwenji* [Proceedings of the International Conference on Jin Yong's Novels], edited by Qiu Gui Wang, 221–35. Taipei: Yuan-Liou Publishing, 1999.

Chen, Jin-Shiow. "A Study of Fan Culture: Adolescent Experiences with Animé/Manga *Doujinshi* and Cosplay in Taiwan." *Visual Arts Research* 33.1 (2007): 14–24.

Chen, Lingchei Letty. *Writing Chinese: Reshaping Chinese Cultural Identity*. New York: Palgrave Macmillan, 2006.

Chen Mo. *Renwu Jin Yong* [Characters of Jin Yong]. Beijing: Oriental Publishing, 2008.

Chen, Peifeng. "Enka no zaichika: Jūsōtekina shokuminchibunka kara no jijosaisei no michi" [The localization of Enka: The road from the multicolonial culture to self-helping rebirth]. In *Higashiajia sinjidai no nihon to Taiwan* [Japan and Taiwan in the new age of East Asia], edited by Jun Nishikawa and Hsinhuang Hsiao, 239–300. Tokyo: Akashi book, 2010.

Chen, Pingyuan. *Wuxia xiaoshuo leixing yanjiu* [Genre studies of martial arts novels]. Beijing: People's Literature Publishing, 1992.

Chen, Xiaomei. *Occidentalism: A Theory of Counter-discourse in Post-Mao China*. Lanham, MD: Rowman & Littlefield, 2002.

Chen, Yizhen. *A Research on Johnny's Fans in Taiwan*. Tokyo: Seikyusha, 2014.

Chiang, Howard, "Archiving Peripheral Taiwan: The Prodigy of the Human and Historical Narration." *Radical History Review* 120 (2014): 204–25.

———. "(De)Provincializing China: Queer Historicism and Sinophone Postcolonial Critique." In *Queer Sinophone Cultures*, edited by Howard Chiang and Ari Larissa Heinrich, 19–51. New York: Routledge, 2014.

———, ed. *Transgender China*. New York: Palgrave Macmillan, 2012.

Chin, Bertha, and Lori Hitchcock Morimoto. "Towards a Theory of Transcultural Fandom." *Participations: Journal of Audience and Reception Studies* 10.1 (2013): 92–108.

China News. "Meili wudi: *Xiao'ao Jianghu* shinian beigaibian N ci" [The unparalleled charm: *The Smiling, Proud Wanderer* has been remade for n times within four decades]. July 10, 2013. http://finance.chinanews.com/it/2013/07-10/5025779.shtml.

Ching, Leo. "'Japanese Devils': The Conditions and Limits of Anti-Japanism in China." *Cultural Studies* 26.5 (2012): 710–22.

Chou, Wah Shan. *Tongzhi: Politics of Same-Sex Eroticism in Chinese Societies*. New York: Haworth Press, 2000.

Chow, Kai-wing. "Narrating Nation, Race, and National Culture: Imagining the Hanzu Identity in Modern China." In *Constructing Nationhood in Modern East Asia*, edited by Kai-wing Chow, Kevin M. Doak, and Poshek Fu, 47–83. Ann Arbor: University of Michigan Press, 2001.

Chow Wah Shan. *Tongzhi lun* [On *tongzhi*]. Hong Kong: Hong Kong Homosexual Research Society, 1995.

———. *Tung zi leon* [On *tongzhi*]. Second edition. Hong Kong: Hong Kong Queer Press, 1997.

Chow, Yiu Fai, and Jeroen de Kloet. *Sonic Multiplicities: Hong Kong Pop and the Global Circulation of Sound and Image*. Bristol: Intellectual, 2013.

Chu, Roland. "*Swordsman II* and *The East Is Red*: The 'Hong Kong Film', Entertainment, and Gender." *Bright Lights: Film Journal*, January 1, 2001. Accessed July 14, 2015. http://brightlightsfilm.com/swordsman-ii-east-red-hong-kong-film-entertainment-gender.

Chua Beng Huat. *Structure, Audience and Soft Power in East Asian Pop Culture*. Hong Kong: Hong Kong University Press, 2012.

Chua Beng Huat, and Koichi Iwabuchi, eds. *East Asian Pop Culture: Analysing the Korean Wave*. Hong Kong: Hong Kong University Press, 2008.

Chung Jui-ping. "Tongxinglian manhua duzhe zhi texing yu shiyong dongji zhi guanlianxing Yanjiu" [A study of the relationship between the characteristics and users' motivation of readers of homosexual manga]. MA thesis, Chinese Culture University, 1999.

Chung, Ting-yiu Robert, Ka-lai Karie Pang, and Wing-Yi Winnie Lee. *Survey on Hong Kong Public's Attitudes towards Rights of People of Different Sexual Orientations*. Hong Kong: Public Opinion Programme, University of Hong Kong, November 7, 2012. Accessed March 5, 2015. http://hkupop.hku.hk/english/report/LGBT_CydHo/content/resources/report.pdf.

Chung, Ting-Yiu Robert, Ka-Lai Karie Pang, Wing-Yi Winnie Lee, and Joyce Wai-Man Chan. *Hong Kong LGBT Climate Study 2011–12*. Survey Report. Hong Kong: Community Business Limited and Public Opinion Programme, University of Hong Kong, May 14, 2012. Accessed March 5, 2015. http://hkupop.hku.hk/english/report/LGBT2011_12/content/resources/report.pdf.http://hkupop.hku.hk/english/report/LGBT2011_12/content/resources/report.pdf.

Chung, Ting-Yiu Robert, Ka-lai Karie Pang, Wing-Yi Winnie Lee, and Kin-Wing Jasmine Li. *Survey on Hong Kong Public's Attitudes towards Rights of People of Different Sexual Orientations*. Hong Kong: Public Opinion Programme, University of Hong Kong, October 23, 2013. Accessed March 1, 2015. http://hkupop.hku.hk/english/report/LGBT_CydHo2013/content/resources/report.pdf.

Cicioni, Mirna. "Male Pair-Bonds and Female Desire in Fan Slash Writing." In *Theorizing Fandom: Fans, Subculture and Identity*, edited by Cheryl Harris and Alison Alexander, 153–77. Cresskill, NJ: Hampton Press, 1998.

Coonan, Clifford. "China Box Office: 'Tiny Times 4.0' Lead as Local Youth Flicks Dominate." *Hollywood Reporter*, July 13, 2015. Accessed July 15, 2015. http://www.hollywoodreporter.com/news/china-box-office-tiny-times-808489.

Cruz-Malave, Arnaldo, and Martin Manalansan. Introduction to *Queer Globalizations: Citizenship and the Afterlife of Colonialism*, edited by Arnaldo Cruz-Malave and Martin Manalansan, 1–10. New York: New York University Press, 2002.

Daai DQ. "[Erciyuan] gongkai jihu wuma18/jing tongrenzhi Taiwan tongren zuozhe beibu" [Two-dimension publicizing almost uncensored 18/forbidden *Dōjinshi* Taiwanese author was arrested]. *tgbus*, August 22, 2013. Accessed July 20, 2015. http://bbs.tgbus.com/thread-5196325-1-1.html.

DeAngelis, Michael. *Gay Fandom and Crossover Stardom: James Dean, Mel Gibson, and Keanu Reeves*. Durham, NC: Duke University Press, 2001.

Davis, Deborah S. "On the Limits of Personal Autonomy: PRC Law and the Institution of Marriage." In *Wives, Husbands, and Lovers: Marriage and Sexuality in Hong Kong, Taiwan, and Urban China*, edited by Deborah S. Davis and Sara L. Friedman, 41–61. Stanford, CA: Stanford University Press, 2014.

Davis, Deborah S., and Sara L. Friedman, eds. *Wives, Husbands, and Lovers: Marriage and Sexuality in Hong Kong, Taiwan, and Urban China*. Stanford, CA: Stanford University Press, 2014.

Denton, Kirk A. "Horror and Atrocity: Memory of Japanese Imperialism in Chinese Museums." In *Re-envisioning the Chinese Revolution: The Politics and Poetics of Collective Memories in Reform China*, edited by Ching Kwan Lee and Guobin Yang, 245–86. Stanford, CA: Stanford University Press, 2007.

Ding, Naifei. "Parasites and Prostitutes in the House of State Feminism." *Inter-Asia Cultural Studies* 1.2 (2000): 305–18.

Dollase, Hiromi Tsichuya. "Mad Girls in the Attic: Louisa May Alcott, Yoshika Nobuko and the Development of Shojo Culture." PhD diss., Purdue University, 2003.

Doty, Alexander. *Making Things Perfectly Queer*. Minneapolis: University of Minnesota Press, 1993.

Duffett, Mark. "Celebrity: The Return of the Repressed in Fan Studies?" In *The Ashgate Research Companion to Fan Cultures*, edited by Linda Duits and Koos Zwaan, 163–80. Farnham, UK: Ashgate, 2014.

———. *Understanding Fandom: An Introduction to the Study of Media Fan Culture*. New York: Bloomsbury Academic, 2013.

Duggan, Lisa. "The New Homonormativity: The Sexual Politics of Neoliberalism." In *Materializing Democracy: Toward a Revitalized Cultural Politics*, edited by Russ Castronovo and Dana D. Nelson, 175–94. Durham, NC: Duke University Press, 2002.

Durham, Meenakshi Gigi. "Constructing the 'New Ethnicities': Media, Sexuality, and Diaspora Identity in the Lives of South Asian Immigrant Girls." *Critical Studies in Media Communication* 21.2 (2004): 140–61.

Dyer, Richard. *Gays and Film*. New York: Zoetrope, 1984.

Eng, Lawrence. "Anime and Manga Fandom as Networked Culture." In *Fandom Unbound: Otaku Culture in a Connected World*, edited by Mizuko Ito, Daisuke Okabe, and Izumi Tsuji, 158–78. New Haven: Yale University Press, 2012.

Engebretsen, Elisabeth Lund. *Queer Women in Urban China: An Ethnography*. New York: Routledge, 2014.

Erni, John Nguyet. "Marriage Rights for Transgender People in Hong Kong." In *Wives, Husbands, and Lovers: Marriage and Sexuality in Hong Kong, Taiwan, and Urban China*, edited by Deborah S. Davis and Sara L. Friedman, 189–217. Stanford: Stanford University Press, 2014.

Equal Opportunities Committee, Hong Kong Special Administrative Region Government. *Study on Public Perception of Portrayal of Female Gender in the Hong Kong Media—Executive Summary*. Hong Kong: Social Sciences Research Centre, University of Hong Kong, commissioned by the Equal Opportunities Commission, 2009. Accessed March 1, 2015. http://www.eoc.org.hk/eoc/upload/20096111239594027760.pdf.

Fang, Xindong, Kewu Pan, Zhimin Li, and Jing Zhang. "Zhongguo hulianwang ershinian: Sanci langchao he sanda zhuangxin [2]" [Twenty years of China's Internet: Three waves and three innovations (2)]. *People*, Accessed July 20, 2015. April 21, 2014. http://media.people.com.cn/n/2014/0421/c40606-24922639-2.html.

Fauna. "Wang Jiayun: Chinese Blow-Up Doll Becomes Famous in Korea." *ChinaSMACK*. Last modified February 23, 2011. Accessed October 7, 2014. http://www.chinasmack.com/2011/pictures/wang-jiayun-chinese-blow-up-doll-becomes-famous-in-korea.html.

Featherstone, Mike. *Global Culture: Nationalism, Globalization and Modernity*. London: Sage, 1990.

Feng, Jin. "'Addicted to Beauty': Consuming and Producing Web-Based Chinese *Danmei* Fiction at Jinjiang." *Modern Chinese Literature and Culture* 21.2 (2009): 1–41.

———. *Romancing the Internet: Producing and Consuming Chinese Web Romance*. Boston: Brill, 2013.

Fincher, Leta Hong. *Leftover Women: The Resurgence of Gender Inequality in China*. London: Zed Books, 2014.

Fiske, John. "Act Globally, Think Locally." In *Planet TV: A Global Television Reader*, edited by Lisa Parks and Shanti Kumar, 277–85. New York: New York University Press, 2003.

———. *Reading the Popular*. Boston: Unwin Hyman, 1989.

Fuhr, Michael. "Voicing Body, Voicing Seoul." In *Vocal Music and Contemporary Identities: Unlimited Voices in East Asia and the West*, edited by Christian Utz and Frederick Lau, 267–84. New York: Routledge, 2013.

Fujimoto, Yukari. "Shōjo manga ni okeru 'Shōnen-ai' no imi" [The significance of "Shōnen-ai" in Shōjo manga]. *Nyū feminizumu rybyū* [New feminism review] 2 (May 1991). Unpublished translation by Taeko Yamada. Accessed March 23, 2015. http://www.matt-thorn.com/shoujo_manga/fujimoto.php.

———. *Where Is My Place? Reflections of the Heart in Shōjo Manga*. Translated by Taeko Yamada. Tokyo: Gakuyō Shobō, 1998.

Fung, Anthony. "Faye and the Fandom of a Chinese Diva." *Popular Communication: International Journal of Media and Culture* 7.4 (2009): 252–66.

Fung, Anthony, and Eric Ma. "Formal vs. Informal Use of Television and Sex-Role Stereotyping in Hong Kong." *Sex Roles* 42.1/2 (2000): 57–81.

Galbraith, Patrick W. "Fantasy Play and Transgressive Intimacy among 'Rotten Girls' in Contemporary Japan." *Signs* 37.1 (2011): 211–32.

———. "Moe: Exploring Virtual Potential in Post-millennial Japan." In *Researching Twenty-First Century Japan: New Directions and Approaches for the Electronic Age*, edited by Timothy Iles and Peter C. D. Matanle, 343–65. Lanham, MA: Lexington Books, 2012.

———. *The Moe Manifesto: An Insider's Look at the Worlds of Manga, Anime, and Gaming*. Singapore: Tuttle Publishing, 2014.

———. *The Otaku Encyclopedia: An Insider's Guide to the Subculture of Cool Japan*. New York: Kodansha International, 2009.

Garcia, Angela Cora, Alecea I. Standlee, Jennifer Bechkoff, and Yan Cui. "Ethnographic Approaches to the Internet and Computer-Mediated Communication." *Journal of Contemporary Ethnography* 38.1 (2009): 52–84.

Ge, Zhaoguang. *Zhaizi zhongguo: Chongjian youguan "Zhongguo" de lishi lunshu* [Dwelling in the middle of the country: Reestablishing historical narratives of "China"]. Beijing: Zhonghua shuju, 2011.

Giddens, Anthony. *The Transformation of Intimacy: Sexuality, Love, and Eroticism in Modern Societies.* Stanford, CA: Stanford University Press, 1992.

Goldman, Andrea S. *Opera and the City: The Politics of Culture in Beijing, 1770–1900.* Stanford, CA: Stanford University Press, 2012.

Gould, Stephen Jay. "A Biological Homage to Mickey Mouse." Accessed August 27, 2014. http://faculty.uca.edu/benw/biol4415/papers/Mickey.pdf.

Green, Shoshanna, Cynthia Jenkins, and Henry Jenkins. "Normal Female Interest in Men Bonking: Selections from *The Terra Nostra Underground* and *Strange Bedfellows.*" In *Theorizing Fandom: Fans, Subculture and Identity*, edited by Cheryl Harris and Alison Alexander, 9–38. Cresskill, NJ: Hampton Press, 1998.

Grossberg, Lawrence. "Is There a Fan in the House? The Affective Sensibility of Fandom." In *The Adoring Audience: Fan Culture and Popular Media*, edited by Lisa A. Lewis, 50–65. London: Routledge, 1992.

Gunnels, Jen. "'A Jedi Like My Father before Me': Social Identity and the New York Comic Con." *Transformative Works and Cultures* 3 (2009). Accessed August 9, 2014. http://journal.transformativeworks.org/index.php/twc/article/view/161/110.

Halberstam, Judith. *Female Masculinity*. Durham, NC: Duke University Press, 1998.

———. *In a Queer Time and Place: Transgender Bodies, Subcultural Lives*. New York: New York University Press, 2005.

Hall, Alexis. "Gay or *Gei*? Reading 'Realness' in Japanese *Yaoi* Manga." In *Boys' Love Manga: Essays on the Sexual Ambiguity and Cross-Cultural Fandom of the Genre*, edited by Antonia Levi, Mark McHarry, and Dru Pagliassotti, 211–20. Jefferson, NC: McFarland and Company, 2010.

Halperin, David M. *Saint Foucault: Towards a Gay Hagiography*. New York: Oxford University Press, 1995.

Harrington, C. Lee, and Denise D. Bielby. "Flow, Home, and Media Pleasures." *Journal of Popular Culture* 38.5 (2005): 834–54.

———. *Soap Fans: Pursuing Pleasure and Making Meaning in Everyday Life*. Philadelphia: Temple University Press, 1995.

He, Chengzhou. "Trespassing, Crisis and Renewal: Li Yugang and Cross-Dressing Performance." *Differences: A Journal of Feminist Cultural Studies* 24.2 (2013): 150–71.

Hellekson, Karen, and Kristina Busse, eds. *Fan Fiction and Fan Communities in the Age of the Internet*. Jefferson, NC: McFarland, 2006.

———. *The Fan Fiction Studies Reader*. Iowa City: University of Iowa Press, 2014.

Hernanadez, Vittorio. "Chinese Drama 'Nirvana in Fire' Catches Interest of South Korean TV Viewers." *yibada*, April 13, 2016. Accessed May 8, 2016. http://en.yibada.com/articles/116157/20160413/chinese-drama-nirvana-in-fire-catches-interest-of-south-korean-tv-viewers.htm.

Herold, David K., and Peter Marolt, eds. *Online Society in China: Creating, Celebrating and Instrumentalising the Online Carnival*. London and New York: Routledge, 2011.

Hills, Matt. *Fan Cultures*. Oxon: Routledge, 2002.

———. "Media Academics as Media Audiences." In *Fandom: Identities and Communities in a Mediated World*, edited by Jonathan Gray, Cornel Sandvoss, and C. Lee Harrington, 33–47. New York: New York University Press, 2007.

Hine, Christine. *Virtual Ethnography*. London: Sage, 2000.

Hinsch, Bret. *Passions of the Cut Sleeve: The Male Homosexual Tradition in China*. Los Angeles: University of California Press, 1990.

Hjorth, Larissa. *Mobile Media in the Asian-Pacific: Gender and the Art of Being Mobile*. New York: Routledge, 2009.

Ho, Josephine Chuen-juei. "From Spice Girls to *Enjo Kosai*: Formations of Teenage Girls' Sexualities in Taiwan." *Inter-Asia Cultural Studies* 4.2 (2003): 325–36.

———. "Queer Existence under Global Governance: A Taiwan Exemplar." *positions: east asia cultures critique* 18.2 (2010): 537–54.

———. "Self-Empowerment and 'Professionalization': Conversations with Taiwanese Sex Workers." *Inter-Asia Cultural Studies* 2.2 (2000): 283–99.

Ho, Loretta Wing Wah. *Gay and Lesbian Subculture in Urban China*. New York: Routledge, 2010.

Ho, Sik Ying, and Ka Tat Tsang. "The Things Girls Shouldn't See: Relocating the Penis in Sex Education in Hong Kong." In *Gendering Hong Kong*, edited by Anita Kit-wa Chan and Wai Ling Wong, 690–708. Hong Kong: Oxford University Press, 2004.

Hoad, Neville. "Between the White Man's Burden and the White Man's Disease: Tracking Lesbian and Gay Human Rights in Southern Africa." *GLQ* 5.4 (1999): 559–84.

Homer, Sean. *Jacques Lacan*. London and New York: Routledge, 2005.

Hong Kong Commercial Daily. "Tongxinglianjie zao jingjingfang tuxi fengbi" [The Gay Festival was cracked down on and closed by the Beijing police]. December 27, 2005. Accessed July 20, 2015. http://3g.xici.net/d33726324.htm.

Hongo, Jun. "Comike, Where Otaku Come to Share the Love." *Japan Times*. Last modified December 19, 2013. http://www.japantimes.co.jp/culture/2013/12/19/general/comiket-where-otaku-come-to-share-the-love.

Honig, Emily. "Maoist Mappings of Gender: Reassessing the Red Guards." In *Chinese Femininities / Chinese Masculinities: A Reader*, edited by Susan Brownell and Jeffrey N. Wasserstrom, 255–68. Berkeley: University of California Press, 2002.

Horie, Shunichi. "Futatsu no 'Nihon': Hakkaminkei wo chūshin tosuru Taiwanjin no 'Nihon ishiki'" [Two "Japans": The Taiwanese Hakka people's "consciousness of Japan"]. In *Sengo Taiwan niokeru nihon: Shokuminchi keiken no renzoku, henbō, riyō* ["Japan" in the postwar Taiwan: The continuity, transformation and appropriation of the colonized experiences], edited by Masako Igarashi and Yuko Mio, 121–54. Tokyo: Fukyosya, 2006.

Huang, Hans Tao-Ming. *Queer Politics and Sexual Modernity in Taiwan*. Hong Kong: Hong Kong University Press, 2011.

———. "State Power, Prostitution and Sexual Order in Taiwan: Towards a Genealogical Critique of 'Virtuous Custom.'" *Inter-Asia Cultural Studies* 5.2 (2004): 237–62.

Huang, Shuling. "Nation-Branding and Transnational Consumption: Japan-Mania and the Korean Wave in Taiwan." *Media, Culture & Society* 33.1 (2011): 3–18.

Huang, Xiaoyan. "From Survival to Profit: A Canadian Book Publishers' Guide to China, the World's Largest Market." MA thesis, Simon Fraser University, 2005.

Works Cited

Huang, Xin. "From 'Hyper-feminine' to Androgyny: Changing Notions of Femininity in Contemporary China." In *Asian Popular Culture in Transition*, edited by Lorna Fitzsimmons and John A. Lent, 133–55. New York: Routledge, 2013.

Huang, Zhihui. "Posutokoroniaru Taiwan ni okeru jūsōkōzō: Nihon to chūka" [The multilayered structure in postcolonial Taiwan: Japan and China]. In *Higashi ajia shinjidai no nihon to Taiwan* [Japan and Taiwan in the new era of East Asia], edited by Jun Nishikawa and Hsinhuang Hsiao, 159–93. Tokyo: Akashi Shoten, 2010.

Idea, Nimfa May. "*Lost in Thailand* Filmmakers Brainstorm with Audience to Ensure Movie's Success." *yibada*. June 18, 2015. Accessed March 10, 2016. http://en.yibada.com/articles/39365/20150618/lost-in-thailand-lost-in-hong-kong-highest-grossing-films-in-china-filmmakers-in-china-best-comedy-movie-in-china.htm.

International Federation of the Phonographic Industry (Hong Kong Group) Limited. "IFPI Hong Kong Top Sales Music Award Presented [2001–2014]." Last Modified January 14, 2014. http://www.ifpihk.org/hong-kong-top-sales-music-award-presented-01-14/hong-kong-top-sales-music-award-presented/2014.

Israel, Tania, and Jonathan J. Mohr. "Attitudes toward Bisexual Women and Men." *Journal of Bisexuality* 4.1/2 (2004): 117–34.

Ito, Mamoru. "90 nendai no nihon no terebidorama ni miru joseisei no hyōshō" [The representation of femininity in Japanese TV drama in the 1990s]. In *Global Prism*, edited by Koichi Iwabuchi, 39–62. Tokyo: Heibonsha, 2003.

Ito, Mizuko. Introduction to *Fandom Unbound: Otaku Culture in a Connected World*, edited by Mizuko Ito, Daisuke Okabe, and Izumi Tsuji, xi–xxxi. New Haven: Yale University Press, 2012.

Ito, Mizuko, Daisuke Okabe, and Izumi Tsuji, eds. *Fandom Unbound: Otaku Culture in a Connected World*. New Haven: Yale University Press, 2012.

Iwabuchi, Koichi, ed. *Feeling Asian Modernities: Transnational Consumption of Japanese TV Dramas*. Hong Kong: Hong Kong University Press, 2004.

———. "Purposeless Globalisation or Idealess Japanisation? Japanese Cultural Industries in Asia." *Culture and Policy* 7.1 (1996): 33–42.

———. *Recentering Globalization: Popular Culture and Japanese Transnationalism*. Durham, NC: Duke University Press, 2002.

———. "Return to Asia? Japan in the Asian Audiovisual Market." In *Consuming Ethnicity and Nationalism: Asian Experiences*, edited by Kosaku Yoshino, 177–99. London: Curzon Press, 1999.

———. *Transnational Japan*. Tokyo: Iwanami Shoten, 2001.

———. "Uses of Japanese Popular Culture: Trans/nationalism and Postcolonial Desire for 'Asia.'" *Emergences* 11.2 (2001): 199–206.

Jackson, Peter A. "Bangkok's Early Twenty-First-Century Queer Boom." In *Queer Bangkok: Twenty-First-Century Markets, Media, and Rights*, edited by Peter A. Jackson, 17–42. Hong Kong: Hong Kong University Press, 2011.

———. "Capitalism and Global Queering: National Markets, Parallels among Sexual Cultures, and Multiple Queer Modernities." *GLQ: A Journal of Lesbian and Gay Studies* 15.3 (2009): 357–95.

———. *Dear Uncle Go: Male Homosexuality in Thailand*. Bangkok: Bua Luang Books, 1995.

———. "An Explosion of Thai Identities: Global Queering and Re-imagining Queer Theory." *Culture, Health & Sexuality* 2.4 (2000): 405–24.

———. "Global Queering and Global Queer Theory: Thai [Trans]genders and [Homo] sexualities in World History." *Autrepart* 49 (2009): 15–30.

Jacobs, Katrien. *The Afterglow of Women's Pornography in Post-digital China*. New York: Palgrave Macmillan, 2015.

Jagose, Annamarie. *Queer Theory: An Introduction*. New York: New York University Press, 1996.

Jamison, Anne, ed. *Fic: Why Fanfiction Is Taking Over the World*. Dallas, TX: BenBella Books, 2013.

Japp, Phyllis M., Mark Meister, and Debra K. Japp, eds. *Communication Ethics, Media, and Popular Culture*. New York: Peter Lang, 2005.

Jenkins, Henry. "Acafandom and Beyond: Concluding Thoughts" (blog). October 22, 2011. Accessed January 11, 2016. http://henryjenkins.org/2011/10/acafandom_and_beyond_concludin.html.

———. *Convergence Culture: Where Old and New Media Collide*. New York: New York University Press, 2008.

———. "The Cultural Context of Chinese Fan Culture: An Interview with Xiqing Zheng (Part One)" (blog). February 1, 2013. Accessed May 9, 2015. http://henryjenkins.org/2013/02/the-cultural-context-of-chinese-fan-culture-an-interview-with-xiqing-zheng-part-one.html.

———. *Fans, Bloggers, and Gamers: Exploring Participatory Culture*. New York: New York University Press, 2006.

———. "Pop Cosmopolitanism: Mapping Cultural Flows in an Age of Media Convergence." In *Fans, Bloggers, and Gamers: Exploring Participatory Culture*, edited by Henry Jenkins, 152–72. New York: New York University Press, 2006.

———. *Textual Poachers: Television Fans and Participatory Culture*. New York: Routledge, 1992.

Jenkins, Henry, Sam Ford, and Joshua Green. *Spreadable Media: Creating Value and Meaning in a Networked Culture*. New York: New York University Press, 2013.

Jin, Yong. *Xiao'ao jianghu* [The smiling, proud wanderer]. Hong Kong: Minghe she, 2006.

Jinghua Shibao [Beijing Times]. "Yuenan fengsha wailai yanqing danmei xiaoshuo, zhongguo wangluo wenxue bizhong da" [Vietnam bans foreign romance and *danmei* novels]. May 27, 2015. Accessed May 1, 2016. http://culture.ifeng.com/a/20150527/43847161_0.shtml.

Johnson, Mark. "Global Desirings and Translocal Loves: Transgendering and Same-Sex Sexualities in the Southern Philippines." *American Ethnologist* 25.4 (1998): 695–711.

Jones, Carol. "Lost in China? Mainlandisation and Resistance in Post-1997 Hong Kong." *Taiwan in Comparative Perspectives* 5 (2014): 21–46.

Jones, Sara Gwenllian. "Histories, Fictions, and *Xena: Warrior Princess*." *Television & New Media* 1.4 (2000): 403–18.

Joseph, May, and Jennifer N. Fink, eds. *Performing Hybridity*. Minneapolis: University of Minnesota Press, 1999.

Jung, Sun. *Korean Masculinity and Transcultural Consumption: Yonsama, Rain, Oldboy, K-Pop Idols*. Hong Kong: Hong Kong University Press, 2011.

———. "K-Pop beyond Asia: Performing Trans-nationality, Trans-sexuality, and Trans-textuality." In *Asian Popular Culture in Transition*, edited by Lorna Fitzsimmons and John A. Lent, 108–30. New York: Routledge, 2013.

———. "The Shared Imagination of *Bishōnen*, Pan–East Asian Soft Masculinity: Reading DBSK, Youtube.com and Transcultural New Media Consumption." *Intersections: Gender and Sexuality in Asia and the Pacific* 20 (2009). Accessed December 27, 2014. http://intersections.anu.edu.au/issue20/jung.htm.

Kam, Lucetta Yip Lo. "Desiring T, Desiring Self: 'T-Style' Pop Singers and Lesbian Culture in China." *Journal of Lesbian Studies* 18.3 (2014): 252–65.

———. "Recognition through Mis-recognition: Masculine Women in Hong Kong." In *AsiaPacifiQueer: Rethinking Genders and Sexualities*, edited by Fran Martin, Peter A. Jackson, Mark McLelland, and Audrey Yue, 99–116. Urbana: University of Illinois Press, 2008.

———. *Shanghai Lalas: Female Tongzhi Communities and Politics in Urban China*. Hong Kong: Hong Kong University Press, 2012.

———. "This Gender Called TB (TB 這性別)." *E-journal on Hong Kong Cultural and Social Studies* 2 (2002). Accessed September 25, 2008. http://www.hku.hk/hkcsp/ccex/ehkcss01/frame.html?mid=1&smid=1&ssmid=7 (site now defunct).

Kaneda, Junko. "Yaoi ron, asu no tameni sono 2" [The theory of *yaoi*: For the future 2]. *Yuriika* December 2007, 48–54.

Kang, Wenqing. *Obsession: Male Same-Sex Relations in China, 1900–1950*. Hong Kong: Hong Kong University Press, 2009.

Kim, Youna. *Korean Media in a Digital Cosmopolitan World*. New York: Routledge, 2013.

Kinsella, Sharon. "Cuties in Japan." In *Women, Media and Consumption in Japan*, edited by Lise Skove and Brian Morean, 220–54. Richmond: Curzon, 1995.

———. "Amateur Manga Subculture." In *Adult Manga: Culture and Power in Contemporary Japanese Society*, 10–238. Richmond: Curzon Press, 2000.

Kitada, Akihiro. "Japan's Cynical Nationalism." In *Fandom Unbound: Otaku Culture in a Connected World*, edited by Mizuko Ito, Daisuke Okabe, and Izumi Tsuji, 68–84. New Haven: Yale University Press, 2012.

Ko, Yufen. "The Desired Form: Japanese Idol Dramas in Taiwan." In *Feeling Asian Modernities: Transnational Consumption of Japanese TV Dramas*, edited by Koichi Iwabuchi, 107–28. Hong Kong: Hong Kong University Press, 2004.

———. "Nihon no aidoru dorama to taiwan niokeru yokubō no katachi" [The Japanese idol drama and the shape of desire in Taiwan]. In *Global Prism*, edited by Koichi Iwabuchi, 151–82. Tokyo: Heibonsha, 2003.

Kong, Shuyu, "The 'Affective Alliance': *Undercover*, Internet Media Fandom, and the Sociality of Cultural Consumption in Postsocialist China." *Modern Chinese Literature and Culture* 24.1 (Spring 2012): 1–47.

Kong, Travis S. K. *Chinese Male Homosexualities: Memba, Tongzhi and Golden Boy*. Oxon: Routledge, 2011.

———. "A Fading *Tongzhi* Heterotopia: Hong Kong Older Gay Men's Use of Spaces." *Sexualities* 15.8 (2012): 896–916.

Kong, Travis S. K., Hoi Leung Lau, and Cheuk Yin Li. "The Fourth Wave? A Critical Reflection on the *Tongzhi* Movement in Hong Kong." In *Routledge Handbook of Sexuality Studies in East Asia*, edited by Mark McLelland and Vera Mackie, 188–201. London: Routledge, 2015.

Kort, Michelle. "Welcome Back to L World." *Advocate*, February 1, 2005. Accessed April, 1, 2010. http://www.advocate.com/news/2005/01/18/welcome-back-l-world.

Lai, Rainsta. "Dialogue Two: Rose/Mary/Rose-Mary; The Blurring of Gender Boundaries." In *Fe/male Bodies*, edited by Daryl Cheung, Chun Chun Lai, Krebs Lee, Josette Tang, and Tommy Tse, 56–61. Hong Kong: Kubrick, 2005.

Lamerichs, Nicolle. "The Cultural Dynamic of *Doujinshi* and Cosplay: Local Anime Fandom in Japan, USA and Europe." *Participations* 10. 1 (2013): 154–76.

———. "Stranger Than Fiction: Fan Identity in Cosplay." *Transformative Works and Cultures* 7 (2011). Accessed April 1, 2016. http://journal.transformativeworks.org/index.php/twc/article/view/246.

Larson-Wang, Jessica A. "What Are You, Five? Chinese Women and *Sa Jiao*." Last modified December 21, 2012. Accessed October 27, 2014. http://www.echinacities.com/news/What-are-You-Five-Chinese-Women-and-Sa-Jiao.

Lavin, Maud. *Push Comes to Shove: New Images of Aggressive Women*. Cambridge, MA: MIT Press, 2010.

Lavin, Maud, and Xiaorui Zhu. "Alexter: Boys' Love Meets Hong Kong Activism." *fnewsmagazine*, November 17, 2014. Accessed July 20, 2015. http://fnewsmagazine.com/2014/11/alexter-boys-love-meets-hong-kong-activism/.

Lee, Iyun. "The Conflict between the Reality and Illusion—the Implication of the Re-emergence of the Japanese Image on Postwar Taiwan, 1945–1949." *Journal of Information Studies, Interfaculty Initiative in Information Studies the University of Tokyo* 69 (2005): 137–60.

———. "The Japanese Image Made by the Japanese Dramas in Taiwan." *Journal of Mass Communication Studies* 69 (2006): 108–25.

Lee, Ming-Tsung. "Qinri de qinggan jiegou yu hari de zhuti: Yige kuashidai rentong zhengzhi de kaocha" [The "pro-Japan" emotional structure and the "Japanophile" subjects: A study on diachronous identity politics]. Paper presented at the annual meeting for the Taiwanese Sociological Association, Xinchu, Tsinghua University, December 4–5, 2004.

Lee, Tzuyao. "Dongman yuzhaizu de huanxiang shijie: Yi Taiwan de tongren chuangyan huodong wei yanjiu duixiang" [A fantasy theme criticism of *dōjinshi* and cosplay in Taiwan]. MA thesis, Fu Jen Catholic University. 2004.

Lei, Weizhen. "Cong 'yishi' dao 'paidui': Hulianwang dui 'meijieshijian' de chonggou" [From "ritual" to "orgy": Reconstruction of "media events" by the Internet]. In *Xinmeiti shijian yanjiu* [New media events research], edited by Jack Linchuan Qiu and Joseph Man Chan, 66–94. Beijing: Renmin University Press, 2011.

Lent, John A. "Comics in East Asian Countries: A Contemporary Survey." *Journal of Popular Culture* 29.1 (1995): 185–98.

———. "Local Comic Books and the Curse of Manga in Hong Kong, South Korea and Taiwan." *Asian Journal of Communication* 9.1 (1999): 108–28.

Leonard, Sean. "Progress against the Law: Animation and Fandom, with the Key to the Globalization of Culture." *International Journal of Cultural Studies* 8.3 (2005): 281–305.

Leung, Helen Hok-Sze. "Loving in the Stillness of Earthquakes: Ho Yuk—Let's Love Hong Kong." In *Ho Yuk—Let's Love Hong Kong: Script and Critical Essays*, edited by Ching Yau, 57–61. Hong Kong: Youth Literary Press, 2002.

———. "Thoughts on Lesbian Genders in Contemporary Chinese Cultures." In *Femme/Butch: New Considerations of the Way We Want to Go*, edited by Michelle Gibson and Deborah T. Meem, 123–34. New York: Harrington Park Press, 2002.

———. *Undercurrents: Queer Culture and Postcolonial Hong Kong*. Vancouver: University of British Columbia Press, 2008.

Levi, Antonia, Mark McHarry, and Dru Pagliassotti, eds. *Boys' Love Manga: Essays on the Sexual Ambiguity and Cross-Cultural Fandom of the Genre.* Jefferson, NC: McFarland, 2010.

Li, Eva Cheuk-Yin. "The Absence of Fan Activism in the Queer Fandom of Ho Denise Wan See (HOCC) in Hong Kong." In "Transformative Works and Fan Activism," edited by Henry Jenkins and Sangita Shresthova. Special issue, *Transformative Works and Cultures* 10 (2012). doi:10.3983/twc.2012.0325.

———. "Approaching Transnational Chinese Queer Stardom as Zhongxing ('Neutral Sex/Gender') Sensibility." *East Asian Journal of Popular Culture* 1.1 (2015): 75–95.

———. "Exploring the Productiveness of Fans: A Study of Ho Denise Wan See (HOCC) Fandom." MPhil Thesis, University of Hong Kong, 2011.

Li, Hongmei. "Parody and Resistance on the Chinese Internet." In *Online Society in China: Creating, Celebrating and Instrumentalising the Online Carnival*, ed. David Kurt Herold and Peter Marolt, 71–88. London and New York: Routledge, 2011.

Li, Shubo. "The Online Public Space and Popular Ethos in China." *Media, Culture & Society* 32.1 (2010): 63–83.

Li, Siu Leung. *Cross-Dressing in Chinese Opera.* Hong Kong: Hong Kong University Press, 2003.

Li, Yannan. "Japanese Boy-Love Manga and the Global Fandom: A Case Study of Chinese Female Readers." MA thesis, Indiana University, 2009.

Li, Yinhe. *Xingquanli yu fa* [Sexual rights and law]. Beijing: Science Studies Publishing House, 2009.

Li, Yinhe, and Xiaobo Wang. *Tamen de shijie: Zhongguo nantongxinglian qunluo toushi* [Their world: China's homosexual male community]. Taiyuan: Shanxi People's Publishing House, 1993.

Lim, Song Hwee. *Celluloid Comrades: Representations of Male Homosexuality in Contemporary Chinese Cinemas.* Honolulu: Hawai'i University Press, 2006.

———. "How to Be Queer in Taiwan: Translation, Appropriation, and the Construction of a Queer Identity in Taiwan." In *AsiaPacifiQueer: Rethinking Genders and Sexualities*, edited by Fran Martin, Peter A. Jackson, Mark McLelland, and Audrey Yue, 235–50. Urbana: University of Illinois Press, 2008.

Lin, Tiara. "Men Succumb to Women's Sajiao Spell." *Global Times*, last modified January 17, 2013. Accessed February 4, 2015. http://www.globaltimes.cn/content/756586.shtml.

Lin, Yi-min. "Why Are They 'Obsessed'? An Exploration of the *Tong-Ren-Zhi* Phenomenon among Teenagers in Taiwan." *Inter-Asia Cultural Studies* 2.3 (2001): 447–53.

Liu, Li-jen. "Fei neirong fenji ershao shangwang gai fanghu jigou" [Content ratings abolished; children and youth to be protected online by an organization, instead]. *Liberty Times Net*, May 17, 2012. Accessed February 18, 2015. http://news.ltn.com.tw/news/life/paper/584380.

Liu, Lydia H. *Translingual Practice: Literature, National Culture, and Translated Modernity China, 1900–1937.* Stanford, CA: Stanford University Press, 1995.

Liu, Petrus. "Queer Marxism in Taiwan." *Inter-Asia Cultural Studies* 8.4 (2007): 517–39.

———. "Why Does Queer Theory Need China?" *positions: East Asia Cultures Critique* 18.2 (2010): 291–320.

Liu, Ping-chun. "Jiegou liuxing wenhua de quanli guiji: Shixi Taiwan manhua wenhua" [Deconstructing the power trajectory of popular culture: An analysis of manga culture in Taiwan]. PhD diss., National Cheng-chi University, 2003.

Liu, Pinzhi. "Funü de huanxiang yu wang/wangxiang" [A study on *fujoshi*'s queer reading experience]. MA thesis, National Kaohsiung Normal University. 2014.

Liu, Ting. "Conflicting Discourses on Boys' Love and Subcultural Tactics in Mainland China and Hong Kong." *Intersections: Gender and Sexuality in Asia and the Pacific* 20 (2009). Accessed October 22, 2014. http://intersections.anu.edu.au/issue20/liu.htm.

Longhurst, Brian, Gaynor Bagnall, and Mike Savage. "Place, Belonging, and the Diffused Audience." In *Fandom: Identities and Community in a Mediated World*, edited by Jonathan Gray, Cornel Sandvoss, and C. Lee Harrington, 125–38. New York: New York University Press, 2007.

Loo, John, ed. *New Reader for Chinese Tongzhi*. Hong Kong: Worldson, 1999.

Lorenz, Konrad. *Studies in Animal and Human Behavior*. Vol. 2. Translated by Robert Martin. Cambridge, MA: Harvard University Press, 1971.

Lothian, Alexis. "An Archive of One's Own: Subcultural Creativity and the Politics of Conservation." *Transformative Works and Cultures* 6 (2011). Accessed January 20, 2016. http://journal.transformativeworks.org/index.php/twc/article/view/267/197.

Louie, Kam. *Theorising Chinese Masculinity: Society and Gender in China*. Cambridge: Cambridge University Press, 2002.

Lu, Guojing. "Danmei wenhua yu tongrennü qunti yanjiu" [Studies on Boys' Love culture and the fangirl community]. MA thesis, Suzhou University, 2011.

Lunsing, Wim. "*Yaoi Ronsō*: Discussing Depictions of Male Homosexuality in Japanese Girls' Comics, Gay Comics and Gay Pornography." *Intersections: Gender, History and Culture in the Asian Context* 12 (January 2006). Accessed December 1, 2016. http://intersections.anu.edu.au/issue12/lunsing.html.

Lunning, Frenchy. "Cosplay, Drag, and the Performance of Abjection." In *Mangatopia: Essay on Manga and Anime in the Modern World*, edited by Timothy Perper and Marthan Cornog, 71–88. Santa Barbara, CA: Libraries Unlimited, 2011.

Mackie, Vera, and Mark McLelland. "Introduction: Framing Sexuality Studies in East Asia." In *Routledge Handbook of Sexuality Studies in East Asia*, edited by Mark McLelland and Vera Mackie, 1–17. New York: Routledge, 2014.

MacWilliams, Mark W. Introduction to *Japanese Visual Culture: Explorations in the World of Manga and Anime*, edited by Mark W. MacWilliams, 3–25. Armonk: M. E. Sharpe, 2008.

Mak, Anson Hoi Shan. *Soeng sing cing juk* [Bisexual desires]. Edited by Mary Ann Pui Wai King. Hong Kong: Hong Kong Women Christian Council, 2000.

Martin, Fran. *Backward Glances: Contemporary Chinese Cultures and the Female Homoerotic Imaginary*. Durham, NC: Duke University Press, 2010.

———. "Comics as Everyday Theory: The Counterpublic World of Taiwanese Women Fans of Japanese Homoerotic Manga." In *Cultural Theory and Everyday Practice*, edited by Katrina Schlunke and Nicole Anderson, 164–76. Oxford: Oxford University Press, 2008.

———. "The Gender of Mobility." *Intersections: Gender and Sexuality in Asia and the Pacific* 35 (2014). Accessed January 5, 2016. http://intersections.anu.edu.au/issue35/martin.htm.

———. "Girls Who Love Boys' Love: Japanese Homoerotic Manga as Trans-national Taiwan Culture." *Inter-Asia Cultural Studies* 13.3 (2012): 365–83.

———. *Situating Sexualities: Queer Representation in Taiwanese Fiction, Film and Public Culture*. Hong Kong: Hong Kong University Press, 2003.

———. "Transnational Queer Sinophone Cultures." In *Routledge Handbook of Sexuality Studies in East Asia*, edited by Mark McLelland and Vera Mackie, 35–48. New York: Routledge, 2014.

Martin, Fran, and Larissa Heinrich, eds. *Embodied Modernities: Corporeality, Representation, and Chinese Cultures*. Honolulu: University of Hawai'i Press, 2006.

Martin, Fran, Peter A. Jackson, Mark McLelland, and Audrey Yue. Introduction to *AsiaPacifiQueer: Rethinking Genders and Sexualities*, edited by Fran Martin, Peter A. Jackson, Mark McLelland, and Audrey Yue, 1–28. Urbana: University of Illinois Press, 2008.

Martin, Fran, Peter A. Jackson, Mark McLelland, and Audrey Yue, eds. *AsiaPacifiQueer: Rethinking Genders and Sexualities*. Urbana: University of Illinois Press, 2008.

Mathews, Gordon. *Ghetto at the Center of the World: Chungking Mansions, Hong Kong*. Chicago: University of Chicago Press, 2011.

Mathews, Gordon, and Yang Yang. "How Africans Pursue Low-End Globalization in Hong Kong and Mainland China." *Journal of Current Chinese Affairs* 41.2 (2012): 95–120.

Matsushita, Keita. "Diffusion of Japanese Media Culture and Forming 'Japanese Image' in Taiwan." *Mejiro Journal of Humanities* 4 (2008): 121–34.

McLean, Kirsten. "Inside, Outside, Nowhere: Bisexual Men and Women in the Gay and Lesbian Community." *Journal of Bisexuality* 8.1/2 (2008): 63–80.

McLelland, Mark. "Australia's Proposed Internet Filtering System: Its Implications for Animation, Comics and Gaming (ACG) and Slash Fan Communities." *Media International Australia* 134 (February 2010): 7–19.

———. "Australia's 'Child-Abuse Material' Legislation, Internet Regulation and the Juridification of the Imagination." *International Journal of Cultural Studies* 15.5 (2012): 467–83.

———. "The Love between 'Beautiful Boys' in Japanese Women's Comics." *Journal of Gender Studies* 9.1 (2000): 13–25.

———. "Sex, Censorship and Media Regulation in Japan: A Historical Overview." In *Routledge Handbook of Sexuality Studies in East Asia*, edited by Mark McLelland and Vera Mackie, 402–13. Oxford: Routledge, 2014.

———. "The World of *Yaoi*: The Internet, Censorship and the Global 'Boys' Love' Fandom." *Australian Feminist Law Journal* 23 (2005): 61–77.

McLelland, Mark, Kazumi Nagaike, Katsuhiko Suganuma, and James Welker, eds. *Boys Love Manga and Beyond: History, Culture, and Community in Japan*. Jackson: University Press of Mississippi, 2015.

McLelland, Mark, and Seunghyun Yoo. "The International *Yaoi* Boys' Love Fandom and the Regulation of Virtual Child Pornography: The Implications of Current Legislation." *Sexuality, Research, and Social Policy* 4.1 (March 2007): 93–104.

Meyer, Uli. "Hidden in Straight Sight: Trans*gressing Gender and Sexuality via BL." In *Boys' Love Manga: Essays on the Sexual Ambiguity and Cross-Cultural Fandom of the Genre*, edited by Antonia Levi, Mark McHarry, and Dru Pagliassotti, 232–56. Jefferson, NC: McFarland and Company, 2010.

Meyers, Erin. *Dishing Dirt in the Digital Age: Celebrity Gossip Blogs and Participatory Media Culture*. New York: Peter Lang, 2013.

Miyake, Toshio. "Doing Occidentalism in Contemporary Japan: Nation Anthropomorphism and Sexualized Parody in *Axis Powers Hetalia*." *Transformative Works and Cultures* 12 (2013). doi:10.3983/twc.2013.0436.

Mizoguchi, Akiko. "Male-Male Romance by and for Women in Japan: A History and the Subgenres of *Yaoi* Fictions." *U.S.-Japan Women's Journal* 25 (2003): 49–75.

———. "Theorizing Comics/Manga as a Productive Forum: *Yaoi* and Beyond." In *Comics Worlds and the Worlds of Comics: Towards Scholarship on a Global Scale*, edited by Jaqueline Berndt, 143–68. Kyoto: International Manga Research Centre, Kyoto Seika University, 2010. Accessed April 21, 2016. http://imrc.jp/lecture/2009/12/comics-in-the-world.html.

Mori, Yoshitaka. "*Winter Sonata* and Cultural Practices of Active Fans in Japan: Considering Middle-Age Women as Cultural Agents." In *East Asian Popular Culture: Analysing the Korean Wave*, edited by Chua Beng Huat and Koichi Iwabuchi, 127–42. Hong Kong: Hong Kong University Press, 2008.

Morreall, John. "Cuteness." *British Journal of Aesthetics* 31.1 (1991): 39–47.

Morris, Rosalind C. "Three Sexes and Four Sexualities: Redressing the Discourses on Gender and Sexuality in Contemporary Thailand." *Positions* 2.1 (1994): 15–43.

Muñoz, José Esteban. *Cruising Utopia*. New York: NYU Press, 2009.

———. *Disidentifications: Queers of Color and the Performance of Politics*. Minneapolis, University of Minnesota Press, 1999.

Munt, Sally. *Heroic Desire: Lesbian Identity and Cultural Space*. New York: New York University Press, 1998.

Music Dream: Ho Denise Wan See. Directed and written by Winnie Ho. Produced by RTHK. TVB Broadcasting, June 13, 2010.

MVA Hong Kong Limited. *Survey on Public Attitudes towards Homosexuals, Report Prepared for the Home Affairs Bureau, Hong Kong Special Administrative Region Government*. March 2005. Accessed March 5, 2015. http://www.legco.gov.hk/yr05-06/english/panels/ha/papers/ha0310cb2-public-homosexuals-e.pdf.

Nagaike, Kazumi. "Do Heterosexual Men Dream of Homosexual Men? BL *Fudanshi* and Discourse on Male Feminization." In *Boys Love Manga and Beyond: History, Culture, and Community in Japan*, edited by Mark McLelland, Kazumi Nagaike, Katsuhiko Suganuma, and James Welker, 189–209. Jackson: University Press of Mississippi, 2015.

———. "Elegant Caucasians, Amorous Arabs, and Invisible Others: Signs and Images of Foreigners in Japanese BL Manga." *Intersections: Gender and Sexuality in Asia and the Pacific* 20 (2009). Accessed December 25, 2014. http://intersections.anu.edu.au/issue20/nagaike.htm.

———. "Perverse Sexualities, Perversive Desires: Representations of Female Fantasies and *Yaoi* Manga as Pornography Directed at Women." *U.S.-Japan Women's Journal* 25 (2003): 76–103.

Nagaike, Kazumi, and Tomoko Aoyama. "What Is Japanese 'BL Studies'? A Historical and Analytical Overview." In *Boys Love Manga and Beyond: History, Culture, and Community in Japan*, edited by Mark McLelland, Kazumi Nagaike, Katsuhiko Suganuma and James Walker, 119–40. Jackson: University Press of Mississippi, 2015.

Nakamura, Karen, and Matsuo Hisako. "Female Masculinity and Fantasy Spaces: Transcending Genders in the Takarazuka Theatre and Japanese Popular Culture." In *Men and Masculinities in Contemporary Japan: Dislocating the Salaryman Doxa*, edited by James E. Roberson and Nobue Suzuki, 59–76. New York: Routledge Curzon, 2003.

Nava, Mica. *Visceral Cosmopolitanism: Gender, Culture and the Normalisation of Difference*. Oxford: Berg, 2007.

Neuliep, James W. *Intercultural Communication: A Contextual Approach*. Sixth edition. Los Angeles: Sage, 2015.

Newman, Michael Z. 2012. "Free TV: File-Sharing and the Value of Television." *Television & New Media* 13.6 (2012): 463–79.

Ng, Margaret. *Jin Yong xiaoshuo de nanzi* [The men in Jin Yong's novels]. Taipei: Yuan-Liou Publishing, 1998.

Ng, Wai-ming. "A Comparative Study of Japanese Comics in Southeast Asia and East Asia." *International Journal of Comic Art* (Spring 2000): 45–56.

———. *The Impact of Japanese Comics and Animation in Asia*. Last modified 2002. Accessed September 10, 2003. http://www.jef.or.jp/en/jti/200207_006.html.

Ning, Ke. "Zhongguo danmei xiaoshuo zhong de nanxing tongshehui guanxi yu nanxing qizhi" [Male homosocial bonding and masculinity in Chinese *danmei* fiction]. PhD diss., Nankai University, 2014.

NPR. "How to Measure a Crowd, without the Political Numbers." October 5, 2014. Accessed November 28, 2016. http://www.npr.org/2014/10/05/353849607/how-to-measure-a-crowd-without-the-political-numbers.

Nütong Xueshe. "Zeoi 'hung tung' kek zaap syun geoi" [Voting for the most homophobic television drama]. N.d. Accessed December 2, 2016. https://sites.google.com/site/gayvotetvb/home.

Ogi, Fusami. "Gender Insubordination in Japanese Comic (Manga) for Girls." In *Illustrating Asia: Comics, Humour Magazines, and Picture Books*, edited by John A. Lent, 171–86. Honolulu: University of Hawai'i Press, 2001.

Oh, Chuyun. "The Politics of the Dancing Body: Racialized and Gendered Femininity in Korean Pop." In *The Korean Wave: Korean Popular Culture in the Global Context*, edited by Yasue Kuwahara, 53–83. New York: Palgrave Macmillan, 2014.

Ong, Aihwa. *Flexible Citizenship: The Cultural Politics of Transnationality*. Durham, NC: Duke University Press, 1999.

———. "On the Edge of Empires: Flexible Citizenship among Chinese in Diaspora." *Positions* 1.3 (1993): 745–78.

Orbaugh, Sharalyn, ed. "Manga." Special issue, *U.S.-Japan Women's Journal* 25 (2003): 3–7.

Pagliassotti, Dru. "Better Than Romance? Japanese BL Manga and the Subgenre of Male/Male Romantic Fiction." In *Boys' Love Manga: Essays on the Sexual Ambiguity and Cross-Cultural Fandom of the Genre*, edited by Antonia Levi, Mark McHarry, and Dru Pagliassotti, 59–83. Jefferson, NC: McFarland, 2010.

———. "GloBLisation and Hybridisation: Publishers' Strategies for Bringing Boys' Love to the United States." *Intersections: Gender and Sexuality in Asia and the Pacific* 20 (2009). Accessed October 22, 2014. http://intersections.anu.edu.au/issue20/pagliassotti.htm.

Pan, Suiming. "Tongxinglian he women" [Homosexuality and us]. In *Zhongguo xing geming zonglun* [Sex revolution in China: Its origin, expressions and evolution], 201–34. Gaoxiong: Wanyou Publishing House, 2006.

Parker, Andrew. "Foucault's Tongues." *Mediations* 18.2 (1994): 80–88.

Penley, Constance. "Brownian Motion: Women, Tactics and Technology." In *Technoculture*, edited by Constance Penley and Andrew Ross, 135–62. Minneapolis: University of Minnesota Press, 1991.

———. "Feminism, Psychoanalysis, and the Study of Popular Culture." In *Cultural Studies*, edited by Lawrence Grossberg, Cary Nelson, and Paula A. Treichler, 479–500. New York: Routledge, 1992.

———. *NASA/Trek: Popular Science and Sex in America*. London: Verso, 1997.

Perper, Timothy, and Martha Cornog, eds. *Mangatopia: Essays on Manga and Anime in the Modern World*. Santa Barbara, CA: Libraries Unlimited, 2011.

Phelan, Shane. "Public Discourse and the Closeting of Butch Lesbians." In *Butch/Femme: Inside Lesbian Gender*, edited by Sally R. Munt, 191–99. London: Cassell, 1998.

Pratt, Marnie. "This Is the Way We Live . . . and Love!" In *Gender, Race, and Class in Media: A Critical Reader*, edited by Gail Dines and Jean M. Humez, 341–48. Thousand Oaks, CA: Sage, 2011.

Qiu, Linchuan, and Joseph Chan, eds. *Xinmeiti shijian yanjiu* [New Media Events Research]. Beijing: Renmin University Press, 2011.

Qiu, Zitong. "Cuteness as a Subtle Strategy: Urban Female Youth and the Online *Feizhuliiu* Culture in Contemporary China." *Cultural Studies* 23.2 (2013): 225–41.

Republic of China. Laws & Regulations Database. Regulations for the Rating of Internet Content (Abolished). Accessed February 18, 2015. http://law.moj.gov.tw/LawClass/LawContent.aspx?PCODE=P0050021.

Rofel, Lisa. *Desiring China: Experiments in Neoliberalism, Sexuality, and Public Culture*. Durham, NC: Duke University Press, 2007.

———. "Grassroots Activism: Non-normative Sexual Politics in Post-socialist China." In *Unequal China: The Political Economy and Cultural Politics of Inequality*, edited by Wanning Sun and Yingjie Guo, 154–67. New York: Routledge, 2013.

———. *Other Modernities: Gendered Yearnings in China after Socialism*. Berkeley: University of California Press, 1999.

Rogoff, Irit. "Gossip as Testimony" (1996). In *The Feminism and Visual Culture Reader*, edited by Amelia Jones, 268–76. New York: Routledge, 2003.

Rubin, Gayle. "Thinking Sex: Notes for a Radical Theory of the Politics of Sexuality." In *The Lesbian and Gay Studies Reader*, edited by Henry Abelove, Michèle Aina Barale, and David M. Halperin, 100–33. London: Routledge, 1993.

Russ, Joanna, ed. *Magic Mommas, Trembling Sisters, Puritans & Perverts: Feminist Essays*. New York: Crossing Press, 1985.

———. "Pornography by Women, for Women, with Love." In *Magic Mommas, Trembling Sisters, Puritans and Perverts*, 79–99. New York: Crossing Press, 1985.

Russo, Julie Levin. "Textual Orientation: Queer Female Fandom Online." In *The Routledge Companion to Media and Gender*, edited by Cynthia Carter, Linda Steiner, and Lisa McLaughlin, 450–60. New York: Routledge, 2014.

Sabucco, Veruska. "Guided Fan Fiction: Western 'Readings' of Japanese Homosexual-Themed Texts." In *Mobile Cultures: New Media in Queer Asia*, edited by Chris Berry, Fran Martin, and Audrey Yue, 70–86. Durham, NC: Duke University Press, 2003.

Sandvoss, Cornel. Fans: The Mirror of Consumption. Cambridge: Polity Press, 2005.

Sang, Tze-Lan D. *The Emerging Lesbian: Female Same-sex Desire in Modern China*. Chicago: University of Chicago Press, 2003.

Schilt, Kristen, and Laurel Westbrook. "Doing Gender, Doing Heteronormativity: 'Gender Normals,' Transgender People, and the Social Maintenance of Heterosexuality." *Gender & Society* 23.4 (August 1, 2009): 440–64.

Schodt, Frederik L. "Regulation versus Fantasy." In *Manga! Manga! The World of Japanese Comics*, edited by Frederik L. Schodt, 120–37. Tokyo: Kodansha International, 1983.

Scodari, Christine, and Jenna L. Felder. "Creating a Pocket Universe: 'Shippers,' Fan Fiction, and the *X-Files* Online." *Communication Studies* 51.3 (2000): 238–57.

Sedgwick, Eve Kosofsky. *Between Men: English Literature and Male Homosocial Desire*. New York: Columbia University Press, 1985.

———. *Epistemology of the Closet*. Berkeley: University of California University, 1990.

Seidman, Steven. "From Identity to Queer Politics: Shifts in Normative Heterosexuality and the Meaning of Citizenship." *Citizenship Studies* 5.3 (2001): 321–28.

Shandong Shangbao [Shandong Business Daily]. "*Taizifei shengzhiji* xiaxian le!" [*Go Princess Go!* Taken offline!]. January 21, 2016. Accessed April 21, 2016. http://news.163.com/16/0121/14/BDS1BL3R00014Q4P.html.

Sharp, Luke. "Maid Meets Mammal: The 'Animalized' Body of the Cosplay Maid Character in Japan." *Intertext* 15.1 (2011): 60–78.

Shi, Liang. *Chinese Lesbian Cinema: Mirror Rubbing, Lala, and Les*. Lanham: Lexington Books, 2015.

Shih, Shu-mei. "The Concept of the Sinophone." *PMLA* 126.3 (2011): 709–18.

———. *Visuality and Identity: Sinophone Articulations across the Pacific*. Berkeley: University of California Press, 2007.

Shirk, Susan L. *China: Fragile Superpower*. New York: Oxford University Press, 2008.

Shohat, Ella. "Notes on the Post-colonial." *Social Text* 31/32 (1992): 99–113.

Silvio, Teri. "BL/Q: The Aesthetics of Pili Puppetry Fan Fiction." In *Popular Culture in Taiwan: Charismatic Modernity*, edited by Marc L. Moskowitz, 149–66. London: Routledge, 2013.

———. "Informationalized Affect: The Body in Taiwanese Digital Video Puppetry and Cosplay." In *Embodied Modernities: Corporeality, Representation, and Chinese Cultures*, edited by Fran Martin and Larissa Heinrich, 195–217. Honolulu: University of Hawai'i Press, 2006.

Sina Entertainment. "Dianshiju wangluo dianjilü" [The online click ratio of TV dramas]. April 16, 2013. Accessed December 26, 2014. http://ent.sina.com.cn/v/m/2013-04-16/14283901301.shtml.

———. "Qiong Yao qisu Yu Zheng chaoxi" [Qiong Yao has sued Yu Zheng for plagiarism]. December 26, 2014. Accessed July 14, 2015. http://ent.sina.com.cn/f/v/qyjbyz/.

Sina Ladies. "He Yunshi faqi chengtongzhi fanqishi yundong" [Ho Wan See launches a movement of 'supporting homosexuals and opposing discrimination']. January 15, 2013. Accessed December 27, 2014. http://eladies.sina.com.cn/qg/2013/0115/15441207565.shtml.

Sina News. "Dianshiju nianchanliang" [The annual output of TV dramas]. August 27, 2013. http://dailynews.sina.com/gb/ent/tv/sinacn/20130827/02294909558.html.

Sina Weibo. "Zheshi yige gaoji de shidai!" [This is an era of engaging in gay love!]. February 16, 2013. Accessed December 27, 2014. https://freeweibo.com/weibo/3546426354853926.

Sing kei luk zau hon [Saturday Magazine]. "Ho bat ci ngo—ho wan si" [Why not be like me—Denise Ho]. March 29, 2003.

Singer, June. *Androgyny: Toward a New Theory of Sexuality*. London: Routledge, 1976.

Sinnott Megan. *Toms and Dees: Transgender Identity and Female Same-Sex Relationships in Thailand*. Honolulu: University of Hawai'i Press, 2004.

Sohu. "Meiju meiying gaoshou dayin yinyuwang zimuzu hunzhan yijiu" [Guru of American media hiding online: The tangled fight between fansubbing groups]. Last modified November 8, 2009. Accessed November 1, 2013. http://yule.sohu.com/20091108/n268043090.shtml.

Stychin, Carl. *A Nation by Rights: National Cultures, Sexual Identity Politics and the Discourse of Rights*. Philadelphia, PA: Temple University Press, 1998.

Suen, Yiu-tung, et al. *Study on Legislation against Discrimination on the Grounds of Sexual Orientation, Gender Identity and Intersex Status*. Hong Kong: Equal Opportunities Commission, 2016. Accessed June 1, 2016. http://www.eoc.org.hk/eoc/upload/ResearchReport/20161251750293418312.pdf.

Sullivan, Andrew. *Virtually Normal*. New York: Vintage Books, 1995.

Sung, Sang-Yeon. "Constructing a New Image: Hallyu in Taiwan." *European Journal of East Asian Studies* 9.1 (2010): 25–45.

Suzuki, Kazuko. "Pornography or Therapy? Japanese Girls Creating the *Yaoi* Phenomenon." In *Millennium Girls: Today's Girls around the World*, edited by Sherrie A. Inness, 243–67. Lanham, MD: Rowman & Littlefield, 1998.

Suzuki, Midori. "The Possibilities of Research on *Fujoshi* in Japan." *Transformative Works and Cultures* 12 (2013). doi:10.3983/twc.2013.0462.

Taiwan Ministry of Culture. "Chuban pinji luying jiemudai fenji guanli banfa" [Measure for the management of ratings systems for publications and video programs]. 2012. Accessed February 18, 2015. http://www.moc.gov.tw/law.do?method=find&id=363.

Tam, Arthur. "HOCC: Gay . . . and Happy!" *Time Out Hong Kong*, December 19, 2012.

Tan, Dazheng. *Xingwenhua yu fa* [Sexual culture and law]. Shanghai: Shanghai People's Publishing House, 1998.

Tan, See Kam. "Global Hollywood, Narrative Transparency, and Chinese Media Poachers: Narrating Cross-Cultural Negotiations of *Friends* in South China." *Television and New Media* 12.3 (2011): 207–27.

Tan, Shzr Ee. "Beyond the 'Fragile Woman': Identity, Modernity, and Musical Gay Icons in Overseas Chinese Communities." In *Popular Culture in Asia: Memory, City, Celebrity*, edited by Lorna Fitzsimmons and John A. Lent, 183–205. Basingstoke, UK: Palgrave MacMillian, 2013.

Tang, Denise Tse-Shang. *Conditional Spaces: Hong Kong Lesbian Desires and Everyday Life*. Hong Kong: Hong Kong University Press, 2011.

———. "An Unruly Death: Queer Media in Hong Kong." *GLQ: A Journal of Lesbian and Gay Studies* 18.4 (2012): 597–614.

Taylor, Insup, and Martin M. Taylor. "Spoken Chinese." In *Writing and Literacy in Chinese, Korean and Japanese*. Revised edition. Philadelphia, PA: John Benjamins Publishing Co., 2014.

Tetsuy, Akiko. *Yongyuan de Lin Qingxia* [The last star of the East: Brigitte Lin Ching Hsia and her films]. Taipei: Locus Publishing, 2008.

Theweleit, Klaus. *Male Fantasies*. Vol. 1, *Women, Floods, Bodies, History*. Translated by Chris Turner et al. Minneapolis: University of Minnesota Press, 1987.

Thomas, Bronwen, and Julia Round, eds. *Real Lives, Celebrity Stories: Narratives of Ordinary and Extraordinary People across Media*. New York: Bloomsbury, 2014.

Thorn, Matthew. "Girls and Women Getting Out of Hand: The Pleasure and Politics of Japan's Amateur Comics Community." In *Fanning the Flame: Fans and Consume Culture in Contemporary Japan*, edited by William W. Kelly, 169–88. Albany, NY: State University of New York Press, 2004.

Thornton, Sarah. *Club Cultures: Music, Media and Subcultural Capital*. Oxford: Polity Press, 1995.

To, Sandy. *China's Leftover Women: Late Marriage among Professional Women and Its Consequences*. Abingdon, Oxon: Routledge, 2015.

Tong, Carmen Ka Man. "Being a Young Tomboy in Hong Kong: The Life and Identity Construction of Lesbian Schoolgirls." In *AsiaPacifiQueer: Rethinking Genders and Sexualities*, edited by Fran Martin, Peter A. Jackson, Mark McLelland, and Audrey Yue, 117–30. Urbana: University of Illinois Press, 2008.

Tongmeng, Shahulu. *Taiwan azhai qishilu* [Taiwan *otaku* apocalypse]. lightnovel.cn. September 8, 2010. Accessed July 20, 2015. http://www.lightnovel.cn/thread-214503-1-1.html.

Tsai, Chih-Lan. "Nüxing huanxiang guodu zhong de chuncui aiqing—lun Taiwan BL xiaoshu" [The pure love in the kingdom of women's fantasy—on BL novels in Taiwan]. MA thesis, National Taiwan Normal University, 2011.

Tsai, Eva. "Existing in the Age of Innocence: Pop Stars, Publics, and Politics in Asia." In *East Asian Pop Culture: Analyzing the Korean Wave*, edited by Chua Beng Huat and Koichi Iwabuchi, 217–42. Hong Kong: Hong Kong University Press, 2008.

Tsai, Jintang. "The Views of Japan by Taiwanese People Who Had Lived During the Japanese and Kuomintang Colonization Periods." Translated by Takuju Mizukuchi. In *Sengo Taiwan niokeru nihon: Shokuminchi keiken no renzoku, henbō, riyō* ["Japan" in postwar Taiwan: The continuity, transformation and appropriation of the colonized experiences], edited by Masako Igarashi and Yuko Mio, 19–60. Tokyo: Fukyosya, 2006.

Ueno, Chizuko. *Hazujō sōchi* [The apparatus of eroticism]. Tokyo: Chikuma Shobō, 2002.

Valentine, Gill. "Imagined Geographies: Geographical Knowledges of Self and Other in Everyday Life." In *Human Geography Today*, edited by Doreen Massey, John Allen, and Philip Sarre, 47–61. Cambridge: Polity Press, 1999.

Volodzko, David. "Self-Perceptions Strain Hong Kong–Mainland Relations." *Diplomat*, September 14, 2014. Accessed November 29, 2016. http://thediplomat.com/2014/09/self-perceptions-strain-hong-kong-mainland-relations/.

Wang, David. "Xu" [Preface]. In *Jinyong xiaoshuo guoji xueshu yantaohui lunwenji* [Proceedings of the International Conference on Jin Yong's Novels], edited by Qiu Gui Wang, i–v. Taipei: Yuan-Liou Publishing, 1999.

Wang, Ning. "Orientalism versus Occidentalism?" *New Literary History* 28.1 (1997): 57–67.

Wang, Qian. "Queerness, Entertainment, and Politics: Queer Performance and Performativity in Chinese Pop." In *Queer/Tongzhi China: New Perspectives on Research, Activism and Media Cultures*, edited by Elisabeth L. Engebretsen and William F. Schroeder (with Hongwei Bao), 153–78. Copenhagen: NIAS Press, 2015.

Wang, Weibo. "Xinlixue shiye xia de xinxing yawenhua qunti—zhongguo 'tongrennü' xianzhuang jiqi chansheng de shehui xinli genyuan tanxi" [A psychological perspective of an emerging subcultural group: Exploring the socio-psychological causes of Chinese "fangirls"]. MA thesis, Xuzhou Normal University, 2011.

Warner, Michael. "Introduction: Fear of a Queer Planet." *Social Text* 29 (1991): 3–17.

———. *Publics and Counterpublics*. New York: Zone Books, 2002.

———. *The Trouble with Normal: Sex, Politics, and the Ethics of Queer Life*. Cambridge, MA: Harvard University Press, 1999.

Warren, Mary Anne. "Is Androgyny the Answer to Sexual Stereotyping?" In *Femininity, Masculinity and Androgyny: A Modern Philosophical Discussion*, edited by Mary Vetterling-Braggin, 170–86. Totowa: Littlefield, 1982.

Wei, John. "Queer Encounters between Iron Man and Chinese Boys' Love Fandom," *Transformative Works and Cultures* 17 (2014). Accessed July 20, 2015. http://journal.transformativeworks.org/index.php/twc/article/view/561/458.

Wei, Shu-chu. "Shaping a Cultural Identity: The Picture Book and Cartoons in Taiwan, 1945–1980." In *Illustrating Asia: Comics, Humour Magazines, and Picture Books*, edited by John A. Lent, 64–84. Honolulu: University of Hawai'i Press, 2001.

Welker, James. "Beautiful, Borrowed, and Bent: 'Boys' Love' as Girls' Love in Shojo Manga." *Signs: Journal of Women in Culture and Society* 31.3 (2006): 841–70.

———. "Drawing Out Lesbians: Blurred Representations of Lesbian Desire in *Shōjo* Manga." In *Lesbian Voices, Canada and the World*, edited by Subhash Chandra, 156–84. New Delhi: Allied Publishing, 2006.

———. "Lilies of the Margin: Beautiful Boys and Lesbian Identities." In *AsiaPacifiQueer: Rethinking Gender and Sexuality in the Asia-Pacific*, edited by Fran Martin, Peter A. Jackson, Mark McLelland and Audrey Yue, 46–66. Urbana and Chicago: University of Illinois Press, 2008.

Wen, Huike. "'Diversifying' Masculinity: Super Girls, Happy Boys, Cross-Dressers, and Real Men on Chinese Media." *ASIA Network Exchange: A Journal for Asian Studies in the Liberal Arts* 21.1 (2013): 1–11.

Wertime, David. "In China, Shrugs and Sneers for Hong Kong Protesters." *Foreign Policy*, October 2, 2014. Accessed October 22, 2014. http://www.foreignpolicy.com/articles/2014/10/01/in_chinese_mainland_shrugs_and_sneers_for_hong_kong_protesters.

Wikipedia. "Taiwan tongzhi youxing" [Taiwan gay parade]. Last modified October 27, 2014. https://zh.wikipedia.org/wiki/%E5%8F%B0%E7%81%A3%E5%90%8C%E5%BF%97%E9%81%8A%E8%A1%8C.

Williams, Raymond. "Dominant, Residual and Emergent." In *Marxism and Literature*, edited by Raymond Williams, 121–27. Oxford: Oxford University Press, 1978.

Wilson, Ara. "Queering Asia." *Intersections: Gender, History and Culture in the Asian Context* 14 (2006). Accessed September 20, 2013. http://intersections.anu.edu.au/issue14/wilson.html.

Wilson, Magnus. "Didactic Escapism: New Viewing Practices among China's Digital Generation." In *Asian Popular Culture in Transition*, edited by Lorna Fitzsimmons and John A. Lent, 77–96. New York: Routledge, 2013.

Winge, Teresa. "Costuming the Imagination: Origins of Anime and Manga." In *Mechademia 1: Emerging Worlds of Anime and Manga*, edited by Frenchy Lunning, 65–76. Minneapolis: University of Minnesota Press, 2006.

Women's Commission, Hong Kong Special Administrative Region Government. *Findings of Survey on Community Perception on Gender Issues*. Hong Kong: Women's Commission, 2009. Accessed March 1, 2015. http://www.women.gov.hk/download/research/Community-perception-survey-findings.pdf.

Wong, Alvin Ka Hin. "From the Transnational to the Sinophone: Lesbian Representations in Chinese-Language Films." *Journal of Lesbian Studies* 16.3 (2012): 307–22.

Wong, Day. "(Post-)identity Politics and Anti-normalization: (Homo)sexual Rights Movement." In *Remaking Citizenship in Hong Kong*, edited by Agnes S. Ku and Ngai Pun, 195–214. Oxon: RoutledgeCurzon, 2004.

———. "Rethinking the Coming Home Alternative: Hybridization and Coming Out Politics in Hong Kong's Anti-homophobia Parades." *Inter-Asia Cultural Studies* 8.4 (2007): 600–16.

Wong, Nicholas. "Dialogue Two: From Rose Mary to Rolls Royce; Denise Ho X Wyman Wong Queerness in Denise Ho's Music." In *Fe/male Bodies*, edited by Daryl Cheung, Chun Chun Lai, Krebs Lee, Josette Tang, and Tommy Tse, 62–68. Hong Kong: Kubrick, 2005.

Wong, Wai Ching Angela. "The Politics of Sexual Morality and Evangelical Activism in Hong Kong." *Inter-Asia Cultural Studies* 14.3 (2013): 340–60.

Wood, Andrea. "'Straight' Women, Queer Texts: Boy-Love Manga and the Rise of a Global Counterpublic." *Women's Studies Quarterly* 34.1/2 (2006): 394–414.

Wu, Cuncun. *Homoerotic Sensibilities in Late Imperial China*. New York: RoutledgeCurzon, 2004.

Wu, Di. "Yiru danmei shensihai—wo de geren 'danmei tongren' shi" [Once entering *danmei*, it is as deep as sea—my personal *"danmei/*fanfic" history]. In *Wangluo wenxue pinglun* [Web literature review]. Vol. 1, edited by Guangdong Provincial Writers' Association and Guangdong Web Literature Institute, 150–67. Guangzhou: Huacheng chubanshe, 2011.

Xiao, Hui Faye. "Androgynous Beauty, Virtual Sisterhood." In *Super Girls, Gangstas, Freeters, and Xenomaniacs: Gender and Modernity in Global Youth Cultures*, edited by Susan Dewey and Karen Brison, 104–24. Syracuse, NY: Syracuse University Press, 2012.

Xinhua Net. "Leiju *Xiao'ao Jianghu* weihe hong? Jiulinghou: Mei Yu Zheng shei shi Jin Yong" [Why is the shocking drama swordsman so popular? The post-1990s: We wouldn't know Jin Yong if there were no Yu Zheng]. February 27, 2013. Accessed July 14, 2015. http://education.news.cn/2013-02/27/c_124393012.htm.

Xu, Hailong, and Lewen Zhang. "'Zhongqu de dansheng—jinlai yangshichunwan xiaoping dui danmei yawenhua de shoubian" [The birth of "a middle stage": The incorporation of *tanbi* subculture into CCTV *Spring Festival Gala*]. *Journal of Nanyang Normal University (Social Sciences)* 13.10 (2014): 51–55.

Xu, Peixian. *Taiyang qixia de mofa xuexiao: Rizhi Taiwan xinshi jiaoyu de dansheng* [The magic school under the sun flag: New style of education in Taiwan during the colonial period]. Taipei: Dongcun, 2012.

Xu, Yanrui, and Ling Yang. "Forbidden Love: Incest, Generational Conflict, and the Erotics of Power in Chinese BL Fiction." *Journal of Graphic Novels and Comics* 4.1 (2013): 30–43.

———. "Zhongguo danmei (BL) xiaoshuo zhongde qingyu shuxie yu xing/bie zhengzhi" [Erotic desires and gender/sexuality politics in Chinese boys' love (BL) fiction]. *Taiwan shehui yanjiu jikan* [Taiwan: A radical quarterly in social studies] 100 (2015): 91–121.

Yan, Jiayan. *Jinyong xiaoshuo lungao* [Essays on Jin Yong's novels]. Beijing: Peking University Press, 2007.

Yan, Mei Ning. "Regulating Online Pornography in Mainland China and Hong Kong." In *Routledge Handbook of Sexuality Studies in East Asia*, edited by Mark McLelland and Vera Mackie, 387–401. London: Routledge, 2015.

Yang, Guobin. "The Internet and the Rise of a Transnational Chinese Cultural Sphere." *Media, Culture & Society* 25.4 (2003): 469–90.

———. "Lightness, Wildness, and Ambivalence: China and New Media Studies." *New Media & Society* 14.1 (2012): 170–79.

———. *The Power of the Internet in China: Citizens Activism Online*. New York: Columbia University Press, 2009.

———. "Technology and Its Contents: Issues in the Study of the Chinese Internet." *Journal of Asian Studies* 70.4 (2011): 1043–50.

Yang, Lijun, and Yongnian Zheng. "*Fen Qings* (Angry Youth) in Contemporary China." *Journal of Contemporary China* 21.76 (2012): 637–53.

Yang, Ling. "All for Love: The Corn Fandom, Prosumers and the Chinese Way of Creating a Superstar." *International Journal of Cultural Studies* 12.5 (2009): 527–43.

———. "'Nongwan de' luomansi: Chaonü tongrenwen, nüxing yuwang yu nüxing zhuyi" ["Bent" romance: *Super Girl* slash literature, women's desires, and feminism]. *Wenhua yanjiu* [Cultural Studies] 9 (2010). Accessed April 8, 2012. http://wlwx.literature.org.cn/Article.aspx?ID=46197.

Yang, Ling, and Hongwei Bao. "Queerly Intimate: Friends, Fans and Affective Communication in a *Super Girl* Fan Fiction Community." *Cultural Studies* 26.6 (2012): 842–71.

Yang, Ling, and Yanrui Xu. "*Danmei*, Xianqing, and the Making of a Queer Online Public Sphere in China." *Communication and the Public* 1.2 (2016): 251–56.

———. "'The Love That Dare Not Speak Its Name': The Fate of Chinese *Danmei* Communities in the 2014 Anti-porn Campaign." In *The End of Cool Japan: Ethical, Legal, and Cultural Challenges to Japanese Popular Culture*, edited by Mark McLelland, 163–83. London: Routledge, 2016.

———. "Queer Texts, Gender Imagination, and Popular Feminism in Chinese Web Literature." In *Queer/Tongzhi China: New Perspectives on Research, Activism, and Media Cultures*, edited by Elisabeth L. Engebretsen and William F. Schroeder (with Hongwei Bao), 131–52. Copenhagen: NIAS Press, 2015.

Yang, Mayfair. "From Gender Erasure to Gender Difference: State Feminism, Consumer Sexuality, and Women's Public Sphere in China." In *Spaces of Their Own: Women's Public Sphere in Transnational China*, edited by Mayfair Mei-hui Yang, 35–67. Minneapolis: University of Minnesota Press, 1999.

———, ed. *Spaces of Their Own: Women's Public Sphere in Transnational China*. Minneapolis and London: University of Minnesota Press, 1999.

Yang, Qian. "Guonei meiti dui tongxinglian xianxiang de fenxi" [An analysis on the news of homosexual phenomena in the Chinese mass media]. *Xinwen Aihaozhe* [Journalism Lover] 2 (2011): 54–55.

Yang, Tianhua. "Tongxinglian qunti de meijie xingxiang jiangou" [The construction of the image of homosexual groups in the mass media]. *Sex-Study*, August 1, 2012. Accessed May 20, 2015. http://www.sex-study.org/news.php?isweb=2&sort=158&id=1134

Yang, Yuxi, and Boyin Liu. "Quanmeiti shidai de miwenhua yanjiu—yi danmei miqun weili" [Fan cultural studies in an age of digital media—using *danmei* fandom as an example]. *Xinwen Aihaozhe* [Journalism Lover] 3 (2012): 15–16.

Yano, Christine R. "Kitty Litter: Japanese Cute at Home and Abroad." In *Toys, Games, and Media*, edited by Jeffrey Goldstein, David Buckingham and Giles Brougère, 55–71. Mahwah, NJ: Lawrence Erlbaum Associates, 2004.

———. "Wink on Pink: Interpreting Japanese Cute as It Grabs the Global Headlines." *Journal of Asian Studies* 68.3 (2009): 681–88.

Yau, Ching. "Bridges and Battles." *GLQ* 12.4 (2006): 605–07.

———. "Dreaming of Normal While Sleeping with Impossible: Introduction." In *As Normal as Possible: Negotiating Sexuality and Gender in Mainland China and Hong Kong*, edited by Ching Yau, 1–14. Hong Kong: Hong Kong University Press, 2010.

———. *Xingbie guangying: Xianggang dianying zhong de xing yu xingbie wenhua yanjiu* [Sexing shadows: Gender and sexualities in Hong Kong cinema]. Hong Kong: Hong Kong Film Critics Society, 2005.

Yi, Erika Junhui. "Reflection on Chinese Boys' Love Fans: An Insider's View." *Transformative Works and Cultures* 12 (2013). doi:10.3983/twc.2013.0424.

Young, Marilyn B. "Chicken Little in China: Women after the Cultural Revolution." In *Promissory Notes: Women in the Transition to Socialism*, edited by Sonia Kruks, Rayna Rapp, and Marilyn B. Young, 233–47. New York: Monthly Review Press, 1989.

Yue, Audrey. "King Victoria: Asian Drag Kings, Postcolonial Female Masculinity, and Hybrid Sexuality in Australia." In *AsiaPacifiQueer: Rethinking Genders and Sexualities*, edited by Fran Martin, Peter A. Jackson, Mark McLelland, and Audrey Yue, 251–70. Urbana: University of Illinois Press, 2008.

———. "Queer Asian Cinema and Media Studies: From Hybridity to Critical Regionality." *Cinema Journal* 53.2 (2014): 145–51.

———. "What's So Queer about *Happy Together*? A.k.a. Queer (N)Asian: Interface, Mobility, Belonging." *Inter-Asia Cultural Studies Journal* 1.2 (2000): 251-64.

Yue, Audrey, and Haiqing Yu. "China's Super Girl: Mobile Youth Cultures and New Sexualities." In *Youth, Media and Culture in the Asia Pacific Region*, edited by Usha M. Rodrigues and Belinda Smaill, 117–34. Newcastle, UK: Cambridge Scholars Publishing, 2008.

Zeitlin, Judith. *Historian of the Strange: Pu Songling and the Chinese Classical Tale*. Stanford, CA: Stanford University Press, 1993.

Zhang, Weiyu, and Chengting Mao. "Fan Activism Sustained and Challenged: Participatory Culture in Chinese Online Translation Communities." *Chinese Journal of Communication* 6.1 (2013): 45–61.

Zhao, Jing Jamie. "Articulating the 'L' Word Online: A Study of Chinese Slash Fandom of *Super Girl*." MA Thesis, University of Wisconsin–Milwaukee, 2012.

———. "Fandom as a Middle Ground: Fictive Queer Fantasies and Real-World Lesbianism in *FSCN*." In "Access/Trespass." Special conference issue, *Media Fields Journal* 10 (2014). Accessed February 10, 2016. http://mediafieldsjournal.squarespace.com/fandom-as-a-middle-ground/.

Zhao, Yuezhi. *Media, Market, and Democracy in China: Between the Party Line and the Bottom Line*. Urbana: University of Illinois Press, 1998.

Zhou, Xiaomeng. "2013 nian disanjidu meiti jiance baogao" [Media monitoring report in the third quarter of 2013]. *Rainbow Awards*. Accessed May 20, 2015. http://www.chinarainbowawards.cn/index.php?m=content&c=index&a=show&catid=5&id=41.

Žižek, Slavoj. *Welcome to the Desert of the Real: Five Essays on September 11 and Related Dates*. New York: Verso, 2002.

Notes on Contributors

Weijung CHANG is a PhD candidate in the Division of Interdisciplinary Gender Studies at Ochanomizu University, Japan. Her research interests include Japanese popular culture, gender, and sexuality. She is currently working on the Japanophilia context in Taiwan and related issues of gender and sexuality. She has presented her works in multiple languages. These include "Analyzing the Construction of Sexuality from 'BL Fantasy': A Case Study of Taiwanese *Fujoshi*'s Fantasy Practice in 'Butler Cafés,'" *Journal of Women and Gender Studies* (2013, published in Chinese), "Analyzing the Relationship with 'Japaneseness' from the Life Story of a Taiwanese Japanophile Girl," *Japan Oral History Review* (2014, published in Japanese), and "Gendered/Sexualized Transformation of Japanophilia: The Symbolization and the Localization of 'Japaneseness' in Taiwan" (2015, presented in English at the annual conference of the North America Taiwan Studies Association).

Shih-chen CHAO earned a PhD in Chinese Studies at the University of Manchester, during which she was the recipient of the Doctoral Dissertation Fellowship awarded by the Chiang Ching-kuo Foundation. Her fields of scholarship are Internet literature, gender and queer studies, and fandom and media studies. She is also interested in digital humanities, which connects the disciplines of humanities with research IT. Her paper on the prosumption of Internet fiction in China was published in the *Journal of the British Association of Chinese Studies*, and her article "Grotesque Eroticism in the *Danmei* Genre: The Case of Lucifer's Club in Chinese Cyberspace" was published in *Porn Studies*. She is currently working as a research IT software engineer at the University of Manchester.

Maud LAVIN is a professor of visual and critical studies and art history, theory and criticism at the School of the Art Institute of Chicago. She has published widely on genders, sexualities, and cultures. Her books include *Push Comes to Shove: New Images of Aggressive Women* (MIT Press, 2010); *Clean New World: Culture, Politics, and Graphic Design* (MIT Press, 2001); and *Cut with the Kitchen*

Knife: The Weimar Photomontages of Hannah Höch (Yale University Press, 1993). She has received a John Simon Guggenheim Memorial Fellowship and a Senior Research Residency at Asia Research Institute, National University of Singapore, among other awards. Her most recent essays have appeared in *Situations: Cultural Studies in the Asian Context*; *Intersections: Gender and Sexuality in Asia and the Pacific*; and *Transformative Works and Cultures*.

Eva Cheuk Yin LI is a PhD candidate in film studies at King's College London. She is the recipient of a Chiang Ching-kuo Foundation Doctoral Dissertation Fellowship and a King's College London Hong Kong Scholarship. She has been trained as a sociological researcher at the University of Hong Kong, from which she obtained a bachelor of social sciences (first class honors) and master of philosophy (awarded outstanding research postgraduate student). She is interested in the interdisciplinary study of media and culture, gender and sexualities, and intimacy in transnational and East Asian contexts. Her doctoral research explores the lived experience of "neutral gender/sex" (*zhongxing*), a substantial gender and mediated phenomenon in postmillennial Chinese societies. Her works have appeared in collected volumes on fandom, gender, and sexuality in both Chinese and English, and also in *East Asian Journal of Popular Culture*, *Graduate Journal of Social Science*, and *Transformative Works and Cultures*.

Fran MARTIN's best-known research focuses on cultural production in contemporary transnational China (the People's Republic of China, Taiwan, and Hong Kong), with a specialization in representations and cultures of gender and queer sexuality. Her publications in this area include *Backward Glances: Contemporary Chinese Cultures and the Female Homoerotic Imaginary* (Duke University Press, 2010); *Mobile Cultures: New Media in Queer Asia* (coedited with C. Berry and A. Yue, Duke University Press, 2003); *Situating Sexualities: Queer Representation in Taiwanese Fiction, Film and Public Culture* (Hong Kong University Press, 2003); *Angelwings: Contemporary Queer Fiction from Taiwan* (University of Hawai'i Press, 2003); *AsiaPacifiQueer: Rethinking Genders and Sexualities* (coedited with P. Jackson, M. McLelland, and A. Yue, University of Illinois Press, 2008); and *Telemodernities: Television and Transforming Lives in Asia* (coauthored with T. Lewis and W. Sun, Duke University Press, 2016). She is an associate professor and reader in cultural studies at the University of Melbourne and an Australian Research Council Future Fellow.

Yanrui XU is an associate professor of communication at Ningbo Institute of Technology, Zhejiang University, China. She received her PhD in literary studies from Capital Normal University in Beijing and was a postdoctoral researcher at the Institute of Communication Studies of Zhejiang University from 2010 to 2013. She is the author of *Contemporary Feminist Literary Criticism in China 1980s–2000s* (Guangxi Normal University Press, 2008) and *Media and Gender: Femininity, Masculinity and the Formulation of Gender in Media* (Zhejiang University Press, 2014). She has published research in Chinese on women's literature and queer culture. Xu is also a BL novelist, and her stories have appeared in Chinese BL magazines and literature websites such as Jinjiang, Lucifer Club, and My Fresh Net.

Ling YANG is an assistant professor of Chinese at Xiamen University, China. She is the author of *Entertaining the Transitional Era: Super Girl Fandom and the Consumption of Popular Culture* (China Social Sciences Press, 2012) and the coeditor of *Fan Cultures: A Reader* (Peking University Press, 2009). She has published articles on fan culture, Internet culture, and youth fiction in *International Journal of Cultural Studies*, *Cultural Studies*, and a number of Chinese journals.

Jing Jamie ZHAO is currently a PhD student in film and television studies at the University of Warwick, UK. She received her first PhD degree in gender studies from the Chinese University of Hong Kong and her MA in media studies from the University of Wisconsin–Milwaukee (UWM). She is the recipient of UWM Chancellor's Scholarships (2010–2012), Louise J. Kordus Scholarships (2011, 2012), a 2015–2016 Global Scholarship for Research Excellence, and the 2015–2016 CUHK Reaching Out Award. Her research spans a diversity of gender- and queer-related topics in media and audience studies, including Chinese fandom, cybercultures, and entertainment TV. She has published in *Media Fields Journal*, *Intersections*, *Feminist Media Studies*, and *East Asian Journal of Popular Culture*.

Egret Lulu ZHOU is a lecturer in the Department of Literature and Cultural Studies and a member of the Center for Popular Culture in the Humanities at the Education University of Hong Kong. She obtained her PhD in cultural studies from the Chinese University of Hong Kong supported by a Hong Kong PhD Fellowship (2010–13). Fandom and stardom, film and television, feminism and queer studies, youth subculture, and modern Chinese literature constitute her research interests in recent years. Her papers have been published in *Theoretical Studies in Literature and Art*, *Cultural Studies*, *Twenty-First Century* (in Chinese), and *Journal of Audience and Reception Studies* (in English), among other venues; she teaches courses on film, TV drama, Internet literature, Jin Yong's characterization, comparative literature, East and West, as well as photomedia at the BA and MA levels.

Shuyan ZHOU is a postdoctoral researcher in the School of Communication and Design at Sun Yat-sen University. She received her PhD in gender studies from the Chinese University of Hong Kong. Her research interests focus on Chinese cyberculture, popular culture, feminism, and psychoanalysis. Recent publications include book chapters in *Transitioning Masculinities: Re-Imagining Male Paradigms* (2015) and *New Trends in Communication Studies* (in Chinese, 2014). She teaches BA and MA courses on creative writing and in gender and cultural studies theory.

Index

The abbreviation "BL" refers to "Boys' Love." Page numbers in italics refer to illustrations.

AC Ailisi Weiniang Tuan (AC Alice Fake Girl Group). *See* Alice Cos Group
ACG (anime, comics, and games): brother-sister bond in, 61n32; cosplay performances, 21–22, 25, 28–29, 38; *danmei* fans, 8–9; fan feelings toward characters, 31; female *vs.* male fans, xii, 30, 41n25; narratives, 30–31; on university bulletin boards, xviii; websites, 8–9. *See also* anime; comic market; *Hetalia: Axis Powers*; manga agency: Chinese queer, xv, 66, 72; netizens', 92, 106; political, 91
Akatsuka, Neal K., 208, 210, 218n43, 230
Alice Cos Group: cuteness (*ke'ai*) of, 20, 28–30, 36–37, 39; group members, 20, 23, *24–28*; Haoge and Xiaohua's web entries, 31–33, 42n42; public performances and videos, xxii, 24, 29–30, 41n21, 41n23; queer dimension of, 38–39; success, 24, 39; Weibo pages, 30, 40n17
Allison, Anne, 36
Altman, Denis, 71
Anderson, Benedict, 46
androgyny: hybridity and, 76; pop music groups, xv–xvi; transnational, xi–xii; TV personalities, xvii; in Western and Chinese contexts, xiv, 75–76, 87n96. *See also* HOCC; Li Yuchun; Moennig, Katherine
anime, xviii, xxviiin6, 4, 9. *See also Hetalia: Axis Powers*
AO3 (archiveofourown.org), 10
Aoyagi, Hiroshi, 36

Appadurai, Arjun, 207–8
Arnold, Matthew, 15, 19n50
Australia, 70, 213
Axis Powers: Hetalia (APH). *See Hetalia: Axis Powers*

Baidu Post Bar, 5, 9, 22, 24; Dongfang Bubai site, 112, 115, 116, 124n7; *Hetalia* fan communities, 46–47; Joe Chen site, 121, 124n7; Li Yuchun site, 158
Bakhtin, Mikhail, 91–93, 104–5, 106
Bao, Hongwei, 161
belonging, cross-border elective, 157–58, 161–62, 168, 171
bin tai, meaning, 163
bisexuality, 145, 155n97
bishōnen (beautiful boy), 51–52
"Blues on the Run" (Rita), 57, 62n42
Blur-F, 139–40, 153n72
Boao Forum for Asia, 62n50
Boys' Love (BL): celebrity matchmaking, 94–98, *95, 98*, 101–6, *103*, 110n48; cross-cultural comparison, xxvi; fantasy of grand union, 45, 58; gender politics of, 10, 205; heterosexual engagement with, xxvi–xxvii; homosexuality discourses on, 203–7; publications, 5–8; TV dramas, xi; writers, xx–xxi. *See also danmei; fujoshi*; Japanese Boys' Love (BL); Taiwanese Boy's Love (BL)
Boys' Love (BL) fandom: access to information, xviii; censorship, 96, 108n22; cultural appropriation of, 105–6; failure of, 101–2; folk theories

on, 204, 217n34; in mainland China, xviii, xxii, xxvi; male homosexual fantasies, 94–100, 103–5, 110n47, 179, 184, 193n27; origin, 93–94; scholarly works on, xiv. *See also* online fandom

Boys' Love (BL) manga: censorship and restrictions, xxi, 179, 195–96, 211–12; fantasy worlds, 209–11, 218n44; *fujoshi* consumption of, 179, 184–87, 188; gender and sexual identity and, 205–7; girl characters in, 204; history of, 196–97; in mainland China, 93–94; piracy, xviii, xxi, 197–98; *seme* and *uke* principles of, 9, 50; subgenres, 199–202, 216n26; in Taiwanese market, 197; *tongrenzhi* works, 198–99. *See also* manga

Bury, Rhiannon, 64–65

butchness: of Katherine Moennig, 66, 74, 76–78; normative, 75, 79

Butler, Judith, 38, 44n71

carnival, xxii–xxiv; Bakhtin's concept, 91–93, 104–5, 106; official media and, 100, 102; pleasures of, 103–4

celebrities: BL matchmaking of, 94–98, 95, 98, 102; consumerism and, 105–6; privacy, 83n23; queer readings of, xviii, 64, 65, 70; rumors of, 96, 99–100, 104, 110n48; supermodels, 70; transgender, xvi–xvii; *weiniang* (fake girl), 22–23, 33

censorship: of BL fan sites, 96, 108n22; by CCTV, 100–102, 104; of *danmei* content, xxi, 4, 6, 11, 13; evasion tactics, xxi–xxii; fan circulation practices and, 63; of film, xvi, 108n19; Internet, xxv, 212–13; in mainland China, xiii, xxi, 12, 94, 96; of manga, xxii, 179, 197, 211–12; of TV dramas, xvi, 116

Chang, Jing, xvii

Chang, Shihyun, 183

Chang, Weijung, xxv

Chao, Shih-chen, xxii

Chen, Joe, xxiv, 112, 115, 119, 123, 126n37

Chen, Lingchei Letty, 76

Chen, Xiaomei, 72–73

Chen, Yizhen, 183

Chen Chiao-En. *See* Chen, Joe

Cheng, Sammi, 139, 153n69

Cheung Kwok Wing, Leslie, xv

Chiang, Howard, xix

Chin, Bertha, 11

China: culture, 91–93, 132; cuteness in, 37; empire/nation-state identity, 53; Japanese relations, 48, 56–57; language, 31, 40n12, 42n35; Manchu regime, 52; Marxist indoctrination, 61n37; "proper" gender expressions in, 20; publishing industry, 5, 17n11; *seme* and *uke* representations of, 49–51, 60n20; Soviet ties, 54–56; Taiwanese relations, 52; television industry, xvi–xvii, 114–15. *See also* Hong Kong-mainland China relationship

China's Got Talent (*Zhongguo daren xiu*), 23

Chinese Central Television (CCTV/CCTV-1), xvii, 108n27, 110n44, 116; "Looking for Leehom" saga, 93, 100–102, 105–6; *Spring Festival Gala*, xxiii, 93, 97–100, 103–4, 106

Chinese/Chineseness, word usage, xix

Chinese poems, 100, 109n37

Chinese women: innocent/sexualized identity of, 37–38, 39; "leftover women," 118–19; socialist androgyny of, 75–76

Chow Wah Shan, 114

Chu, Roland, 114

Chua Beng Huat, 7

Chung, Jui-ping, 201

cisgender, meaning, 150n24

comic market, 6, 14, 17n14, 215n13

communism, 55–56, 113

Confucius, 45–46

consumption: of BL manga, 179; of celebrities, 103, 105–6; cultural/transcultural, xxv, xxvi, 52, 65–66; of cuteness, 35; of *danmei*, 8, 11, 14; of *funü* subculture, 101; of "Japaneseness," 180, 183, 184, 208; of male homosexuality, 110n47; in queer politics, 132; spaces, 137; of Western media, 63–64

cosmopolitanism, 172n6; Chinese gayness and, 72; Li Yuchun and, xxiv, 158, 160–61, 164, 167, 171; "pop," 14, 66; in *Pravda Remix*, 54, 56

cosplay (costume play): crossplay-performances, 21–22; definition and origin, xxviiin5, 21, 192n9; of *Hetalia* characters, 47; websites, 22; *weiniang*, 22–23. *See also* Alice Cos Group

Index

251

cross-dressing: in Chinese opera, 44n75; of cosplayers, 21–23, 33, 38; in manga, 196–97
cultural economy, 15
cuteness: babyish, 34–35; Japanese "*kawaii*," 35–36; physical attributes of, 28–29; sexualized femininity and, xxii, 36–37; South Korean "*aegyo*," 36–37, 44n63
cyberculture, 91–93

Danlan, xx
danmei: artists and writers, 6–7, 8, 10, 14; circles, 8–11, 15, 18n23; as a cultural commons, xxii, 8, 16; Euro-American circle (*oumei quan*), 8, 10, 15; female fans of, 15, 17n10; as a form of low-end globalization, xxi, 7, 14; free resources, 7–8, 9; Japanese circle (*rixi quan*), 8–9, 15; magazines and publishers, 5–6; origin and term usage, 3, 8, 16n1; popularity of, 3, 4; transnational distribution network, xxi, 4, 14; websites and social media, 4–5, 7, 9–10
democracy, 132; Hong Kong, xi, 12–13, 157, 160
disidentification, 73, 74, 81, 173n26
dōjinshi. See *tongrenzhi*
Dongfang Bubai (DFBB): gay reading of, xxiv, 116–17; gender change, 112, 119; heterosexual reading of, 117–18; lesbian reading of, *121*, 121–23; popularity and adaptations, 111–12; in *The Smiling, Proud Wanderer*, 112–13; subcharacters and fan-made stories of, 119, *120*, *121*, *122*, 126n37; in *Swordsman*, 114–15; in *Swordsman II*, 113–14
Doty, Alexander, 123
Due South, 64
Duffet, Mark, xviii
Duggan, Lisa, 132
Dyer, Richard, 79

Erichsen, Freja Beha, 70
Erni, John Nguyet, 163

fandom, definition, 133
fandom studies, xiv, xxviiin9, xxxiin62, 111, 172n5; on academic fans

(aca-fans), 167–69, 172n4; transnational, 14
fanfic (fan fiction): Asian family-themed, 57; *Pravda* series, 54, 58; slash, 8, 10, 31, 65, 123; studies, 119, 126n36; writers, 5
fansubs (fan-made subtitles), xviii, xxii
fantasy-reality relationship, 105, 106, 138, 210–11
fanzines, See *tongrenzhi*
femininity: butchness and lesbian, 74–78, 87n96; cuteness and, 22, 36–37; Liu Zhu's view of, 33; masculinity and, 50; normative, 210; performing, 20–21, 32, 38; sexualized, 37, 206
feminism, 117–19; cultural politics, 204, 205
femslash, 140–41. See *also* slash studies
Feng Nong, 6, 7
film industry: censorship in, xvi, 108n19; festivals, xx; in Hong Kong, 72; in mainland China, xvi–xvii; in Thailand, xvii
Fincher, Leta Hong, 118
Fiske, John, 71
forums, fan: *danmei*, 4, 5, 9–10, 11, 14, 15; Dongfang Bubai, 115; *Hetalia*, 46–47, 49; HOCC International Fan Club, 133, 138–40, 150n18, 153n68; *The L Word*, 63–64, 82n9; *South of Nowhere* (*SON*), 82n10
fu, meaning, xii
Fuhr, Michael, 36, 44n63
Fujimoto, Yukari, 196–97, 210, 218n43
fujoshi (female BL fans): ACG narratives and, 30–31; BL fantasies, 184–85, 188, 190, 193n27; Japaneseness/ Japanophilia contexts of, xxv–xxvi, 179–80, 184–87; new notions of sexuality and, xxvii; profile of interviewees, *181*, *182*, 191n6; term origin and usage, 17n10, 30, 179, 191n3. See *also funü*
funü (rotten women): celebrity consumption, 106; male homosexual fantasies of, 94–99, 101, 105, 108n21; meaning, 30, 93, 191n3. See also *fujoshi*

Galbraith, Patrick W., 184
Garden of Eden Subtitling Group (Yidianyuan Zimuzu; GE), 73, 87n96; fan surveys, 67–69; gossip about

Katherine Moennig, xxiii, 67, 80; *The L Word* fan forum, 63–64, 77; overview of services, 63
gay passion (*jiqing*), 97, 108n28
gender flips (*xingbie fanzhuan*), xi
gender norms, 33–34, 39, 50, 147; Chinese expressions for, 77; tomboy, 166–67, 169. See also heteronormativity
gender performance: of Alice Cos Group, 20–21, 34, 38–39, 44n75; of HOCC, 146; in Maoist China, 75–76. See also performativity
gender politics: activism, 117; Chinese female, 75–76, 79; of *danmei*, 10; discussions on online forums, 14, 73; geopolitics and, 46, 50–51; of Taiwanese BL fans, 203–4
geopolitics: of China, 53; gender politics and, 46, 50–51
Ge Zhaoguang, 53
Giddens, Anthony, 188–89
Girls' Generation, 27, 29–30, 36–37
Girls' Love (GL): definition, 16n3; scholarly works on, xiv; TV representations, xi; unpopularity of, 218n43. See also lesbians/lesbianism
globalization: accelerating, 207; China and, 58; cultural, 15, 63; hybridity and, 76; of Japanese popular culture, 179; low-end and high-end, xxi, 7, 14; of queer culture, 71–72
gong/shou coupling, 179, 188, 191n2, 200–201, 215n18. See also *seme/uke* roles
Go Princess Go! (*Taizifei shengzhiji*), xi
gossip: on female models, 70; as women's practice, 67; on HOCC, xxiv, 134–35; on Katherine Moennig, xxiii, 65, 69, 77–78, 80; on Li Yuchun, 160–61, 168–71; repressed desires and, 66; value of, 175n55; on Wang and Li, 104
Gould, Stephen Jay, 34–35
Great Cultural Revolution (1966–1976), 75, 113
Guess (*Wocai wocai wocaicaicai*), xvii
Guo Jingming, 94–95, *95*

Halberstam, Judith, 75, 79
Han Han, 94–95, *95*
Han Yi, 13
hegemony, 53, 54, 71, 91

Hello Kitty, 35
Hetalia: Axis Powers, 60nn16–17; Asian family themes, 57; *Born to be Dragon* fanzine, 51–54, 58, 61n31, 61n40; events, 47, 60n13; online fan communities, 46–47; popularity and controversy, xxii–xxiii, 47–48, 59n7; *Pravda Remix* fanzine, 54–56, 58, 61n42, 62n52; *seme* and *uke* allegories, 49–51; series overview, 45–46
heteronormativity, 83n23, 102, 105, 131; *danmei* and, 3; familial, 136, 141, 148; of fan forums, 138–39; of female bodies, 142; homoeroticism and, 203; internalization of, 143, 147; lesbianism and, 79, 142, 146–47; meaning, 132
heteropatriarchy, xxiii, 66, 76, 79, 80; Chinese family and, 136, 148. See also patriarchy
heterotopia, xiv
Himaruya, Hidekaz, 47, 49, 55, 59n11, 61nn31–32
Ho, Denise Wan-See. See HOCC
Ho, Josephine Chuen-juei, 213
HOCC: ambivalence of her sexuality, xxiv, 132, 138; antidiscrimination activism, 117, 144, *145*, 154n74, 155n96, 160; blog, 153n66; coming-out, xxv, 143–45, 151n37, 151n39; femslash on, 140–41; gender representation, 134–35, *135*, 150n22; history and music career, 133–34, 151nn32–33, 154n75; International Fan Club (IFC), 133, 138–40, 150n18, 153n68; lesbian embodiment, 145–47, 148; nickname, 140, 154n81; sexuality and relationships, 135–36, 141–42, 148
homoeroticism, xii, xvi, xxviiin9, 83n23; characterizations of Japan, 65, 187; Chinese female gender and, 79–80; female, xi, 68, 71, 74; of Western celebrities, 65, 67, 70, 76, 80
homonormativity, 132, 147
homophobia, xxiv, 73, 100, 153n61; in fan-made stories, 122–23; in Hong Kong, 132, 137; normalizing, 145
homophobic prohibition, 102, 104–5, 106, 110n44
homosexuality: BL discourses on, 204–7; decriminalization, xx, 96, 132, 136–37; female fantasies of male, 93–94, 97,

99–100, 101, 104–6; film industry and, xvi, 108n19; and homosociality, xvi, 94–96, 103–4, 179; liberal attitudes on, 203–4; trivialization of female, 75; in TV discourses, 117; Western countries and, 70. *See also* lesbians/lesbianism
Hong Kong: antidiscrimination legislation, 144; class inequality, 162; evangelical activism, 136–37, 144; languages spoken in, 149n7; mainland-born residents, 157; media, xvii, 137–38, 141; music industry, 134, 150n28; prodemocracy movement, 12–13; queer politics, 114, 132–33, 137–38; sex education in, 141; social movements, xi, xx, 132, 136; tourists, 163, 173n28
Hong Kong–mainland China relationship: bigotry, 157–58, 163–64, 172n5; cross-border friendships, 161–62, 166, 171; fan perceptions of Li Yuchun, xxiv–xxv, 164–67; handover, 52, 157
Hunan Satellite TV, xvii, 33, 41n23; *Kuaile nansheng* (Happy male voice), 22; *Super Girl*, xvi, 159; *Swordsman*, 115, 116
hybridity, 66, 76, 80, 180, 191
hyperfemininity, 32, 76, 134, 200
hypermasculinity, 78–79

identities: China's, 53; coming-out, 201–2; cross-gender/transgender, xv, xxi; fans/fannish, xiii, xv, 138, 142, 158; gay, 116, 207; gender and sexual, 22, 33–34, 38, 68–69, 204, 206–7; lesbian, xxiii, 68, 69–70, 78, 79, 87n96; national, 14, 15; paradoxes and complexities of, xxvi, xxvii; politics of, 133; virgin/whore, 36–37
If You Are the One (*Feicheng wurao*), xvi
imaginaries: fannish, 161; female homoerotic, 68, 70–71, 80, 83n23, 200; gendered, 76; of Japan, 64, 183, 184, 188, 196; transnational, 213; Western queer, xxiii, 65, 70–72
imagined geography, 64–65, 196, 207, 211, 218n44
incest, 121
Internet: anonymity of, 4; Chinese, 11, 91–92, 97, 103; connections and access, xvii–xviii; protection/regulation measures, 212–13, 218n50; Taiwanese, 212; *tongrenzhi* sales networks, 14; usage, xxixn9. *See also* forums, fan; online fandom
Ito, Mizuko, 3
Iwabuchi, Koichi, 58, 187, 193n31, 208

Jackson, Peter A., 71
Japan: aggression against China, 48, 53; colonial rule of Taiwan, xxv, 187–88; consumer culture/cultural products, 35–36, 189–90, 208, 218n42; *otaku* culture, xii, 183; "soft power," 15–16; tourists, 209; in World War II, xxiii, 192n10
Japanese Boys' Love (BL): aesthetics and conventions of, 9; Chinese *danmei* fans of, xxii, 5–6, 8–9; cross-cultural consumption of, xiv; popularity in the United States, 208; translation of works, xxi, 8. *See also* Boys' Love (BL) manga
Japanese language, 31, 42n35, 185–86, 192n25, 193n26
Japaneseness: consumption of, 180, 189–90; foreignness of, 189; in *fujoshi* practices, xxv–xxvi, 184–86; ideals in BL fantasies, 188–89; Japanophiles' desire for, 183–84; recognized by Taiwanese manga readers, 208–11; Taiwanese colonial history and, 187–88
Japanophilia: definition, 179–80; *fujoshi* culture and, xxi, xxvi, 179–80, 186–87; media attention to, 180, 183, 192n10; role of Japaneseness in, 183–84, 186, 188, 190
ji, meaning, xii
Jinjiang Literature City, 4–5, 9–10, 94. *See also* Xianqing
Jin Yong (Louis Cha), xvii, xxiv, 111–13, 115, 119, 124n3; studies of his works, 111, 123
Jones, Carol, 163

Kam, Lucetta Yip Lo, 75
kawaii (cute/adorable), 22, 31; in Japanese culture, 35–36
ke'ai (cuteness): *jiaomei* (coquettish), 37–38; origin and contemporary contexts, 20, 37; performed by Alice Cos Group, 20, 32, 38, 39
Keenan, Zee Mattanawee, xvii

Kim, Youna, 43n62
kimonos, 190, 194n40
Kinsella, Sharon, 36
Ko, Yufen, 183
K-pop, xxii, 20, 43n62, 51; Girls' Generation, 27, 29–30, 36–37

Lacan, Jacques, 104
Lau, Wilfrid, 135–36, 143
Lavin, Maud, xxiv
Lee, Iyun, 183, 189
Lee, Ming-Tsung, 191n4
Lee, Tzuyao, 183
Lei, Weizhen, 92
Leo, Ching, 56
lesbian, gay, bisexual, transgender, and queer (LGBTQ): celebrities, xvi–xvii; identity, xv, 131; new forms of sexuality and, xxvii; pop artists, xv; PRC government's attitude toward, xvi, 96; social and political activities, xx. *See also specific group*
lesbians/lesbianism: celebrities, 64, 69–70, 78, 80; in Dongfang Bubai context, *121*, 121–23; in fan-made webisodes, 121–23; feminine/masculine roles, 75–79, 87n96, 142, 146–47; in Hong Kong, 137–38, 155n100; "proper" embodiment of, 132, 145–47, 148; universal appeal of, 68; Western ideals and, 66, 74. *See also* butchness; *L Word, The*; tomboy
Les+ magazine, xx
LeTV, xi, 117
Leung, Helen Hok-Sze, 75, 114
Li, Eva Cheuk Yin, xxiv, 171
Li, Hongmei, 91–92, 95
Li, Shubo, 13
Lin, Brigitte, xxiv, 113–14
linguistic barriers, 10–11
literature websites, 7, 9–10
Liu, Lydia H., 35n43
Liu, Pinzhi, 184
Liu, Ting, 7
Liu Qian, 100–102
Liu Zhongde, 159
Liu Zhu, 22, 33–34, 40n14, 42n44, 43n47
Li Yuchun: commercial success, 159–60; gender and sexual ambiguity, xxv, 158, 160–61, 162–63, 169–71; gossip about, 168–69; Hong Kong–based mainlander fans (Corns), xxiv, 157–58, 164–67, 171n1
Li Yundi: BL fantasies of, *98*, 98–100, *103*, 103–6; "Looking for Leehom" saga, 93, 100–102, 110n48; piano career, 108n23; sexual identity, xxv, 99–100, 102, 104; *Spring Festival Gala* performance (2012), xxiii, 97
Lofter.com, 5
Lohan, Lindsay, 78–79
Long March (1934–1935), 56
Lorenz, Konrad, 34
Lost in Thailand (Renzai jiongtu zhi taijiong), xvi
Louie, Kam, 32
love: romantic and confluent, 188–89, 204, 207; subgenres in BL manga, 199–202
L Word, The (TLW): criticism on lesbian representations, 74, 146–47; fan survey, 67, 69; online forum, 63–64, 82n9; plot, 155n101; portrayal of gender and sexuality, 68; translation and distribution of, 63. *See also* Moennig, Katherine

manga: aesthetics and conventions of, 9; BL and GL origins in, xii, 93–94, 179; cosplay performances of, xxii; piracy, 46, 197–98; publishers, 179; restrictions and censorship, xxii, 179, 197; *shōjo*, 196, 214n3; *shōnen-ai*, 196–98, 215n15; Taiwanese readers, 197–98, 208–11; translation of, 8, 48; on university bulletin boards, xviii; websites, 8–9; women authors, 196. *See also* Boys' Love (BL) manga; *Hetalia: Axis Powers*
Mao Zedong, 113, 114, 115, 118, 125n20
maps, 58
markets: *danmei*, 5–6, 7; Japanese, 36; overseas, 15
marriage, 118, 151n39, 155n96; same-sex, 137
Martin, Fran, xxv, xxvii, 64–65, 68, 187
masculinity: butchness and lesbian, 74–78, 87n96; female, xvi, 75, 78–79; soft, 51–52; in relation to femininity, 50; soft, 51–52; in *wen/wu* archetypes of, 32
Mathews, Gordon, xxi, 7
Matsuo, Hisako, 210, 218n43

Index

McLelland, Mark, 213
media industry: Chinese, 72, 91–92, 104; grassroots *vs.* top-down, xiv; Japanese, 180, 183; mainstream, 94, 96, 99, 101, 104; power relations in, 103; Taiwanese, 183; Western, xviii, xxii, 57, 63–64. *See also* film industry; television industry
Mei Lanfang, 33, 42n42
meili, meaning, 32
meng, meaning, 30–31
Meyer, Uli, 94
Meyers, Erin, 175n55
Mickey Mouse, 34–35
minoritarian sexuality, 159, 162
MissTER, xvi
Mizoguchi, Akiko, xxvii, 195, 197
moe, term usage, 31, 185–86, 192n23
Moennig, Katherine: fan gossip about, xxiii, 65, 69, 77–78, 80; personal life and sexual orientation, 66–67, 70, 74–75, 78–79; role on *The L Word*, 65, 74, 76
moeru, meaning, 31
Mongkok, 147, 156n103
Morimoto, Lori Hitchcock, 11
Morreall, John, 34
Muñoz, José Esteban, 73, 76, 173n26
myfreshnet.com, 7

Nakamura, Karen, 210, 218n43
nationalism: on *danmei* forums, 12–14, 15; of *Hetalia* fans, xxv, 54; queer, 46
Nava, Mica, 158, 172n6
neta, meaning, 61n41
netiquette, 47
netizens, 108n27, 114; BL matchmaking and, 94–95, 98; gay, 110n47; parody and carnival practices, 91–93, 99–100, 103–6
neutrosexuality, xiv, xvi. See also *zhongxing*
Nirvana in Fire (*Langya bang*), xix
normal, concept, 132, 138; queer relations, xxiv, 141, 143, 147, 148, 155n95. *See also* heteronormativity
Nütong Xueshe, 153n61

Occidentalism, xxvi, 49, 65; Chinese queer imaginings of, xxiii, 71; official and antiofficial, 72–73

Occupy Central movement, 12–13, 151n39
Oh, Chuyun, 36
online fandom: Dongfang Bubai fan community, 116–19, *120*, 121–23; *Hetalia* fan community, 46–47; HOCC discussions, 133, 138–40, 144–47, 150n18, 150n22, 153n68; influence on offline media, 96–97, 101–2; *The L Word* fan demographics, 67–68; political debates, 12–13, 73; transcultural activities, 10–11; Wang and Li forums, 93, 99–100; *weiniang* community, 22. *See also* forums, fan
otaku: culture, xiv, 3, 183; meaning, xii; sexuality, xxvii
otoko no ko (male daughter), 22, 40n9. See also *weiniang* (fake girl)
Otomedream.com, 8–9
Ozaki, Minami, 198, 216n20

Palace of Desire (*Daming gongci*), xvi
parody and spoof: in BL matchmaking of Wang and Li, 97, 99, 100–102, *103*; in *Hetalia*, 47–48, 61n37; pleasure of, 94–95; political potential of, 91–93
patriarchy, 38, 117–19, 204. *See also* heteropatriarchy
peer-to-peer (P2P) networks, xviii, 63
People's Republic of China (PRC) government: attitude on LGBTQ, xvi, 96; censorship practices, xxi; democratic movement (1989), 12; Dongfang Bubai and, 114; restrictions on foreign media, xxii
Perfect Sky (*Feitian*), 5
performativity: Butler's definition, 38, 73–74; gender, 20–21, 38–39, 44n71, 146–47; lesbian, 74, 170
piracy, xviii, xxi, 46, 64, 197–98
Pivi.net, 9
politics. *See* gender politics; queer politics
popular culture: Chinese-speaking, xi, xiii, xxviiin9, 68, 87n96, 94; consumerism in, 105; cuteness in, 35; global, xxvii, 3; Hong Kong, 161, 168; hybridized, 180; Japanese, xxi, xxvi, 3, 179–80; politics and, 117; transnational, 14, 81; utopian dimension of, xxvi; Western/American, xviii, 147
pornography, 4, 201–2, 205, 207, 214n6

power relations, 50, 56, 74, 76; in different forms of media, 92, 103, 104
pride parades, xx, 137, 143, *145*

Qiong Yao, 201, 216n24
Qiu Zitong, 37
queer, term usage, xii, xix, 131–32
queer fan cultures: cross-cultural, 64–65; expansion, xix; gender hierarchy, xiv–xv; heterosexual engagement in, xxvi–xxvii; in HOCC fandom, 131–32, 136, 138–43, 148, 150n19, 150n22; queer fantasies of, xii, xxvi, 64–65, 69–71, 73–74
queer light, definition, 162, 167, 169
queerness: appearance of, 162; of Chinese culture, 71–72; commodified, 166, 170; of HOCC, 132, 150n22; performing *ke'ai* and, 20–21, 38–39; Western influence on, 71
queer politics: Anglo-American, 132, 149n10; in Hong Kong, 133; normalization of, 147, 148, 155n95
queer studies, xiii–xiv, xxviiin9, 83n23, 123

rituals, 139, 153n70, 206
Rofel, Lisa, 76
Ronson, Samantha, 78
Rose (actress), xvi
Rotten Manga, 8–9

Sailor Moon, 21, 30
Saito, Tamaki, xxvii
sajiao (coquettishness), 20, 37–38, 39; meaning, 29
scanlation, 9, 48, 185, 192n22. *See also* translation groups
Sedgwick, Eve Kosofsky, 68, 94
selfie photos, 37
seme/uke roles: in BL fan dreamlands, 45; Chinese *danmei* and, 9–10, 15–16; in *Hetalia* context, 46, 49–51, 52–53
Sengoku BASARA, 186, 192n24
sexual competitiveness, 205
S.H.E., xvi
shengnü (leftover women), 118–19
Shih, Shu-mei, xix
Silvio, Teri, 186
Sina Weibo, 5, 99, 115, 158; Alice Cos Group account, 20, *24–28*, 30–32; Dongfang Bubai fans, 112, 124n7; HOCC's account, 143, 154n74; Li Yundi's, 99, 101, 102; *tongzhi* activism on, 116–17
Sinitic-language cultures, xix
Sino-Japanese relationship, 48, 56–57
Sino-Russian relationship, 54–56
slash studies, 65, 83n23, 123, 140, 215n16. *See also under* fanfic (fan fiction)
Smiling, Proud Wanderer, The, xvii, xxiv; adaptations and versions, 111–12, 124n3; plot and characters, 112–13
social movements: in China, 96; in Hong Kong, xi, xx; Occupy Central movement, 12–13, 151n39; *tongzhi* movement, 116–17, 126n31, 132, 136, 144, 147. *See also* Umbrella Movement (*Yusan yundong*)
social networking, 5, 99, 140, 144, 154n74. *See also* Sina Weibo; Twitter
South Korea: cuteness in, 36; pop industry, xxii, 20, 36–37, 43n62, 51; protest of *Hetalia*, 48; queer fan culture, xix
South of Nowhere (*SON*), 82n10
State Administration of Press, Publication, Radio, Film and Television (SAPPRFT), xvi, 33, 100, 108n19, 116
stereotypes, 47, 73, 137, 163, 170; lesbian, 75, 79, 146
student protests, xi, 12, 14
Suiyuanju, 10
Super Girl (*Chaoji nüsheng*), xvi, 159, 164
Super Idol (*Chaoji ouxiang*), xvii
Swordsman, xxiv, 112, 125n12; characters and plot, 114–15; fan-made subcharacters and webisodes, 119, *120*, 121–23, 126n37
Swordsman II, xxiv, 112, 125n12; characters and plot, 113–14

Taiwan: acceptance/negation of homosexuality, xx; colonial history, xxv, 187–88; mainland China relations, 52, 61n32; music industry, xv–xvi, 150n29; politicians, 186, 193n27; pro-Japanese sentiments in, 179, 187–88, 191n4; publishing industry, 6–7, 197–98, 212, 215n13; regulation of cultural production, 213
Taiwanese Boy's Love (BL): BL manga and, xxi, 199–202, 215n18; compared to

Index 257

mainland BL fandom, xxvi; cultural labor of, 202; "double foreign-ness" of, 64–65, 211; gender and sexuality discourses, 202, 204–7, 213n1; generational attitudes, 203; homoerotic imaginings of Japan, 64–65, 196; Internet access and, 212; social function of, 195, 207; transnational imaginary and, 213; "worlding" and, xxv, 211. See also *fujoshi*
Taobao, 24, 54
television industry: Chinese dramas and series, xvi–xvii, 114–15, 116, 118, 125n24; Japanese dramas, 180, 183, 188; singing/talent shows, xvi, 22–23, 33, 159; state regulations, xvi, xxi, 116; Taiwanese talk shows, xvii; translation of shows, 63. See also Chinese Central Television (CCTV/CCTV-1); Hunan Satellite TV
That Year, That Rabbit, Those Events (Nanian natu naxie shi), 60n17
Theweleit, Klaus, 163
Thorn, Matthew, 21
Tianchuang Lianmeng, 14, 47
Tianman BLue (Tianman lanse), 5
Tianya, 48, 50, 99
Tiny Times (Xiao shida), xvi–xvii
To, Sandy, 118
Tokidoki, 35
tomboy, 66, 68, 78, 87n96, 142; HOCC as, 146–47; in Hong Kong culture, 146, 155n100, 160, 166, 169; Li Yuchun as, 158–60, 163, 167; Taiwanese music groups, xv–xvi
tongrennü (BL fan girls), 45–46, 59n3. See also *fujoshi*; *funü*
tongrenzhi (fanzines), 6, 14, 17n14, 183; BL subculture, 196, 198, 202, 211; *Born to be Dragon*, 51–54, 58, 61n31, 61n40; circles, 215n15; definition, 192n8; *Hetalia*, 47, 54; *Pravda* and *Pravda Remix*, 54–56, 58, 61n42, 62n52; "The Prolonged Sleep-over," 52; works in Taiwan, 198–99
tongzhi (gay): activism/movements, 116–17, 126n31, 144, 147; discrimination, 143, 153n61; manga narratives, 201–2, 204; meaning, 149n6; normalization and, 132, 147, 148

transgender, 134; celebrities, xvi–xvii; identities, xxi, 113. See also Dongfang Bubai (DFBB)
translation groups, xviii, 8, 9, 48, 63. See also Garden of Eden Subtitling Group
transnational cultural flows, xii, 4, 14, 15, 58, 76
Tsai, Chih-lan, 183
Tsui, Hark, xxiv, 112–14, 115, 119, 125n20
Tudou, 48, 140
Twitter, 13, 67, 70, 154n74. See also Sina Weibo

U17.com, 5
Umbrella Movement (*Yusan yundong*), Hong Kong, xi, xxv, 157; HOCC's support for, 151n39, 154n74, 155n96
USSR, 54–56
utopianism, xxvi, 80, 92; Confucian, 45–46; love fantasies, 189; queer, 70–71, 72

Valentine, Gill, 64, 207
Vietnam, xix
Volodzko, David, 163

Wang Leehom: BL fantasies of, 98, 98–100, 103, 103–6; "Looking for Leehom" saga, 93, 100–102, 110n48; sexual identity, xxv, 99–100, 102, 104, 108n23; *Spring Festival Gala* performance (2012), xxiii, 97
Warner, Michael, 132, 207
webisodes, 121–23, 122, 126n37
Weibo. See Sina Weibo
weiniang (fake girl): celebrities, 22–23, 33; online fan community, 22, 39, 40n13; performing, 38; physical attributes of, 23; popularity of, 20. See also Alice Cos Group
Weiniang Ba, 22, 40n13
Westernization, 71–73. See also Occidentalism
Williams, Raymond, 217n30
Wong, Faye, xv, xxvi
World War II, xxiii, 47, 192n10
wuxia (martial arts), 164

Xianqing Forum: female aggressiveness of, 15; overseas users, 11–12; political discussions, 12–14; topics and jargon, 11; Wang and Li threads, 97, 99

Xiao Can, 23
Xu, Yanrui, xxi

Yahoo!, 153n66
Yang, Guobin, 11, 91–92
Yang, Lijun, 13
Yang, Ling, xxi, xxii, 159, 161
Yano, Christine R., 36
yaoi, xxvii, 94, 179, 197; term origin, 214n6. *See also* Boys' Love (BL)
Yaoi Society, 6
Yau Ching, 114, 132
Yes or No, xvii
Yoshiya, Nobuko, 214n3
Youku, 24, 29–30, 140
Youngster C (C *qingnian*) stories, 49–50, 51, 54
YouTube, 140, 154n76

Yung, Joey, 151n37, 153n66; fan discussions on, 138–40, 153n67; HOCC break-up, 143–45, 154n76; nickname, 135–36, 154n81
Yu Zheng, xxiv, 112, 115, 116, 119

zhai, meaning, xii
Zhao, Jing Jamie, xxii
Zheng, Yongnian, 13
zhongxing (neutrosexuality), 87n96; HOCC's association with, 141–42, 146, 148; Li Yuchun's association with, 158, 161, 164, 166–67. *See also* androgyny; tomboy
Zhou, Egret Lulu, xxi, xxiv
Zhou, Shuyan, xxi, xxiii
Zhuxi Candang, 208
Žižek, Slavoj, 105